CW00818800

IRAN'S RISE AND RIVALRY WITH THE US IN THE MIDDLE EAST

IRAN'S RISE AND RIVALRY WITH THE US IN THE MIDDLE EAST

MOHSEN M. MILANI

A Oneworld Book

First published by Oneworld Publications Ltd in 2025

ISBN 978-0-86154-842-2
eISBN 978-0-86154-843-9

Typeset by Geethik Technologies Pvt Ltd
Printed and bound in Great Britain by Clays Ltd, Elcograf S.p.A.

Oneworld Publications Ltd
10 Bloomsbury Street
London WC1B 3SR
England

Stay up to date with the latest books,
special offers, and exclusive content from
Oneworld with our newsletter

Sign up on our website
oneworld-publications.com

To Ramak, the love of my life and my best friend
and to Shayda, Doniya, and Ava, the greatest treasures of my life

I dedicate this book to the people of Iran and the United States,
with hopes for peace and lasting friendship.

Contents

Introduction: The Riddle of Iran's Rise   1

1 Pax Americana in Iran and Roots of Anti-Americanism   7
2 Revolutionary Iran's Regional Policy: Anti-Americanism
   on Steroids   23
3 Iran–Iraq War: Laying the Foundation for Iran's Rise   41
4 Invading Iraq: America's Unintended Strategic Gift to Iran   72
5 Iran's Power Play in Lebanon: Hezbollah as the Key Strategic
   Asset   102
6 Iran's Enduring Alliance with Syria   138
7 Iran's Yemen Policy: Operating in the Grey Zone   173
8 Iran's Evolving Relations with Hamas and the Palestine Islamic
   Jihad   202

Conclusion: Iranian Regional Policies at a Perilous Crossroads   240
Acknowledgements   254
Select Bibliography   257
Notes   265
Index   341
About the Author   354

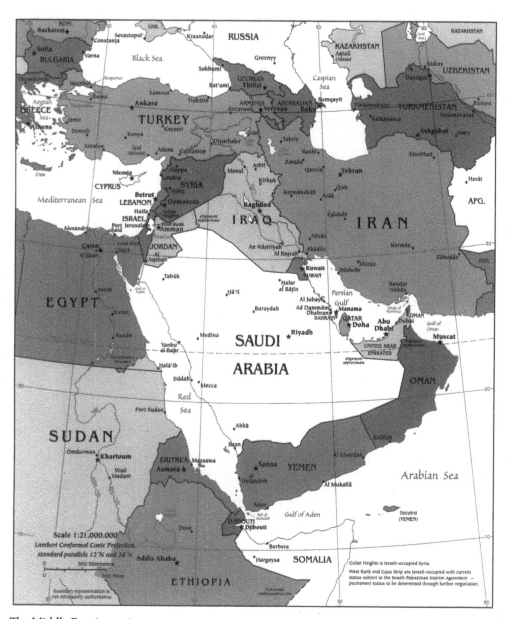

The Middle East in 2008

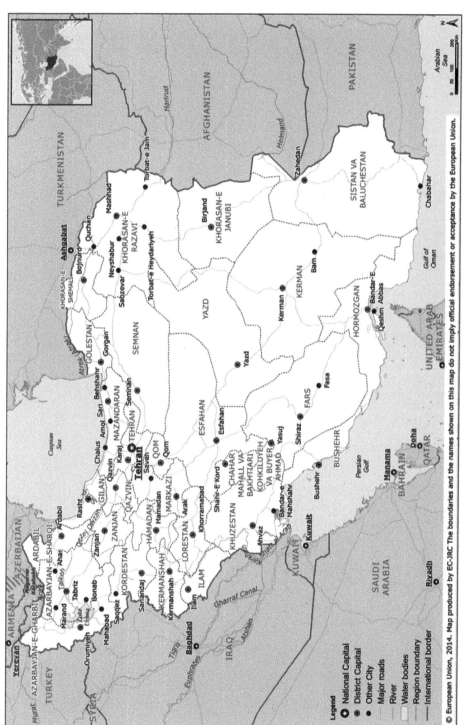

© European Union, 2014. Map produced by EC-JRC. The boundaries and the names shown on this map do not imply official endorsement or acceptance by the European Union.

Modern Iran and its borders

The Safavid Empire's greatest extent, 1588–1629

Introduction

The Riddle of Iran's Rise

When General Qasem Soleimani arrived at Baghdad International Airport in the early hours of 3 January 2020, nothing was amiss. On the tarmac, a convoy of two vehicles awaited the general's arrival, ready to escort him to his scheduled meeting with Iraq's prime minister. But the convoy never left the airport. Fifteen minutes after the plane landed, an MQ-9 Reaper drone armed with Hellfire missiles launched several rounds – engulfing the vehicles in flames and killing all ten passengers. Soleimani was dead – his charred body in pieces. He was identified by the red carnelian ring he always wore – a gift from Ayatollah Seyyed Ali Khamenei, Iran's Supreme Leader.[1]

Speaking from Mar-a-Lago in Florida, President Donald Trump claimed responsibility for the strike. He denounced the general as the world's 'number-one terrorist' whose hands were stained with American blood.[2]

Hailing from the obscure village of Qanat-e Malek (b. 1957) in Iran's south-central province of Kerman, Soleimani enlisted in the Islamic Revolutionary Guard Corps (IRGC) following the 1979 Islamic Revolution and steadily climbed the ranks to become the country's most powerful and celebrated military leader.[3] In 1999, Khamenei appointed him to command the elite Quds Force of IRGC and oversee Iran's overseas military and security operations. Ten years later, in 2019, Soleimani became the first commander since the 1979 Islamic Revolution to receive the Order of Zulfaqar, Iran's highest medal of honour.

The assassination on foreign soil of an active-duty Iranian general, revered by some Iranians as a national hero, sent shockwaves through Iran. As millions of mourners flooded the streets, Khamenei vowed to exact 'hard revenge' against the US and 'expel' US forces from the Middle East. In response, Trump threatened to decimate fifty-two historical Iranian sites if Tehran retaliated. The IRGC paid no heed to this warning and audaciously launched a dozen ballistic missiles at the Ayn al-Assad base in western Iraq, where American troops were stationed. Despite extensive property damage, there were no fatalities. The US did not follow through on Trump's threat. But it was on a knife-edge. General Kenneth McKenzie Jr, then Commander of the United States Central Command, told me that 'the US would have used overwhelming force against Iran had there been huge American casualties'.[4]

Amid the haze and fog of this heightened period of tension, mere hours after the missile attacks in Iraq, the IRGC tragically shot down a civilian Ukrainian aeroplane departing from Tehran, resulting in the deaths of all 176 innocent passengers, the majority of whom were Iranian. That January, Iran and the US stood on the precipice of a hot war but chose to de-escalate the situation.

In this era marked by their lingering conflicts, it is easy to overlook the fact that Iran and the US were once fast friends. In December 1977, President Jimmy Carter met with Iran's reigning king, Mohammad Reza Shah Pahlavi, in the grand Niavaran Palace in Tehran. Making a New Year's Eve toast, he praised the monarch for creating an 'island of stability' in the troubled Middle East. Just over twelve months later, an epochal revolution with universalist pretensions toppled his seemingly invincible regime, propelling this once powerful leader into exile, as he wandered from one country to another in search of political sanctuary. And amid revolutionary chaos in November 1979, misguided militants stormed the US embassy in Tehran, holding all its personnel hostage. The egregious assault marked the end of Pax Americana in

Iran, spanning from 1953 to 1979, and heralded the beginning of a cold war between the erstwhile allies. Meanwhile, Iran has gradually and ironically emerged as a formidable anti-American power in three strategic regions: the Persian Gulf, the Levant, and the Arabian Peninsula.

In his 2018 congressional testimony, former US Secretary of State Henry Kissinger characterised Iran as 'the key' challenge in the Middle East and 'the most consistently cohesive power of the region'. He also expressed alarm about Iran's potential to resurrect the Persian empire and build 'a belt of Iranian influence stretching from Tehran through Baghdad and Damascus all the way to Beirut'.[5] While Kissinger may have exaggerated the prospect of a Persian empire revival, he accurately highlighted the dramatic rise in revolutionary Iran's power.

Iran's ascendancy in the Middle East has been most conspicuously displayed in Iraq, Syria, Lebanon, Yemen, and to a much lesser extent, most recently, in the Gaza Strip. How has Iran managed to successfully navigate the minefields and expand its power as the champion of anti-Americanism, despite enduring US containment efforts, sanctions, constant threats of regime change in Tehran, potential military attacks, and US-sponsored regional alliances against it? The question becomes even more perplexing when we consider that Iran's rise has occurred in a strategically important region that has cost the US more in blood and expenditure than anywhere else since the conclusion of the Vietnam War in 1975.

It is hardly surprising that Iran's ambition to expand its regional power has placed it on a collision trajectory with the US. Before the dawn of the last century, Samuel Huntington, one of the most celebrated political scientists of his generation, presciently recognised Iran as a rising regional power that would likely challenge what he called 'American superpowerdom'.[6] Building upon Huntington's formulation, I hypothesise that the lingering cold war between the US and Iran, fiercely waged across Middle Eastern battlegrounds, is primarily driven by a clash of geopolitical interests rather than ideological disputes or Washington's concerns over the Islamic Republic's human rights violations. More precisely, it is a cold war between an aspiring country, seeking a new regional balance of power through reliance on Islam, and the US, the world's pre-eminent superpower and guarantor of the status quo.[7]

Iran's ambition to expand its regional power is not new, nor is the pursuit of power an anomaly in international relations. Indeed, power, broadly defined as the capacity to impose one's will upon others, through coercion, persuasion or other means, serves as the 'mother's milk' of international relations. Power is, as Machiavelli put it, 'the pivot on which everything hinges'. Picking up where Machiavelli left off in the sixteenth century, scholars from realist and neorealist schools of thought in international relations, from Hans Morgenthau to Kenneth Waltz to John Mearsheimer, have maintained that all states relentlessly strive to expand power, ensure their survival, and safeguard their security. The result, as Waltz observed, is that in the international system, characterised by many competing sovereign states and lacking a system of law enforcement, where each state pursues its own interests, conflict and wars become inevitable.[8] Over four decades of conflict between Iran and the United States, coupled with persistent demonisation campaigns, validate Waltz's sobering observation.

This book tells the intriguing story of revolutionary Iran's gradual rise in Iraq, Syria, Lebanon, Yemen, and the Gaza Strip, against the backdrop of its cold war with the US, its 'shadow war' with Israel, and its intense regional rivalry with Saudi Arabia. I will answer four critical questions: First, why and how did Iran adopt anti-Americanism and anti-Israeli policies as the central tenets of its regional policy? Second, what is the strategic logic behind Iran's regional policies, as expressed by Tehran, and what methods has it employed to expand its power? Third, what are the consequences of Iran's geostrategic rivalry with the US in each of these four countries and in Gaza, and how has Tehran developed asymmetric deterrence capabilities against the US and its regional allies? Finally, has the Islamic Republic's deterrence mechanism against the United States proven effective, and is its rise sustainable, serving Iran's national interests?

The Islamic Republic's regional strategy is closely tied to its perception of the US as an existential threat. Since the Iranian revolutionaries rose to power and decided to challenge the United States in the Middle East, they have been keenly aware of the significant military disparities between

Iran and the US. Iran's 'forward defence' strategy, a cornerstone of its regional policies, aims to level the playing field and mitigate disparities, expand Iranian influence, and build deterrence by extending the theatre of conflict with the US beyond its borders, potentially targeting vital US interests. In pursuit of this strategy, the Islamic Republic employs asymmetric or unconventional warfare methods, aiming to cultivate an indigenous and self-sustaining military capability to achieve its objectives.

To analyse Iran's gradual rise over the past four decades in four countries and Gaza, we will examine the intricate interplay of several pivotal factors. These include the transformative impact of the Islamic Revolution and the subsequent eight-year war with Iraq; the formation and evolution of a clandestine regional network that became the Axis of Resistance; the strategic repercussions of the 2003 US invasion of Iraq; Iran's proactive involvement in civil and sectarian conflicts across Iraq, Syria, Lebanon, Yemen, and Gaza; and Iran's alliances with Syria, its close relations with post-Saddam Iraq, and its tactical alliance with Russia during the Syrian civil war.

This book diverges in several ways from the approach of many valuable volumes that delve into the broad principles guiding Iran's foreign policy, and its bilateral relationships, by offering a comprehensive overview and the big picture of Iran's complex regional policies towards four countries and Gaza. Drawing on the extensive literature on Iranian foreign policy, my previous writings, dozens of interviews with prominent experts and diplomats, recently declassified US government and CIA documents, and Persian-language sources, I explore the interrelationships between Iran's regional policy and its fierce domestic factional rivalries.[9] Moreover, the book presents a comparative analysis that underscores major elements of continuity and change in Iran's foreign policy towards the United States, Israel, Iraq, Syria, Yemen, Lebanon, and Palestinian organisations, spanning both the pre-revolutionary and revolutionary eras. This book moves beyond 'presentism', linking the past with the present, and uncovering recurring patterns in the policies and behaviour of the Iranian state. This exploration of the past enriches our understanding of current events, revealing the dynamic forces shaping the international arena, and it allows us to develop a more informed perspective on potential future trajectories.

Finally, I have strived to incorporate both Iranian and US viewpoints in my analysis. As the British philosopher John Stuart Mill succinctly said:

> He who knows only his own side of the case, knows little of that. His reasons may be good, and no one may have been able to refute them. But if he is equally unable to refute the reasons on the opposite side; if he does not so much as know what they are, he has no ground for preferring either opinion. He must be able to hear them from persons who actually believe them; who defend them in earnest, and do their very utmost for them.[10]

Adhering to Mill's sage advice, I have endeavoured to go beyond the often sensationalised narratives of Iranian foreign policy, offering a more nuanced and balanced perspective.

Our journey begins with an analysis of the historical roots of anti-Americanism in pre-revolutionary Iran and why it became the main pillar of revolutionary Iran's regional policy.

Chapter 1

Pax Americana in Iran and Roots of Anti-Americanism

On the eve of the 1979 Islamic Revolution, the imposing American embassy in Tehran stood as the iconic symbol of US pre-eminence and its strategic alliance with Mohammad Reza Shah. Just a stone's throw away from where I was born, this red-brick building in one of Tehran's most desirable neighbourhoods served as the hub where the US managed its extensive and multifaceted relations with Iran during the Cold War. Ambitious Iranian politicians and entrepreneurs vied for access to the embassy, hoping to climb the ladder of power. The US Mission consisted of 'around 1,400 Americans', 1,200 of them in the army Mission-Military Assistance Advisory Group, and 800 locals. Moreover, there were over 45,000 Americans living and working in Iran.[1] At that time, Iran was one of the US's premier strategic allies in the Middle East.

How did the US navigate the byzantine politics of Iran in the postwar era to replace Britain as its dominant foreign power? How and why did the Shah leverage his alliance with the US to consolidate his rule at home and expand his power abroad? And why did anti-Americanism take root in pre-revolutionary Iran and intensify dramatically after the 1979 revolution?

Relations between the US and Iran could have been more enduring and mutually beneficial had Washington policymakers been more sensitive to Iranian sovereignty. Iran's turbulent history, characterised by periods of both grandeur and defeat, has left an indelible imprint on the collective psyche of its people, who cherish their sovereignty. This has nurtured a profound distrust of foreign powers, a sentiment not easily dispelled through diplomatic efforts alone. Iranians have good reasons to question the intentions and policies of major global powers.

The Weight of Past Empires: Iran's Struggle for Sovereignty

Iran's pre-Islamic story, which has profoundly influenced its national identity, began with the Achaemenid empire (circa 546–334 BC), the largest empire the world had ever seen.[2] At its greatest extent, it stretched from modern-day Macedonia and Thrace in the west to Punjab in the east, from Uzbekistan in the north to Oman in the south. This mighty empire collapsed after Alexander the Great defeated the Persian armies in 334 BC, and its vast expanse was divided among his generals after his death. After less than a century of rule, Alexander's successors were defeated by the Persian Parthians, who established another empire (247 BC to AD 224). After the demise of the Parthians, Iran then became the seat of the large Sassanid empire (224–651 CE), which rivalled Rome and Byzantium.

The course of Iranian history changed when the Islamic army, led by Caliph Umar ibn Khattab, defeated the Sassanids and conquered parts of Persia in 651. Over time, Iranians gradually abandoned Zoroastrianism, the country's official religion, and converted to Islam, while protecting the integrity of their distinct culture and language. They played a pivotal role in expanding the Islamic empire during the Abbasid Caliphate (750–1258). During the Golden Age of Islam from the eighth to the thirteenth century, eminent Persians like Khwarizmi (780–850) revolutionised mathematics with Hindu-Arabic numerals and algebra, and Avicenna (980–1038) produced what was the standard textbook for medicine for centuries. However, the flowering of Islamic culture drew to a close following devastating invasions by the Mongols. In 1220–21, Bukhara, Samarkand, Herat, Tus and Nishapur were razed by Genghis Khan's army. In the words of a Persian eyewitness: 'They came, they sapped, they burnt, they slew, they plundered and they departed.'[3] In 1258, Genghis Khan's grandson, Hulagu Khan, conquered Baghdad and ended the Abbasid dynasty. Despite experiencing the rise and fall of various foreign dynasties, who largely became Persianised, Iran saw remarkable cultural flourishing from the Mongol invasion until the early sixteenth century.

Finally, under the Safavid dynasty (1501–1722), Iran experienced a remarkable resurgence, with the country unified and transformed into a hub of culture and commerce. The Safavids not only established Shia Islam as the state religion but also expanded their empire well beyond Iran's current borders. This territorial expansion continued during the reign of Nader Shah Afshar, who ruled from 1736 until his assassination in 1747, representing the zenith of Iran's regional influence.

During the rule of the Qajar dynasty (1789–1925), Iran's decline as a regional power began. The onset of their rule coincided with new challenges from European powers and Russia. Fuelled by industrialisation and democratisation, and buoyed by vibrant capitalist economies, European powers sought to either colonise weaker nations or bring them under their sway. Consequently, the power imbalances between Europe, and even Russia, and Iran became glaringly evident and seemingly insurmountable. In that era, Britain and Russia emerged as dominant foreign powers in the country. Although they could not colonise Iran, Britain and Russia colluded to undermine its sovereignty and territorial integrity and keep it subordinate to their imperial interests. Following two disastrous wars with Russia in the early nineteenth century, Iran ceded several fertile provinces on its northern frontiers. Additionally, Britain forced Iran to cede Herat to Afghanistan in 1857, establishing it as a buffer to protect its prized colony in India while solidifying its dominance over the Persian Gulf, historically considered Iran's backyard. Finally, the secret Anglo-Russian Convention in 1907 effectively partitioned Iran into Russian and British spheres of influence, leaving it crippled in protecting its interests. Iran at the turn of the twentieth century was a failing state, sovereign in name only.

Iran's powerlessness became devastatingly clear when, despite its declaration of neutrality, it was invaded by the British, Russian, and Ottoman troops during the First World War. The occupation not only violated Iranian sovereignty but also exacerbated a severe famine that ravaged the country between 1917 and 1919, coinciding with the spread of plague, cholera, and typhus. It is estimated that at least one million, out of an estimated total population of nine million, perished from disease and famine.[4] However, some sources provide a higher estimate of two million lives lost.[5]

Yet this situation was soon to change. Russia, rocked by the Bolshevik Revolution in 1917 and the subsequent civil war, no longer had any interest in exercising influence in Iran, or the capacity to do so. This created a propitious opportunity for Britain, one of the victors of the First World War, to step in and consolidate its position as Iran's sole dominant foreign power. Lord George Curzon, the British Secretary of State for Foreign Affairs, recognised Iran's potential pivotal role in preventing the spread of communism to the Middle East and serving British interests, provided it had a strong, pro-Western leader capable of restoring internal tranquillity. As the author of a two-volume book called *Persia and the Persian Question*, Curzon was intimately familiar with Iran and its strategic importance. His ideas profoundly shaped British strategy towards Iran.

Iran's politics began to gradually transform when William Knox D'Arcy, a British subject who was granted a lucrative concession by the Qajar king, discovered oil in Iran in 1907–8 and established the Anglo-Persian Oil Company. In 1914, Winston Churchill, serving as the First Lord of the Admiralty, directed the Royal Navy to shift from coal to oil as its primary source of fuel. This decision not only increased the significance of oil but also enhanced Iran's importance for British imperial ambitions. And so the Cossack army officer Reza Khan, with tacit British approval, staged a coup against the ineffectual Qajar king in 1921. Four years later, he overthrew the Qajar dynasty and crowned himself as Reza Shah, establishing the Pahlavi dynasty (1925–1979).[6] This marked the first time in Iranian history that a new dynasty ascended to power peacefully and with the approval of an elected parliament.

Reza Shah was a ruthless yet visionary Iranian patriot who accomplished a great deal during his brief reign. He ruled with an iron fist, and suppressed his opponents. He was supported by a circle of intellectuals who were united in their ambition to modernise Iran without democratising it. Reza Shah restored internal order, embarked on a bold industrialisation and secularisation project, modernised the armed forces, reformed Iran's antiquated educational and judicial systems, and introduced progressive social reforms, including banning women from wearing hijab. To bolster revenues for his ambitious developmental projects, an indignant Reza Shah, determined to reduce foreign influence, voiced his discontent with the existing oil agreement with Britain and pushed for renegotiation. After extensive negotiations, Reza Shah acquiesced, in 1933, to a new agreement that extended the oil concession for another sixty years and delivered only a modest increase in profits for Tehran, an outcome he undoubtedly found disappointing.[7]

Despite his impressive domestic achievements, Reza Shah could not expand Iranian regional power as he feared retribution from Britain and the Soviet Union, who believed Iran needed to be contained. His weakness became glaringly apparent when Britain carved out a new state, Iraq, along Iran's western borders, without so much as consulting Iran.

Ultimately, Reza Shah's fortunes would tragically unravel during the Second World War. Iran was invaded in 1941, this time by Soviet, British and American troops, rendering its official declarations of neutrality meaningless and making a mockery of its sovereignty. During this period of occupation and chaos, the US became strategically and economically drawn to Iran.[8]

Sovereignty Undermined: The 1953 Coup against Mosaddegh

For years, Britain had been apprehensive about Reza Shah's determination to reduce British influence, whereas the Soviets were unforgiving of his anti-communism. After invading Iran in 1941, both states promptly engineered Reza Shah's humiliating abdication, only one month after they had put troops on the ground. To justify their blatant intervention in the affairs of a sovereign country, they accused the king of pursuing pro-Nazi policies and inviting thousands of German advisors to the country. In fact, to safeguard the country's sovereignty, Reza Shah had been using Germany as a counterweight against Britain and Russia. When faced with pressure, he attempted to appease both London and Moscow by quickly ordering the expulsion of German advisors, but it proved to be in vain. The truth was that the two foreign powers saw Reza Shah as a strong leader who could challenge them and potentially disrupt the flow of supplies between Britain and the Soviet Union during the war. They preferred to deal with a country in chaos and engage with a weaker leader, who would be dependent on them for his survival. Consequently, they unceremoniously put Reza Shah on board a British ship, the *SS Bandra*, exiling him first to Mauritius and ultimately to South Africa, where he became a prisoner under British surveillance.[9] He would die there in July 1944, far away from the land he truly loved.

The occupying powers agreed to allow Reza Shah's 22-year-old son, Mohammad Reza, to inherit the Peacock Throne.[10] The young king's first major crisis came when the Soviet Union refused to withdraw its troops from Iran, as mandated by the Tripartite Treaty Alliance, signed by London, Moscow, and Tehran in 1942. Adding insult to injury, the Red Army helped establish two puppet republics in Kurdistan and Azerbaijan provinces in 1945, seemingly as the first step towards their annexation. Thanks to President Truman's strong support and deft diplomacy by Prime Minister Ahmad Qavam and the Shah, the Red Army eventually withdrew, leading to the collapse of the two fake republics upon the arrival of the Iranian armed forces.[11]

Washington's commitment to Iran's territorial integrity at that critical juncture significantly augmented its popularity as an exceptional and benevolent Western power that harboured no irredentist ambitions and had a legacy of successful opposition to British colonialism. Vivid in the minds of Iranians was the heroism of Howard Baskerville, an American missionary who lost his life defending the 1905 Constitutional Movement, Iran's first encounter with democracy.[12] Equally engrained was the memory of Arthur Millspaugh, an enlightened American appointed by the Iranian government in 1922 to reform its corrupt and foreign-controlled finance ministry.

Mohammad Reza Shah was cognisant of public support in Iran for the US. He also had his own motives for moving closer to Washington, hoping to forge a strategic alliance with the US to consolidate his shaky rule and counter the influence of Britain and the Soviet Union, two countries that had humiliated his father and showed no signs of relinquishing their hold over Iran. As the Shah watched Britain being forced to cede control of its once mighty empire, one state at a time, he jumped on the bandwagon of the US, which was clearly in the ascendant.

The young Shah faced another major crisis in 1951, when Prime Minister Mohammad Mosaddegh nationalised the British-controlled Anglo-Iranian Oil Company (AIOC). A French-educated Qajar aristocrat, Mosaddegh (1882–1967) firmly believed that Iran could not exercise its sovereignty unless it exercised full control over its own oil industry – the major source of revenue for the Iranian state – and put an end to Britain poking its nose into Iran's affairs. His bold call for the nationalisation of the oil industry ignited Iran's first popular, democratic, nationalist, and fiercely pro-sovereignty movement, quickly turning him into the father of liberal nationalism in Iran. It not only shook the very foundation of British power in Iran but also served as inspiration for other anti-British movements, such as Egypt's nationalisation of the British- and French-controlled Suez Canal in 1956. In response, Britain resorted to various machinations, including imposing crippling sanctions on Iran and making military threats to undermine Mosaddegh. In turn, Mosaddegh sought support from the US, which he saw as a natural ally. He even met with President Harry Truman in Washington in October 1951, and – in vain – requested a loan to improve Iran's economy that was suffocating under British sanctions. While Truman sympathised with Mosaddegh, he proposed that Iran should compensate Britain for nationalising the AIOC. Mosaddegh, however, rejected the offer, and the Anglo–Iranian dispute intensified, with Britain continuing to subvert him. Determined to weaken the entrenched British intelligence network in Iran, Mosaddegh finally took the audacious step of formally severing diplomatic relations with Britain in October 1952 and expelled British diplomats.

The dynamics of the Anglo–Iranian dispute changed when General Dwight Eisenhower assumed the presidency in January 1953. He extended a helping hand to British Prime Minister Winston Churchill, who harboured strong animosity towards Mosaddegh. The two leaders skilfully framed their vehement opposition to Mosaddegh within the context of the unfolding Cold War. They portrayed Mosaddegh as a demagogic and ailing nationalist leader who would inevitably align Iran with Russia. It did not matter that Mosaddegh was not a communist, but rather a quintessential Iranian liberal patriot with no enmity towards the West, under whose rule democracy and freedom flourished.[13] Nor did it matter that the communist forces, represented by the pro-Moscow Tudeh party, lacked widespread support and were unlikely to prevail over Mosaddegh. The prime minister's cardinal sin was nationalising the AIOC, challenging British dominance of his country, and advocating a new foreign policy paradigm based on safe-guarding Iran's sovereignty and non-alignment during the emerging Cold War.[14]

Eventually, with support from pro-Shah elements in Iran and the acquiescence of a significant segment of the Shia clerical establishment, Mosaddegh was overthrown in a joint CIA-MI6 coup d'état, codenamed Operation Ajax, in August 1953.[15] The Peacock Throne was saved when the Shah, who had earlier fled the country, returned home and reas-sumed leadership. Mosaddegh was subsequently arrested, imprisoned for three years, and then placed under house arrest until he died in his ancestral village of Ahmadabad in 1967. His powerful legacy, however, has inspired generations of Iranian patriots.

The coup proved to be a Pyrrhic victory for the US and the Shah, as it sowed the seeds of the 1979 revolution. They may have removed a trou-blesome prime minister, but the Shah was tainted as being beholden to Washington, making the US a toxic brand among many Iranian nation-alists and leftists. Many middle-class and nationalist Iranians began to look at the US as a typical Western power, primarily concerned with expanding its own imperial power and indifferent to Iran's sovereignty. The coup also popularised anti-Americanism among intellectuals and leftist activists. In this new political environment, four months after the coup, Vice President Richard Nixon visited Tehran and met with the Shah, triggering protests by students at the University of Tehran in which three students were killed by the police. Since then, the day of their deaths, the 16th of Azar in the Persian calendar, has been commemo-rated as 'Student Day' in Iran.

Although the Shah lost some degree of legitimacy in the eyes of many Iranians, he continued to rely on his alliance with the US to sustain his rule and counter external threats. Iran resumed diplomatic relations with Britain and joined the US security architecture in the Middle East, becoming a US ally in containing the Soviet Union during the Cold War. The Iranian oil industry was denationalised, and a Western-dominated oil consortium was established, with American companies holding a major share – perhaps a reward for the US for staging the 1953 coup. Additionally, the US expanded its economic ties to Iran and began to modernise its armed forces.[16] Emboldened by his alliance with the US, the Shah swiftly consolidated his authoritarian rule while granting considerable social, cultural, and religious freedoms. The US, for its part, became Shah's accomplice, playing a major role in the creation of Iran's secret police (SAVAK) in 1957, which grew to become a feared and powerful force accountable only to the king.

A decade after the coup, the Shah's rule seemed impregnable, with the US firmly entrenched as Iran's predominant foreign power.

Khomeini's Debut on the National Stage

But beneath the surface of apparent internal stability, political tension was simmering. Under pressure from the Kennedy administration, the Shah implemented a series of reforms in 1963, collectively known as the 'White Revolution'. The linchpin and the most controversial and progressive provisions of these reforms were land reforms aimed at curtailing the power of the landed upper class and granting suffrage to women.[17] At this juncture, Ayatollah Ruhollah Mousavi Khomeini, a relatively obscure religious leader, audaciously challenged both the Shah and the US.

Khomeini (1900–1989) was born into a religious family in the village of Khomein in Iran in 1900.[18] After completing his religious studies at the Arak and Qom seminaries in Iran, he began teaching and writing. In 1941, following the abdication of Reza Shah, he published his first major treatise, a book called *Kashf al-Asrar*, or 'Secrets Unveiled'. In it, he wrote a scathing criticism of Reza Shah's secularisation policies and his compulsory unveiling of women. With his book, Khomeini emerged as a reformer who criticised Reza Shah's policies while defending the institution of monarchy, asserting, 'No one from this class [Shia clerics] has ever opposed the principle of kingship.'[19] However, the book failed to make any political impact. It was Khomeini's political courage that brought him to national attention in the early 1960s, when he declared war on the Shah and his policies.[20]

Khomeini used the pulpit as a platform to denounce the Shah's land reform and women's enfranchisement. The government arrested the ayatollah on 4 June 1963, sparking large protests in Tehran and a few other cities the next day – the largest and deadliest since the 1953 coup. Official government reports claimed twenty people were killed, yet opposition forces estimated several hundred fatalities. While under house arrest, it is alleged, although denied by the Islamic Republic, that Khomeini conveyed a secret message to the United States through an intermediary. The message purportedly stated that 'he was not opposed to American interests in Iran', and that 'the US presence was necessary as a counterbalance to Soviet and possibly British influence'.[21]

Following the violent suppression of the June Uprising, calm prevailed, albeit briefly. During this period, a new generation of pro-American and American-educated politicians and technocrats emerged on the political scene. Prime Minister Hassan Ali Mansur, who assumed office in March 1964, epitomised this promising wave of leadership. While an increasing number of US military personnel and advisors went to Iran to modernise its armed forces, the Majles, supported by Mansur, passed the Status of Forces Agreement in 1964, granting legal immunity to Americans and their dependants living in Iran. In exchange, Iran received a $200 million loan from the US to purchase American weapons.

At that critical juncture, when the cantankerous Khomeini was released from house arrest, he vehemently criticised the Status of Forces Agreement, labelling it a 'capitulation agreement'. Addressing him as 'Mr Shah', a disrespectful reference to the king, Khomeini accused him of 'selling out' the country and turning it into a 'US colony', where 'an American cook' would have 'more rights in Iran than its Shah and Ayatollahs'.[22]

The government could no longer put up with his presence in Iran: Khomeini was deported to Turkey in November 1964, and from there to Najaf, Iraq, in 1965, where he resided until October 1978, when he moved to France. This did nothing to dampen his popularity as a brave and uncompromising opponent of the Shah and the United States, nor did it diminish his organisational skill. Just two months after Khomeini's exile, a covert network he had formed in Iran assassinated Prime Minister Mansur, who had supported the Status of Forces Agreement legislation. Some of the architects of this plot would later occupy key government positions in the Islamic Republic.

In the fifteen-year interregnum, between the June 1963 uprising and the onset of the revolutionary movement in 1978, the Shah remained securely seated on his throne. However, a paradigm shift in the *modus operandi* of the opposition forces against the Shah occurred in the 1960s. While the 1953 coup had triggered anti-American sentiments among leftist and nationalist forces, the June 1963 uprising sparked fervent anti-Americanism among Islamist forces, the traditional middle class, and a pro-Khomeini segment of the Shia clerical establishment. This marked the beginning of more radical and widespread opposition to the Shah and the US. At the same time, many young Iranian activists, concluding that the Shah's regime was incorrigible and could not be reformed, resorted to armed struggle against him.

American Eagle and Iranian Lion in the Persian Gulf

Neither Mosaddegh nor Khomeini managed to derail the Shah from his alliance with the US. Now that the Shah felt his house was in order, he focused on expanding Iranian power abroad and bolstering deterrence against perceived foreign threats.

Iran signed the bilateral defence cooperation agreement with the US in March 1959, granting it considerable latitude to reshape the Iranian armed forces. However, fearing Moscow's retribution for his alliance with the United States, the Shah signed the 1962 Non-Aggression Treaty with the Soviets, prohibiting foreign powers, including the US, from using Iranian territory to launch missiles or nuclear weapons against the Soviet Union. Although relations with Moscow improved after the treaty, the Shah secretly permitted the US to install its most sophisticated electronic listening devices along Iranian–Soviet border to monitor Moscow's missile and space activities, cementing his alliance with the US.[23]

The Shah also viewed the Soviet-backed communists, pan-Arabism, and the new republic established in Iraq in 1958 as grave threats both to Iran and to regional stability, an assessment Washington often considered exaggerated. In the 1960s, he helped empower the marginalised Shias as a counterforce against pan-Arabism in Lebanon, while also providing military assistance to anti-Gamal Abdel Nasser loyalists in the North Yemen civil war.

Beginning in the late 1960s, conditions became increasingly favourable for the Shah to expand Iran's regional power and neutralise perceived threats. Around the time Britain withdrew its forces from the Persian Gulf in 1968, the Organization of the Petroleum Exporting Countries (OPEC), an oil cartel controlling about one third of global oil production, dramatically raised the price of crude oil under the leadership of the Shah. The economic windfall from OPEC's oil price increases provided the Shah with the crucial breathing space and financial independence needed to embark on an ambitious and nationalist foreign policy. Consequently, the Shah became a junior US partner. In this new environment, armed with strong will, he quickly established himself as the dominant indigenous power in the Persian Gulf, a region that was the lifeline for the oil-hungry industrialised world.

President Richard Nixon played an instrumental role in enabling his friend, the Shah, to expand Iranian power. Deeply engaged in the Vietnam War, the US had no appetite to become militarily involved in the Persian Gulf and fill the power vacuum created after British withdrawal. As early as 1971, the US adopted the Twin Pillars policy, delegating the responsibility for maintaining stability in the region to Iran and Saudi Arabia.[24] Recognising Iran's much larger population, economy, and superior armed forces, the US acknowledged it as the 'policeman of the Persian Gulf'.[25] To bolster Iran's military capabilities, Nixon approved the transfer of the most advanced military technologies to Iran, only stopping short at nuclear weapons. For many years in the 1970s, Iran was the world's number-one buyer of American weapons, accounting for 25 per cent of all FMS (Foreign Military Sales) orders between 1970 and 1978.[26] This massive build-up of military power under peacetime conditions was described by an American official as the most rapid 'in the history of the world'.[27]

In the 1970s, the stars began to align for the emergence of the Shah as one of the most powerful figures in the Middle East, if not the most powerful.[28] He demonstrated more independence from Washington than ever before, to the extent that even some of his most radical enemies conceded that he was pursuing an independent and nationalistic foreign policy. According to a CIA report, the Shah was well versed in foreign policy and military matters, adopting a 'classical realpolitik approach' that emphasised 'the primacy of national power'.[29] To that end, he cultivated friendly relations with Syria and provided financial support. He ended years of hostility with Iraq and deployed troops to Oman, successfully quelling a communist rebellion in Dhofar province. He envisioned that Iran could attain the status of a 'Great Civilisation' within a decade or so, surpassing Western nations and remaining 'free from the blemishes' of (Western) society.[30] He commanded the world's fifth largest armed forces, with indisputable military superiority in the Persian Gulf. At the same time, Iran was experiencing phenomenal economic growth, unprecedented in its modern history. American and European companies eagerly competed to sign lucrative contracts with Iran. In 1975, the US and Iran signed a huge economic agreement worth $15 billion.[31] But the economic boom proved to be a mixed blessing. Impressive as Iran's growth was in the 1970s, it also widened the already substantial gap between the rich and the poor, overheated the economy, caused bottleneck shortages, and exacerbated corruption.

Powerful Abroad, Vulnerable at Home

The Shah was also expanding Iranian power beyond the Persian Gulf to the Indian Ocean, pledging to provide financial assistance to Sri Lanka, Pakistan, and India.[32] The Shah's military power and control of vast oil wealth raised concerns among some American politicians and military officers. In 1974, William Simon, Secretary of the Treasury, referred to the Shah as 'a nut'.[33] A few years later, General George S. Brown, former chairman of the Joint Chiefs of Staff, expressed concerns that the Shah's ambitious military programme 'just makes you wonder whether he doesn't have visions of the Persian Empire'.[34]

At home, the Shah also faced mounting criticism for his massive purchases of advanced weapons from the United States and his human rights violations. While the divided opposition against the Shah was checkmated by the SAVAK, President Jimmy Carter's human rights policy gave it a new lease of life. Carter believed that his human rights advocacy would 'remove the reasons for revolutions that often erupt among those who suffer from persecution'.[35] Therefore, starting in 1977, he began to pressure the Shah to liberalise his closed political system. In response, the Shah granted amnesty to some political prisoners, promised to stop torturing dissidents, pledged to enhance press freedom, and committed to hold free and fair parliamentary elections. These reforms made the opposition more assertive. From Iraq, Khomeini wrote to the clerics in Iran that 'today in Iran, a break is in sight. Take advantage of this opportunity and write about these difficulties and declare to the world the crimes of the Shah.'[36] And in January 1978, the government poured petrol on the fire when a Tehran newspaper published an article denouncing Ayatollah Khomeini as a reactionary fanatic of Indian ancestry. In protest, seminary students took the lead in organising demonstrations that shut down the schools, shops, and the bazaar in Qom. These demonstrations were violently suppressed, further galvanising the secular and Islamic opposition to the Shah to continue protesting for democratic rights. Now strikes and protests flared up all over Iran.

During that critical year, Carter struggled to balance his human rights advocacy with protecting the enormous economic and strategic interests of the US in Iran. This reflected the division within his own cabinet, with one faction supporting further liberalisation while the other called on the Shah to pursue an iron-fisted approach towards the revolutionaries. Carter oscillated between these two camps. The vacillations in Carter's position only intensified the Shah's own indecisiveness. The Shah appeared to hold the delusion that he could preserve his throne by ruling as an 'autocratic democrat', alternating between offers of concessions to appease the opposition forces one day and ordering the police to use brute force against them the next.[37] He failed to recognise that revolutionary times require a resolute course of action from the incumbent: one path or the other must be taken decisively. At the height of the revolutionary movement, the Shah stunned the nation by declaring in a televised address to the nation that he had 'heard the voice of their revolution', admitted to having made mistakes in the past and promised to rectify them. In a sense, he legitimised the revolution that sought to overthrow his regime.

Yet, instead of relinquishing some of his absolute power and collaborating with moderate forces against the radical factions of the revolutionary movement, the Shah appointed the ineffectual General Gholamreza Azhari to lead a military government. At that very moment, he effectively penned his own political suicide note. His debilitating lack of resolution, exacerbated by his terminal cancer and coupled with Washington's inability to speak with one voice, played a key role in the rapid disintegration of the Pahlavi regime.

Unlike the Shah, Khomeini knew what needed to be done and acted decisively. He had forged a broad, multi-class and multi-generational coalition against the Pahlavi regime: he came to preside over a truly national revolution. Yet, in many ways, Khomeini did not win the revolution; rather, it was the Shah who lost it.

Even the Shah's alliance with the US could not save him, nor could his armed forces. A 1976 CIA report pointed out that: 'The Shah doubts the US would prove a reliable ally in case of a regional conflict not involving a communist power.'[38] However, since there was no regional conflict involving a communist power, the question of whether the US would have assisted him remains unanswered. What we do know is that when he required robust support from the United States in the final year of his rule, he did not receive it. Although he had become one of the most powerful leaders in the Middle East and successfully prevented foreign incursions on Iranian territory, he lacked the capacity or the will to deal effectively with his domestic enemies. His problem was that while he modernised Iran's economy and society, the country's politics remained archaic and autocratic.

Mohammad Reza Shah was forced into exile on 16 January 1979. After a year and a half of wandering from country to country in search of refuge, he succumbed to cancer and grief. His fate mirrored that of his father: broken and exiled, he died in Egypt on 27 July 1980, at the age of sixty, far from the homeland he served and loved.

Khomeini not only toppled the Shah, he also dismantled a monarchy that had endured in Iran for over 2,500 years. In a bewildering turn of events, he established a theocratic order in this modern age – an Islamic republic – and brought about a fundamental shift in Iranian foreign policy that changed the landscape of the Middle East, as will be explored in the next chapter.

Chapter 2

Revolutionary Iran's Regional Policy: Anti-Americanism on Steroids

> It is a quality of revolutions not to go by old lines or
> old laws, but to break up both and make new ones.
> — Abraham Lincoln

The Islamic Revolution of 1979 stands as one of the most transformative events in the second half of the twentieth century, fundamentally transforming Iran's foreign policy and reshaping the geopolitical dynamics of the Middle East. On 4 November 1979, militant Iranians stormed and occupied the American embassy in Tehran and took sixty-three personnel hostage. By 20 January 1981, when the hostages were finally released, Pax Americana lay in the dust. The US would no longer be Iran's respected partner and principal arms supplier, becoming instead its number-one enemy.

The embassy, once a symbol of American power, was now derided as the 'Den of Spies', and Khomeini's moniker for the United States as 'the Great Satan' had captured the popular imagination. When the compound fell under the control of the IRGC, it was transformed into a museum, complete with a small bookstore, dedicated to recounting 'American crimes against Iran' to the world.

Why and how did the Tehran hostage crisis fundamentally change Iranian foreign policy? More specifically, what strategic rationale underlies Tehran's regional policies, and how has the ongoing factional power struggle shaped its fluctuations?

Revolution in a Revolution: The Tehran Hostage Crisis

After the 1953 coup, the Shah and the US became politically entwined. It was only a matter of time before the revolutionaries directed their rage towards the US. Signs were emerging on the horizon in the 1960s and 1970s that a wave of anti-Americanism was about to crest. Leftist and Islamist guerillas killed several Americans living in Iran, and occasional cultural clashes erupted between the 45,000 Americans, often living in secluded communities, and the more religious and traditional segments of the population. Espousing anti-Americanism had become a rite of passage among dissident intellectuals and activists.

Despite these anti-American sentiments, the primary target of the wrath of the anti-Shah coalition led by Ayatollah Khomeini was not the US. Studies of the hundreds of slogans chanted during the massive demonstrations in the last year of the Pahlavi rule confirm that only a negligible number of slogans targeted the US. The overwhelming majority were against the Shah and in support of Khomeini and Iranian sovereignty.[1] This lack of explicit anti-American sentiment is understandable. As the Shah's grip on power loosened, Khomeini grew increasingly concerned about a potential coup by the US-trained Iranian armed forces to save the Shah, and therefore did not want to antagonise the US. In fact, he authorised his top advisors to secretly meet with American officials to discuss the mechanics of power transfer to the revolutionaries.[2] Ten days after the Shah's exile and prior to his return to Iran, Khomeini conveyed a message to the US through Ebrahim Yazdi, one of his top advisors who later became Iran's foreign minister. Khomeini suggested that it would be 'advisable' for the US to dissuade the armed forces from supporting Shapour Bakhtiyar, the last prime minister of the Pahlavi period. He added that 'the activities and works of Bakhtiyar and the present leaders of the army are not only harmful for Iranians but also are very harmful for the American government and especially for the future of the Americans [that means for the Americans in Iran]'.[3] Khomeini implied a veiled threat of potential harm or danger to Americans residing in Iran should the army initiate a crackdown. Khomeini's manoeuvre bore fruit. Merely ten days after his triumphant return to Iran on 1 February 1979, the Iranian armed forces declared their neutrality, marking the end of the monarchy in Iran.[4]

Khomeini swiftly appointed Mehdi Bazargan (1907–1995) as the prime minster of the Provisional Revolutionary Government. A devout Shia who had served in the Mosaddegh administration, Bazargan led the Liberation Movement, the same organisation Khomeini had earlier authorised to negotiate covertly with the US regarding the status of the armed forces. Bazargan had to craft the country's foreign policy within the constraints of the prevailing sentiment, encapsulated in the most popular slogan of the revolution: *'Esteqlal, Azadi, Jomhuri-ye Eslami'* (independence, freedom and the Islamic Republic). This fervent desire to safeguard the country's independence was later distilled into the slogan of 'No East, No West' as the cornerstone of the country's non-aligned foreign policy. This slogan is prominently inscribed on the entrance of the country's Foreign Ministry in Tehran.[5]

Bazargan pledged to maintain friendly relations with the US while restructuring the bilateral relationship to accommodate the more radical elements within the revolutionary coalition. While he declared his plan to keep US military advisors in Iran, he also emphasised that Iran would reduce its purchases of US weaponry. He emphatically stated that Iran would no longer play the role of the 'policeman of the Persian Gulf'. Concurrently, Iran joined the Non-Aligned Movement, signalling its neutrality in the Cold War.

Bazargan's reforms fell short of satisfying the insatiable appetite of the revolutionaries for radical change, causing the country to lurch dangerously towards anti-American sentiments. The dominant political discourse was primarily shaped by secular leftists and intellectuals, communists, and, to a lesser extent, radical Islamists, all vying to establish their bona fides as genuine anti-American champions. These forces demanded the expulsion of American military advisors and severing relations with the US. In fact, Marxist forces attacked the American embassy in Tehran in February 1979. They quickly vacated the compound and released the hostages they had taken after Khomeini expressed his disapproval.

Meanwhile, with Khomeini's blessing, Bazargan was in secret talks with Washington to chart a new course for bilateral relations. One of the most contentious bilateral issues was the fate of the exiled Shah, who had requested entry to the US for cancer treatment. Against Bazargan's advice, President Carter reluctantly admitted the Shah to the US,[6] prophetically asking his advisors, 'What are you guys going to advise me to do if they [Iranians] overrun our embassy and take our people hostage?'[7] Disappointed with Carter's decision, Bazargan nonetheless 'pledged to help if the American embassy was attacked'.[8]

Amid covert negotiations between the US and Iran, it was revealed that Bazargan and US National Security Advisor Zbigniew Brzezinski had met in Algeria. This revelation ignited widespread hysteria among anti-American factions and dramatically altered the revolution's trajectory. At that time, a few hundred militant Islamists, who later called themselves the 'Students Following the Line of Imam [Khomeini]', seized the opportunity to capture the mantle of anti-Americanism from the secular leftists.[9] On 4 November 1979, they stormed the American embassy in Tehran, seizing its personnel hostage. This date coincided with the fifteenth anniversary of Khomeini's exile from Iran by the Shah – a day President Carter wrote in his memoir that he 'will never forget'.[10] Hojatolislam Seyyed Mohammad Mousavi Khoeiniha, 'the spiritual advisor' of the hostage takers, told me in Tehran that the militant Islamists believed Bazargan was moving dangerously 'close to Washington', and that the Shah's entry to the US was a 'conspiracy concocted by the US to restore the Shah back to power', as it had done in 1953 through a coup.[11]

Initially silent about the embassy takeover, Khomeini glorified the attack as a new 'revolution' against the 'Great Satan' once his son, Ahmad, assured him that the hostage takers were devoted to him.[12] In contrast, Prime Minister Bazargan denounced the attack and demanded the hostages' immediate and unconditional release. When the militant students ignored his prudent plea, Bazargan resigned.

As Iran stubbornly refused to release the hostages, Carter imposed an arms embargo on Iran, prohibited US companies from buying Iranian oil, froze Iran's bank accounts and assets in the US, and broke diplomatic relations. He even launched Operation Eagle Claw to release the hostages. A small Delta Force team, led by Colonel Charles Beckwith, was tasked with freeing the hostages. Their mission, as he put it, was not to arrest the Iranian guards but 'to shoot them right between the eyes'.[13] However, the operation encountered serious technical hurdles in Tabas, Iran, and was aborted following the loss of eight US service members.

All US actions to release the hostages proved futile as they were mere pawns in a ferocious power struggle among rival forces jostling for control of the Iranian state. Khomeini himself saw an opportunity to consolidate his power by prolonging the crisis. To survive and thrive, revolutions need an enemy, and Khomeini had found that enemy in the US. Amid the national hysteria caused by the hostage crisis, a new constitution was approved through a referendum. The document enshrined the doctrine of the *Velayat-e Faqih*, or rule by an Islamic jurist, as the foundation of the Islamic Republic's governance, giving extraordinary power to Khomeini. The hostage takers meticulously pieced together the shredded documents they had seized from the US embassy. Dubbed 'Documents of the Spy Den' (and published under the title *Documents from the U.S. Espionage Den*), they were selectively released by the militants to disparage Khomeini's opponents as spies. While Khomeini masterfully utilised the hostage crisis to marginalise or force many of his moderate critics into exile, the leftists, particularly the Soviet-backed Tudeh party, celebrated the hostage crisis, oblivious to the fact that they were next on the ayatollah's target list.[14]

Finally, when the Islamic Republic was institutionalised and the hostage crisis no longer served Khomeini's interests, Iran and the US signed the Algiers Accords, resulting in the release of the hostages after 444 days of captivity on 20 January 1981 – mere minutes after Ronald Reagan had been inaugurated as the new president. The accords included commitments by the US to not intervene in Iran's affairs, to unfreeze its assets, and to lift the sanctions – pledges that have been largely ignored by the United States.

While the hostage crisis was a boon for Khomeini's personal rule, it was an utter disaster for Iran's national interests. Iran now gained a reputation as a rogue state and as a violator of international law and the established norms of diplomacy. The resulting isolation on the global stage may well have emboldened Iraq to invade Iran in September 1980, while the hostages remained in captivity. Most importantly, Tehran and Washington were now embroiled in a cold war – a conflict that would shape Middle Eastern history over the next four decades.

The Deep State and Iran's Foreign Policy

The hostage crisis revealed the significance of non-state actors in revolutionary Iran and how foreign policy decisions were made. In the early chaotic days of the revolution, American policymakers struggled with their limited understanding of Iran's decision-making process and its new leaders. After all, to maintain its friendly relationship with the Shah, the United States had minimal contact with the Iranian opposition. As a result of this limited knowledge, America's chargé d'affaires for Iran, Bruce Laingen, who was the most senior American official to be held hostage at the embassy, lamented that American policymakers utterly failed to 'realise where the real power rested in Tehran'.[15] In his interview, he told me that many embassy personnel 'hardly knew the leading figures of the revolutionary movements, particularly among the clerics'.[16]

Beneath the apparent disorder in decision making, however, lay a concealed order. Like the Shah before him, Khomeini stood at the apex of the country's power structure, as the ultimate decision maker. In fact, real power did not reside in the regular state. Instead, it rested with a deep state, meticulously created and controlled by Khomeini. Appreciating how it operates is indispensable to understanding Iran's foreign policy.

The foundation of the deep state was laid shortly before the downfall of the Pahlavi state. While in exile in France, Khomeini established the secret Council of the Islamic Revolution in early January 1979. He appointed trusted clerics alongside prominent lay politicians to this small council, which effectively served as an extension of his authority.[17] Gradually, the secret body was superseded by a deep state that operated parallel to, but independent of, the regular state.

The deep state maintained its own armed forces in the IRGC, operating independently from the regular armed forces. The IRGC was established by Khomeini in May 1979 and served as the revolution's praetorian guard. Its primary roles included preserving order, preventing potential coups by remnants of the Imperial Armed Forces, safeguarding the Shia integrity of the Islamic Revolution in Iran, and spreading the Islamic Revolution throughout the Islamic world.[18]

The deep state established its own police forces through thousands of neighbourhood 'committees' formed across the country following the collapse of the monarchy. These committees, managed by armed vigilantes, worked to suppress the opponents of the Islamic Republic. Moreover, the deep state wielded considerable legal power, sometimes surpassing even the regular judiciary. Its autonomous Revolutionary Courts struck fear among the 'enemies of the revolution' through prosecutions and summary executions. The deep state also achieved financial autonomy by seizing properties and private foundations from the old regime.

Atop this intricate nationwide network stood Khomeini's small and modest office. It not only oversaw the deep state but also maintained its own 'kitchen cabinet', comprised of his 'eyes and ears' who reported to him and provided counsel.

Prime Minister Bazargan consistently lamented the duality of power. He described how the unending interference by the deep state had rendered his government powerless, akin to a 'knife without a blade'. During an interview in Tehran, he confided to me that Khomeini had 'intentionally constructed a complex web of parallel and rival institutions, creating a labyrinthine structure that allowed him to control the system and made infiltration by foreign agents exceedingly challenging'.[19] Mir Hossein Mousavi, a devoted follower of Khomeini who served as prime minister during the Iran–Iraq War, also voiced his complaints about the dual power structure to President Ali Khamenei. He explicitly stated in August 1988 that some 'operations' were conducted outside Iran without his knowledge, a direct allusion to the deep state's involvement during the war.[20] To manage this dualism in the decision-making process, the Supreme National Security Council was established in 1989. Consisting of top government, military and intelligence officials, the council makes the key decisions, subject to approval by the Supreme

Leader. The council reduced but did not eliminate the dynamic of dual power. In fact, the power of the deep state has expanded significantly under Ayatollah Khamenei. In 2021, Foreign Minister Javad Zarif acknowledged that the IRGC sometimes operates in secrecy, formulating and executing regional policies without consulting the Foreign Ministry.[21]

The deep state's pivotal role in shaping foreign policy remains the primary determinant for Iran's strategic consistency. Successive elected presidents have wielded significant influence over the tactical aspects of the Islamic Republic's foreign policy. However, they have remained unable to alter its core strategic orientation, a responsibility exclusively reserved for the Supreme Leader by the constitution.

The decision-making style in pre-revolutionary and revolutionary Iran exhibits remarkable similarities. Mohammad Reza Shah made key foreign and security decisions without significant input from his prime ministers or the Majles. These decisions were made without any meaningful public discussions. In the cabinet, the prime minister and the foreign minister alone enjoyed the exclusive privilege of holding regular weekly meetings with the king.[22] The Shah also exercised direct and absolute control over the country's military, security, and intelligence agencies.

In 1921, at the onset of his meteoric rise to power, Reza Khan issued a decree that began with 'Farman Meedaham' or 'I So Order', establishing his role as the country's new strongman.[23] As king, he wielded absolute authority over Iran's foreign policy, a pattern continued by his son, Mohammad Reza Shah, and by Khomeini and Khamenei. In both imperial and revolutionary Iran, the king and the Supreme Leader issue *farman*, and the system, using different methods and institutions, follows suit, demonstrating the continuity of centralised power and hierarchical structures.

Iran's Strategic Goals: Power and Deterrence

Revolutionary Iran's primary objectives in the region include expanding its power by empowering marginalised forces and Islamising the political landscape, reducing US influence and, ideally, expelling US troops from the region and opposing, and if possible, eradicating Israel. Concurrently, Iran is actively engaged in building deterrence against the United States.[24] These core goals are influenced by Iran's threat perception. Tehran has employed various methods to achieve its core objectives in Iraq, Syria, Lebanon, Yemen, and Gaza.

While Iran has historically aspired to extend its influence beyond its volatile neighbourhood, the Islamic Revolution provided the country with an additional motivating force: expanding the tentacles of its power in the name of Islam and the export of its revolution. The 1979 constitution embodies the interventionist ethos of the revolution and its aversion to the United States, albeit without explicit mention. It calls for 'the complete elimination of imperialism and the prevention of foreign influence' (Article 3, Chapter I), and stipulates that while Iran must refrain from interfering in the internal affairs of other nations, it must also support 'the just struggles of the *mustadh'afun* [the downtrodden] against the *mustakbirun* [arrogant] in every corner of the globe' (Article 154, Chapter X).[25] The Islamic Republic's hardliners have used this article to justify the Islamic Republic's intervention in the internal affairs of other countries.

The aspirations of Iranian revolutionaries to expand their power and the United States' determination to thwart it are also consistent with the historical precedent of past revolutions. Following revolutions in France in 1791 and Russia in 1917, global powers, in collaboration with their regional allies, swiftly moved to prevent their spread and to preserve both the regional and the global order. The United States also promptly recognised the urgency of containing the potential destabilising impact of the Islamic Revolution and the subsequent Soviet invasion of Afghanistan in 1979. In 1980, President Carter established the Rapid Deployment Force, which later evolved into the US Central Command. Consistent with the Carter Doctrine, which was designed to defend the United States' interests in the Persian Gulf, the primary mission of Central Command was to 'serve as a hedge against the expansionist goals of Iran'.[26] Iraq's invasion of Iran in September 1980 was also a bold attempt to halt, or at least slow down, the spread of the Islamic Revolution. However, this war with Iraq served as the motor for expanding Iran's regional influence. The littoral countries of the Persian Gulf were equally concerned about the spread of the Islamic Revolution and the Iran–Iraq War. To protect themselves against the export of the Islamic Revolution, Saudi Arabia, Kuwait, the United Arab Emirates (UAE), Qatar, Bahrain, and Oman joined forces to establish the Gulf Cooperation Council in February 1981.[27]

Against the backdrop of opposition from the US and its regional allies, as well as the war with Iraq, the Islamic Republic formulated an evolving strategy to achieve its broad objectives in the region, based on four pillars.[28]

The first pillar of Iran's strategy is expansion of power. Both Khomeini and Khamenei, like the Shah before them, recognised the crucial role of power in international politics. However, unlike the Shah, they perceived that national power is best realised through the promotion of Islam and in opposition to the United States. Before he assumed the role of the Supreme Leader, Khamenei, as Iran's president (1981–1989), addressed the United Nations General Assembly in 1988, declaring that 'Global hegemonies [US and USSR] do not understand anything but force and power, and it is necessary to use the language of power when confronted with their language of power.'[29] As commander of the Iranian armed forces, Khamenei has sought to bolster Iranian power, asserting that any threat against Iran must be met with a corresponding threat, and that the era of 'hit and run' attacks against Iran has ended.[30] The IRGC has elevated Khamenei's philosophy of 'threat against threat' into one of the central pillars of Iran's regional policies, as evidenced by its adoption of the 'forward defence strategy'.[31] In the early days of the revolution, Iran employed this strategy sparingly when it dispatched IRGC forces to Syria to assist in establishing Hezbollah in Lebanon. However, it has become a key component of Iran's regional policies over the past two decades. This strategy assumes that the likelihood of hostile actions by the US and its Middle Eastern allies, such as targeting Iran's nuclear infrastructures, decreases when Iran extends its power beyond its borders, or establishes strategic depth in regions where it could potentially undermine vital US interests. Khamenei has encapsulated the essence of this strategy by asserting that Iran's enemies oppose its presence in the region because it 'gives us strategic depth and much more national power'.[32]

The second pillar of Iran's regional strategy involves establishing a covert regional network, originally built during the Iran–Iraq War. The IRGC and Iran's itinerant Shia clerics leveraged religious sensibilities, along with deeply engrained anti-colonial and anti-Western sentiments prevalent in the region, to mobilise the historically disenfranchised Shias and others and weaponise their grievances.[33] The IRGC established an ideologically cohesive network of allies and militias trained in asymmetric and hybrid warfare, skills they had mastered during the Iran–Iraq War.[34] Irregular warfare is often the preferred and cost-effective choice for the weaker party against the powerful, as it avoids the risk of escalation to conventional war.

What has made this network exceptionally effective is what Mohiaddin Mesbahi calls 'anthropology of death-martyrdom' or the willingness of its members to face martyrdom.[35] Another important factor contributing to the resiliency of this network is the belief among its members that their fate is inextricably tied to the survival of the network itself. They are anti-American and anti-Israel, often operating in grey areas outside the jurisdiction of the states where they reside and willing to commit acts of terrorism. This network has provided a cost-effective, human-based deterrence mechanism against the US and its allies.[36] Initially comprising exclusively Shia groups, the network has evolved into the Axis of Resistance, now encompassing Sunni organisations such as Hamas and the Palestinian Islamic Jihad.[37] While these groups are often branded as Iran's proxies, implying they are mere mercenaries devoid of agency, the reality is more complex and nuanced.[38] These non-state actors are deeply embedded in the societies where they operate, enjoying varying degrees of autonomy from Tehran, although they all rely on Iran's weapons and multifaceted support. They possess significant independence in addressing local issues according to their own discretion. Nevertheless, they often align with Tehran's broad priorities.[39]

The third pillar of Iran's strategy is built on balancing and counterbalancing strategies aimed at both expanding its power and mitigating its threat perception. Iran forged an enduring alliance with Syria, based on what Walt terms a 'balance of threat'.[40] They joined forces against their perceived common threats from Iraq, Israel, and the US. Iran also formed a tactical military alliance with Russia during the Syrian civil war in 2015 to counterbalance the forces aligned against President Bashar Assad, including the US. This tactical alliance with Russia was a component of Iran's broader 'counterbalancing' strategy against the US, which involved its recent pivot towards Russia and China.[41] This pivot accelerated after President Trump's unilateral withdrawal from the Iran nuclear deal in 2018.

The fourth pillar of Iran's regional strategy is founded on the establishment of a relatively self-sufficient military-industrial complex. Its construction began during the Iran–Iraq War, a period when the US and other Western powers imposed an arms embargo on Iran while allowing Iraq to be heavily armed. Recently, this complex, which oversees Iran's nuclear programme, has been producing advanced missiles and drones, serving as the cornerstone of Iran's defence doctrine. It is from this complex that Iran has armed and equipped its regional network.

Dissecting the essence of Iran's regional strategy also requires acknowledging the role of its perception of threats.[42] The importance of threat perception in international relations should not be underestimated.[43] As recently highlighted by Melvyn Leffler, President George W. Bush's perception that Iraq possessed weapons of mass destruction played an important role in his decision to invade Iraq in 2003 – a point that is rejected by some observers.[44] Since its founding in 1979, the Islamic Republic's regional policy has been profoundly influenced by its threat perception, which is a blend of genuine concerns and exaggerations.

Insecurity is a congenital and lingering ailment of the Islamic Republic, stemming from constant fears of a popular uprising and perceived US machinations to overthrow it.[45] In an interview, Prime Minister Bazargan told me that Khomeini 'was shocked to see how swiftly the Shah's regime fell and feared that remnants of the Imperial Army, in collusion with the US, might attempt to restore the monarchy. He felt insecure, even when he was securely in power.'[46] Khomeini's paranoia reached its peak when he issued an unprecedented edict emphatically asserting that the preservation of Iran's theocracy was the foremost duty of the faithful, even if it entailed violating some fundamental pillars of Islam. However, some of his fears were justified. The early years of the Islamic Republic were marked by the spread of separatist movements, insurgencies, mass uprisings, targeted assassinations of officials, and coup attempts. This period of instability was further complicated by regional geopolitical shifts, including the 1979 Soviet invasion of Afghanistan and Iraq's invasion of Iran in 1980. This sense of insecurity persisted beyond Khomeini's death. In 1989, Iraq invaded Kuwait, leading to the deployment of hundreds of thousands of US troops in the Persian Gulf. This was followed by the US invasions of Afghanistan in 2001 and Iraq in 2003. By that time, US forces had virtually encircled Iran. At the same time, there were calls for bombing Iranian nuclear facilities and its military infrastructure.[47]

Presently, the US maintains military bases or facilities in Iran's neighbours in countries such as Iraq, Kuwait, Oman, Qatar, Saudi Arabia, the UAE, and Turkey. Furthermore, within a radius of approximately 2,000 kilometres from Iran, there are three nuclear-armed nations: Pakistan, India, and Israel.[48] Adding to Iran's apprehensions has been the US support for various opposition groups against the Islamic Republic, along with the imposition of economic, financial, and military sanctions by Western powers.[49]

Ayatollah Khamenei once remarked that 'the Americans and their allies always threaten Iran, meanwhile, they expect that Iran reduce its defensive power. Is this a joke? Isn't that ridiculous?'[50] His strategic thinking focuses on expanding Iranian power, both defensively and offensively, in the region as insurance for the survival of the Islamic Republic and as a deterrent against adversaries.[51]

Factional Rivalry and Iranian Regional Policies

The foreign policy of the Islamic Republic, reflecting its internal politics, has swung from radicalism to pragmatism, and more recently to militarisation.[52] These shifts were the outcomes of factional rivalries among the elites, Iran's relations with the US, and regional developments.[53]

Since the onset of the Islamic Revolution, the debate regarding Iran's relationship with the US and the extent to which the Islamic Republic must adhere to pan-Shia and pan-Islamic principles have profoundly influenced Iran's foreign policy. There are two paradigms at play, each represented by a powerful political faction. Hardliners advocate for an interventionist foreign policy primarily rooted in an unwavering commitment to pan-Shia and pan-Islamic principles and, secondarily, in safeguarding the country's national interests. They view the US as an imperialist power dedicated to maintaining its global dominance. Consequently, they resist establishing normal relations with the US, often citing Khomeini's analogy of US–Iranian relations resembling those between a ravenous wolf and a fat sheep. In a way, being anti-American and anti-Israel has become part of their identity. [54] In contrast, moderates advocate for a less ideological and more realistic foreign policy that carefully balances the enhancement of Iranian national interests with its commitment to pan-Shia principles. They contend that establishing normal relations with the US is essential for Iran's integration into the global economy and the welfare of its people.

The tumultuous radical phase of Iranian foreign policy coincided with the consolidation of power by Ayatollah Khomeini in the 1980s. During this phase, a new generation of radical, idealistic, ambitious, inexperienced, and mostly young Iranians assumed control of the country's foreign policy establishment. Mesmerised by the revolutionary spirit, pro-Khomeini forces suppressed the voices of secular nationalists and leftists. At the same time, they rewarded unbridled radicalism, fervent anti-Americanism, and strong anti-Israeli policies. The Tehran hostage crisis and Iraq's invasion of Iran further radicalised the domestic scene, sparked a cold war with the US, and ignited an eight-year war of attrition with Iraq. Iran's primary objective – and its obsession – was to win the war against Iraq. Concurrently, Iran built a regional network, helped establish Hezbollah in Lebanon, formed an alliance with Syria, and bolstered its deterrence capabilities against Iraq, the US, and Israel. To protect the revolution, Khomeini maintained a balance between hardliners and moderates, ensuring that neither faction could prevail over the other.

The moderate phase of Iran's regional policies began when the revolutionary fever abated somewhat, following the ceasefire between Iran and Iraq in 1988 and the passing of Ayatollah Khomeini in 1989. [55] One day after Khomeini's death, the Assembly of Experts for Leadership voted to make Hojatolislam Khamenei, the incumbent president, the Supreme Leader. Two weeks later, Hojatolislam Ali Akbar Hashemi Rafsanjani (1934–2017) was voted in as president. Rafsanjani, arguably Iran's most powerful leader after Khomeini's death, played a crucial role in the selection of Khamenei as successor to Khomeini. Rafsanjani ultimately came to regret his pivotal support of Khamenei. He perhaps initially believed that by establishing a strong, imperial presidency and leveraging the vast national network he had built during his leadership of the Majles, he could out-manoeuvre Khamenei, who had a narrow base of popular support, and position himself as Iran's strongman. He was proven wrong.

Recognising the fatigue and apathy of Iranians, desperate for normalcy after a long war, Khamenei and Rafsanjani collaborated to ensure a smooth transition of power.[56] While Khamenei quietly and diligently focused on consolidating his power by bringing the deep state, the IRGC, and other security forces under his control, Rafsanjani moved swiftly to revitalise the country's struggling economy and moderate its foreign policies to attract foreign investments.[57] Khamenei followed Khomeini's precedent and maintained a delicate equilibrium between rival factions, though not for too long.

During this moderate phase, Iran improved relations with the Persian Gulf's littoral states, consolidated its position in Lebanon, strengthened its alliance with Hafez Assad, and established ties with the Houthis in Yemen. Tehran also welcomed the auspicious disintegration of the Soviet Union, which removed a major threat from its northern borders and allowed it to reallocate resources to the Middle East.[58] Rafsanjani orchestrated an ill-fated rapprochement with the US, despite the American policy of 'dual containment' to restrain both Iran and Iraq.[59] In that vein, Iran maintained neutrality during the First Persian Gulf War, despite its vehement opposition to the deployment of hundreds of thousands of US troops in the region. Rafsanjani even reached a tentative agreement with Conoco, an American oil company, for a potentially game-changing $1 billion deal in 1995 – a first since the revolution. The agreement was scuttled when President Bill Clinton issued an executive order.

Pragmatism in foreign policy continued beyond Rafsanjani's presidency. President Mohammad Khatami tried to reshape the Islamic

Republic into a more tolerant, transparent, and representative state. Committed to fostering a 'Dialogue Among Civilisations' as the corner-stone of his foreign policy, Khatami improved relations with Iran's neigh-bours and the West. Most notably, Iran reached a tentative nuclear agree-ment with Germany, England, and France.

Despite his best intentions, Khatami's attempted reforms ultimately failed. Significantly, for the first time, the balance of factional power began to visibly shift towards hardliners. When massive protests erupted in response to the closure of a popular reformist newspaper in July 1999, leading to the deaths of between four to seven students, twenty-four IRGC commanders, including Qasem Soleimani, issued a letter to Khatami. They warned him that they would take matters into their own hands unless Khatami prosecuted the protestors – and they did.[60] Subsequently, Khatami faced increased marginalisation by the deep state. Despite this, he remained popular, as the public recognised that unelected officials were undermining his reforms. Consequently, Khatami easily won re-election in 2001. However, in his second term, he was even less effective in governing or reforming Iranian foreign policy than during his first term.

The current militarisation phase of Iran's regional policies took root following the US invasions of Afghanistan in 2001 and Iraq in 2003. This period also saw a significant shift in the factional balance of power in favour of the hardliners and the deep state, a process that had begun during Khatami's tenure. The shift accelerated after 2005, when, in a contested presidential election, Mahmoud Ahmadinejad claimed victory over Hashemi Rafsanjani, the Islamic Republic's most powerful voice of moderation. However, the pivotal year for this power shift was 2009, during Ahmadinejad's re-election campaign. Prior to the presidential campaign, his arch-enemy Rafsanjani penned a missive to Khamenei, warning that Iran was teetering on the edge of turmoil without free elec-tions.[61] His prediction proved to be accurate. Following the election, Ahmadinejad's principal rivals, former prime minister Mir Hossein Mousavi and former speaker of the Majles Mehdi Karroubi, accused Ahmadinejad of orchestrating an 'electoral coup', triggering massive protests that gave rise to the Green Movement. While the movement sought to democratise the Islamic Republic, government forces forcefully suppressed it, leading to a significant schism within the governing elites and further weakening both the pragmatic and reformist factions. Both Rafsanjani and Khatami supported the Green Movement. In response, Khamenei publicly aligned himself with Ahmadinejad against Rafsanjani and the reformists. For all intents and purposes, the decades-long friendship between Rafsanjani and Khamenei came to an end, dealing an irreparable blow to the forces of moderation that could have tempered the radical impulses in Iranian foreign policy. Thereafter, the Islamic or non-elected components of the Islamic Republic were progressively strengthened, while its republican elements weakened. Moreover, the drive towards homogenising the elites began in earnest, paving the way for the dominance of hardliners backed by the deep state and the IRGC. Although the election of pragmatic Hassan Rouhani, a protégé of Rafsanjani, to the presidency in 2013 resulted in the landmark nuclear deal between Iran and six global powers in 2015 (the Joint Comprehensive Plan of Action – JPCOA), it did not result in a significant change in Iran's regional policies.

In tandem with the major shift in the factional balance of power in favour of hardliners, the civil wars in Iraq, Syria, and Yemen further fuelled this militarisation. Khamenei and Soleimani were pivotal in steering and leading Iran's regional policies towards militarisation, prioritising security, and military objectives over diplomatic and economic imperatives. With hundreds of thousand US and NATO troops deployed around Iran's eastern and western borders, Iran saw itself as encircled and threatened. Tehran's fears deepened further when President George W. Bush announced his new 'preventive war' strategy, granting the US the authority to pre-emptively attack other countries to eliminate imminent threats to its national interests.[62] President Trump's 'maximum pressure' policy spurred Iran on, as normal relations with the US seemed off the table. Trump unilaterally withdrew from the JPCOA nuclear deal in May 2018 and reimposed sanctions to destabilise Iran and compel it to negotiate a new nuclear deal. Secretary of State Mike Pompeo candidly stated that the US will 'crush Iran … until we achieve' our goals.[63]

Throughout all three phases, the Islamic Republic actively pursued the objectives of expanding its power and building deterrence. The foundation for these twin goals, however, was laid during the Iran–Iraq War, which served as the military cornerstone of Iran's rise. Now, let's delve deeper into this intricate dynamic.

Chapter 3
Iran–Iraq War: Laying the Foundations for Iran's Rise

In peace, sons bury their fathers. In war, fathers bury their sons.
— Herodotus

Monday, 22 September 1980, will forever be etched in Iran's history as a day of infamy. While Iran was still reeling from its revolution, Iraq launched an invasion. Before the invasion, President Saddam Hussein confided in his generals that 'We have to stick their [Iranians'] noses in mud so we can impose our political will over them.'[1] With striking audacity, Iraq launched surprise airstrikes on Iran's ten major airports, aiming to cripple its air force. Subsequently, Iraq deployed ground troops at multiple points along the 904-mile-long border between the two countries. It is plausible that Iraq sought to replicate Israel's successful military strategy during its Six-Day War against Egypt, Jordan, and Syria in June 1967. In that war, Israel astounded its enemies with its lightning-fast pre-emptive airstrikes, which effectively disabled much of their air forces. Simultaneously, Israel's ground offensives captured substantial Arab territory, resulting in a decisive victory in mere six days. But Iraq was no Israel. Its overly optimistic pursuit of a swift and conclusive victory turned into a nightmare, ultimately culminating in one of the twentieth century's longest and deadliest conventional wars.

What triggered this war with Iraq – the most destructive and deadly for Iran in at least three centuries? What were its ramifications, what role did the US play in it, and how did it lay the military foundation for Iran's rise in the Middle East?

Pre-revolutionary Iran's Uneasy Relations with Iraq

Persia has cast a long shadow over Iraq (which was part of former Mesopotamia) for many centuries. In antiquity, most of that region was ruled by three Persian empires – the Achaemenids, the Parthians, and the Sassanids. Ctesiphon, situated near Baghdad, served as the Sassanids' capital (224–651). Today, the remains of the old palace, Ayvan-e Kasra, distinguished by its towering clay arch, continue to be a popular tourist attraction.[2]

In the early modern period, Iraq was caught between the Sunni Ottoman and Shia Safavid empires, with control of Baghdad changing hands several times. After the signing of the Treaty of Qasr-e Shirin in 1639 (also known as the Treaty of Zuhab), the Persian and Ottoman empires brought an end to their protracted, intermittent wars by establishing a demarcated boundary between them.[3] Consequently, Iran relinquished its ambition to control Baghdad and southern Mesopotamia. Iraq's status as an Ottoman stronghold subsequently obstructed Iran's expansion westward towards the Levant and south-west towards the Arabian Peninsula. This balance of power between the Persian and Ottoman empires would be upturned when the British captured Baghdad in 1917. As the victorious powers carved up a new Middle East order in the aftermath of the First World War, the British moved to establish Iraq as a nominally independent state.

Iran's religious bonds with Iraq are strong as well. The two countries represent the two largest Shia-majority countries in the Middle East, with between 61 to 64 per cent of Iraq's population being Shia.[4] The mausoleums or shrines of many of the most revered Shia imams are in Iraq. The Najaf *Hawza*, the oldest and most iconic Shia seminary, was founded by the Persian theologian Sheikh Mohammad ibn al-Hasan al-Tusi (995–1067) in the eleventh century. Moreover, a large community of Persians and Persian-Iraqis has resided in southern Iraq for centuries, coexisting with a network that still connects the clerical establishments of the two countries. The confluence of these factors has created a situation in which Iran's ambition to expand its power in Iraq and beyond has been linked to its capacity to leverage 'the Shia card'. But why didn't Iran play this card when Iraq was established in 1921?[5]

When the League of Nations granted Britain a mandate to rule over Iraq in 1920, the country's majority Shia population rebelled against British rule.[6] These protestors drew inspiration from a *fatwa*, a religious decree, issued by Sheikh Mohammad-Taqi Shirazi, an Iranian cleric in Iraq, which forbade non-Muslim rule over Iraq. In 1921, following the violent suppression of these protests, Britain installed Faisal bin Hussein as king.[7]

Interestingly, Britain had backed a coup by Reza Khan in Iran six months prior to installing Hussein in Iraq. Both of these developments were integral to a broader British strategy to establish and sustain a new Middle Eastern order, protect its oil investments in the region, and integrate both Iraq and Iran into its security architecture against the growing menace of Russian communism.[8]

Reza Khan had his reasons for standing back while Iraq's Sunni minority, supported by Britain, consolidated control over the nascent state at the expense of the Shia majority. On a personal level, he harboured ambitions of eventually ascending to the throne as king and could not afford to antagonise Britain, which was then Iran's dominant foreign power. From a political standpoint, he staunchly opposed empowering Shias in Iraq, fearing it might embolden their brethren in Iran, just as he prepared to modernise the country and curtail the power of Shia clerics.

Ironically, Reza Khan's passive approach towards developments in neighbouring Iraq stemmed partly from his realism and nationalism. He recognised that Iran lacked the capability to challenge Britain, yet remained steadfast in safeguarding Iran's territorial integrity, particularly in the oil-rich Khuzestan province. In that province, with its significant Iranian-Arab population, Sheikh Khaz'al bin al-Ka'bi, a corrupt and ambitious Iranian-Arab ruler supported by the British, was plotting to establish an independent country.[9] Aware of Khaz'al's scheme, Reza Khan and his troops advanced into Khuzestan, swiftly dismantling Khaz'al's small fiefdom. The conniving sheikh was later arrested and placed under house arrest in Tehran until his death.[10] Shortly thereafter, the Majles, impressed by Reza Khan's triumph in Khuzestan, approved the end of the Qajar dynasty and the establishment of the Pahlavi dynasty in December 1925, thereby proclaiming him as Reza Shah.

During Reza Shah's reign, Iraq and Iran maintained a friendly yet uneasy relationship. The most contentious dispute centred around the question of sovereignty over the Arvand Rood, or Shatt al-Arab, a crucial waterway connecting both countries to the Persian Gulf. Supported by Britain, Iraq claimed full sovereignty over the waterway based on the 1913 Constantinople Protocol, which had been signed between the Persian and Ottoman empires. In contrast, Iran contended that the protocol lacked legal validity because Tehran had signed it under pressure from the Ottomans, Britain, and Russia. Instead, Iran demanded joint sovereignty over the waterway, drawing from the Thalweg Doctrine, which delineates boundary lines along the centre of navigable waterways. Ultimately Reza Shah capitulated and signed the 1937 treaty, granting Iraq sovereignty over the lower estuary of the waterway, except for a few square kilometres near Iran's major oil installations.[11] This outcome was a setback for Iran and a victory for Iraq, but it was not the end of the story.

Mohammad Reza Shah's Triumph: The Algiers Accords

Relations between Iran and Iraq remained generally friendly until Brigadier Abdul al-Karim Qasem orchestrated a bloody coup in Iraq in July 1958. Inspired by Egyptian President Gamal Abdel Nasser's pan-Arabism, which advocated the unification of the Arab world, Qasem overthrew the monarchy, brutally killed the young King Faisal II and many others, and established a republic.

The Shah was 'shocked and frightened'[12] by the possibility that the coup in Iraq could inspire Iranian military officers to stage a coup against his dynasty.[13] The American embassy in Tehran portrayed the Shah's palace as if it were a war zone, noting that the 'Palace Guard has been strengthened by transfer of tanks'.[14] The Shah's fears were not entirely unwarranted, as the CIA had not dismissed the likelihood of a coup against him. His perception of threat was amplified when Iraq withdrew from the anti-Soviet Baghdad Pact and moved closer to the Soviet sphere of influence. Over the next decade, Iraq's rhetoric and actions became more provocative. Baghdad called for the 'liberation' of Khuzestan from the 'Persian occupiers' and became a haven for Iran's outlawed Tudeh party,[15] as well as for General Teymur Bakhtiyar. A former ambitious head of SAVAK, now a disgruntled figure, Bakhtiyar was actively hatching plots against the Shah.[16] In his missive to President Lyndon Johnson in 1964, the Shah asserted that Iran had unearthed 'centres of Arab espionage in Khuzestan', allegedly supported by Iraq and 'international communism'.[17] When his warnings were dismissed by Washington, he played hardball with Iraq.[18] He called for joint sovereignty over the Arvand Rood and the renegotiation of the 1937 treaty. Iraq rebuffed this entreaty and became more aggressive.

Following the British withdrawal of forces from the Persian Gulf in 1968, Iran and Iraq became deeply embroiled in a rivalry for regional dominance. The Shah, a staunch opponent of the Western military presence in the Persian Gulf, was determined to replace Britain as the dominant power in the region.[19] He believed that 'each major power should have an acknowledged zone of influence. Iran's zone is the Persian Gulf', where it 'will ultimately work for the elimination of both the Soviet and US military presence'.[20] Viewing Iraq as the primary obstacle to his ambitions, the Shah pursued unusually assertive policies aimed at undermining Iraq.[21]

The Shah's opening manoeuvre in his power play was to demand that Iraq engage in renegotiation to revisit the 1937 agreement concerning sovereignty over the Arvand Rood. Iraq rejected this demand, and, in a display of its determination, threatened to use force to compel Iranian vessels to lower their flags while navigating the Arvand Rood. In a remarkable response, the Shah unilaterally withdrew from the 1937 agreement.[22] He then ordered Iranian fighter jets to escort a ship adorned with the Iranian flag as it traversed the Arvand Rood. This bold move caught Iraq off guard, and the the vessel was allowed to pass through unimpeded.

Iraqi Kurds and the SAVAK–CIA–Mossad Axis

The linchpin of the Shah's strategy to undermine Iraq was to leverage the Iraqi Kurds, comprising approximately 18 per cent of Iraq's population, as a proxy to destabilise Baghdad.[23] He ordered Colonel Mujtaba Pashaei, chief of SAVAK's Middle East operations, to provide military and financial support to Mullah Mustafa Barzani, the pre-eminent leader of his generation and the head of the Kurdistan Democratic Party.[24] Despite harbouring suspicions about Barzani, who earned the moniker the 'Red Mullah' after spending twelve years as a political refugee in the Soviet Union, the Shah opted to support him.[25] The Shah armed the Kurds to pressure Iraq into recognising joint sovereignty over the Arvand Rood and to divert Iraqi troops north-west, thereby allowing Iran to strengthen its position in the Persian Gulf. As Iran's ally, Israel played a crucial role in the Shah's strategy to support the Kurds, as Tel Aviv hoped the Kurds would 'distract the Iraqi government from anti-Israel activities'.[26]

Baghdad, which had decided to use the army 'to seek a final solution' to the Kurdish problem, was aware of the Shah's plan and took measures to neutralise it.[27] Initially, Saddam Hussein, an ambitious Ba'ath party apparatchik and vice president of Iraq's Revolutionary Command Council, reached a tentative agreement with Barzani in March 1970, granting substantial concessions to the Kurds. However, the informal agreement faltered, partly because the Shah increased his military and financial assistance for the Kurds, coupled with his commitment to lobby for US backing for the Kurdish cause, a goal Barzani had tirelessly pursued for years but failed to achieve. Initially, the US was hesitant to assist the Kurds, as Washington was attempting to mend relations with Baghdad and prevent its further alignment with the Soviet Union. In due course, President Nixon reversed his stance, and, in August 1972, instructed the CIA to covertly support the Kurds. This marked the formation of the axis of SAVAK–CIA–Mossad (Israel's intelligence agency) to use Iraqi Kurds against Baghdad. Iran, however, played the pivotal role in this axis, both militarily and financially. During the peak of the military operations against Baghdad in 1974, Iran contributed $75 million to Barzani, overshadowing the CIA's contribution of $18 million.[28] Iran also maintained a more substantial military presence in Iraq's Kurdistan than the US and Israel. In fact, Iranian forces had crossed into Iraqi territory, introducing 'artillery and air defence units directly into the fighting inside Iraq'.[29] Despite deploying its troops extensively to the northern region, Iraq's army was unable to subdue the Kurds, resulting in a stubborn stalemate and substantial casualties on both sides.

Ultimately, in March 1975, the Shah and Saddam Hussein met in Algiers and signed the Algiers Accords, ending years of hostility between the two countries.[30] The agreement also abruptly terminated Iran's support for the Iraqi Kurds.[31]

Without Iranian support, Iraq's army quickly subdued the Kurdish resistance. As a result, the Shah faced scathing criticisms in the US for 'ditching the Kurds'.[32] Israel, too, expressed dissatisfaction with the Shah.[33] Uri Lubrani, Israel's unofficial ambassador to Iran, conveyed to the American embassy in Tehran that Israel was displeased with the Shah's decision to sign the Algiers Accords and abandon the Kurds.[34] Israel would have preferred the Iraqi army to focus on suppressing the Kurdish insurgency rather than engaging with Israel.

Iraqi Kurds understandably felt betrayed by the Shah. To appease the Kurds, the monarch met Barzani in Tehran in March 1975, promising to provide him and thousands of Kurdish Peshmerga (militias) a sanctuary in Iran along with financial support.[35] These gestures by the Shah, however, did not alleviate the Kurds' sense of betrayal.[36] Isa Pejman, a former SAVAK official, alleged that the Kurds were so incensed that they distributed weapons to the revolutionaries who overthrew the Shah in 1979.[37]

Despite these criticisms, the Shah displayed prudence and served Iranian national interests by signing the Algiers Accords.[38] This represented a major victory for him and reinforced his position as a major regional power.[39] Iraq finally yielded to Iran's demand for joint sovereignty over the Arvand Rood, based on the principle of *thalweg* – an achievement that had eluded his father, Reza Shah. The Shah's strategy worked as intended. Following the signing of the accords, Sa'dun Hammadi, Iraq's former foreign minister, conceded that Iraq either had to accept the Algiers Accords or 'lose the north of the country' to the Kurds.[40]

Most importantly, the Shah wisely averted a potential war with Iraq. He astutely conveyed to the Ford administration that: 'It was not in Iran's interest any longer to send out troops to the other side of the border.'[41] He was right. In the November 1974 President's Daily Brief, we learned that 'the possibility of larger scale fighting between Iraqi and Iranian troops is increasing'.[42] Furthermore, the Shah recognised that normalising relations with Iraq would not only bolster his personal standing in the Arab world, where he faced criticism for his support of Israel, but also serve as a necessary step towards expanding Iranian power beyond the Persian Gulf and into the heart of the Arab world. Egyptian President Sadat assured the Shah that such normalisation would integrate Iran into the 'Arab mainstream' and reduce Iraq's dependence on Moscow.[43]

Following the signing the Algiers Accords, Iran and Iraq enjoyed a brief period of peace. Saddam Hussein even visited the Shah in Tehran. This was the calm before the storm, however, as the Iranian revolution unleashed a tidal wave of change, transforming the two neighbours into bitter adversaries.

Invading Iran: Iraq's Deadly Miscalculations

It is unclear precisely when Saddam Hussein made the fateful decision to invade Iran in September 1980. However, it seems that he had been preparing for the war for months in advance.[44]

Relations between Iran and Iraq rapidly deteriorated following the Islamic Revolution, steadily pushing the two countries towards an inevitable confrontation.[45] Tehran accused Iraq of engaging in border ambushes and skirmishes, arming the opponents of the Islamic Republic, and attempting to destabilise the country. At the same time, radical Iranian Islamists unleashed vitriolic rhetoric against President Saddam Hussein and recklessly incited their Iraqi Shia brethren to overthrow him. Iran also began to arm and train anti-Saddam forces on its soil.[46]

Threatened by the Islamic Revolution, Saddam Hussein consolidated power and prepared for an eventual clash with the Islamic Republic.[47] He was mindful of Khomeini's animosity towards him, as he had expelled the septuagenarian ayatollah from Iraq in 1978 at the urging of the Shah. He assumed the presidency by forcing President al Bakr into resigning in July 1979, and purged the Ba'ath party. He then began to eliminate his Shia opponents. His security forces killed Ayatollah Mohammad Baqer al-Sadr, Iraq's popular Shia leader, along with his sister. They arrested, killed, and forced into exile many members of the al Dawa party, Iraq's largest Shia organisation. They forcibly expelled thousands of the estimated '250,000 Shias of Iranian ancestry'.[48]

Saddam Hussein also provided financial and logistical support to exiled opponents of Khomeini. His true intentions came to light two months prior to the invasion, when he reportedly lent financial support to the failed Nojeh coup against Khomeini, resulting in the death and purges of thousands of officers. The attempted coup was orchestrated to overthrow the revolutionary government and was organised by the remnants of the Imperial Armed Forces, in collaboration with former prime minister Shapour Bakhtiyar, who was living in Paris at the time, and seemed to have enjoyed some support from the United States.[49] As Wright observed, 'The war [against Iran] was an extension in Saddam's mind of the coup [Nojeh] that failed.'[50]

Ultimately, Saddam Hussein made the decision to invade because he believed that Iran had become exceptionally vulnerable and isolated. He correctly recognised Iraq's notable military advantage over Iran. The CIA estimated that Iraq enjoyed 'a 2-to-1 advantage in the number of modern aircraft ... a 3-to-1 advantage in operational tanks and a nearly 2-to-1 advantage in operational armoured personnel carriers'.[51] He was aware that the revolutionaries had ruthlessly eliminated the top leadership of the Iranian armed forces, while the US arms embargo had significantly eroded their operational capabilities. He was receiving the same pessimistic assessment of Iran's preparedness from former Iranian military officials. Bruce Riedel, the CIA's Iran desk officer at the start of Iraq's invasion, recalled that General Gholam Ali Oveissi, the last commander of Iran's Imperial Army, confided in him that he had personally informed Saddam Hussein that Iran had become 'too weak' after the revolution.[52]

It is inconceivable that Saddam Hussein would have launched the invasion without being thoroughly convinced that the US and the Soviet Union would not vehemently oppose it. He had cultivated friendly relations with the Soviet Union, which was the primary supplier of weapons to Iraq. He probably assumed that Moscow, especially after its invasion of Afghanistan in 1979, would not take punitive measures against Baghdad. Moreover, he may have calculated that as long as American hostages were held in captivity in Iran, the US might not only refrain from opposing the invasion but might even welcome it. In addition to these considerations, Saddam Hussein was aware that the Arab countries of the Persian Gulf, which were genuinely alarmed by the potential export of Iran's revolution, would not oppose the invasion. He allegedly even secured the promise of financial support from Saudi Arabia, intended to lubricate Iraq's war machine.[53]

In his assessment, Saddam Hussein seemed to have underestimated Iran's significant manpower advantage, its steadfast commitment to safeguarding territorial integrity, preserving national honour, and restructuring its armed forces.[54] He was also ignorant of the dynamics of revolutions: wars waged against revolutions have historically invigorated them rather than quelled them. A decade of revolutionary wars between France and Austria, Prussia, Britain, and others (1792–1802) consolidated the French Revolution and ultimately led to the rise of Napoleon Bonaparte as the French Emperor in 1804. In Iran, Iraq's invasion sparked a remarkable surge in nationalism and a renewed dedication to Shiism, culminating in the institutionalisation and further radicalisation of the nascent theocratic order, while also laying the foundation for Iran's later ascendancy.

Saddam Hussein publicly justified his naked aggression against Iran as 'preventive and pre-emptive', to neutralise what he described as an imminent threat from Iran. But far greater ambitions lay beneath these excuses. His decision was shaped by myriad factors, including his desire to impose Iraq's sovereignty over the Arvand Rood, to acquire or annex territories in Iran's oil-rich provinces with the potential of installing a puppet government in those areas, to take the place formerly held by the Shah as the dominant power in the Persian Gulf, and, if possible, to dismantle the Islamic Republic.[55]

Building a Regional Network

When Iraq launched its surprise air and ground offensives, Iran found itself utterly unprepared to mount an effective defence. Initially, Iraqi forces made impressive advances, capturing several small towns. It took Iran thirty-four days fully to grasp the danger to its territorial integrity when, on 26 October 1980, Iraq captured the strategic port city of Khorramshahr in southern Iran and rapidly advanced towards Abadan, home to its largest oil refinery. However, despite early initial Iraqi successes, Iran's armed forces did not crumble, and its air force remained operational, shattering Iraq's illusion of achieving a quick victory. In fact, the air force, a legacy of Mohammad Reza Shah's modernisation of the armed forces, managed to hit some 'high-visibility targets' inside Iraq,[56] despite facing severe shortage of 'jet fuel and spare parts' for its American-made fighter aircraft.[57] Only four months after the start of the war, in December 1980, the CIA presciently concluded that Iraq could not achieve 'its ambitious strategic objectives in the near future'.[58]

It took seventeen months for Iran to mobilise all its forces and commence offensive operations against Iraq, thereby changing the course of the war in its favour. During this crucial period, Ayatollah Khomeini made four critical decisions that put the country on a war footing. First, he expedited the release of the American hostages 125 days after Iraq's invasion. He recognised that Iran could not sustain both a hot war with Iraq and a cold war with the US simultaneously. Second, in October 1980, he centralised war decision making by establishing the Supreme Defence Council, and instructed the paramilitary *Baseej* organisation to recruit volunteers from all corners of the country for deployment to the war fronts. Third, Khomeini intervened to resolve the dispute between President Abol Hassan Bani Sadr (1933–2021, the first elected president of the Islamic Republic) and the IRGC, which was compromising the effectiveness of Iran's military operations. Bani Sadr, once an advisor to Khomeini, believed that the professional regular army, rather than the inexperienced IRGC, should spearhead Iran's war efforts.[59] He lost that battle. In June 1981, Bani Sadr was impeached by the Majles and fled the country; he was eventually granted political asylum by France. Subsequently, the IRGC's role in the war steadily expanded.

The fourth major initiative by Ayatollah Khomeini was to authorise the Islamic Republic to build a covert regional network of exclusively Shia militias and allies while partially pivoting towards the Levant. In retrospect, this appears to be Iran's first practical step in pursuing a 'forward defence' strategy, with a focus on the Levant. The process of network building began with Iran supporting established Iraqi Shia organisations fighting against Saddam in Iraq, while also facilitating the formation of new Iraqi Shia organisations. Iran then extended this process to the Levant, establishing Hezbollah in Lebanon in 1982 with support from Syria. By the third year of the war, Iran had established a covert regional network, crucial for expanding its regional influence and undermining Iraq.

Iran made substantial investments in supporting and arming al Dawa, or Hizb ad-Da'wa al-Islāmiyya, a Shia organisation founded in Iraq decades before the Islamic Revolution. Some of its members sought refuge in Iran after Iraq accused the party of being Iranian collaborators and declared it illegal in the late 1970s.[60] In response, the party moved its headquarters to Tehran, and the IRGC established a training camp for al Dawa in Ahwaz, close to the war front with Iraq. Al Dawa was not and is not an Iranian puppet or proxy. It is an authentic Iraqi party that shared Iran's goal of toppling Saddam Hussein. Al Dawa did not even embrace the doctrine of the *Velayat-e Faqih*, which is the foundation of Iranian political system.

Al Dawa's first operation was the attack on the Iraqi embassy in Beirut in December 1981, causing significant damage.[61] This was followed by an attempted assassination of Saddam Hussein in Dujail, a small Iraqi town,

in July 1982. In response, Saddam executed 148 individuals and prosecuted around 800 others.[62] Al Dawa also was implicated in the terrorist
bombing of the US and French embassies in Kuwait in December 1983,
resulting in six deaths (with no American casualties). One of the motivations behind these attacks could have been to intimidate those who were
supporting Iraq during the war. While the Islamic Republic's involvement in these operations remains unclear, they were aligned with Iran's
strategic goals.

Iran also played a pivotal role in the formation of the Supreme Council
of Islamic Revolution in Iraq (SCIRI) in 1982. Established in Tehran,
SCIRI served as a critical bridge connecting the Shia clerical establishments in Iraq and Iran. In 1982, the IRGC played the key role of creating
the SCIRI's military wing, known as the Badr Brigade, which gradually
evolved into one of Iran's closest Iraqi militias.[63] Unlike al Dawa, the
Badr Brigade maintained close military and ideological ties to Tehran, as
Ayatollah Khomeini harboured a deep mistrust of any organisation he
had not created and could not control. Unlike al Dawa, SCIRI aspired to
import the Islamic Revolution to Iraq by creating an Islamic government
mirroring that of Iran's Islamic Republic.[64]

Both the armed wing of al Dawa and the Badr Brigade provided
multifaceted assistance to Iran during the war, reportedly including
fighting alongside Iranian soldiers and gathering intelligence. However,
the precise extent of their contribution remains unclear. Nonetheless,
these two Iraqi organisations played a significant role in Iran's expansion
of power in Iraq following the US invasion in March 2003.

To End or Escalate the War

In May 1982, Iran achieved its first major battlefield victory by liberating
the important city of Khorramshahr. After this victory, Iran found itself at
a crossroads: whether to end the war or escalate it by advancing into Iraqi
territory. Ultimately, Ayatollah Khomeini made the monumental decision to take the war into Iraqi territory, thereby squandering an auspicious opportunity to bring the conflict to a close from a position of
strength. There are varying narratives surrounding the rationale behind

this decision. Mohsen Rezaei, IRGC commander, argued that both IRGC and army commanders favoured taking the war into Iraq.[65] President Khamenei, who also served as chair of the Supreme Defence Council, appeared to favour the continuation of the war, advocating for the defeat of Saddam Hussein while emphasising that Iran had no intention of annexing any part of Iraqi territory.[66] However, Rafsanjani, who served as the acting commander of the Iranian armed forces, presented a convoluted interpretation. While Khomeini had instructed Rafsanjani 'to continue the war until victory', he also voiced concerns about entering Iraq, fearing that with such action 'the world will condemn Iran as aggressor'.[67] Rafsanjani appeared to suggest that Khomeini opposed advancing into Iraqi territory. Regardless of the veracity of these conflicting narratives, the responsibility for the decision rested squarely with Khomeini.

Iran's decision to take the war into Iraq changed the dynamics of the conflict. Based on the mistaken intelligence that Iraq's army was teetering on the brink of collapse, Tehran recalibrated its war strategy with the objective of capturing Basra, a Shia-dominated, strategically vital port in Iraq. Tehran aimed to cut off Iraq's oil exports from Basra, in the hope that this would trigger a tsunami of protests across Iraq, ultimately leading to the overthrow of Saddam Hussein. The Iranian offensive was launched in July 1982, accompanied by Khomeini's highly publicised call for the 'Iraqi nation and army' to unite with Iranian forces to overthrow Saddam.[68] However, Khomeini's call fell on deaf ears, as Iraqis rallied behind their flag, much as the Iranians had when their country was invaded. The offensive faltered, resulting in Iranians sustaining 'extremely heavy casualties in human wave assaults'.[69] Despite the tremendous price paid, capturing Basra remained an elusive goal that Iran pursued throughout the rest of the war.

By the third year, a stubborn stalemate had taken hold, with no breakthrough on the horizon for either side. In February 1984, Iran captured territory in the Majnoon Islands, a key hub for Iraq's oil production.[70] However, Iraq quickly regained control of this territory through the extensive use of the illegal chemical weapon tabun, a nerve agent that can cause death by asphyxiation or cardiac arrest within minutes.[71] Emboldened by the lack of repercussions for its illegal use of chemical weapons, Iraq initiated the 'war of the cities' in 1984. The objective was to pressure the Iranian government into ending the war by terrorising the populations of its major urban areas. Iran reciprocated by launching artillery bombardment of Basra and firing rockets into Iraqi cities.

More consequential than the 'war of the cities' was the 'tankers' war' in the Persian Gulf, which had far-reaching effects on international oil markets and significantly reduced the oil revenues of both countries. Iraq started to attack ships in 1981 due to Iran's successful efforts to disrupt its oil export capacity and Syria's closure of Iraq's oil pipelines to the Mediterranean Sea, which was done at Iran's behest. Gradually, Iraq escalated its attacks on tankers carrying Iranian oil. In response, Tehran threatened to close the vital Strait of Hormuz in the Persian Gulf, a crucial passage for millions of barrels of oil destined for international markets. Iran also began targeting oil tankers from Kuwait and Saudi Arabia, pressuring these countries to cease their financial support for Iraq. To reduce tensions in the Persian Gulf, the United Nations Security Council passed a resolution in 1984 condemning the attacks on Kuwaiti and Saudi tankers, without explicitly naming Iran.[72] The resolution refrained from condemning Iraq, despite its fifty-three attacks on ships compared to Iran's eighteen hits in 1984.[73]

The 'tankers' war' caused significant damage to the Iranian economy. In March 1985, the Iraqi air force destroyed a sizeable portion of Iranian oil installations on Khark Island.[74] Iraq's capability to execute such destructive attacks was bolstered by its acquisition of Mirage F-1 fighter aircraft from France, one of Iraq's main suppliers of advanced weaponry. These fighters were configured to carry the deadly Exocet missiles.[75] However, Iraq's success in inflicting serious damage on Iran's economy and infrastructure was insufficient to shake its determination to persist in the war. Ayatollah Khomeini declared that as long as 'one person stays alive in this country, this war will continue'.[76] And so it did.

Iraq responded by escalating its attacks on ships and attempting to draw the US into the conflict. Its gambit proved successful; the US cited the tankers' war as the *casus belli* for its intervention in the Persian Gulf, a move that altered the trajectory of the war.

America's Shadow on the War

The United States profoundly influenced the course and denouement of the Iran–Iraq War. In fact, it achieved most of its strategic goals with minimal costs and casualties, which stands as one of its most successful political-military interventions in decades. When Iraq invaded Iran, Khomeini promptly accused the US of 'instigating' the conflict and condemned Saddam as 'a US proxy', imposing a war on Iran at America's behest. While there is no verifiable evidence that substantiates US instigation, Washington possessed intelligence regarding Iraq's impeding invasion and chose not to take preventive measures.[77] Nor did the US condemn Iraq for invading Iran, which was holding Americans hostage in Tehran. The official American position from the onset of the war until its conclusion was one of 'neutrality'. However, the US changed its stance several times during the conflict and was never truly neutral. Initially, it seems the United States hoped for a quick Iraqi victory and an end to the hostilities. However, by mid-1982, as it became increasingly evident that Iraq was unlikely to win the war, the US covertly shifted towards supporting Iraq. In February 1982, the United States removed Iraq from the list of state sponsors of terrorism to eliminate legal obstacles to providing multifaceted assistance, including financial aid, and to facilitate the resumption of diplomatic relations.[78] By the fourth year of the war, the United States appeared to have once again concluded that Iraq couldn't win, and that the Iraqi government could potentially disintegrate in the face of Iranian offensives. As early as April 1984, President Reagan signed the National Security Decision Directive (NSDD 139), instructing the US government to devise a plan of action designed to avert an Iraqi collapse.[79] In the last few years of the war, the US goal was to prevent an Iranian victory.

US support for Iraq and opposition to Iran was glaringly evident by its arms sales policy directed towards both countries. On one hand, the US unilaterally imposed a crippling arms embargo on Iran, whose armed forces were largely equipped with US weapons and desperately in need of American spare parts to maintain their effectiveness. Moreover, Washington launched Operation Staunch to impede other countries from selling weapons and essential spare parts to Iran. On the other hand, the US turned a blind eye as the Soviet Union, global arms suppliers, and certain NATO members, most notably France, armed Iraq to the teeth with sophisticated weaponry.

The US refusal to condemn Iraq's extensive use of illegal chemical weapons against Iranians epitomised not only its support for Iraq but also one of the most egregious aspects of its policy during the war.[80] In flagrant violation of the 1925 Geneva Protocol, Iraq brazenly used banned chemical agents to kill, incapacitate, and demoralise defenceless Iranian forces. The US, a signatory of the protocol, was fully aware of Iraq's illegal use of chemical weapons at least as early as 1983, if not earlier.[81] Moreover, the US knew that Iraq had 'acquired a CW [chemical weapons] production capability, primarily from Western firms, including possibly a US foreign subsidiary'.[82] Even more troubling was the US's knowledge that Saddam Hussein felt no compunction and feared no retribution from the US for using chemical weapons. A US official from Baghdad sent a cable to Washington with the chilling message that an Iraqi military spokesman had warned Iran in early 1983 that 'the invaders should know that for every harmful insect there is an insecticide capable of annihilating it whatever their number and Iraq possess[es] this annihilation insecticide'.[83]

Washington refrained from taking any punitive measures against Iraq because its strategic goals were to resume diplomatic relations with that country, which had close ties with the Soviets, integrate it into its sphere of influence, and use it as a counterweight against revolutionary Iran. To achieve these goals, Donald Rumsfeld, the US Special Envoy, visited Saddam Hussein in Baghdad in March 1984, personally delivering a letter from President Reagan. In it, Reagan proposed improving bilateral relations and jointly opposing Iran and Syria.[84] The visit was successful. As these secret negotiations were unfolding, Iraq, believing it was immune from US retribution, escalated its deadly use of chemical weapons against Iranians. Only under international pressure did the US reluctantly issue symbolic condemnation of Iraq's deployment of chemical weapons in March 1984, without taking any punitive action. A mere eight months later, the US and Iraq re-established diplomatic relations. Thereafter, the US further increased its intelligence sharing with Iraq, providing Baghdad with various resources, including maps and satellite imagery from its sophisticated Airborne Warning and Control System, which could have revealed the positions of Iranian forces.[85]

Tehran was aware of US support for Iraq. Consequently, pro-Iran non-state actors and proxies within its clandestine regional network engaged in multiple acts of terrorism against US and Western interests in Lebanon and elsewhere, aiming to increase the cost of US support for Baghdad.

McFarlane in Tehran

Ironically, while the US was drawing closer to Iraq, it was also engaged in secret negotiations with Tehran in the mid-1980s. Throughout the war, Iran consistently faced acute shortages of advanced weaponry and essential spare parts for its primarily American-built weapons systems. Reports began to surface as early as 1981 that, despite imposing an arms embargo on Iran, the US had sold limited quantities of American-made weapons and spare parts to Iran – an allegation that Iran and the Reagan administration vehemently refuted. However, Gary Sick has argued that these sales were the result of a secret, informal deal between the Reagan team and Iranian officials in Europe during the 1980 American presidential campaign, while the American hostages were still captive in Iran. In this alleged deal, Tehran, seeking retribution against President Carter for supporting the Shah, purportedly agreed to withhold the release of American hostages until after the US elections, in exchange for the Reagan team's pledge to provide arms to Iran if Reagan won the election.[86] Notwithstanding the accuracy of Sick's allegation, Israeli Prime Minister Menachem Begin reportedly approved the sale of 'tires for Phantom fighter planes as well as weapons for the Iranian army' as early as 1980. In exchange, Khomeini allowed some Jews to leave Iran for the US.[87] It is unlikely that the US was unaware of these sales. The limited sale continued until 1985, according to a CIA report.[88]

However, these alleged Israeli sales were inadequate to meet Iran's military needs. Therefore, Iran's frantic pursuit of American weapons on global black markets continued, eventually leading it to the White House.[89] During the mid-1980s, several Americans, including William Buckley, the CIA station chief in Beirut, were held captive by pro-Iranian groups in Lebanon. The imperative to secure their release weighed heavily on President Reagan's mind. Simultaneously, his National Security Advisor Robert McFarlane, a seasoned Cold War warrior, believed that the US should actively curtail the expanding influence of the Soviets in Iran. He advocated for bolstering the moderate/pragmatic faction within the Islamic Republic as a crucial first step towards a potential rapprochement with Tehran.[90] To pursue this goal, McFarlane issued a National Security Directive in June 1985 authorising limited arms sales to Iran. Just a month later, President Reagan gave his approval for McFarlane to engage with Tehran directly and secretly, a move Israel also supported. This audacious move set in motion a series of covert negotiations between the two countries, spanning sixteen months. These negotiations, subsequently known as the 'Iran–Contra' affair, developed into an 'arms-for-hostages' arrangement with Iran. This complex arrangement involved the unlawful diversion of funds generated from arms sales to the Islamic Republic, which were then used to aid the Contra counter-revolutionaries in their battle against the Sandinistas' revolutionary government in Nicaragua.

In mid-June 1985, when McFarlane issued his National Security Directive, President Rafsanjani was in Damascus, hoping to persuade President Hafez Assad to provide Iran with Russian-made missiles, which he could not. Rafsanjani recalled that the Speaker of the Syrian parliament confided in him that the Americans had conveyed to Assad that if the hostages from the hijacked TWA aircraft were released from Lebanon, Israel would release Lebanese prisoners. Rafsanjani claimed to have informed Hezbollah's leaders to try to resolve the crisis.[91] This raises the important and yet unexplored question of whether Rafsanjani, who was open to the idea of a rapprochement with the US, might have changed the initial proposal of a 'hostages-for-prisoners' deal between

Israel and Hezbollah to a 'hostages-for-arms' arrangement between Iran and the US. What is known is that approximately two months after Rafsanjani's visit to Syria, in August 1985, the first shipment of 100 TOW missiles was dispatched from Israel to Iran, followed by delivery of additional 400 more TOWs in September. In exchange, Reverend Benjamin Weir was released from Lebanon by his captors.[92] More significantly, nine months later, Reagan signed a Presidential Finding, authorising direct US arms sales to Iran, marking the first official arms sales to that country since the 1979 revolution.

During these negotiations, McFarlane took the unprecedented risk of secretly travelling to Tehran to meet with the Islamic Republic's most senior decision makers. Against the backdrop of radical forces passionately chanting anti-American slogans on Iranian streets, he delivered a plane loaded with spare parts for Hawk missiles to Iran. Ayatollah Khomeini unexpectedly, and for reasons still undisclosed, prohibited Iran's most senior officials from meeting with McFarlane. A disappointed McFarlane still met with Iranian officials, reportedly conveying to them that the US was determined to 'commence a new chapter' with Iran.[93] At the height of the Cold War, he reportedly urged Tehran to consider distancing itself from the Soviets, warning that the Russians could not be trusted and would persist in arming Iraq because: 'If Iraq loses the war, it will tarnish their reputation and credibility.'[94]

After McFarlane's return to Washington, limited US arms sales to Iran continued, as did the secret negotiations between the two countries. Lieutenant Colonel Oliver North met with an Iranian delegation in Frankfurt in October 1986. As a symbol of the US commitment to improving relations with the Islamic Republic, North presented them with a Bible personally signed by President Reagan.[95] Less than a month later, US–Iran secret negotiations came to an abrupt halt when *Al Shiraa*, a Lebanese newspaper, exposed them on 3 November 1986. Pierre Razoux claims that in 'fifteen months the United States had obtained the release of three hostages (out of five), in exchange for delivering Iran 2,500 TOW missiles and the equivalent of 300 Hawk missiles.'[96] The Iran–Contra fiasco, however, left an indelible impact on US policy towards the Iran–Iraq War.

Iran's Advances in Faw and US Alarm

The disclosure of Iran–US secret negotiations triggered political earth-quakes in both Tehran and Washington. The alleged source of the leak to the Lebanese newspaper was Mehdi Hashemi, a radical IRGC officer and the brother-in-law of Ayatollah Hossein-Ali Montazeri, the designated heir apparent to Ayatollah Khomeini. Hashemi was found guilty of trea-son by the Special Court for the Clergy and executed in 1987.[97] Hashemi's close association with the Montazeri family set the stage for Ayatollah Montazeri's eventual ousting by Khomeini. However, the pragmatists who favoured rapprochement with the US emerged unscathed from the revelations and retained their positions of power.

In Washington, Reagan faced a major political crisis. Despite his earlier vow never to negotiate with hostage takers and his ban on American allies selling arms to Iran, he was caught red-handed engaging in both. To exonerate himself from allegations of hypocrisy, he argued that his overarching objectives in reaching out to Iran were to secure the release of American hostages and to forge a 'strategic opening' with the country. But the possibility of that strategic opening was now swiftly discarded to appease his domestic critics. At a crucial point, when Iran's chances of winning the war were at their highest, the US provided more support to Iraq than at any other time since the beginning of the Iran–Iraq war.

While the US–Iran talks were ongoing, Iran executed the Al-Fajr VIII operation, with the objective of capturing the Faw Peninsula in Iraq in February 1986. Despite Iraq's extensive use of prohibited chemical weap-ons, Iranian forces surprised Iraq by successfully crossing the Arvand Rood and advancing through the unforgiving terrain of the peninsula. They managed to seize Faw, thereby depriving Iraq of its only access to the Persian Gulf, effectively rendering the country landlocked. This perhaps marked Iran's most impressive victory since the liberation of Khorramshahr in June 1982.

Iran's victory at Faw had already set off alarm bells in Washington prior to the exposure of the US–Iran secret negotiations. In a series of reports, the CIA cautioned that Iran stood at the brink of winning the war. One report described the Faw victory as a 'watershed' moment for Iran and an 'ominous' development for Iraq. It highlighted the possibility that Iran could establish a puppet 'Islamic republic' in Faw.[98] Another report observed that Iraq had failed 'to exploit its many military advantages over Iran' and was likely to 'lose the war over the long term'.[99] Most importantly, a third CIA report foresaw that, upon winning the war, 'Iran would clearly be the dominant regional actor'.[100]

Instead of leveraging their victory in Faw to negotiate an end to the war from a position of strength, Iran's obstinate leaders were fixated with the delusion of 'War, war, until victory'.[101] Mohsen Rezaei envisioned 'a long war' with Iraq, expressing confidence that his 'people-oriented war strategy' could succeed.[102] Had Ayatollah Khomeini not rejected this plan, Iran would have encountered financial ruin and undergone trans-formation into a garrison state.

Emboldened with its victory in Faw, Iran escalated its targeted attacks on oil tankers in the Persian Gulf. In response, Kuwait requested US protection for its ships in December 1986.[103] The US agreed to reflag Kuwaiti ships, irrevocably changing the course of the war. This should have come as no surprise, as it was the United States' policy 'to undertake whatever measures may be necessary to keep the Strait of Hormuz open to international shipping'.[104]

When explaining the rationale for reflagging to the House of Representatives, Michael Armacost, Under Secretary of State for Political Affairs, emphasised that while the US was committed to its neutrality in the war, it was concurrently applying pressure on the belligerents to bring an end to the conflict. He added that: 'It is fundamentally counter to US interest for Iran –with its current policies and anti-American ideology to control or have permanent influence over this oil supply'.[105] Shortly after his testimony, the US House Joint Resolution 216 cautioned that the continuation of the war 'could result in an Iranian breakthrough which could threaten the stability of the entire region and would not be in US interest'.[106]

Both Armacost's testimony and Resolution 216 confirm one of the main contentions of this book: that the cold war between Iran and the

US is primarily driven by a clash of geopolitical interests and, more specifically, by Iran's pursuit of regional power.

By 1986–7, the US was determined to prevent an Iranian victory, apply pressure on Iran to end the war, and bolster Iraq once again as a counterbalance against Iran. Consequently, the US pursued a dual strategy involving aggressive diplomatic initiatives alongside a robust naval intervention in the Persian Gulf.

The US reflagging of ships in the Persian Gulf commenced in July 1987, with the first reflagged vessel falling victim to an Iranian mine, rendering it inoperative. Reciprocal escalation characterised the confrontation between the overwhelmingly superior US naval forces with Iran's smaller naval fleet. Interestingly, US operations against Iran began just two months after Iraq had fired two French-made Exocet missiles at the Frigate USS *Stark* in May 1987, killing thirty-seven crew. The US accepted Iraq's assertion that the missile attack was unintentional.

In response to Iran's mining activities and the threat posed by the IRGC's fleet of speedboats surrounding American vessels, the US launched Operation Prime Chance. It resulted in the sinking of *Iran Ajr*, the death of five, and the capture of twenty-six crew members.[107] As a reprisal, Iran targeted another reflagged ship with missiles, causing damage and injuries to a few crew members. In response, the US launched Operation Nimble Archer, resulting in the destruction of two more Iranian oil platforms. Iran then moved to lash out more aggressively: the Frigate USS *Samuel B. Roberts* struck an Iranian mine, coming close to sinking on 18 April 1988. This incident resulted in the injury of ten Americans. In response, the US executed Operation Praying Mantis, destroying one more Iranian oil platform, and damaging another, along with sinking two Iranian ships (*Joeshan* and *Sahand*) and disabling a third (*Sabalan*). In this confrontation, two Americans and at least a dozen Iranians were killed.[108]

Facing these losses in the Persian Gulf did not cause any reconsideration of Iran's war strategy. Invigorated by maintaining control over Faw, Iran made strides towards capturing Basra, a long-desired goal. In a 1987 memorandum to President Reagan titled 'At the Gates of Basrah [Basra]', the Defense Intelligence Agency warned that Iran could capture

Basra and emerge victorious in the war. President Reagan, taking note of this sobering assessment, wrote on the margin of the memo, 'An Iranian victory is unacceptable.'[109]

While the US continued its naval operations against Iran, Iraq launched an effective ground offensive to retake Faw in April 1988. Whether these simultaneous US naval and Iraqi ground operations were the result of collusion or merely 'an amazing coincidence', they marked the beginning of the end of the war.[110] Engaging with the US at sea and Iraq on land simultaneously proved to be an unmitigated disaster for Iran.

The unexpected fall of Faw triggered a sequence of disorientating events for Iran. According to President Hassan Rouhani, Mohsen Rezaei, who oversaw the operations in Faw, believed that Iran's dominance over Faw was so entrenched that only an atomic bomb could dislodge its control over the territory.[111] Despite holding Faw for twenty-six months, Iran lost its grip in a mere thirty-six hours after Iraq launched its offensive. While not yet verified, it is possible that Washington could have shared crucial intelligence with Baghdad regarding the positions of Iranian forces in Faw. What remains certain is that Iraq, once again, used banned chemical agents against Iranian forces without fearing reprisal from the US, which was closely monitoring the situation in Faw. While Iraqi troops were sufficiently equipped to protect themselves, unfortunate Iranians 'died by hundreds, desperately injecting atropine to counter the effects of the nerve agents'.[112] There were heavy casualties.

The loss of Faw, coupled with the destruction of parts of Iran's small navy by the US Navy, delivered a devastating blow. To stop the momentum of Iraqi advances, Iran shifted some of its forces to the northern battlefields in the Kurdish region of Iraq in March 1988. Collaborating with the Patriotic Union of Kurdistan, a Tehran-friendly Kurdish party, they captured the town of Halabja in Iraqi Kurdistan, positioning themselves only 155 miles from Iraq's oil field in Kirkuk. Two days after Iranian troops entered Halabja, Iraq once again resorted to deploying chemical weapons. This time, an estimated 3,500 to 5,000 defenceless people, primarily consisting of Kurdish civilians and children, were killed. This operation was part of Iraq's genocidal 'Anfal' campaign to eradicate the Kurds, marking the deadliest chemical attack ever launched during the Iran–Iraq War. Following the American occupation of Iraq, Ali Hassan al Majid, the former spy chief and a trusted henchman of Saddam Hussein who had earned the sobriquet of Chemical Ali, defiantly and unabashedly defended the use of chemical weapons at his trial: 'The orders were given as the region was full of Iranian agents. We had to isolate these saboteurs. We know that Iran had taken a lot of our land ... almost more than the size of Lebanon.... You know historically what they have done with Iraq.... I am not apologising. I did not make (any) mistake.'[113] Once again, the US and the international community took no punitive action against Iraq's clear war crimes.

Drinking Poison from the Chalice

Amid these challenging times for Iran, the USS *Vincennes* fired missiles at an Iranian civilian Airbus on a routine commercial flight from Bandar Abbas to Dubai on 3 July 1988, resulting in the deaths of all 290 passengers. Iran quickly accused the US of 'committing a war crime' by deliberately targeting a civilian aircraft. Tehran insisted that the aircraft was in the country's territorial waters and ascending, signalling it posed no imminent threat to the American warship. The US, however, rejected these claims, contending that the Iranian aircraft was in international waters and that the crew of USS *Vincennes* operated under the fog of war, and had mistakenly identified the Airbus as an F-14 fighter jet and attacked in error. The international community's failure to condemn the US for this tragedy deeply troubled Tehran and revealed its international isolation.

By mid-July 1988, Iran finally buckled under the stark reality that victory in the war was beyond its grasp. In a secret letter to Rafsanjani, IRGC Commander Rezaei lamented that unless Iran could substantially increase its troop deployment and have access to modern weapons, including laser and even atomic weapons, victory in the war would be unlikely.[114] After enduring a tumultuous revolution and a devastating war, all within a single decade, Iranians were drained. They were eager to embrace peace and put their shattered lives back together. Their country's infrastructure lay in ruins, the economy was in disarray, and basic foodstuffs like rice and meat were subject to rationing; the standard of living for its people had significantly deteriorated since the revolution.

Under these dire circumstances, a visibly disheartened Khomeini finally accepted the ceasefire Resolution 598 on 18 July 1988. He told the nation that he had to drink 'poison' from the chalice for making this painful but necessary decision.[115] Just two days earlier, he had written a confidential letter to the country's top leaders, lamenting that the military leaders had informed him that Iran was no longer capable of winning the war or even 'procuring one-tenth of the weapons Iraq had acquired'. He scorned those who still harboured fantasies about continuing the war in the face of a disenchanted population and a bankrupt state.[116] Rafsanjani claimed he played a major role in persuading Ayatollah Khomeini to accept the ceasefire, stating that Khomeini even contemplated stepping down as the country's Supreme Leader when he agreed to end the war.[117] In his memoirs, Rafsanjani wrote that the Americans: 'had sent a message to Tehran expressing interest in reestablishing official relations with Iran and were prepared to address our [Iran's] weapons needs'.[118] Regrettably, the cold war between the two countries continued.

After Iran had accepted the ceasefire, the Mojahedin-e Kahlq Organisation launched the final military operation of the Iran–Iraq War.[119] This Iranian opposition group had collaborated with Iraq against Iran during the war and had relocated its headquarters from France to Iraq in 1986. The Mojahedin-e Khalq, with Iraq's logistical support, crossed over onto Iranian soil in July 1988 with their 7,000-strong 'National Liberation Army'.[120] However, the Iranian forces surrounded and crushed them.

Winners and Losers: The IRGC Comes of Age

The ceasefire was neither a defeat nor a victory for Iran, but it was certainly a loss for Iraq, which had started the war. Iraq failed to achieve its major strategic objectives: the destruction or containment of the

Islamic Revolution, the acquisition of Iranian territory, and the imposition of its hegemony over the Persian Gulf. Saddam Hussein's ambitions and his irrational optimism about a quick victory over Iran bankrupted and ruined his country. His ignorance and hubris blinded him to the fact that he was being manipulated as a 'useful idiot' by Western powers and his Arab supporters and financiers, who sought to make him powerful enough to counterbalance Iran but not dominant enough to control the region.

For its part, Iran paid an incredibly heavy price in both blood and treasure. However, it had one consolation: in this war, unlike many of its past wars, Iran did not cede any territory. This was no small achievement, given that Iran often stood defiantly alone against Iraq and its Western and Arab supporters. The boundless idealism and naïveté of the Islamic Republic's leaders, coupled with their failure to match their ambitions with the country's capabilities, prevented them from recognising that, in an era when oil was the lifeblood of the industrialised world, the US would never have permitted Iran, an avowedly anti-American state, to win the war and impose dominance over the oil-rich Persian Gulf. Moreover, in 1982, Iran had an opportunity to end the war but instead chose to advance into Iraqi territory, believing victory was within reach. Many years after the war's conclusion, Mohsen Rezaei candidly acknowledged that entering Iraqi territory in 1982 was a mistake.[121] However, he was unwilling to admit that this mistake of historic proportions led to thousands of deaths and unfathomable economic destruction. The estimated death toll for Iran alone ranges from 262,000 to 600,000, with millions seriously left injured and displaced.[122] Iraq's deployment of chemical weapons resulted in the death of nearly 5,000 people and caused injuries to more than 100,000 Iranians.[123] The economic costs surpassed the total oil revenues the two countries had earned from the time oil was discovered in Iran in 1907 until 1988, amounting to over $1.1 trillion.[124]

Despite its bewildering destructiveness, the war with Iraq gave the Iranian state a sense of direction, fostered national unity, reshaped the society, and formed *Weltanschauung* of the country's leaders.

The war bequeathed another legacy: the laying of the military foundation for Iran's eventual ascent as a regional power. The single most consequential byproduct of the war was the emergence of the IRGC as the country's foremost and most potent military and security force. Paralleling how the Second World War produced a new generation of leaders who would shape American foreign policy for decades, the veterans of the Iran–Iraq War have dominated Iranian politics for the past three decades.

At the war's outset, the IRGC was an assortment of small groups of revolutionary volunteers. It lacked discipline, operated in a decentralised manner, and had limited experience in warfare and strategy, although some of its leaders had received training in guerrilla tactics in Lebanon and Syria during the Pahlavi era. However, the war changed the IRGC's trajectory, reshaping it into a battle-tested fighting force.[125] This transformation was largely attributable to Ayatollah Khomeini's preference for the IRGC over the regular armed forces. There were compelling reasons behind Khomeini's trust and confidence in the IRGC. Khomeini was an institution builder who harboured profound mistrust towards any institution that he could not control or that had ties to the West. In contrast to the Imperial Army, whose senior leaders often received their education in Western military colleges and training from Western powers, the IRGC was a home-grown and ideological cohesive force characterised by passionate commitment to Khomeini and Shiism. It had been created, trained, and managed by Iranians.

Faced with Iraq's significantly better-equipped armed forces, sheer strategic necessity compelled both the IRGC and the regular army to work towards establishing parity with Iraq. They achieved this by learning, mastering, and employing the art of asymmetric and hybrid warfare through trial and error on the unforgiving battlefields of the Iran–Iraq War, rather than in the comfortable classrooms of war colleges. Having created a regional network of militias and Shia activists, primarily from Iraq and Lebanon, the IRGC also trained and armed them in asymmetric warfare. To circumvent the stringent American arms embargo, the IRGC also built a small indigenous military-industrial complex to fulfil the country's military needs, including reverse-engineering missiles, as we shall see.

But the war's real victor was the US. It achieved its strategic objectives through meticulous planning and prudence, all while incurring minimal costs. The US prevented Iran from prevailing in the war, stopped the war from spreading, ensured the safe and uninterrupted flow of oil from the Persian Gulf for the most part, and cultivated closer relations with the littoral Arab countries of the region, including Iraq. Most significantly, it laid the groundwork for a security architecture to replace the UK as the dominant foreign power in the Persian Gulf. This process had been under way since at least 1983, when the US began exploring 'measures to establish a long-term framework for US security cooperation with the Gulf states'.[126] The final step in this process was completed after Iraq invaded Kuwait, prompting the US to deploy troops on the ground in the region for the first time.

Active Neutrality in the Persian Gulf War

After the conclusion of the Iran–Iraq War, the two countries chose different paths. Saddam Hussein invaded Kuwait just two years after the war with Iran ended. This invasion dashed any hope that Hussein was committed to regional peace, proving that he presided over a deadly and expanding war machine.[127] In Iran, pragmatism in foreign policy began to dominate after the end of the war. The fervour for exporting the Islamic Revolution had waned, as the Islamic Republic shifted its primary focus to consolidating regional power and reconstructing the country's devastated infrastructure and fragile economy.

Following their accepting the ceasefire in 1988, Iran and Iraq accepted living in a state of 'no peace, no war'. While they engaged in direct talks, withdrew their troops to the internationally recognised borders, and exchanged prisoners, they failed to reach an agreement regarding the status of the Arvand Rood. Nor did Iraq agree to begin negotiations regarding war reparations to Iran.

Iraq came out of the war with a large and battle-tested army, along with 'the largest and most experienced air force in the Middle East'.[128] However, its economy was in ruins, its treasury depleted, and it carried substantial foreign debts, mostly from Saudi Arabia and Kuwait. When Saddam Hussein's plea to Kuwait and Saudi Arabia for debt forgiveness fell on deaf ears, he invaded Kuwait in August 1990, earning the ignominious distinction of invading two neighbours within a single decade.[129] President George H.W. Bush condemned the invasion and called for Iraq's unconditional withdrawal. When Saddam disregarded this demand, the US assembled a formidable international coalition against Iraq, which ultimately led to the deployment of hundreds of thousands of US military personnel to the Persian Gulf. After forty-two days of relentless air strikes, followed by one hundred hours of ground operations, Iraq was compelled to withdraw its troops. As a result, much of Iraq's armed forces were destroyed and its civilian infrastructure degraded to the level of a 'pre-industrial age'.[130] The victorious American-led forces did not advance beyond Kuwait to overthrow the Iraqi government, partly because President Bush believed that, despite all his flaws, Saddam Hussein could serve as a counterbalance to Iran.

As soon as Iraq invaded Kuwait, Iran unhesitatingly condemned it. Tehran dreaded the prospect of permanent deployment of US forces in the region. Consequently, Tehran proposed various approaches, including the creation of an Islamic force to facilitate Iraq's withdrawal, all with the aim of preventing the deployment of US forces to the region. When Tehran concluded that the US had strategically opted to establish a permanent military presence in the Persian Gulf, it pursued a policy of 'active neutrality' during the Persian Gulf War. This policy was designed to avoid any military confrontation with either Iraq or the US.

Saddam Hussein, aware of Iran's strong opposition to the presence of US troops in the region, wrote several letters to Rafsanjani to persuade Iran to form an alliance with Iraq against the US.[131] While preparing for the invasion of Kuwait, he suggested a summit between the two presidents to address areas of mutual interest. Rafsanjani chose not to respond. A day after invading Kuwait, Saddam Hussein sent another letter, warning Iran that the invasion of Kuwait was an 'Arab problem', and that Persians should stay uninvolved. This time, Rafsanjani responded. He brushed aside Saddam's empty threat and instead emphatically stated that acceptance of the 1975 Algiers Accords was the only basis for establishing peace between the two countries. As the US accelerated its massive deployment of forces to the Persian Gulf, a desperate Saddam Hussein wrote to Rafsanjani once again. This time, he accepted the 1975 Algiers Accords – an agreement he had previously signed with the Shah in 1975. He wrote that, 'Now that you have gotten everything you have asked for ... we must work together to expel the foreign troops.'[132] He embraced the Algiers Accords because of his concern that, as he was deploying troops to Kuwait, Tehran could be tempted to make incursions inside Iraq. Rafsanjani welcomed Iraq's acceptance of the Algiers Accords but rebuffed any collaboration with Iraq against the US.

Thanks to its pragmatic policy of active neutrality, Iran's relations with the US temporarily improved after Iraq's invasion of Kuwait. The US partially reimbursed Iran for the undelivered weapons it had purchased during the Pahlavi era and began to buy Iranian oil. However, Iran's relations with both the US and Iraq underwent a significant transformation following the US invasion of Iraq in March 2003, an event that served as a catalyst for Iran's rise.

Chapter 4

Invading Iraq: America's Unintended Strategic Gift to Iran

The US invasion of Iraq in March 2003 struck the Middle East's strategic landscape like an earthquake, exposing its fault lines and triggering aftershocks that reshaped the region's political dynamics. The moment US Marines and Iraqis toppled the statue of Saddam Hussein in Baghdad's Firdos (Paradise) Square less than one month after the start of Shock and Awe operation, the political rivalry between the US and Iran over the future of Iraq began in earnest. Iran greeted Iraq's invasion with mixed feelings. On the one hand, Tehran welcomed the US overthrow of its arch-enemy, Saddam Hussein, and the dismantling of his expansionist war machine. On the other hand, the invasion heightened Iran's threat perception, as it positioned the US, with a substantial troop presence in Iraq, as Iran's new western neighbour. With a massive troop deployment in Afghanistan, which shares an eastern border with Iran, US troops effectively encircled Iran. This, in turn, intensified the cold war between the US and Iran, with Iraq as a key battleground.

In 1921, when the state of Iraq was first carved out by the British, a weak Iran could not leverage its influence in that country to expand its power or challenge Britain. But now, with another historical regime change looming, Iran was prepared to use all of its assets to secure a sphere of influence in Iraq and undermine the US. How did Iran manoeuvre through Iraq's deadly fault lines to expand its power and build deterrence despite the presence of a massive number of American troops? And how did Tehran manage to use Iraq as a springboard to expand its regional power?

Iran's Strategic Goals in Iraq and Threat Perception

At the dawn of the new century, Iraq had transformed into a caricature of the menace it once posed to Iran. While United Nations (UN) weapons inspectors were effectively disarming Iraq, the US and Britain had imposed two no-fly zones with the aim of expanding their own power and protecting the Kurds in the north and the Shias in the south. Furthermore, the draconian UN sanctions had resulted in a staggering loss of life and widespread stagnation and poverty in Iraq. And, to Tehran's satisfaction, Saddam Hussein had become an international pariah.

Iraq's destiny and the nature of its relationship with Iran profoundly changed following the al-Qaeda attacks on the United States on 11 September 2001, which resulted in the deaths of nearly three thousand men, women and children. In Iran, President Mohammad Khatami publicly denounced these brazen acts of terrorism, while thousands of people spontaneously held candlelight vigils in sympathy with the US. Washington promptly and accurately identified the Taliban government in Afghanistan as responsible for harbouring al-Qaeda and sought to overthrow it. In pursuit of this legitimate goal, the US sought Iranian support. Ayatollah Khamenei authorised Iran's limited collaboration with the US, as he perceived the Taliban as a grave security threat to Iran.[1] The US had compelling reasons to seek Iranian support in its quest to oust the Taliban. Tehran had a deep understanding of Afghanistan's intricate political landscape, as well as its rich cultural tapestry and complex ethnic dynamics.

More importantly, Iran had been providing military support to the Northern Alliance in its ongoing struggle against the Taliban.[2] Given the

US's limited familiarity with Afghanistan's political terrain, collaborating with the Northern Alliance was a reasonable route to toppling the Taliban. The convergence of US and Iranian interests in Afghanistan became evident when General Qasem Soleimani's Quds Force actively collaborated with US military personnel and the Northern Alliance, providing critical intelligence to facilitate the overthrow of the Taliban.[3] Following the Taliban's removal in December 2001, Iran continued its diplomatic cooperation with the US at the Bonn conference, which ultimately led to the selection of Hamid Karzai as Afghanistan's provisional leader.

This unprecedented and promising cooperation between the Islamic Republic and the US in Afghanistan ended abruptly when Israel seized the *Karine A* ship in the Red Sea in January 2002. Allegedly the ship was carrying arms from Iran to the Palestinian Authority. Despite Iran's denial of the allegation, the seizure triggered a forceful reaction from President George W. Bush. He declared that Iran, Iraq, and North Korea constituted 'an axis of evil' that 'threatened the peace of the world'. That presidential declaration undermined Iranian–American cooperation in Afghanistan.

During the occupation of Afghanistan, the US also began covert discussions with Iraqi dissidents regarding the possibility of a US invasion of Iraq.[4] Among those engaged in these talks was Ayatollah Mohammad Baqer Hakim, an ally of Iran and the leader of the SCIRI, an organisation Tehran helped create in 1982. Hakim's plan, presented to the US, involved Iraqi dissidents themselves overthrowing Saddam Hussein with the backing of the US. Washington rejected Hakim's proposal as it had its own plan to invade Iraq.[5] As time went on, the calls for this invasion became increasingly loud and bombastic in the US. After the 9/11 attacks and the ensuing 'war on terrorism', there were largely unsuccessful attempts to link Saddam Hussein to terrorist organisations. Ultimately, Washington strategically framed its invasion as a national security imperative to eliminate Iraq's alleged possession of weapons of mass destruction.

Tehran supported the overthrow of Saddam Hussein, a goal it had pursued but failed to achieve during its eight-year war with Iraq. However, it vehemently opposed the US invasion and the deployment of American forces in Iraq and the Persian Gulf, viewing them as significant threats to its national security. To forestall the invasion, Tehran proposed that the US seek authorisation from the UN Security Council and challenged the credibility of American allegations regarding Iraq's possession of weapons of mass destruction.[6] While US hawks confidently asserted that 'liberating Iraq would be a cakewalk',[7] Hezbollah's Hassan Nasrallah, an ally of Iran, cautioned Americans that Iraqi people would not 'welcome you with roses and jasmine' but 'with rifles, blood, and martyrdom operations'.[8] However, Iran's manoeuvres had no impact on the determination of the US to invade and occupy Iraq.

The US invasion of Iraq in March 2003 elevated Tehran's threat perception to its highest level.[9] The astonishing speed at which the Shock and Awe military operation toppled Saddam sent chills down the spine of Iranian leaders. Tehran's apprehensions were further compounded by Bush's doctrine of pre-emptive US strikes against imminent threats.[10] The possibility of a US attack on Iran's nuclear facilities, or even a direct incursion into Iran, was a significant factor in prompting Iran to suspend its military nuclear weapons programme in 2003.[11]

Initially Tehran cautiously interfered in Iraq. However, as the anti-US insurgency operations rapidly escalated and Tehran concluded that the US had become mired in an inescapable quagmire in Iraq, Iran pursued more interventionist policies.

Since the US invasion of Iraq, Iran has pursued four strategic goals in Iraq, deeply rooted in Realpolitik, aimed at expanding its power, establishing deterrence, and ensuring the survival of the Islamic Republic. Iran's foremost priority has been to prevent the re-emergence of an anti-Iran government in Baghdad. The enormous losses incurred during the Iran–Iraq War made it imperative for the Republic to ensure that there is no possibility of Iraq invading Iranian territory ever again or posing serious threats. To mitigate this risk, Tehran has supported the establishment of a Shia-dominated and Tehran-friendly government in Baghdad, viewing Iraqi Shias as its potential natural ally. The second objective has been to expand Iranian power and develop asymmetric deterrence against the US in Iraq. Militarily, Iran has bolstered its covert network in Iraq, which it had built during the Iran–Iraq War. Tehran also trained and armed anti-American Iraqi Shia militias while avoiding direct military confrontation with the US. Politically, unlike many regional Arab allies of the United States, Tehran supported the active participation of its allies in the US-sponsored state formation. Iran's third goal has been to prevent the establishment of a permanent US military presence in Iraq and dissuade Baghdad from forming a strategic alliance with Washington. Iran's final objective has been to prevent the disintegration and Balkanisation of Iraq along ethnic lines, as such a partitioning would pose a threat to its own territorial integrity, with restive independence movements waiting in the wings.

Iran's Paradox: Insurgency and State Formation in Iraq

A harbinger of the rivalry between the US and Iran over the future of Iraq surfaced when Iran objected to President Bush's appointment of Paul Bremmer to lead the Coalition Provisional Authority (May 2003 to June 2004), then the highest civilian US authority in Iraq. Iran insisted that Iraqis, rather than Americans, should govern Iraq. However, Iran was not as intemperate as the US's Arab allies, who had vehemently opposed Saddam Hussein's overthrow and refused to extend a helping hand to Washington; instead, Tehran encouraged its partners in Iraq to collaborate with the US in the state-building process.

Bremmer, with no prior Middle East experience, made two imprudent decisions that laid the groundwork for the subsequent chaos in Iraq and opened the door for Iran to expand its power. With a stroke of the pen in May 2003, he dissolved Iraq's army and its intelligence services, all the while supporting the de-Ba'athification of state apparatuses. These two decisions resulted in the loss of jobs for many Sunni Ba'ath party apparatchiks, military officers, soldiers, and intelligence personnel, intensifying the sectarian conflict between Shias and Sunnis. Simultaneously, droves of Shias, including those close to Iran, rushed to fill the vacant government positions. The lack of sound judgement exhibited by Bremmer becomes evident when juxtaposed with Khomeini's decisions concerning the Imperial Armed Forces in 1979. Khomeini didn't dissolve the armed forces; he simply purged its leadership, leaving thousands of army officers and regular soldiers on the state payroll with no cause to resent him. This gave him the breathing space necessary to build the IRGC.

The establishment of the Governing Council by the US in July 2003 further intensified the US–Iran rivalry. The council marked the initial phase in transferring limited sovereignty to Iraq. Iran became the first country in the region to recognise the council and sent a delegation to meet with its members.[12] Nevertheless, Tehran expressed dissatisfaction with the US decision to appoint Ayad Alawi to the council. Alawi, a prominent secular Shia politician and former Ba'athist, was known for his vocal criticism of Iran's interference in Iraq. Tehran saw the Alawi appointment as a veiled attempt by Washington to fracture the Shia ranks and undermine the Iranian position. Iran, of course, had its own allies in the council who opposed Alawi. Among them was Ahmad Chalabi, who was a renowned advocate of the US invasion and received praise from American neoconservatives as Iraq's George Washington.[13] The conflict between Alawi and Chalabi escalated in April 2004 when the US established the Iraqi National Intelligence Services and appointed General Mohammad Abdullah Al-Shahwani, a former officer of the Republican Guard, as its director, much to Chalabi's dismay.[14] Shahwani's decision to reintegrate some members of Saddam Hussein intelligence agency, who were known for their anti-Iranian activities, constituted a major development that did not go unnoticed in Tehran. Meanwhile, Chalabi was accused of passing sensitive intelligence to Tehran, which resulted in raids on his home and offices and a gradual decline of his influence. His relations with Tehran, however, remained amicable until his death from a heart attack in 2015.

The nature of Iran's two-track Iraq policy quickly became evident.[15] On one front, Iran cautiously supported the US-sponsored state-building efforts, augmenting its influence within the state apparatuses. On the other front, it sought to create its own sphere of influence beyond the Iraqi state by providing support and weapons to anti-US militias, which Tehran hailed as the commencement of a new *intifada* (uprising) against the US. In turn, the US accused Tehran of arming both Shia and Sunni militant groups, including the Ansar-e Islam, an al-Qaeda affiliate.

The Mystery of Muqtada Sadr

In its infancy, the anti-US Shia insurgency was led by a young firebrand cleric named Muqtada Sadr.[16] Born in Iraq in 1973, he came from a distinguished family and inherited vast wealth and an extensive network from his father, who was a popular ayatollah assassinated by Saddam Hussein's goons. Sadr enjoyed widespread popularity among the poor, who received financial aid through his charitable network. Despite his lack of religious erudition, Sadr could not be disregarded. Fearless, fiercely independent, a master of rhetoric, ardently nationalistic, and vehemently against American occupation, he commanded a formidable militia known as the Mahdi Army, or the Jaysh al-Mahdi.[17] While an enigma to the US, Sadr was well-known in Iran's Shia circles. Tehran regarded him as a loose cannon who required support and management, but he turned out to be more unpredictable, cunning, and challenging than anticipated.

The US and many Iraqi politicians accused Iran of providing military support to Sadr, portraying him as Iran's puppet. However, Sadr's relationship with Tehran can't be boiled down in this way. Far from being a mere puppet, he exploited his collaboration with Tehran to serve his own interests, which were not always aligned with Iran's, while Tehran leveraged him to advance its agenda. Iran was also accused of supporting the 'Special Groups' controlled by Sadr, which were notorious for their violent actions against US-led forces, former Iraqi Ba'athists, and even some Iraqi Shias. Iraq's former prime minister Nouri al-Maliki appeared to confirm this allegation. He reportedly informed his American interlocutors in 2009 that during his meeting with Ayatollah Khamenei and General Soleimani in Tehran, he emphasised that Iran's support of the Special Groups was hurting the image of Iran:

> Soleimani had asserted that the training and weapons supply must have been done 'without authorization' and would be investigated. The Supreme Leader had sworn 'by every oath he knew' (Maliki said he attached no credibility whatsoever to all this) that he had issued a fatwa against any activities that could harm the security of Iraq....

Maliki said it was a 'mistake' to see Soleimani as an independent actor. 'He follows Khamenei's line completely and without Khamenei, he would be nothing.'[18]

While there is strong circumstantial evidence that Tehran supported Sadr and his Special Groups, the extent of that support remains unclear.[19]

At times, Sadr's radicalism and his refusal to engage in the US-sponsored state-building efforts clashed with Iran's tacit support for that very process. In April 2004, during a confrontation between Sadr's militias and the US-backed security forces in Najaf, Tehran advised him to cease the fighting quickly, as he was destined to lose. Ayatollah Khamenei conveyed a message to Ayatollah Ali Sistani, Iraq's most popular ayatollah, lamenting that: 'If Sadr dies, people will blame the Shia clerics for having done nothing to save him.' Sistani responded by affirming that he had cautioned Baghdad against acting against Sadr.[20] Tehran was also keen to avoid any situation that could serve as a pretext for delaying the parliamentary elections scheduled for 2005, in which Tehran's allies were set to participate. In the end, Tehran achieved its short-term objectives: Sadr survived, and the parliamentary elections proceeded as planned.

During the escalating anti-US insurgencies in 2004–2005, two bomb-shell developments severely tarnished American credibility and enhanced the position of anti-American and pro-Iranian forces. First, it was confirmed that the US had committed blatant human rights viola-tions in Iraq's notorious Abu Ghraib prison by subjecting detainees accused of terrorism to torture, including waterboarding. This revelation infuriated many Iraqis who had witnessed the US claiming the moral high ground over Saddam Hussein for his human rights abuses. The second, and more consequential development was the release of the final report by Charles Duelfer, the Special Advisor to the Director of Central Intelligence on Iraq's weapons of mass destruction. This report concluded that Iraq possessed no weapons of mass destruction, shattering the primary public rationale for the US invasion of Iraq.[21] Former American ambassador to Iraq Chris Hill told me that: 'One glaring misstep was our intelligence failure concerning Iraq's alleged possession of weapons of mass destruction. This error severely damaged our credibility on the international stage. It also exposed a critical lapse in our intelligence gathering and assessment.'[22]

Elections and Shia Ascendancy

In the aftermath of these two scandals, Iraqi public opinion turned sharply against the US. To change the conversation, the US focused on its democracy-promotion project, centred on holding elections. This was another unintentional gift from the US to Iran. Tehran greeted this new initiative with enthusiasm because it opened a fresh venue for expanding its power and influence. Tehran believed that, through elections, the Shia majority could secure long-term dominance over Iraq's electoral landscape, thereby indirectly bolstering Iranian influence within the state apparatuses.

The validity of this assessment was proven in the 2005 elections for the Transitional National Assembly, in which Tehran could claim a resounding victory. The United Iraqi Alliance, a coalition of the SCIRI, al Dawa, and Chalabi's Iraqi National Congress – all Iran's friends – secured enough seats to confirm Ibrahim al-Jaafari from the al Dawa party as prime minister. In a rare moment of consensus, both Washington and Tehran welcomed the selection of Jaafari as the new prime minister. Born into a prominent Shia family in Iraq, Jaafari, a physician by training, had sought refuge in 1980 to escape persecution by Saddam Hussein's regime. During his short tenure (May 2005–May 2007), Iran–Iraq relations were friendly. Iran reopened its embassy in Baghdad, and Jaafari appointed pro-Iran Iraqis from al Dawa and SCIRI to important government positions. In 2007, the Supreme Council of Islamic Revolution in Iraq made a major political decision by removing 'Islamic Revolution' from its title, rebranding itself as the Islamic Supreme Council of Iraq (ISCI). This move signalled a clear departure from its earlier advocacy for establishing an Islamic republic in Iraq, reaffirming its commitment to operating within the country's emerging legal framework. By that time, Iran's allies, al Dawa and the ISCI, had become integral components of the new power structure established by the US.

Jaafari visited Tehran and signed several agreements with the Islamic Republic. Iran also pledged to give a $1 billion loan to Iraq to buy Iranian products. Furthermore, during the US-sponsored Madrid Donor Conference in 2005, Iran pledged to contribute 'electricity, gas supplies and oil export facilities' to Iraq.[23]

Jaafari was so closely aligned with Tehran that even the temperate President Jalal Talabani, a Kurdish friend of Iran, criticised him for his 'dictatorial administrative style' and for ordering 'the release of all Iranian detainees' held in Iraq on charges of supporting the insurgency 'without due diligence'.[24] A red flag was raised in Washington when Mowaffak al-Rubai, Iraq's National Security Advisor, informed the US that Jaafari was considering forming a 'strategic security alliance with Iran to assist Iraq in combating the Sunni insurgency'.[25] Furthermore, Jaafari did not support the US policy of crushing the Shia insurgents. Instead, he believed the insurgents were part of 'Iraq's de facto reality' and must be incentivised to participate in electoral politics.[26] Ultimately, he was compelled to resign in 2007 after weeks of deadlock over forming a new government, during which his Shia allies urged him to quit. US pressure clearly played an important role. While Jaafari's selection as prime minister revealed Iran's growing influence, his resignation showed its limited ability to promote its priorities. Moreover, it demonstrated that the United States called the shots, exposing the unequal power balance between Tehran and Washington.

Iran and the Sectarian Civil War

Following Jaafari's resignation, the rivalry between the US and Iran over the choice of a new prime minister escalated. However, after extensive deliberations, the National Assembly appointed Nouri al-Maliki to this position – supported by both the US and Iran. Born in 1950 in Iraq, Maliki, was active in the al Dawa party during his youth. Like some of his contemporaries in that party, he fled to Syria when Saddam Hussein launched his crackdown on Shias in 1979. Three years later, he moved to Iran and stayed there until 1990 before moving to Syria, where he remained until the fall of Saddam Hussein in 2003.

Washington's assessment of Maliki's past relations with Iran may have played a pivotal role in its decision to support his premiership. He was praised by some staff of the American Embassy as a devout Shia nationalist who held 'a dark assessment of Iran's ambitions toward Iraq'. They believed that Maliki ostensibly relocated from Iran to Syria to 'avoid falling under Tehran's sway'.[27] Such assessments may have been accurate before Maliki came to power. However, the acquisition of state power often changes politicians' temperament and calculations. Upon assuming office, Maliki recognised the crucial importance of Iran's support for the survival of his government, while conversely, Iran acknowledged the necessity of Maliki's cooperation to advance its agenda. Furthermore, Maliki, who had his own policy disagreements with Washington, viewed Iran as a counterforce against the US that he could effectively leverage to secure concessions from Washington. As a result, Maliki often accommodated both Washington and Tehran.

During Maliki's tenure as Prime Minister (May 2006–September 2014), the relationship between Tehran and Baghdad was friendly but not devoid of tension. Both sides pursued the strategic imperative of ensuring the continued dominance of Shia forces within the Iraqi state, while concurrently endeavouring to hinder the Sunnis from reclaiming the power they had previously held. Moreover, during Maliki's tenure, the sectarian civil war between Shias and Sunnis endangered Iraq's internal cohesion and territorial integrity, pushing Tehran and Baghdad closer. Ambassador Chris Hill told me that, 'Prior to the invasion of Iraq, policymakers in Washington failed to fully comprehend the volatile sectarian divisions between Shias and Sunnis in Iraq. This failure complicated our efforts to successfully stabilise Iraq. The ensuing sectarian conflict greatly hindered our plans for the country, leading to prolonged instability and security challenges.'[28] Hill was certainly right. Following the US invasion, as Sunnis began to lose much of their power, many of them gradually embraced a conspiratorial narrative that the real US goal was to collaborate with Shias against them, or to de-Sunnify Iraq.[29] Consequently, some of them forged an unholy and informal alliance with al-Qaeda in Iraq (AQI) against both the US and Shias. The mastermind of this alliance was Abu Musab al-Zarqawi.

Born in Jordan, he had previously fought against the Soviets in Afghanistan before relocating to Iraq, where he established the AQI following the US invasion. Notoriously anti-Iran and anti-Shia, he referred to Shias as 'the lurking snake, the crafty and malicious scorpion, the spying enemy', whose goal was to 'establish a Shia state stretching from Iran through Iraq, Syria, and Lebanon and ending the cardboard kingdoms of the Gulf'.[30] He sought to foment a bloody civil war between Shias and Sunnis in Iraq. He indiscriminately killed Shias and US troops while recruiting Sunnis from across the Arab world to join him on Iraq's battlefields. In retaliation, Shia militias mercilessly attacked Sunni strongholds, killing many people. Matters came to a climax in February 2006, when bombs exploded and destroyed the Golden Dome of the al-Askari Shrine in Samarra – the burial site of the tenth and eleventh Shia imams. Sectarian violence now erupted into an uncontrollable civil war.

Iran was careful not to fan the flames in its response, while attributing the responsibility for the attacks to the American occupation of Iraq. Although it continued to mobilise Shia forces, Tehran had no interest in prolonging a civil war that could have easily metastasised to its own Sunni-populated provinces along its porous borders with Iraq, potentially undermining its territorial integrity. So, while Iran officially remained aloof from the ongoing conflict, it nonetheless funded a range of Shia militias. Consequently, the US and many of its allies accused Tehran of playing a cynical role, alternating between exacerbating and mitigating the conflict as it suited the Islamic Republic.

Not only was Iran deeply concerned about the escalating civil war in Iraq, but it also vehemently opposed the presence of the Mojahedin-e Khalq (MEK) there. Originally an Islamic organisation, the MEK gradually embraced a peculiar blend of Islam and Marxism. In the 1970s, they engaged in guerrilla activities and killed several Americans living in Iran. While they initially supported Khomeini against the Shah, they quickly turned against Khomeini's rule, leading to the killing of hundreds of officials of the Islamic Republic, and in effect starting a mini civil war that they lost. As Khomeini presided over a violent crackdown, MEK organisers fled to France and subsequently to Iraq in 1983, where Saddam Hussein welcomed them with arms, money, and their very own military base, Camp Ashraf. Even more unforgivably in Tehran's eyes, the Mojahedin-e Khalq had collaborated with Hussein in the Iran–Iraq War. Following the overthrow of Saddam Hussein, Tehran persistently urged Baghdad to expel the group, but its efforts were unsuccessful, even though the US had designated the Mojahedin-e Khalq as a Foreign Terrorist Organisation. Tehran accused the organisation of being a 'terrorist US proxy'.

Maliki extended a helping hand to Tehran to address its security concern about the Mojahedin-e Khalq operations in Iran. In April 2011, Iraqi forces entered Camp Ashraf in Diyala province, where at least 4,500 members of the Mojahedin-e Khalq were housed, resulting in the deaths of three members.[31] Despite this, the group persisted in their covert activities against the Islamic Republic. For reasons that are not entirely clear, in September 2012 the US removed the MEK from its list of Foreign Terrorist Organisations.[32] However, in another raid in September 2013, Iraqi forces killed fifty-two members, with several Iraqis injured.[33] Finally, the Mojahedin-e Khalq were deported to Albania in 2016.[34] Today they remain the most organised opposition force against the Islamic Republic.

Tehran and the US–Iraq Strategic Agreements

Despite his cooperation with Tehran regarding the status of the Mojahedin-e Khalq, Maliki and Tehran had significant differences concerning the status of US troops in Iraq and the Shia insurgency.

During his first term in office, Maliki became deeply involved in negotiations with the US regarding the future of US troops in Iraq and their legal status. By the time these delicate negotiations commenced, the US had already made the decision gradually to withdraw its troops. After extensive negotiations and despite Iran's strong opposition, Maliki signed the Status of Forces Agreement (SOFA) and the Strategic Framework Agreement (SFA) with the US. These two agreements provided legal immunity to US military personnel in Iraq, mandated the withdrawal of all US combat troops by December 2011, laid the framework for strategic cooperation between the two countries, and allowed the US to maintain a residual force for counterterrorism efforts, as well as for training and arming Iraq's security forces. There was significant opposition in Iraq to these agreements. During the signing ceremony in Baghdad, attended by President Bush and Maliki in December 2008, Muntadhar al Zaidi, an Iraqi journalist, famously threw shoes at the president, narrowly missing his intended target.

Tehran also exerted strong yet ultimately futile pressure on Maliki to avoid signing strategic agreements with the US, advocating instead for the immediate withdrawal of all American troops from Iraq. Tehran reminded Baghdad of Ayatollah Khomeini's denunciation of the Shah for signing a similar version of the SOFA with the US in 1963. To appease Tehran, Maliki visited Ayatollah Khamenei. Upon returning from Tehran, he conveyed to the American embassy that, 'Khamenei was strongly opposed to SOFA/SFA agreement on both political and religious grounds, but had suggested that it was Maliki's decision to make.'[35] Apparently one of Khamenei's main concerns was the potential use of Iraq by the US 'as a platform to attack other countries in the region', specifically Iran.[36] To placate Tehran, Maliki shrewdly endorsed including a clause in the final SOFA agreement, stating that 'Iraqi land, sea, and air shall not be used as a launching or transit point for attacks against other countries.' Following the signing of the two agreements, the US commended Maliki for displaying 'backbone in the face of Iranian pressure on the US–Iraq Security Agreement'.[37] The signing of these two agreements once again demonstrated the US dominance over Iraq and underscored the limits of Iranian power.

The second point of contention between Tehran and Maliki concerned the Shia insurgency. Both the US and the Maliki government took decisive measures to quell the Shia insurgency amid the civil war. Maliki, in fact, assumed a leadership role in this regard, potentially putting him at odds with Iran. Together, the US and Maliki government pursued a two-pronged approach. First, the US initiated a security dialogue with Iran to address the deteriorating situation in Iraq, with the hope of pressuring Tehran to cease its support for the Shia insurgency. The Iran Study Group, mandated by Congress to provide policy recommendations about the situation in Iraq, proposed that, given Iran's significant role in

Iraq, the US 'should try to engage them [Iran and Syria] constructively'.[38] However, the US administration's genuine commitment to implement- ing the recommendations of the Iran Study Group remains questionable. American Ambassador Crocker, who met with his Iranian counterpart in Baghdad, told me that his meetings with the Iranians were unproduc- tive because he believed that 'Iran consistently undermined the Maliki government and lent its support to the Shia insurgency'.[39] When these meetings failed to yield results, the US raided Iran's consulate general in Erbil in January 2007 and 'abducted five Iranian consular officers', although they were subsequently released.[40] Despite these efforts by the US, Iran continued its support for Shia militias.

Tehran and the Inter-Shia War

Tehran and Maliki were also at odds over the Shia insurgency. With US support, Maliki launched Operation Knight in March 2007, focused on disarming Shia militias in Basra. After the British withdrew their forces in 2007, the port city of Basra became the battleground for a power struggle between Sadr's Jaysh al-Mahdi and the Badr Organisation, which was known as the Badr Brigades until the American invasion and was created with Iranian assistance in 1980. Both groups were profiting immensely from smuggling gas and oil. However, beneath the surface, the conflict in Basra was also an extension of a long-standing animosity between Maliki and Sadr – two ambitious politicians with vastly differ- ent visions for Iraq.[41] While Sadr, in contrast to Maliki, advocated for the immediate and complete withdrawal of US troops from Iraq, Maliki viewed Sadr as a rebellious leader, lacking in vision and intentionally undermining his government's efforts to stabilise the country.

The Basra fighting placed Iran in a delicate position as it was simulta- neously supporting Jaysh al-Mahdi, the Badr Organisation, and the Maliki government. Moreover, this inter-Shia conflict had the potential to fracture the coalition that had enabled the Shias to maintain control over the Iraqi state. Consequently, Tehran took swift action to resolve the feud. Haidar al-Abadi, one of Iran's closest allies, conveyed to his

American interlocutor that Tehran viewed the Basra conflict as 'a plot' orchestrated by the US and 'Maliki to eliminate the Sadrists' as a major political force, something Iran strongly opposed.[42] As the violence escalated, General Soleimani stepped in to mediate and halt the bloodshed. In Tehran, he held meetings with Sadr, who was residing in Iran at the time, Hadi al Amiri, the leader of the Badr Organisation, and Ali al-Adeeb, a member of Maliki's al Dawa party.[43] Soleimani played a key role in brokering a ceasefire, reportedly pressuring Sadr to accept the ceasefire or risk losing Iran's support.[44]

The Basra ceasefire strengthened the position of the Maliki government but did not appear to have a negative impact on the Badr Organisation. However, Sadr seemed to have been temporarily weakened. He announced his intention to 'suspend' the Jaysh al-Mahdi and restructure it into a 'cultural and religious force'.[45] This announcement was met with scepticism, as Sadr, who was attending a Shia seminary in Iran to establish his religious credentials, appeared to be buying time to recover from the setback in Basra. A year after the hostilities ceased, Colonel Hazam, head of the Iraqi Intelligence Service's Fusion Center for Basra, warned that the Jaysh al-Mahdi still posed 'the biggest security threat in southern Iraq', emphasising this as evidence of 'Iran's ill intentions toward Iraq'.[46]

Having established relative calm in Basra, a more self-assured Maliki found himself in a strong position in a country desperate for peace. The American embassy reported that Maliki's standing among Iraqis had significantly improved because of his 'routing of Shi'a militias', which 'has soothed many Iraqis' worries that he was but a pawn of Tehran'.[47] Confident, he made his second bid for premiership in 2011. However, the election results shocked him. In the National Assembly elections, Ayad Alawi, his main rival, reportedly secured more seats than Maliki, who quickly accused Alawi of electoral fraud. President Obama, intent on preventing an election dispute that would complicate the planned withdrawal of US troops from Iraq in 2011, sided with Maliki.[48] So did Tehran, given that Alawi was no friend of the Islamic Republic. Thus, Maliki secured a second term. What he did not anticipate was the astonishing rise of ISIS (Islamic State of Iraq and Syria) in Iraq.

Soleimani Meets ISIS

During his second term in office, Maliki appeared poised to emerge as Iraq's new strongman – a Shia reincarnation of Saddam Hussein.[49] But while Maliki had been attempting to reconcile the different Shia factions, he had overlooked the rise of ISIS next door in Syria. By January 2014, ISIS had managed to conquer Fallujah. Six months later, Iraq was shocked when Mosul, its second largest city, also fell to ISIS. As details of the battle leaked out, revealing the ineffectiveness of Iraqi security and armed forces, many of whom were trained by the United States, Iraqis began to point the finger at Maliki. Suddenly, Maliki became friendless, echoing President John F. Kennedy's famous statement: 'Victory has a thousand fathers, but defeat is an orphan.' His de-Ba'athification campaign had estranged the Sunnis, while his resistance to granting greater autonomy to the Kurds had left them disheartened. Furthermore, his crackdown on the pro-Sadr militias had significantly eroded his support among the Shias. The US had also lost confidence in Maliki, conditioning its critical support on his commitment to making his government less sectarian and more inclusive by integrating American-backed Sunni armed groups into Iraqi state. Both ayatollahs Sistani and Khamenei also urged Maliki to step down for the 'sake of Shiism and Iraq'.[50] Maliki's second term, therefore, was swiftly cut short.

The National Assembly promptly chose Dr Haider al-Abadi as the new prime minister in September 2014. Abadi, a trained physician, was, like Maliki, a member of the al Dawa party. During the 1980s, he sought refuge in the West to escape persecution by Saddam Hussein, only to return to Iraq after the US invasion.

During Abadi's tenure (September 2014 to October 2018), Iraq's relations with Iran significantly improved as both countries collaborated closely to counter the ominous security threat posed by ISIS.[51] As President Obama noted, ISIS was the 'direct outgrowth of al-Qaeda in Iraq that grew out of our invasion, which is an example of unintended consequences, which is why we should generally aim before we shoot'.[52] The terrorist organisation was led by Abu Bakr al-Baghdadi, an Iraqi-born militant who had previously been incarcerated by the US in Iraq.

He shrewdly exploited the anxieties and fears of Sunni Iraqis about the US occupation and their marginalisation in the post-Saddam Hussein era. An influential Iraqi sheikh candidly described al-Baghdadi 'as the defender of 15 million Iraqi Sunnis'.[53] Al-Baghdadi swiftly imposed his reign of terror over millions of people across Iraq and Syria. With millions of dollars looted from Mosul's banks and an extensive cache of weapons confiscated from the fallen city's barracks, ISIS established an 'Islamic State', with al-Baghdadi as its caliph. Functioning as an outlaw state, ISIS levied taxes and enforced strict Sharia laws in the territories it controlled. With each ISIS victory, thousands of inspired jihadists from the Islamic world and Europe joined the caliphate, turning it into a formidable force.[54] The international community finally recognised the gravity of the ISIS threat when the group released a video in August 2014, showing one of its members beheading James Foley, an American journalist.

The Islamic Republic denounced ISIS, a Sunni organisation with a declared anti-Iran and anti-Shia ideological stance, as a significant threat that could potentially foment chaos in its Sunni-populated provinces along the border with Iraq and undermine Iran's regional standing. At one point, Tehran claimed that ISIS had advanced within 60 miles of Iran's border.[55] Admiral Ali Shamkhani, Chair of Iran's Supreme National Security Council, stated that: 'If we don't defeat ISIS [today], they will be inside our borders tomorrow.'[56] To undermine the credibility of its regional rival, Saudi Arabia, and the United States, Tehran sought to link both al-Qaeda and ISIS to them. Ayatollah Khamenei minced no words and, without providing supporting evidence, declared that, 'they [the United States and Israel] created al-Qaeda and Daesh [ISIS] to sow seeds of discord among Muslims and oppose the Islamic Republic, but now they also suffer the consequence'.[57] Foreign Minister Javad Zarif labelled ISIS the 'ideological sibling' to al-Qaeda.[58] Tehran insisted that the ideological underpinnings of both groups were deeply rooted in Wahhabism, a Sunni fundamentalist movement inspired by Abd al Wahhab in the eighteenth century that holds sway in Saudi Arabia today. Given its direct engagement with al-Qaeda-linked terrorists in the Syrian civil war, Iran was resolute in its determination to combat ISIS in Iraq.

A *Fatwa* that Changed Iraq

Iran's direct and extensive engagement in Iraq to counter ISIS began after Ayatollah Ali Sistani issued a *fatwa*, a religious decree, in June 2014, following the fall of Mosul.[59] The *fatwa* urged Iraqis to defend their country and its sacred shrines. In response, thousands of volunteers and several Shia organisations joined forces and formed the Popular Mobilisation Units (PMU), also known as al Hashd al-Sha'bi.[60] At the invitation of Iraq's government, Iran extended assistance to Iraq in its hour of need when others were hesitant to do so. Iran promptly began training and arming select units within the PMU for low-intensity, asymmetric warfare in both urban and rural environments. Tehran supplied arms and ammunition, not only to the Iraqi government but also to the beleaguered Kurds under siege by ISIS. Former prime minister Nouri al-Maliki has been quoted as saying that Baghdad would have likely fallen to ISIS without Iranian support, which he believed would have triggered the collapse of the entire region.[61] At the same time, the rise of ISIS provided Iran with yet another opportunity to expand its power in Iraq, reinforce its relations with its militias, and strengthen its ties to its politicians and military leaders. However, while there is compelling evidence of Iran's crucial role in defeating ISIS in Iraq, it is important to refrain from overstating the impact of its involvement.[62]

Soleimani was the architect and commander of Iran's military and security operations in Iraq and Syria.[63] He conveyed a cell phone message to General David Petraeus, commander of US forces in Iraq, asserting that he controlled 'the policy for Iran when it comes to Iraq and also Syria, Lebanon, Gaza and Afghanistan'.[64] Soleimani closely collaborated with select units in the PMU, particularly with the Kata'ib Hezbollah and the Badr Organisation. Unlike many military leaders, he took a significant risk by venturing onto the battlefields and forging personal and religious bonds with the troops he led, often praying with them. His relationship with the PMU was rooted more on 'mentorship' than 'direct command and control', yet he had considerable influence over their activities.[65] Soleimani's closest ally and his comrade-in-arms was Jamal Jaffar Mohammad Abumahdi, known as Mohandes (1954–2020), who led the PMU operations.[66] Mohandes, who headed the Kata'ib Hezbollah, reportedly and perhaps expectedly suggested that the liberation of Mosul in October 2016, which was a turning point in the battle against ISIS, would not have been possible without Iranian backing. Soleimani also had a close personal relationship with Hadi al Amiri, the leader of the Badr Organisation, the largest PMU militia. Amiri, who had Iranian citizenship and led the Badr Brigade when it was first established in Iran in 1982, effusively praised Soleimani for helping the PMU, backed by the Iraqi troops, liberate Fallujah, Mosul, and Tikrit (the birthplace of Saddam Hussein).[67]

Like his supporters, Soleimani believed that the US was not serious about combating ISIS and was capitalising on the situation to push its own agenda.[68] Moreover, he believed that Iraq's armed forces were improperly trained to effectively combat a nimble jihadist entity such as ISIS in an urban setting.[69] To provide training for Iraqi militias, he deployed Lebanese Hezbollah commandos to Iraq. Iraj Masjedi, Iran's ambassador to Iraq, recalled that Soleimani brought sixty Lebanese Hezbollah commanders to Iraq from Lebanon to share their expertise with their fellow Iraqi Shias as soon as Ayatollah Sistani issued the *fatwa* against ISIS.[70] However, he does not disclose the number of IRGC officers engaged in training Iraqi militias or the number of IRGC operating in Iraq.

Soleimani's hallmark approach towards ISIS was distinguished by swift and decisive military offensives. He believed that no town, village, or neighbourhood should be conceded to ISIS, and any foothold they establish must be promptly attacked and uprooted. Empowered with full authority by Ayatollah Khamenei, he bypassed time-consuming deliberations with Tehran and made instant, on-the-spot decisions on critical matters.[71] Former prime minister Maliki recalled that Soleimani managed to deliver Iraq's requested arms within a single day, a feat that would have taken much longer if requested from the US.[72]

While Iraqi government and PMU forces were making strides against ISIS, an auspicious opportunity emerged for the US and Iran to move towards a potential détente. They both recognised ISIS as a mutual enemy that must be crushed. Nevertheless, their divergent perspectives on Iraq's future hindered direct collaboration, leading to sporadic, indirect, and brief cooperation in some operations against ISIS. Hence, the US, engaged at the time in secret negotiations with Iran over its nuclear programme, showed minimal concern regarding the presence of the Iranian forces in Iraq, even extending air support for specific anti-ISIS operations led by the PMU, which were also supported by the IRGC.

When Iraq and Iran jointly declared victory over ISIS in Iraq in 2017, it came at heavy price: at least 2,000 PMU members and 40 IRGC advisors had lost their lives.[73] In 2016, Iraq's National Assembly brought the PMU under government jurisdiction. As of 2018, the cost of Iran's assistance to the PMU was estimated at around $20 million annually.[74] Despite the integration of the PMU into the state apparatus, Iran maintained substantial influence over some of its units, which have joined Iran's Axis of Resistance. Consequently, Iran's campaign against ISIS not only safeguarded its national security but also expanded its power in Iraq and bolstered its capacity for retaliating against the US.

To the Rescue of Kaka Masoud

To counter ISIS in Iraq, Iran also provided support to the Kurdish Regional Government (KRG). With a population of 3.5 million Kurds, who are ethnically non-Arab and predominantly Sunni, the KRG holds a semi-autonomous or federal status according to the 2005 Iraqi constitution. At first, the Kurds were hesitant to engage ISIS, possibly because they felt secure in their fortified enclaves. Yet while the Kurds might not have been interested in fighting ISIS, ISIS was interested in fighting them. It was not until mid-2014, when ISIS was advancing towards the Kurdish capital city of Erbil, that Kurds finally recognised the imminent danger posed by ISIS.[75] At this critical juncture, a frantic Masoud Barzani, the president of the KRG, urgently appealed to the US and a few other countries for military assistance but received no immediate response. Desperate to defend Erbil, Barzani turned to Soleimani, who reportedly told him, 'Kaka [brother] Masoud, just hold on to the city for one night.'[76]

By the following morning, Soleimani and his entourage arrived in Kurdistan. The Islamic Republic has not disclosed how many fighters were dispatched or deployed, or what kind of weapons they carried or provided to the Kurds. Soleimani reportedly played an important role in assisting the Kurdish Peshmerga in repelling ISIS and saving Erbil from falling to ISIS.[77] There were historical reasons why Masoud Barzani reached out to Tehran. Born in Mahabad, Iran, in 1946, is the son of the famed Mulla Mustafa Barzani, who collaborated with Mohammad Reza Shah to undermine Baghdad in the early 1970s. He later acknowledged that, in his hour of need, 'Iran was the first country to provide us with weapons and ammunition.'[78] To show his gratitude, he penned a missive to the Iranian president, expressing appreciation for Iran's unwavering support.[79] Iran continued its assistance by deploying Iranian fighters to aid the 'Peshmerga to take back Jalawla in Diyala Governorate from ISIL [ISIS]'.[80] Additionally, Soleimani encouraged Iranian-backed Asa'ib Ahl al-Haq and Kata'ib Hezbollah militias to collaborate with the Iraqi army and the Peshmerga 'to break the ISIL [ISIS] siege of Amerli in Saladin Governorate'. The operation was backed by the US Air Force.[81]

As the ISIS threat against the Kurds diminished, a more confident Barzani seized the opportunity and called for a referendum on Kurdish independence in September 2017. The United States wisely urged Barzani to reconsider or delay the referendum.[82] He likely believed that Iraq's central government was too fragile to oppose his bold move and that Israel and the US might support the Kurdish bid for independence. Barzani gambled big and lost big.

Both Tehran and Baghdad issued stern warnings to Barzani that holding the referendum would cross their red line and would not be tolerated. Nezam Omar Dabbagh, the KRG representative in Iran, recalled that Soleimani specifically cautioned Barzani that if the referendum were to proceed, he would be unable to prevent the Hashd al-Sha'bi from launching an assault on the Kurds. Even Jalal Talabani, Iraq's president and the leader of a powerful Kurdish political party, expressed his displeasure with the proposed referendum, dismissing the Kurdistan independence as a 'royaye sha'eraneh' or poetic delusion.[83]

President Barzani disregarded these admonitions and defiantly held the referendum in September 2017. As anticipated, over 92 per cent of

Kurds voiced their support for independence. However, this victory for Barzani proved to be fleeting.

Tehran saw the Kurdish referendum as the initial move in a plot to fragment Iraq into discrete entities, potentially even redrawing the national borders of the region. With its own restive Kurdish population of between eight to ten million, Iran feared that the establishment of an independent Iraqi Kurdistan would inevitably embolden separatist Kurds in Iran to pursue their own autonomous state, thereby undermining Iranian territorial integrity.[84] In fact, a few months prior to the Kurdish referendum, in June 2017, ISIS affiliates had attacked the iconic shrine of Ayatollah Khomeini and the parliament in Tehran, killing more than a dozen people. Five of the terrorists were Iranian Kurds. Iran's apprehensions about the KRG extended further. The increasing presence and influence of Israel in Iraqi Kurdistan, coupled with the allegation that Israel had been 'recruiting and training … Iranian dissidents from Iraqi Kurdish region', caused alarm in Tehran.[85] Significantly, Israel stood alone in the Middle East in endorsing Kurdish independence. This further exacerbated Iranian concerns that Israel, with US backing, was leveraging its connections to Iraq's Kurdistan and the Iranian opposition based there to destabilise the country.

Ayatollah Khamenei condemned the Kurdish referendum as 'an act of treason' and called on the KRG to annul its result. Tehran responded by conducting military manoeuvres along its borders with Iraqi Kurdistan and closing its air space to the KRG. It also increased its collaboration with Turkey, a staunch opponent of the referendum, to undermine Barzani and push for a change in policy.

However, the most significant development came when, in the aftermath of the referendum, the Iraqi army, with support from the Hashd al-Sha'bi, advanced towards the strategically important city of Kirkuk, which serves as a major source of oil revenues for the KRG. Soleimani warned the Kurdish Peshmerga that it would 'be a fatal mistake' to confront the Iraqi forces. He pleaded with them to peacefully withdraw from Kirkuk, and they heeded his counsel.[86] Following the fall of Kirkuk, Barzani had no alternative but to resign, relegating the referendum to a mere footnote in the Kurds' ongoing quest for independence.

The General Was No More

By the end of 2016, owing in part to direct Iranian involvement, the threat of ISIS in Kurdistan and in other parts of Iraq had subsided. Furthermore, as the nuclear negotiations between the US and Iran proceeded, Tehran and Washington cautiously started to move towards rapprochement as early as 2014, easing the tensions stemming from their rivalry in Iraq.[87] They even indirectly collaborated against ISIS. However, the inauguration of President Trump in January 2017 marked a turning point in this promising trajectory. During the presidential campaign, Trump often spoke of shredding the JCPOA to pieces. As president, he followed through on his promise by unilaterally withdrawing from the JCPOA in 2018 and imposing draconian sanctions on Iran. In reaction to his strategy of 'maximum pressure', designed to push Iran into agreeing to a more favourable nuclear deal with the US and to modifying its regional policies, Iran adopted a confrontationist policy of maximum resistance towards the US. Consequently, Iraq once again found itself as the battleground of the US–Iran cold war.

Both the US and Iran took several escalatory actions that brought the two countries to the brink of war. In 2017, Secretary of State Rex Tillerson demanded that the 'Iranian militias that are in Iraq … those militias need to go home', likely referring to the IRGC officers.[88] Two years later, the US took the unprecedented step of designating the IRGC, an official component of the armed forces of a sovereign country, a 'Foreign Terrorist Organisation', and even imposed sanctions on the office of Ayatollah Khamenei.[89] In response, Iran designated US Central Command 'a terrorist entity'. Furthermore, Washington exerted pressure on Iraq to enforce unilateral sanctions imposed by the US on Iran. Prime Minister Al-Mahdi resisted these efforts, affirming that Iraq 'is not a part of the framework of anti-Iran sanctions by the US' and would act 'in accordance with its national interests'.[90]

In a bold move, Iran then shot down a highly sophisticated, unmanned Navy RQ-4 Global Hawk surveillance aircraft valued at $220 million over the Strait of Hormuz in June 2019. While the US decried this as an 'unprovoked attack', Tehran insisted that the aircraft had intruded into

Iranian airspace.[91] As reprisal, the US launched cyber-attacks and imposed more sanctions on Iran. At the same time, the Iran-backed Iraqi militias were persistently targeting Baghdad's Green Zone, where the American embassy is located. Secretary Pompeo issued a stern warning that any attacks by Iran or its proxies would be met with 'a decisive US response'.[92] When a missile struck the Kirkuk military base in December 2019, leading to the death of a civilian contractor and injures to four US troops, the US swiftly retaliated by targeting the base of Kata'ib Hezbollah, a close Iranian ally, killing twenty-five militia members. Iraq and Iran condemned the attacks, emphasising that the targeted group was a lawful part of the PMU.

During this spiralling conflict, President Trump authorised an American drone to target General Soleimani's convey as it was leaving the parameters of the Baghdad International Airport on 2 January 2020. The strike instantaneously killed Soleimani and his entourage. Shocked by the event, the IRGC denounced the US as 'terrorists',[93] while Khamenei hailed Soleimani as a 'great martyr'.[94] Ultimately, the IRGC launched Operation Martyr Soleimani on 8 January 2020, firing over a dozen ballistic missiles at the Ayn al-Asad and Erbil airbases in Iraq, where US forces were stationed. The US did not retaliate. Amir Ali Hajizadeh, the commander of the IRGC Aerospace Force overseeing the attacks, stated that the objective was not to 'cause casualties'.[95] At the same time, General Salami, IRGC's commander, stressed that the missile attacks served as a deterrent, warning the US that any future strikes on Iran would come at a cost.[96]

Conflicting narratives surround Iran's missile attacks. General McKenzie told me that 'the US had credible intelligence indicating a possible Iranian missile attack, prompting us to relocate many of our assets from the Ayn al-Assad base'. He noted that the attacks were 'remarkably precise, destructive, and seriously damaged some of our assets'. McKenzie emphasised that the 'Iranians had the capability to target the US Embassy in Baghdad and potentially cause extensive casualties but refrained from doing so, likely due to fears of our retaliation.'[97] Former foreign minister Javad Zarif has presented a different perspective. He stated that, 'The US learned about the attacks on the Ayn al-Assad earlier than I did. Forty-five minutes before the attacks, two

Quds Force [IRGC] officers visited the office of Iraq's prime minister [al-Mahdi] to inform [Iraq] that Iran would imminently attack a base in Iraq', presumably as an alert to the US.[98]

The assassination of Soleimani delivered a disorienting blow to the Islamic Republic and its regional strategy. He was a charismatic soldier and an effective military leader with a deep understanding of the complex landscapes of Iraq, Syria, Lebanon, Yemen and Gaza. Over two decades, he was uniquely positioned to foster close personal connections with Iran's foreign allies and clandestine regional network. Despite Ayatollah Khamenei's immediate appointment of General Ismail Ghaani, who had long served as Soleimani's deputy commander, as the Quds Force commander, the Islamic Republic has not fully recovered from the loss of Soleimani. In fact, Iranian regional power has plateaued, and perhaps even eroded, since his killing.

Even before Soleimani's assassination, there was a surge of violent protests in Iraq against the government and Iran. These protests fractured the Shia bloc in the National Assembly, but they did not end Shia dominance in the country's politics. Enraged protestors were demanding the resignation of Prime Minister al-Mahdi, a close ally of Tehran, and holding him responsible for the country's deteriorating economic conditions and pervasive corruption. During these protests, Iranian consulates in Najaf and Karbala were set ablaze by 'unknown elements'. Iran accused the US of inciting these protests as a prelude to pressuring al-Mahdi to step down from office. Al-Mahdi reportedly stated that the US was pressuring Iraq to sever ties with Iran.[99] Ultimately, under mounting pressure, al-Mahdi resigned.

After contentious negotiations, the National Assembly confirmed Mustafa al Kadhimi as the new prime minister in May 2020. He received strong endorsement from the US.[100] Iran reluctantly supported Kadhimi, apprehensive that Iraqi opposition could provoke further protests against Iranian interference in Iraq.[101] Kadhimi, a seasoned Shia politician, assumed power four months after Soleimani's killing in January 2020. Many in Iran harboured suspicions about Kadhimi's alleged involvement with the US in the plot against Soleimani, given his position as Iraq's intelligence chief at the time of the assassination. Tehran's suspicions grew stronger when al-Abadi claimed that Iraq had granted permission for the two US drones to utilise Iraqi airspace in the operation against Soleimani.[102] Furthermore, al-Mahdi alleged that when Soleimani was killed at Baghdad International Airport, he was carrying a letter from Tehran to Riyadh aimed at restoring diplomatic relations between the two regional rivals.[103]

Despite Tehran's suspicions, bilateral relations remained cordial, albeit marked by significant disagreements. These disputes centred around the role of the PMU militias, the presence of anti-Islamic Republic armed Kurdish groups in Iraq's KRG, and, most importantly, Iraq's friendly relations with the US. Kadhimi attempted to disarm the PMU militias and even temporarily detained some of its commanders. However, his actions neither led to the disarming of the PMU nor to the diminution of Iran's influence over them. With respect to the Iranian dissident Kurds, Tehran was unable to convince Kadhimi to expel them from Iraq or disarm them.[104]

Kadhimi also aimed to maintain a delicate balance in Iraq's relations with both Washington and Tehran. He accurately echoed the sentiment of many Iraqi nationalists, asserting that Iraq should not become the battleground for Iran and the US to settle their differences. Tehran viewed Kadhimi's security agreement with the US in 2021 with suspicion. To downplay the new agreement, he emphasised that the US had reduced the number of US troops in Iraq and was developing a timeline for US withdrawal. However, Tehran remained unconvinced. Many believed that Kadhimi had no interest in a US withdrawal and instead preferred to transform the US mission into one focused on 'advisors and military trainers'.[105] Moreover, Tehran was concerned that Kadhimi was succumbing to pressure from Washington to limit Iraq's import of energy from Iran.[106]

What alarmed Tehran even more than Kadhimi's policy towards the United States was the significant role played by Muqtada Sadr in the resignation of al-Mahdi, the selection of Kadhimi, and the weakening of the Shia bloc. After the defeat of ISIS, Sadr rebranded himself as an Iraqi nationalist who opposed both US and Iranian interference in Iraq. Much to Iran's dismay, he also advocated for the disarmament of the Hashd al-Sha'bi, a significant conduit for Iranian influence in Iraq. Furthermore, he urged President Bashar Assad, Iran's key regional ally, to 'make a historic decision' and step down during the Syrian civil war.[107] Distancing himself from the Islamic Republic, Sadr visited Saudi Arabia, Iran's primary regional rival, and engaged in discussions with Crown Prince Mohammad bin Salman in July 2017, signalling his commitment to improving relations with the kingdom. Recognising Iran's concerns and anger about his recent manoeuvres, Sadr visited Tehran in 2018 to meet with Khamenei and Soleimani, hoping to improve his tarnished image.[108] Nevertheless, mutual mistrust has continued to characterise Sadr's relations with Tehran.

Tehran's uneasy relations with Iraq under Kadhimi improved after the National Assembly appointed Mohammad Shia al-Sudani as prime minister in October 2022. Since then, as a Shia politician, al-Sudani has met with Ayatollah Khamenei and the former president Ebrahim Raisi in Tehran. Much to Tehran's pleasure, he has taken steps to enhance relations with the Hashd al-Sha'bi and has worked to limit the activities of dissident Iranian Kurds against the Islamic Republic within Iraq. Al-Sudani's appointment and his efforts to strengthen ties with Tehran have once again demonstrated Shia dominance in Iraqi politics, and the enduring friendship between Tehran and Baghdad since the fall of Saddam Hussein.

Iran's Successes and Failures in Iraq

In the lead-up to the US invasion of Iraq, there was 'irrational exuberance' in Washington, driven by the belief that toppling Saddam Hussein would lead to a flourishing democracy in Iraq, which would spread to Iran and destabilise the Islamic Republic. The US, American hawks thought, could spread liberal values by means of guns and boots on the ground. None of these predictions ultimately proved accurate, revealing that Washington's policy of forced regime change can produce unintended and potentially harmful consequences for all involved. Indeed, there is a widespread consensus that the US project in Iraq was a strategic disaster, with Iran emerging as the primary beneficiary of the invasion among regional players.

The economic costs of the US invasion of Iraq and its human toll has been staggering. The financial burden placed on US taxpayers during the period from 2003 to early 2023, coupled with the anticipated future

costs for medical care of US Iraq War veterans, amounted to an astonishing sum of approximately $1.79 trillion.[109] In that time span, 280,771
and 315,190 people died directly as a result of war-related violence
attributed to the US invasion, its allies, and Iraqi forces, and it is estimated that several times as many Iraqi civilians may have died indirectly due to the war's repercussions.[110] The US also suffered heavy casualties, even if not of the same magnitude: 4,492 members of the US
armed services were killed, and 32,292 were wounded, making it the
deadliest conflict America has been involved in since the Vietnam
War.[111] From March 2003 to December 2011, when the US withdrew its
combat troops, 'at least 603 US personnel deaths were the result of Iran-
backed militants', accounting for 17 per cent of total US casualties in
Iraq.[112]

When President Bush and Prime Minister Blair initially ordered
troops to Iraq, they likely assumed that Iran would not dare to play an
active role against them in the country. But they were mistaken. In fact,
Iran actively intervened and achieved most of its strategic objectives,
albeit at great cost. For the past two decades, Iraq, which waged one of
the most destructive wars in the modern era against Iran, has had a
Tehran-friendly, Shia-dominated government. Iraq is no longer Iran's
sworn enemy but a potential ally that looks to Iran for support. This
shift is no small feat for Tehran. Additionally, Iran has significantly
expanded its influence in Iraq, built deterrence, and helped the Iraqi
government to defeat ISIS and protect its territorial integrity. Moreover,
Iraq has become one of Iran's major trading partners. Iran's exports to
Iraq increased from $6.1 billion in 2016 to $8.9 billion in 2021, while
Iraq's exports to Iran increased from $63.9 million in 2016 to $1.1
billion in 2021. Both countries expect a substantial increase in trade in
the coming years.[113]

Iran has failed to achieve one key goal, however – and this failure
continues to jeopardise the rest of its power-building project. Despite
Tehran's wishes, more than two decades after its invasion, the US still
stations troops in Iraq and maintains a military presence there. If Iraq
has become Tehran-friendly, it has nonetheless cultivated strategic ties
with the US. In fact, the US wields considerably more power in Iraq
than Iran, even though Iran has become arguably the most influential

regional player in that country. Consequently, Iraq remains a crucial battlefield in the cold war between the US and Iran, much to Iraq's displeasure.

While Iran has been unable to impose its hegemony, it has become a major force to be reckoned with in Iraq. However, its most significant strategic asset beyond its borders is not within Iraq, but rather with Hezbollah in Lebanon – the next stop in our journey.

Chapter 5

Iran's Power Play in Lebanon: Hezbollah as the Key Strategic Asset

On 12 July 2006, Hezbollah militants attacked an Israel Defense Forces (IDF) convoy patrolling the Lebanon–Israel border, killing three soldiers and abducting two. In response, General Dan Halutz, the Chief of IDF General Staff, threatened to 'turn back the clock in Lebanon by 20 years' if the captives were not immediately returned.[1] When the captives were not released, Operation Change Direction started, and Israel was prepared to make Lebanon pay.

On 13 July, the first day of the war, Imad Mughniyeh, considered a notorious terrorist by the US and one of Islam's finest warriors by the Islamic Republic, escorted Qasem Soleimani along a secure route from Syria to Beirut. In Lebanon, Soleimani, Mughniyeh, and Hassan Nasrallah, the leader of Hezbollah, led military operations against Israel from their 'secret war room'.[2] As Israel, the Middle East's strongest and most technologically advanced military force, faced off against Hezbollah, Soleimani regularly toured the battlefields, occasionally on his motorcycle. When Israel targeted the 'secret war room' with airstrikes, Soleimani managed to escape. He quickly went to a new hideout, where he was joined by Nasrallah and Mughniyeh. The trio continued to lead Hezbollah's operations against Israel.

After the guns of war fell silent, Iran inaugurated Bostan-e Iran (Iran's Garden) in the village of Maroun al Ras situated just 1 kilometre from the Israeli border. Designed and financed by the Islamic Republic, the park was built on a mountain overlooking Israel and adorned with large Iranian flags. It also showcased giant portraits of ayatollahs Khomeini and Khamenei, gazing down at Israel. Following Soleimani's assassination by the US in January 2020, a giant statue of him was erected in Bostan-e Iran, with his index finger pointing at Israel.[3]

Today, Hezbollah has become, in the words of Brigadier General Guy Tzur, former chief of the Ground Forces Command of Israel's Defense Forces, 'by far the greatest guerrilla group in the world'.[4] While US Deputy Secretary of State Richard Armitage described Hezbollah as the 'A-Team of terrorism',[5] Tehran hails it as the embodiment of the Shia spirit of martyrdom and resistance against injustice.

Why and how was Hezbollah created, and what is Tehran's rationale for its multifaceted support for the group? What role has the organisation played in advancing Iran's strategic goals in the region, and has supporting Hezbollah served its national interests?

The Islamic Republic's crucial role in helping establish Hezbollah was part of Iran's broader and earlier effort to empower Lebanon's neglected Shias, spearheaded by three prominent Iranian clerics: Imam Musa Sadr, Ayatollah Khomeini, and Ayatollah Khamenei. However, the story's opening acts took place during Mohammad Reza Shah's reign – well before the Islamic Revolution.

Mohammad Reza Shah and Shia Empowerment

Southern Lebanon has long been a primary exporter of Shia theology, so it's small wonder that the Islamic Republic feels an affinity with the region. Although both the Achaemenid and Sassanid empires conquered most of the Levant, it was only during the Safavid dynasty (1501–1726) that Iran forged a religious bond with the Shias of Lebanon.[6] Founded by Shah Isma'il, this dynasty unified Iran and imposed Shi'ism as the state religion, despite the solid Sunni majority. To institutionalise Shi'ism, the

Safavids invited Shia theologians from the Jabal Amil region in southern Lebanon. The region – today one of the strongholds of Hezbollah – was one of the main intellectual homes of Shiism, while many of its clerics were looking to free themselves from the leash of the Sunni Ottoman empire. The Safavids and the clerics were a match made in heaven: the Safavids granted power and security to the marginalised Amili clerics, while the clerics, in turn, contributed to establishing the jurisprudential foundation of Shiism in Iran and legitimising Safavid kings. Subsequently, the émigré clerics assumed important roles in both the affairs of the state and Iran's clerical establishment.[7] Many of them married Iranians and came to serve as intermediaries between the peoples of Iran and Lebanon.

Iran maintained good relations with Lebanon, operating three consulates in Beirut, Sidon, and Tripoli under the Qajar dynasty (1789–1925), a friendship that continued throughout the French Mandate after the First World War.[8] To assert control over culturally and religiously diverse Lebanon, France primarily collaborated with Christian Maronites and the Sunni Arabs who held elite status during Ottoman rule over the Levant. At the same time, the significant Shia population was largely marginalised. As in Iraq in the 1920s, Iran did not help the Shias in Lebanon, having no national interest there and fearing it could jeopardise its good relations with France. Ultimately, in the multi-confessional republic France created after Lebanon gained independence in 1943, Shias were granted considerably less power than others: by convention the most powerful post of president was always reserved for a Maronite, that of prime minister for a Sunni, and the speaker of the National Assembly, the least powerful position, for a Shia.

Initially, Iran had little in the way of official relations with Lebanon after its independence. Its educational encounters with Lebanon, however, were substantial, with affluent young Iranians attending French schools and the prestigious American University of Beirut. Among them were Amir Abbas Hoveyda and Ardeshir Zahedi, who served as prime minister and foreign minister during the Pahlavi era, respectively.[9]

More recently, in the 1950s and 1960s, Mohammad Reza Shah became interested in Lebanon as part of his strategic objective to counter the perceived threat posed by Gamal Abdel Nasser's pan-Arabism. Nasser and Mohammad Naguib orchestrated a coup in Egypt in June 1952, overthrowing King Farouk, whose sister, Princess Fawzia Fuad, had previously married the Shah. The Shah found this danger uncomfortably close. Nasser's anti-colonial policies, demonstrated through audacious actions such as the nationalisation of the British- and French-controlled Suez Canal, coupled with his rejection of monarchical rule, popularised pan-Arabism – a distinctive fusion of Arab nationalism and socialism – to unify the Arab world. The Shah's anxiety further intensified when Egypt and Syria briefly merged to form the United Arab Republic between 1958 and 1961.

As early as 1958, the Shah portrayed Nasser as a 'mad man' who was unleashing an 'Arab imperialism'.[10] He told President Eisenhower that Nasser was an Arab version of Adolf Hitler, seeking to control 'large areas in the Middle East', including Iran's oil-rich Khuzestan.[11] However, the US played down the Shah's concerns, assuring him that Nasser posed 'at most only potential' threat to Iran.[12] What was perceived by the US as a 'potential threat to Iran' looked like real threat to the Shah. As a result, he sought to neutralise the perceived threat posed by Egypt in Iraq and Lebanon, where Nasser enjoyed considerable popularity.

With the goal of expanding power in Lebanon and undermining pan-Arabism, the Shah cautiously played the Shia card by empowering the Shia community in Lebanon. Simultaneously, he developed closer relations with Lebanon's Maronite president, Camille Chamoun.[13] Like the Shah, Chamoun was threatened by Nasser, believing that Nasser's goal was 'gobbling up' Lebanon.[14] In 1958, Chamoun urgently pleaded with President Dwight Eisenhower to deploy US troops in Lebanon to help protect its independence. Eisenhower agreed and dispatched a small contingent of US troops. The Shah welcomed US intervention and instructed the delivery of limited quantities of arms and ammunition from Iran to Lebanon.

Imam Musa Sadr Goes to Lebanon

The Shah directed SAVAK to craft a plan to increase Iranian influence in Lebanon. In response, Major Mujtaba Pashaei devised the Green Path, or *Rah-e Sabz*, in the late 1950s.[15] The blueprint centred on empowering Shias as a countermeasure or antidote to pan-Arabism. Pashaei believed that 'we should combat and contain the threat in the east coast of the Mediterranean to prevent shedding blood on Iranian soil'.[16] Decades later, the Islamic Republic used the same logic as it intervened in the Syrian civil war to fight ISIS.

A young Iranian cleric named Musa Sadr lay at the core of Iran's Shia empowerment initiative. Born in Qom in 1928, he completed his traditional religious studies in Qom and Najaf *Howzeh*.[17] From a young age, he distinguished himself as a trailblazer cleric with aspirations to harmonise Shiism with the exigencies of modernity. He even earned a secular degree in law from the University of Tehran – a taboo among his peers.

Upon the invitation of certain prominent Lebanese Shias, Sadr moved to Lebanon in December 1959 to lead its Shia community. What remains unclear is the role, if any, that SAVAK played in Sadr's decision to relocate to Lebanon. General Teymur Bakhtiyar, the first head of SAVAK, allegedly met with Sadr before he left for Lebanon.[18] However, there is no evidence that Sadr was a SAVAK agent, despite his frequent contact with the Iranian government and its embassy in Beirut. General Mansur Qadar, Iran's Ambassador to Lebanon (1973–1979) and a senior SAVAK official, who harboured deep suspicions of Sadr, is quoted as claiming that Sadr was secretly educated and paid by SAVAK, a claim that many others have denied.[19]

Gregarious and charismatic, Sadr quickly rose to prominence as a celebrity cleric of sorts, becoming the voice and face of the marginalised Lebanese Shias. He was admired as a bridge builder, who sought to foster peace and harmony among Christians, Sunnis, and Shias. He was not a bomb-throwing revolutionary zealot, but an enlightened reformist who operated within Lebanon's political system to bring justice to the Shias, who had been 'treated like animals'.[20] Above all, he was an institution builder, believing that organised, oppressed masses were the most effective catalyst for political change. He established charitable organisations and built medical clinics to help the underprivileged, along with schools for both boys and girls. In 1969, he founded the Supreme Islamic Shia Council, which allowed Shias to have their own state-supported council for the first time, on equal footing with Sunnis and Maronites. Serving as its first elected president, he leveraged the council's resources to improve the dire socioeconomic conditions faced by Shias.

By the end of the 1960s, Sadr had become one of the most celebrated religious leaders in Lebanon. As a result, he was granted an audience with the Shah in Tehran in 1971, asking for financial support to build a hospital and a university in Lebanon, a testament to Sadr's growing influence in the Iranian government. It is unclear how much financial support – if any – Sadr received. Despite this meeting, a rift gradually developed between Sadr and some elements within the Shah's regime. Several factors contributed to this divide. One was the diminishing threat of pan-Arabism. In March 1970, shortly before his passing, Nasser's meeting with Imam Musa Sadr in Cairo raised concerns in Tehran about Sadr's loyalty to the Shah.[21] However, following Nasser's death in September 1970, his successor, President Anwar Sadat, reversed course and rapidly brought about Egypt's reconciliation with Iran, ultimately forging a friendship with the Shah. Consequently, Tehran no longer saw a need for Sadr as a counterbalance against the vanishing influence of pan-Arabism.

Another significant factor contributing to the rift between Tehran and Sadr was his deep involvement in Lebanon's civil war. In September 1971, thousands of fighters from the Palestine Liberation Organisation (PLO), who had been expelled from Jordan, sought refuge in the Shia-dominated regions of southern Lebanon. This influx forced thousands of vulnerable Shias to evacuate their towns and villages.[22] In response, Sadr moved to disentangle the fate of Palestinians from that of Shias.[23] In 1974, he established an organisation called the *Harakat al-Mahrumin* (Movement of the Deprived) to aid displaced Shias. Soon after, as Lebanon descended into a civil war, he established *'Afwaj Mouqawma Al-Lubnaniyya*, or *Amal* (Hope), as an armed militia.[24] Surprisingly, Sadr had taken on the roles of a religious, political, and militia leader all at once. During the civil war, he sided with President Suleiman Frangieh and extended an invitation to Syria to deploy troops in Lebanon in June 1976. Sadr saw in Syria a protector of Shia interests and a counterforce against both the PLO and Israel.

In contrast to Sadr, the Shah maintained a position of neutrality in the Lebanese civil war while quietly urging Israel not to suppress the

Shias. Uri Lubrani, who served as Israel's unofficial ambassador to Iran, recounted that after the Shah's palace lodged a complaint alleging that Israel was causing harm to the Shias, he invited one of the Shah's ministers to visit Israel and south Lebanon. During the visit, the minister 'saw with his own eyes that Israel had not harmed the Shias. Then I understood how important the Lebanese Shiites were to Iran.'[25]

The third factor that exacerbated Tehran's mistrust of Sadr was the increasing uncertainly surrounding his allegiance to the Shah.

General Mansur Qadar alleged that Sadr was an ambitious hypocrite who had collaborated with many opponents of the Shah, including Libya's Muammar Gaddafi. However, Ardeshir Zahedi praised Sadr for extending 'his hand of friendship towards us'.[26] He also told me that Sadr 'loved Iran'.[27]

The final factor that gave Tehran grounds for concern about Sadr was the allegation that he was engaging in a duplicitous game, maintaining good relations with Tehran while facilitating the training of anti-Shah Iranian dissidents in guerrilla warfare in Lebanon. In this case, the Iranian government's suspicions were not unfounded.

A Haven for Anti-Shah Militant Islamists

Lebanon in the 1960s and 1970s left an indelible impact on the ideological orientation of both Islamists and secular opponents of the Shah, many of whom received military training there. Anti-imperialism and particularly anti-Israeli perspectives, and occasionally anti-Semitism, became essential components of their viewpoints.

Musa Sadr played a major role in the establishment of two networks of anti-Shah Islamist militants. These networks would later wield considerable influence over revolutionary Iran's foreign policy and its anti-Israeli orientation.

Sadr created and oversaw the larger network, which held deep connections to Amal and Iran's Liberation Movement – an opposition organisation against the Shah, established by Mehdi Bazargan in 1961.

The intermediaries linking Amal and Iranian dissidents were Dr Mustafa Chamran (1932–1981), who later became the Islamic Republic's defence minister, and Ebrahim Yazdi (1931–2017), who became the Islamic Republic's foreign minister.[28] Chamran, who held a PhD from the University of California, Berkeley, and had been working for Bell Laboratories and NASA's Jet Propulsion Laboratories, left behind a successful life in the US in the mid-1960s to become the director of Amal, an organisation Sadr had created. Over time, Chamran – dubbed Iran's 'Che Guevara' – became Sadr's sworn bother, preparing a generation of anti-Shah activists for a protracted guerrilla struggle.

In 1964, Chamran, Yazdi, and a few other members of Iran's Liberation Movement, formed Sazeman-e Makhsous-e Ettehad va Amal (Special Group for Unity and Action), with the goal of launching armed struggle against the Shah's regime. Through the mediation of a member of the Egyptian embassy in Washington, this small group received an invitation from Nasser's government to move to Egypt for military training, where they were based between 1964 and 1966. In total, over forty members received extensive training in different aspects of warfare.[29] The group relocated to Beirut in 1966, discontented with Nasser's overtly anti-Iran stance.[30]

A smaller, yet more radical, network of Islamist dissidents operating in Lebanon was led by Khomeini's students and supporters. While Sadr facilitated their stay in Lebanon, and they collaborated, members of this network harboured suspicions about Sadr, considering him insufficiently revolutionary, anti-Israel, and pro-Palestinian. These two networks represented contrasting interpretations of Shiism – one moderate and somewhat tolerant, the other radically conservative and far less tolerant. This schism became apparent in the first year of the Islamic Revolution, when the moderate Provisional Revolutionary Government headed by Mehdi Bazargan collapsed and radical Islamists ascended to power.

SAVAK was cognisant of the presence of the dissidents in Lebanon, as well as the role Sadr was playing among them, calling him the 'godfather' of the opposition to the Shah.[31] To monitor their activities, its agents were deployed under the guise of UN Interim Force peacekeepers to Lebanon following Israel's Operation Litani in 1987.[32]

As they kept an eye on these dissidents, the Islamic Revolution was steadily marching towards victory in Tehran. In a surprising move, Sadr penned a short piece for France's *Le Monde* in August 1978, recognising Khomeini as the leader of Iran's revolution.[33] In the eyes of his critics, this letter vindicated their assessment that Sadr was more concerned with advancing his personal interests than any allegiance to allies or principles. In that same month, Sadr left Beirut for Libya at the invitation of Muammar Gaddafi. In a mysterious turn of events that has never been fully explained, he disappeared – and has neither been seen nor heard from again since 31 August 1978. Most believe he and his two companions were killed – the question is by whom. There are those who continue to maintain he may still be alive. Gaddafi's youngest son, Hannibal, has been held in a Lebanese prison by Lebanon's Internal Security Forces since 2015 in connection with Sadr's disappearance, as part of an effort to pressure Libya into providing evidence.[34] Some speculate that Gaddafi killed Sadr because of his betrayal of the Palestinians in Lebanon. Scott Cooper suggests, although without providing verifiable evidence, that Ayatollah Mohammad Beheshti, a close associate of Ayatollah Khomeini, may have asked Gaddafi to eliminate Sadr. This request was reportedly prompted by Sadr's willingness to mediate between the Shah and Khomeini, a plan Beheshti supposedly opposed. Scott Cooper writes that President Sadat alleged that Gaddafi killed Sadr, placing his 'body in a box, sealed in concrete, and dropped it from a helicopter into the Mediterranean [Sea]'.[35] The definitive account of his disappearance is yet to be written.

Imam Musa Sadr vanished, yet his profound impact on both Lebanese and Iranian politics and Shiism persisted. His most enduring legacy lay in the empowerment of Lebanese Shias and his promotion of a tolerant interpretation of Shiism in harmony with modernity. Deftly navigating through Lebanon's byzantine politics, he effectively united 'Islam and Lebanese nationalism together as a counterforce to the left', as the Shah had envisioned.[36] While he did not live to witness the Islamic Revolution, his ideas continued to shape the new regime's policies towards Lebanon and Syria.

Khomeini, Pan-Shiism, and Hezbollah

One of the most consequential shifts in revolutionary Iran's foreign policy in the 1980s was its gradual pivot towards the Levant, particularly Lebanon. This was initially driven not by the hard calculus of national interest, but a genuine commitment to exporting the revolution on pan-Shia and pan-Islamic principles. This pivot occurred during the radical phase of the Iranian foreign policy, when high Islamic ideals often triumphed over the exigencies of Realpolitik. During this chaotic period, Iran's 'deep state' played a central role in formulating Iran's new foreign policy, with minimal democratic input.

The Islamists, who had undergone military training in Lebanon and Syria in the 1960s and 1970s, collectively known in Tehran's foreign policy circles as the 'Lebanon and Syria mafia', played a crucial role in shaping this new foreign policy paradigm. Iran's primary objectives in Lebanon were to expand its power, export the Islamic revolution by mobilising its marginalised Shia population and weaponising their grievances, and undermine the interests of the US and Israel, while championing the Palestinian cause.

By the time the Islamic Revolution took place, Amal had already grown to be a formidable Shia organisation in Lebanon. The stars seemed aligned for Amal and the nascent Islamic Republic to forge a strong alliance. Amal had powerful allies in the Iranian government. Most notably, Chamran, one of the founders of Amal, who now served as the defence minister of the Provisional Revolutionary Government. Amal collaborated closely with Tehran to enhance Iran's regional influence. The CIA reported that Amal's armed militias were 'involved in a series of Iranian-backed terrorist activities against Iraqis' during the Iran–Iraq War.[37] However, Amal's influence in the Islamic Republic began to wane after the storming of the American embassy in Tehran by radical Islamists, which led to the downfall of Bazargan's government in November 1979. And, more importantly, Amal lost its most trusted and powerful advocate and liaison with Tehran after the death of Chamran on the battlefields of the Iran–Iraq War in June 1981.

Even before Amal's influence in Tehran began to diminish, a coalition of radical Iranians, the IRGC, and Lebanese Shias were actively lobbying Ayatollah Khomeini to establish a new and revolutionary Shia organisation in Lebanon. The basic concept of creating a new organisation alongside Amal likely originated within the small network of Khomeini's followers, both Iranian and Lebanese, during the 1970s. These militants looked down on Amal as being too secular, too reformist, too nationalistic, too soft on Israel, and too apathetic towards the Palestinian cause. One of the chief advocates for creating a new organisation was Hojatolislam Ali Akbar Mohtashamipour, who later became Iran's ambassador to Syria and is considered one of the 'founding fathers of Hezbollah'. The other influential figure was the rabble-rouser Mohammad Montazeri, nicknamed 'Ayatollah Ringo' for his cowboy-style adventurism. He not only established a unit within the IRGC to support liberation movements abroad but also pledged to send thousands of Iranian volunteers to support the Shias of Lebanon.

The decisive moment in the creation of a Shia group that eventually became Hezbollah came shortly after Iraq invaded Iran in September 1980, when a delegation of radical Lebanese Shias was granted an audience with Ayatollah Khomeini in Tehran.[38] Included in the delegation were Seyyed Abbas Mousavi, a disgruntled Amal member who later became a Hezbollah leader, and the young Hassan Nasrallah, Hezbollah's current Secretary General.[39] During that meeting, Khomeini approved the formation of a new organisation without naming it, instructing the delegation to rely on self-sufficiency and reject the cynics who believe 'you are too weak' to fight the two superpowers.[40]

Less than a year later, in June 1982, Israel invaded Lebanon in Operation Peace of Galilee. The declared *casus belli* was the assassination attempt on Shlomo Argov, who was Israel's ambassador to Britain, by Abu Nidal Organization, a militant group renowned for its terrorist activities. Israel's invasion had multiple objectives: to expel the PLO from Lebanon, to establish a security zone in south Lebanon to prevent potential attacks on Israel, and to exert pressure on Lebanon's government to sign a peace treaty with Israel.[41] However, Israel's invasion, like all invasions, inevitably had unintended results. Years later, Ehud Barak, Israel's prime minister, observed that when Israel invaded

Lebanon, it was initially 'accepted with perfumed rice and flowers by the Shias in the south. It was *our presence* [my emphasis] there that created Hezbollah.'[42] Regardless of whether Shias welcomed the invasion at first, as Barak suggested, Israel's incursion provided a fertile environment for Tehran to effectively mobilise the population against Israel.

Israel's invasion took place just two weeks after Iran had successfully expelled Iraqi troops from Khorramshahr in May 1982. The significant victory altered the trajectory of the Iran–Iraq War in Iran's favour. For the Islamic Republic, Israel's invasion presented a major dilemma: should it stay true to its commitment to pan-Shiism and assist the besieged Shias in Lebanon, or should it prioritise the country's national interests and allocate all available resources to the ongoing war with Iraq?

Khomeini initially harboured suspicions that the invasion might be part of an Israel–US conspiracy aimed at diverting precious Iranian resources to Lebanon, precisely when it had the opportunity to win the war against Iraq.[43] Reportedly, he said 'We might lose to Saddam [Iraq]' if Iran becomes entangled in Syria and Lebanon.[44]

The IRGC Goes to Syria and Lebanon

While Tehran was deliberating its options to support the beleaguered Shias during its own war with Iraq, a delegation of Lebanese Shias arrived in Tehran to persuade the Islamic Republic to support their brethren in Lebanon.[45] The delegation achieved its mission. Tehran decided to dispatch a small team of IRGC and army officers to Syria, its newfound friend, for the purpose of exploring the possibility of Iran making a military intervention in Lebanon.[46] Following initial consultations with Syria, the team reported back to Tehran that Syria was open to cooperating with Iran against Israel. Subsequently, Iran reportedly deployed an estimated 3,000 to 5,000 troops to Syria in June 1982.

Commanded by a young IRGC officer named Ahmad Motevaselian, the contingent received a warm welcome upon arrival at the Damascus airport by Rifaat Assad – the younger brother of President Hafez Assad, who led the forces that had massacred thousands of Muslim Brotherhood members in the city of Hama four months earlier.[47] After expressing dissatisfaction with their run-down 'filthy headquarters', the Iranian team was relocated to a cleaner facility in Damascus.[48] The IRGC commanders were also taken aback when their weapons were temporarily confiscated prior to their meeting with President Hafez Assad. General Ali Sayyad Shirazi, commander of the ground forces of Iran's army, recalled that the Syrians were perplexed by Iran's interest in waging a war in Lebanon while 'you are fighting a war with Iraq'.[49] Assad prudently conveyed to the Iranians that he had no intention of entering a direct war with Israel. Following this eye-opening meeting with Assad, Tehran abandoned its reckless idea of starting an open conflict with Israel in Lebanon. Reportedly, Khomeini issued an order to 'bring the troops back', with a clear message that 'I take no responsibility if their noses bleed.'[50] This suggests that the troop deployment might have been done without Khomeini's knowledge.[51] This, however, was not the end of the story.

The impulse to intervene in Lebanon in defence of Shias and Palestinians against Israel proved irresistible for Iran's idealistic leaders. As a result, they reached a compromise: instead of dispatching thousands of troops for conventional warfare against Israel, Khomeini approved the deployment of approximately 400 to 600 IRGC officers to Syria to train Lebanese in asymmetric warfare against Israel. At the same time, he popularised the slogan 'The Road to Jerusalem Passes Through Karbala'. The slogan effectively tempered the impulsive calls from radicals who sought immediate confrontation with Israel, redirecting their focus towards a more calculated and patient strategy. In this context, Khomeini's primary objective was to win the war against Iraq, while viewing the liberation of Jerusalem as a long-term goal. Importantly, he was determined to avoid a military confrontation with Israel, emphasising that 'Israel is not Iraq', and that 'the quality of Israeli forces is superior to [that of the] Iraqis'.[52]

The IRGC team deployed in Syria swiftly established its training camps for Shias in the Syrian-controlled Bekaa Valley in Lebanon.[53] While those recruited by the IRGC and their Lebanese associates underwent training in asymmetric guerrilla warfare, a select group also regularly convened at a local seminary in Baalbek to discuss political and ideological issues. These meetings were attended by individuals who comprised the 'who's who' of Hezbollah's future leaders. Members pledged allegiance to Khomeini and stood united in the goal of expelling US and Israeli troops from Lebanon and eradicating Israel.[54] The name Hezbollah was chosen, recalled Sheikh Subhi al-Tufayli, who later became Hezbollah's first Secretary General in 1989, because it 'is a Qur'anic phrase that we kept hearing the Persian commanders use about our group'.[55] Kochek Hosseini, an IRGC officer, stated that Motevaselian founded the group and named it Hezbollah.[56] Up until its official declaration in 1985, the decentralised organisation, consisting of several small groups, concealed its identity for security reasons, using various pseudonyms such as Lebanon's Islamic Resistance.[57]

While the IRGC was building Hezbollah's military infrastructures, Motevaselian and his three Iranian companions were kidnapped in Lebanon.[58] Iran blamed Israel and its Maronite allies for the kidnapping. In retaliation, in July 1982, Hezbollah-aligned forces kidnapped David Dodge, the American acting president of the American University in Beirut. Dodge quickly became a bargaining chip, to be used as a leverage for the release of the captured Iranians. Through Syrian mediation, Dodge was released a year later, but the four Iranians were reportedly executed by their kidnappers. Kidnapping, targeted assassinations, hijacking, and suicide bombing became the prevalent modes of operation for rival groups in Lebanon for years to come.

As Iran was progressively becoming more involved in Lebanon, it simultaneously expanded its charitable services to Shia communities, took steps to mediate and manage the escalating conflict between Hezbollah and its rival, Amal, and initiated important structural changes within Hezbollah. To aid the Lebanese, Tehran established the Imam Khomeini Relief Committee (*Komite-ye Imdad-e Imam*) and other foundations, such as the Martyr Foundation. These foundations operated independently from the Iranian state's jurisdiction and were solely accountable to Khomeini. At the same time, the competition between Hezbollah and Amal for control over the Shia community was growing more intense. While Tehran clearly showed favour towards Hezbollah, it had no compelling interest in the marginalisation of Amal, which was supported by Syria, Iran's ally.[59] As a result, Iran worked closely with

Syria, urging Hezbollah and Amal to resolve their differences. The two groups had vastly different political visions. Hezbollah aspired to create an Islamic government like the Islamic Republic of Iran, while Amal remained committed to operating within Lebanon's constitutional framework. While Hezbollah vociferously opposed the US and Israel, Amal was more pragmatic and conciliatory. In fact, following Israel's invasion, Amal's leader, Nabih Berri, served on a US-backed committee that facilitated the departure of the PLO from Lebanon.[60]

Iran's approach towards Hezbollah changed as well. Shortly after the abduction of the four Iranians, Hossein Dehghan, a top IRGC official, was dispatched to Lebanon to command the IRGC forces in the Levant.[61] Reportedly, he replaced all Iranians in leadership positions within Hezbollah with Lebanese Shias.[62] Additionally, he appointed Hassan Nasrallah to oversee a new military training camp. He also assisted Hezbollah in drafting a constitution, publishing a weekly newsletter, and operating a radio station. Tehran's goal was to make Hezbollah more centralised, cohesive, effective, disciplined, and more in tune with its strategic priorities. This was a herculean task, given that there were some renegade rebel groups operating under the umbrella of Hezbollah. But the loose structure had certain advantages: it made it very difficult for Washington to collect accurate intelligence about Hezbollah's operations.

Geostrategic Rivalry with the US and Israel

Amid Lebanon's tumultuous civil war, Hezbollah gained international notoriety for its spectacular terrorist operations against Western and Israeli interests in the 1980s.[63] Initially, the US lacked clarity regarding the true culprits behind these operations and, more importantly, Iran's precise role in them. Washington often interpreted Iran's involvement in these violent actions through the lens of ongoing factional rivalry. Hardliners were often seen advocating terrorism as 'a legitimate tool of state policy', while pragmatists were believed to support terrorism only 'if it furthered Iranian interests'.[64] Although this interpretation was generally accurate, the reality was more nuanced.

Hezbollah's rise occurred simultaneously with the breakdown of the Lebanese state during the civil war and the rise of sectarian armed militias. The civil war, initially sparked by clashes between the left-leaning Lebanese National Movement and the right-wing Christian Phalangists, spiralled into an all-out sectarian war involving the Phalange, Palestinians, and a variety of Muslim militias. Foreign powers, including Syria, Israel, the United States, and France, also deployed troops to quell the violence.

In these unsettling times, President Amine Gemayel made a risky and bold move by signing a separate peace treaty with Israel in May 1983. This act distinguished Lebanon as the second Arab country, following Egypt, to sign a peace treaty with Israel. The treaty, mediated by the US, called for the withdrawal of both Israeli and Syrian troops, with provisions allowing Israel to establish a security zone in southern Lebanon. The US goal, as articulated by Secretary of State George Shultz, was to maintain 'American dominance of Middle East diplomacy' and exert pressure on both parties to implement the treaty which represented 'a major commitment of US prestige'.[65]

Both Syria and Iran vigorously opposed the peace treaty, viewing it as a surrender of Lebanon's sovereignty. It was at this juncture that Hezbollah emerged from obscurity and made its debut on the international stage.

Israel, whose troops had occupied parts of Lebanon, became the first target of the prevailing anger. In November 1982, a car packed with explosives drove into the Israeli Liaison and Assistance Office in Tyre, which served as the IDF headquarters in Lebanon, resulting in the deaths of seventy-five Israelis, along with more than a dozen Lebanese and Palestinian prisoners. Two groups put themselves on the map by claiming responsibility for the operation, although Israel insisted that the explosion was a result of a gas leak. Only in 2022 did Israel reopen a formal inquiry into the cause of the explosion, which its intelligence suggested was caused by a Hezbollah-aligned group.[66] This attack was followed by another deadly assault at the building of border police in November 1983, which claimed the lives of several dozen Israelis and Lebanese. Israel attributed these attacks to 'Shia extremists, possibly backed by Syria and Iran'.[67]

Deadly Attacks on US Marines

These operations against Israel were only a prelude to more audacious strikes against US and French forces in Beirut.[68] In April 1983, a suicide bomber drove a truck laden with explosive into the US embassy compound in Beirut, resulting in the death of sixty-three people, including Robert Ames, the CIA's chief analyst for the Middle East. Six months later, in October 1983, another suicide bomber steered an explosives-packed truck into the US Marine Headquarters building in Beirut, claiming the lives of 241 military personnel. Simultaneously, a suicide bomber targeted the headquarters of the French troops, resulting in the deaths of fifty-eight servicemen. Responsibility for these two attacks was falsely claimed by the Palestine Islamic Jihad and the Lebanese Resistance Front. But this wasn't the full story.

Initially, with little in way of definitive evidence, Washington couldn't identify the culprits behind these attacks. Five days after the bombings, the National Intelligence Council concluded that:

> The evidence of guilt in the Beirut bombing of the Marine Headquarters falls somewhat short of a smoking gun we would all like. In all likelihood we will never get the smoking gun. The evidence linking Syria to the incident is considerably less than to Iran which has 'clear-cut expressions of intent'.[69]

However, in public declarations, the US accused Hezbollah of carrying out the attacks while condemning Iran and Syria for sponsoring terrorism, an allegation both countries denied. While Khomeini refrained from condemning the attacks, he contended that Lebanese were 'fed up' with their country's occupation and have 'become suicidal'.[70] Supporters of these twin attacks justified them as acts of 'self-determination' against the presence of Israeli and Western troops in Lebanon.

In response, President Ronald Reagan declared that the US 'will not leave Lebanon and [we] don't reward intimidation and terrorism'.[71] However, this position became untenable amidst the ensuing chaos, hysteria, and intense anti-Israel and anti-American sentiment. Therefore, the Lebanese government was forced to abrogate the proposed peace treaty with Israel on 6 March 1984 – merely five months after the attacks on the Marines. And, contrary to Reagan's earlier declaration, the US withdrew its troops from Lebanon, just one day after the abrogation of the treaty with Israel. This was a victory for Hezbollah, Iran, and Syria, and, regrettably, demonstrated the effectiveness of terrorism – or what Tehran termed 'martyrdom operations' – as a tool for achieving political objectives. As David Johnson observed, terrorism or martyrdom operations serve to compensate for 'the military imbalance' between two parties by inflicting painful losses on the more powerful side.[72]

'We Do Not Know Their Names'

While disavowing any role in the attacks on Western troops, Iran hailed them as 'martyrdom' operations in defence of Islam and Lebanon's sovereignty.[73] Although initially responsibility was denied, evidence suggests that Hezbollah may have masterminded and executed the attacks on the US Marines and French troops. In its 1985 manifesto, Hezbollah implicitly accepted responsibility for these attacks. It stated that:

> Our people would not withstand all this treason and decided to confront the infidelity of America, France, and Israel. The first punishment against these forces was carried out on 18 April and the second on 23 October 1983 [the days when US facilities were attacked]. We have risen to liberate our country, to drive the imperialists and the invaders out of it and to determine our fate by our own hands.[74]

Hossein Sheikholeslam, one of Iran's main liaisons with Hezbollah, admitted in 2020 that Hezbollah 'started attacking inside the American bases and killed 212 Americans'.[75] Moreover, a monument was built for the 'martyrs of the Marine Operation' in Tehran's Behesht-e Zahra cemetery in 2004. Inscribed on the monument are the words: 'We do not know their names, but we will continue their path.'[76] Even though the evidence regarding Hezbollah's responsibility for the attacks on the Marines is robust, the role of the Islamic Republic in planning and executing these operations has yet to be a definitively determined. What is undeniable is the Islamic Republic's immense influence over Hezbollah. Some sources have accused Iran of direct involvement in these operations.[77]

Contrary to President Reagan's earlier vow not to 'reward intimidation and terrorism', the US effectively did so when it officially withdrew its troops from Lebanon in March 1984. However, Washington sought to increase pressure on Iran and take proactive measures against future Hezbollah attacks. The US placed Iran on its list of 'states of sponsors of terrorism' in January 1984, imposed additional sanctions on it, and increased its support for Iraq during the Iran–Iraq War. Additionally, President Reagan reportedly authorised the CIA, in late 1984, to train counterterrorism units. In pursuit of that goal, as reported by Bob Woodward, the CIA reached out to the Lebanese intelligence service for operational support, to Branch 40 of the Israeli military intelligence for information about the attacks on the Marines, and to Saudi Arabia for untraceable financial support. Eventually, a car bomb was detonated outside the Beirut residence of Mohammad Hossein Fadlallah, a top Hezbollah leader, killing eighty people. Remarkably, Fadlallah survived the explosion.[78] The US denied any involvement in the operation. However, reports circulated in the US that 'Fadlallah had blessed the man who drove the truck carrying the explosives in the suicide bombing [attacks on the Marines].'[79]

Following the failed assassination attempt, Fadlallah became less visible, while Hezbollah intensified its activities against the West. In June 1985, Hezbollah associates hijacked a TWA flight taking off from Athens, forcing it to land in Beirut. When the hijackers' demand for the release of seven hundred Lebanese Shia prisoners in Israel was rejected, they brutally killed Robert Stethem, a US Navy officer. Three days later the hijackers released some passengers while hiding others as hostages in Lebanon.

An initial CIA assessment was that the hijacking was 'an independent operation' by disgruntled Shias 'that was later taken over by Amal and Hizballah'.[80] Two months later, the CIA concluded that the hijacking 'was planned by the Hizballah'.[81] Another CIA report surmised that Iran 'does not appear to have been involved in planning or carrying out the hijacking', and that Tehran had opposed the hijackings.[82] In a fourth report, it was stated that Iran had expressed concerns about its Lebanese allies occasionally acting independently of Tehran.[83]

When the hijacking took place, Rafsanjani was in Damascus exploring the possibility of obtaining weapons for Iran's war efforts against Iraq. After meeting with President Hafez Assad, he also met with a delegation of Hezbollah and Amal's leaders. He claimed that he advised them that 'terrorism is against Islam', and that 'skyjacking and hostage taking will undermine Lebanon', urging them 'to find a peaceful solution to the resolution of the crisis'.[84] A CIA report, however, contradicts Rafsanjani's narrative, stating that 'we suspect Rafsanjani used the occasion to encourage the radical Shias to prolong the crisis and to refuse to compromise on their demands'.[85] Despite conflicting reports, Iran ultimately played a crucial role in the release of the Western hostages, possibly setting the stage for the secret US–Iran negotiations that evolved into the Iran–Contra fiasco.

Khamenei and Hezbollah: Power and Deterrence

Much like Khomeini, Khamenei has been committed to pan-Shia principles and the empowerment of Hezbollah. However, Khamenei, unlike Khomeini, has taken a more hands-on approach to formulating policy towards Lebanon, where some Twelver Shias follow him as their 'source of emulation', and are thus bound to adhere to his rulings on Islamic law and other issues. Perhaps most importantly, Khamenei has placed considerably greater emphasis on security and strategic considerations in formulating Iran's Levant policy than Khomeini did.

Khamenei's objectives in Lebanon continue to revolve around expanding Iranian power, reinforcing its deterrence capabilities, and strengthening Hezbollah politically, economically, and militarily. To achieve these tripartite objectives, he undertook four key initiatives.

Khamenei's first move as the Supreme Leader was to put pressure on both Amal and Hezbollah to cease their ongoing conflict and form a united front. The issue of how to address Palestinians living in Lebanon was a major point of contention between these two Shia groups. They had been embroiled in the 'War of Camps' since the mid-1980s.[86] Backed by Lebanon's government forces, Amal attacked Palestinian refugee camps, resulting in many casualties, while Hezbollah fought alongside the Palestinians against Amal. At the request of the Palestinian ambassador to Iran, President Rafsanjani intervened and temporarily defused the fighting.[87] However, the conflict between the two rivals rekindled after Hezbollah's 1988 abduction of Lt. Colonel William Higgins, chief of the United Nations Interim Force in Lebanon (UNIFIL) that monitored southern Lebanon's borders with Israel. Amal condemned the kidnapping and cooperated with UNIFIL to rescue Higgins. This resulted in the bloody clashes with Hezbollah in what is known as the War of Brothers.[88] Ultimately, Hezbollah's leader Subhi al-Tufayli and Amal's leader Nabih Berri met with Khamenei in Tehran in July 1989, and issued a joint communiqué reaffirming their commitment to ending the conflict.[89] However, the cold-blooded killing of Higgins, which occurred sometime between July 1989 and July 1990, briefly reignited the violence between the two rivals. The 'War of Brothers' finally ceased in November 1990, when the two groups, under the auspices of Iran and Syria, formally agreed to end their bloodshed. Thereafter, Hezbollah became significantly more engaged in southern Lebanon, where Israeli troops were stationed, while Amal focused on parliamentary politics. By and large this division of responsibilities has persisted until today.

Khamenei's second priority was to centralise Hezbollah's decision-making process and increase Tehran's control over the organisation. The Directorate of Intelligence in the US depicted a nuanced picture of the internal dynamics of Hezbollah in 1987, which ironically explains the rationale behind Khamenei's decision. He stated that:

> Iran has significant influence with the radical Shia Hizballah organisation ... but Tehran does not control Hizballah's activities. Despite Iran's considerable support –which includes money, arms and training – and shared ideological objectives, Tehran does not dictate Hizballah's decisions.[90]

To optimise the organisation's processes, the office of Secretary General of Hezbollah was established in 1989, with Subhi al-Tufayli as its inaugural leader. However, he was removed from his position in April 1991, partly due to his opposition to Hezbollah's decision to participate in Lebanon's electoral politics, and he subsequently became an outspoken critic of Hezbollah and Iran. He was succeeded by Seyyed Abbas Mousavi, whose tenure was abruptly cut short when Israel killed him, along with his young son and four other companions, in a missile strike in February 1992. Israel justified the targeted killing as retaliation for Hezbollah's terrorist actions against Israel.

Ayatollah Khamenei appeared to have played a key role in the selection of Hassan Nasrallah as Hezbollah's third and current Secretary General. Immediately after Mousavi's assassination, Hossein Sheikholeslam recalled that Khamenei appointed a small delegation to visit Lebanon and ensure an expedient and peaceful transition of power to a new leader. On the way to Beirut, the delegation, headed by Ayatollah Ahmad Jannati, who currently chairs the Assembly of Experts for Leadership that chooses the next Supreme Leader, reached a consensus that Nasrallah would be the top choice to lead Hezbollah. Although Sheikholeslam indicated that Khamenei had not influenced the delegation's decision, it is inconceivable that any decision was made without Khamenei's prior approval. Once in Lebanon, the delegation conveyed its preference for the new Hezbollah leader to the Central Committee.[91] Sheikholeslam, who attended the Central Committee meeting, recalled that he had learned from Khomeini that 'when an official is martyred, his replacement must be chosen before he is buried'. Nasrallah was chosen as Hezbollah's new leader before Mousavi was buried.[92] Nasrallah promptly met with Khamenei in Tehran and pledged his allegiance to him. With this new leadership, Iran's influence over a more centralised and unified Hezbollah progressively increased.

Squandered Opportunity: Taif Accords

Khamenei's third priority was to consolidate and expand Iran's power in Lebanon, which became possible following the end of the Lebanese civil war in 1989. The destructive civil war concluded after extensive negotiations sponsored by the US and Saudi Arabia among Lebanese forces.

Saudi Arabia invited members of the Lebanese parliament and several countries to meet in Taif in November 1989. The meeting resulted in the Taif Agreement, which was later approved by the Lebanese parliament as the Taif Accords.[93] The accords demanded the disarmament of all militias, called on Israel to withdraw its troops from Lebanon, and emphasised that 'Syria should not be allowed to constitute a source of threat to Lebanon's security' – a not-so-subtle message to Syria to withdraw its troops. However, both Syria and Israel ignored the call and kept their troops in Lebanon.

Washington and Riyadh excluded Iran from participating in the Taif negotiations. However, there was a modest chance that Iran, if invited, would have moderated its policies towards Lebanon. This opportunity was squandered because the US failed to appreciate the major developments unfolding in post-Khomeini Iran and therefore continued its policy of marginalising the Islamic Republic in postwar Lebanon. The Taif meeting took place five months after Khomeini's death, during a period when Iranian foreign policy had entered its moderate phase. Khamenei had not yet consolidated power, and the pragmatic Rafsanjani was formidable enough to moderate Iran's policy towards Lebanon as a stepping stone for a rapprochement with the US and Saudi Arabia. At this point, Iran's main concern was attracting Western investment to recover from the Iran–Iraq War; it literally could not afford to export revolution.

Despite being excluded from the Taif meeting, Iran neither condemned nor praised the Taif Accords, as it was reluctant to antagonise Syria, which had strongly supported them. However, Iran vehemently opposed disarming Hezbollah, maintaining that Hezbollah was a 'legitimate resistance' force and a defender of Lebanon's sovereignty against Israel's 'illegal occupation of Lebanon'. When Amal voluntarily disarmed, Hezbollah emerged as the most powerful militia in Lebanon, which Tehran welcomed.

One of the most significant changes in Iran's Lebanon policy was its encouragement and support for Hezbollah's participation in the country's parliamentary elections. Consequently, Hezbollah participated for the first time in its history in the parliamentary elections in 1992, winning twelve seats in the parliament along with its allies.[94] This opened a new chapter in Hezbollah's evolution, characterised by its dual allegiances. On one hand, the organisation abandoned its unrealistic objective of establishing an Islamic republic in Lebanon and, instead, began to operate within the confines of Lebanon's constitutional framework. On the other hand, Hezbollah maintained its autonomy from the Lebanese state not only by refusing to disarm but also by receiving an accelerated supply of weapons from Iran. As a result, Hezbollah established a small quasi-state in Lebanon. The Islamic Republic strongly supported this dual structure. Randa Slim captured Iran's change of course when she told me, 'Iran gave a carte blanche to Nasrallah to handle Lebanon's internal politics as he sees fit, but retained veto power over Hezbollah's strategy toward Israel and the US' – an arrangement that appears to have remained in place to this day.[95]

Despite changes in its decision-making mechanisms and its entry into Lebanon's complex electoral politics, Hezbollah did not moderate its strongly anti-American and anti-Israeli stance. In retaliation for Israel's assassination of Hezbollah's Secretary General, Mousavi, the group's new leadership targeted innocent Jewish civilians as far away as Argentina. First, a bomb detonated under the Israeli embassy building in Buenos Aires, killing twenty-nine people in 1992. Two years later, a suicide bomber drove his explosive-packed van into the Jewish cultural centre in Buenos Aires, killing eighty-five people – the deadliest attack then on a Jewish centre since the Second World War. Israel pinned the blame on Hezbollah and Iran. Almost three decades later, an internal investigation by Mossad, Israel's spy agency, concluded that while Iran had 'approved and funded the attacks and supplied training and equipment, the findings counter longstanding assertions by Israel, Argentina, and the United States that Tehran had an operational role on the ground'.[96]

The violence in Argentina further intensified the clashes between Israel and Hezbollah in Lebanon, culminating in Israel's launch of Operation Grapes of Wrath in 1996. This sixteen-day operation was designed to disable Hezbollah's capacity to launch missile strikes on northern Israel. Following substantial bloodshed and the displacement of thousands of Lebanese people, Israel and Hezbollah eventually agreed to a truce.

Ayatollah Khamenei's fourth major initiative regarding Hezbollah was to further strengthen its military capabilities, a process that accelerated following Israel's unilateral withdrawal from Lebanon in 2002.

Soleimani and the 2006 Hezbollah–Israel War

Following the truce between Hezbollah and Amal in the early 1990s, Hezbollah became more deeply entwined in southern Lebanon, leading to increased clashes with the Israeli troops. What would ultimately prove to be an unexpected strategic boon for Hezbollah was Prime Minister Ehud Barak's unilateral decision to withdraw Israeli forces from southern Lebanon on 15 May 2000.

With its claim of victory over Israel, Hezbollah's popularity in Lebanon and the Arab world surged significantly. In the words of Jeffrey Goldberg, Hezbollah became 'the first military force, guerrilla or otherwise, to drive Israel out of Arab territory'.[97] Hezbollah quickly marshalled its resources to fill the power vacuum created from Israel's withdrawal, gradually imposing its dominance over southern Lebanon.[98]

As Hezbollah was adjusting to its new status and popularity, the US invasion of Iraq in March 2003 fundamentally changed the region's dynamics. The invasion emboldened pro-Western forces to undertake the formidable task of disarming Hezbollah and forcing Syria to withdraw its forces from Lebanon. Amid this evolving situation, UN Resolution 1559, co-sponsored by the US and France in 2004, was passed. It explicitly called for the withdrawal of Syrian troops from Lebanon and the 'disbanding and disarmament of all Lebanese and non-Lebanese militias'.[99] Hezbollah, with backing from Syria and Iran, refused to disarm. While navigating Lebanon's complex terrain to find a way to implement the UN resolution, former Lebanese prime minister Rafic Hariri, a close ally of Saudi Arabia and the US, was killed in a devastating truck bomb that targeted his motorcade, leaving a 30-foot wide crater in one of Beirut's most iconic promenades. The Western powers, along with many Lebanese, accused Syria and Hezbollah of masterminding and executing this atrocious act of terrorism. Massive demonstrations broke out in Lebanon condemning Hariri's assassination and demanding Syrian withdrawal, leading to the Cedar Revolution and the resignation of the pro-Syrian prime minister Omar Karami. In response, Hezbollah organised large counter-demonstrations in support of Syria. Once again, Lebanon found itself on the verge of implosion.

Ultimately, the growing public outcry in Lebanon, along with pressure applied to Syria by moderate Arab states and Western powers, compelled President Bashar Assad to order the withdraw of Syrian troops from Lebanon in April 2005. The presence of American troops in neighbouring Iraq, coupled with Assad's anxiety about the possibility of becoming the next target of American military action, likely played a crucial role in his decision. Following the withdrawal of Syrian troops, Damascus heavily relied on Tehran, Hezbollah, and Amal to sustain its influence in Lebanon. As a result, a triple alliance was formed among Iran, Syria, and Hezbollah, with Amal as a supporting partner.

With the Syrian troops out of Lebanon, Hezbollah's military engagements with Israel in southern Lebanon gained even greater significance. There were occasional skirmishes between the two antagonists, with Hezbollah occasionally launching rockets into Israel.[100] Both Israel and Hezbollah adhered to the 'rules of the game' to maintain a 'no war, no peace' status quo. This allowed Iran to lay the groundwork for a strategic presence in southern Lebanon, facilitating potential indirect military and retaliatory actions against Israel. In a way, Iran, through its unwavering support for Hezbollah, was positioning itself as Israel's newest and unwelcome neighbour.

While these major developments were unfolding in Lebanon and the region, General Soleimani was quietly leaving his indelible impact on Hezbollah's military capabilities. One of his first moves in 1999, when he became the commander of the Quds Force, was to bring together the top fifty Hezbollah commanders for a meeting with Ayatollah Khamenei in Tehran, where they formulated strategies for future operations. Soleimani believed that Hezbollah should remain consistently prepared for a potential war with the vastly superior Israeli military. His goal was to transform Hezbollah from a conventional militia into a proficient hybrid force characterised by exceptional agility, capable of not only enduring but effectively countering a military offensive from Israel. For him, avoiding defeat by Israel was a form of victory for Hezbollah. Soleimani assisted Hezbollah in constructing a covert defensive/offensive network that has proven to be resilient. This network was founded on the principle of granting substantial autonomy to individual units, all operating under a centralised leadership. Israeli sources claim that Hezbollah's defensive network was based on 'Iranian military doctrine'.[101]

Soleimani reportedly instructed Hezbollah to develop its first ever three-year plan for a possible war with Israel. Furthermore, he directed Imad Mughniyeh to lead the Seyyed al Shohada project, with the aim of enhancing Hezbollah's missile capability and training new cadres.[102] Over time, rockets and missiles became the cornerstone of Hezbollah's defence strategy and their 'weapons of choice', aimed at establishing parity with the far more powerful Israel. Iranian officials are not shy about admitting that they have shared their military technology and weapons with Hezbollah.

Israel's Hybrid Enemy

On 12 July 2006, Hezbollah fighters conducted an ambush inside Israel, killing three soldiers and abducting two more. The reckless operation was reportedly masterminded by Imad Mughniyeh, possibly to initiate negotiations with Israel for prisoner exchange.[103] Much to Hezbollah's astonishment, its actions prompted Israel to unleash a war that lasted thirty-three days. It appears that Hezbollah, much like Hamas after its October 2023 incursion into Israel, did not anticipate the massive and destructive retaliation by Israel.

Once the war began, the Islamic Republic's threat perception was again elevated. Tehran feared that the destruction or humiliation of the Hezbollah could profoundly undermine its regional position. Soleimani believed that the ultimate goal of the war was to eradicate Hezbollah and alter the demographic landscape of southern Lebanon.[104] Consequently, the Quds Force became entangled in the conflict, though Tehran has not disclosed the full extent of its involvement. Hassan Nasrallah revealed that Soleimani ensured Israel could not intercept and disrupt Iran's continuous logistical support to Hezbollah during the war. Soleimani also coordinated the transfer of weapons from Syria to Lebanon.[105] He was reportedly present in Hezbollah's war room in Lebanon for much of the duration of the war.

In the first phase of the war, Israel primarily relied on airstrikes and artillery to pound Hezbollah's command and control centres, Al-Manar (Hezbollah's television station), and Lebanon's infrastructure. While Hezbollah accused Israel of indiscriminate bombing of civilian locations, Tel Aviv countered by alleging that Hezbollah was using human shields, deliberately concealing its weapons, and conducting many of its operations from populated civilian areas, such as schools and mosques.

It appears that Israel was initially experimenting with a new strategy of warfare in Lebanon. General Dan Halutz, Chief of the IDF General Staff, firmly believed that the relentless use of air power targeting strategic centres, without relying on massive combat troops, could lead to the 'strategic cognitive collapse' of Hezbollah, ultimately resulting in Israeli victory.[106] The aim was to instil internal chaos in Hezbollah by relentless aerial bombardment, pushing it to the point of organisational disorientation and breakdown. Halutz was so optimistic at the end of the first day of the war that he informed Prime Minister Olmert that 'all the long-range rockets [of Hezbollah] have been destroyed. We've won the war.'[107] However, it quickly became clear that Hezbollah would not raise the white flag, and Israel had not won the war. According to Soleimani, Hezbollah had been preparing itself for a war with Israel for years and had designed a war plan that involved showcasing its arsenal and its new strategies at different phases of the war.[108]

Anticipating Israel's strategy to swiftly incapacitate its missiles and rockets during a potential war, Hezbollah constructed an extensive tunnel network to conceal and protect its arsenal and maintain operational capability.[109] Also, it had spread out its rocket launchers, arms caches, and other weapons in 'close to 200 villages in southern Lebanon', reinforced by positioning 'hundreds of improvised explosive devices (IEDs)'.[110] Moreover, Hezbollah used transportable missile/rocket launchers that were difficult for Israel to destroy. Thus, Hezbollah withstood Israel's initial bombardment while launching hundreds of rocket and missile attacks into Israel daily.

Within the first week of the war, Hezbollah managed to surprise Israel on two different occasions, thereby changing the psychological and, to a lesser extent, the military trajectory of the conflict. Merely two days into the war, Hezbollah's anti-ship missile targeted one of Israel's most sophisticated warships, INS *Hanit*, off the coast of Lebanon in the Mediterranean Sea.[111] Four Israeli soldiers were killed, and the frigate was dealt a crippling blow by an allegedly Iranian-built C-802 Noor guided missile.[112] Israel later acknowledged that they lacked the intelligence about Hezbollah's possession of the anti-ship missiles.[113] Soleimani recalled that the anti-ship missiles were transported piece by piece to Lebanon and assembled in secret locations. He recounted that, to debunk the rumour that Hassan Nasrallah had been killed and to gain maximum international attention, Hezbollah had planned to broadcast the moment the missiles would hit INS *Hanit* while Nasrallah was delivering his speech about the war. However, owing to technical complications, the missiles could not be launched during the speech. As a result, Hezbollah recorded a video that was subsequently released to the press, showcasing the actual strike on the warship along with Nasrallah's speech.[114] After this attack on an Israeli warship, Hezbollah also caught Israel off guard as it its rockets struck the train station in the port city of Haifa, Israel's third most populated city, killing eight Israeli civilians. In response, Israeli warplanes bombed targets in Lebanon, killing at least forty-five people.[115]

In the initial phase, when Israel had clearly established its military dominance, Soleimani went to Mashhad to brief Ayatollah Khamenei about the status of the unfolding war. He reported that the bombardment of Lebanon represented 'the pinnacle of Israel's technological intoxication' or prowess. He was in awe of the astonishing precision and the unfathomable destructiveness of Israel's bombing campaign.[116] Khamenei reportedly told him that Israel had been strategising a surprise attack to incapacitate Hezbollah before the abduction of the two Israeli soldiers – an assessment also shared by American investigative journalist Seymour Hersh.[117] Furthermore, Khamenei told Soleimani that the kidnapping of the two Israeli soldiers was a fortunate turn of events, a 'divine blessing', since it forced Israel to play its hand prematurely. His instruction to Soleimani and Hezbollah was to fight until victory.

By the end of the first week, it had become abundantly clear that Israel could not prevail in the war solely by relying on its superior airpower, as it had expected. Five days into the conflict, Israel began deploying large numbers of combat troops in Lebanon. During this phase, the conventional wisdom also suggested that Israel would easily emerge victorious. This confidence was crystallised in Secretary of State Condoleezza Rice's assertion, just ten days after the start of the war, that: 'What we're seeing here is, in a sense, the growing – the birth pangs of a new Middle East.'[118] She was prescient about the emergence of a new Middle East, but it would not be a Middle East to her liking.

In the second phase, Israel combined unremitting airstrikes with the substantial deployment of troops. According to Avi Kober, Israel's air force carried out 11,897 combat sorties, averaging slightly over 360 sorties per day, which was more than 'the number of sorties during the 1973 October War (11,223), and during the 1982 First Lebanon War (6,052)'.[119] Still, Hezbollah kept fighting. It had about '10,000 fighters', but it 'relied almost exclusively on the 3,000 fighters in the Nasr Brigade'.[120] It is estimated that Hezbollah's arsenal consisted of 15,000 missiles and rockets.[121] Hezbollah allegedly launched between 3,970 and 4,220 rockets and missiles to Israel, averaging 127 rocket attacks per day.[122]

If Hezbollah was stunned by Israel's thundering reaction to the abduction of its soldiers, Israel was astounded by Hezbollah's resilience when faced with devastating losses. In confronting Israeli troops, Hezbollah combined modern weapons with asymmetric war strategies and classical guerrilla-style attacks. While Hezbollah was 'well-prepared for an Israeli incursion', David Johnson observed, the IDF had little understanding of Hezbollah as a new 'hybrid adversary'. Hezbollah had concluded that it would be 'best served by focusing fighter training on unconventional means, with an emphasis on fighters operating individually and in small groups'.[123] These small and autonomous groups 'combined the weapons normally associated with states' with guerrilla warfare tactics and contacted each other, 'using sophisticated fibre-optic communications that resisted IDF jamming and interception measures'.[124]

After thirty-three days, with no obvious victor in sight, both Israel and Hezbollah could not sustain continued warfare. On 14 August 2006, they accepted UN Resolution 1701, calling for the cessation of all hostilities and Israel's withdrawal from Lebanon, and for implementation of an earlier resolution stipulating the disarmament of all militias.[125] Israel withdrew from Lebanon over the course of two months, however, Hezbollah refused to disarm.

The Day After

After the end of 33-day war, a delegation of Hezbollah leaders and Amal's Berri met with Ayatollah Khamenei in Tehran. Khamenei referred to war as a historic triumph for the Islamic community and a source of pride for all Muslims. He praised Nasrallah as an exceptional leader and expressed gratitude to Berri for the constructive role Amal had played during the war.[126] However, he neglected to address whether Iran's participation in that devastating war served its national interests or the extent to which Iran had committed its limited resources to both the war and the subsequent reconstruction efforts in southern Lebanon. The war may have been perceived by Hezbollah and its supporters as an ideological or even a military victory, but its costs were undeniably staggering. Years after the end of the war, Nasrallah confessed that had he known the price Lebanon and Hezbollah would have to pay for the war, he might have never started it.

The economic and human toll, especially on Hezbollah and Lebanon, was staggering. The war caused economic damage exceeding $2 billion to both Israel and Lebanon, with a significant portion borne by Lebanon.[127] Approximately 1,200 Lebanese, including 270 Hezbollah fighters, were killed, while 115 Israeli soldiers and 43 civilians lost their lives. Roughly 974,000 Lebanese were displaced, and 125,000 housing units were destroyed or damaged. In Israel, about 300,000 people fled their homes, and 2,000 housing units were destroyed.[128]

The war's outcome proved unfavourable for Israel as well, with some of its objectives being overly ambitious and ultimately unattainable. Prime Minister Ehud Olmert (2006–9) described Israel's goals in the

war as to free the two captured IDF soldiers, force Hezbollah to withdraw its forces from along Lebanon borders and replace them with
Lebanon's national army, and, most importantly, to eliminate Hezbollah
as a militia and demolish its war-making and operational capabilities.[129] The bodies of the two abducted Israeli soldiers were only
returned to Israel two years after the end of the war. In contrast to the
1982 invasion, when Israel successfully expelled the PLO from
Lebanon, this time it was unable to drive Hezbollah out of south
Lebanon. Hezbollah, unlike the PLO, is an indigenous organisation
deeply embedded in Lebanese society. Furthermore, while no regional
power provided military support to the PLO in its confrontation with
Israel in 1982, Hezbollah could count on Iran. If anything, the war
made Hezbollah more powerful in Lebanon and more popular in the
Arab world.

Backed by Syria and Iran, Hezbollah also effectively used the global
media to condemn Israel for its bombing of civilian population centres,
tarnishing its moral credibility in the world's eyes.[130]

Hezbollah did not lose the war, but it certainly did not win, as some
observers contend.[131] This marked the first time in the history of Arab–
Israeli conflict since 1948 when an Arab force did not suffer defeat in a war
against Israel. The Winograd Committee, established by Prime Minister
Olmert to investigate Israel's performance in the war, concluded that:

> Israel initiated a long war, which ended without its clear military
> victory. A semi-military organisation of a few thousand men resisted,
> for a few weeks, the strongest army in the Middle East, which enjoyed
> full air superiority and size and technology advantages.[132]

After the end of the war, Israel seemed to have acknowledged Hezbollah's
effectiveness as a hybrid combat force and its capability to launch missiles
capable of targeting Israeli urban centres and possibly its military installations. Likewise, Hezbollah recognised Israel's superior military power
and its willingness to deploy it to devastate Lebanon's critical
infrastructure.

One of the most significant consequences of the war was the establishment of a delicate and limited deterrence dynamic between Hezbollah

and Israel, and, by extension, between Israel and Iran, which has persisted to the present day. This development, in and of itself, was remarkable.

Post 2006 War: Iran and Lebanon's Evolving Relationship

Impressed by Hezbollah's performance, resilience, and willingness to accept casualties during the war with Israel, Iran escalated its efforts to buttress the organisation, supplying it with more lethal and precise missiles, drones, and other military equipment, in addition to increased financial assistance. The Islamic Republic's investment in Hezbollah yielded significant dividends when the organisation supported the beleaguered Assad regime, Iran's ally, during the Syrian civil war with fighters, advisors, and logistical support in the 2010s.

In the aftermath of the 2006 war, Iran attempted to broaden its ties with Lebanon beyond its special relations with the Hezbollah. However, these initiatives have encountered major obstacles, not just from Lebanese Maronite and Sunni factions, but also from Saudi Arabia, France, and the US – countries with vested economic and strategic interests in Lebanon. When Brigadier General Ahmad Vahidi, Iran's defence minister, offered to bolster Lebanon's army, his offer was courteously declined.[133] Similarly, in 2012, a delegation of high-ranking Iranian officials visited Lebanon, extending an offer to support the country with a dozen developmental projects, including building a hydroelectric dam in Tannourine, a Maronite town.[134] The delegation returned to Tehran empty-handed.

Tehran has no one to blame but itself for Lebanon's lack of enthusiasm in elevating bilateral relations to a higher level. Essentially, the Islamic Republic's policy towards Lebanon has been primarily 'Hezbollah-centric', with minimal attention given to economic and developmental matters concerning the Lebanese state. Today, Lebanon continues to hold its position as one of Iran's least significant trading partners.[135] In 2022, the trade volume between the two countries was meagre. In 2022, Iran exported $103 million to Lebanon.[136] In the same year, Lebanon exported $4 million to Iran.[137]

Iran's 'Hezbollah-centric' policy has also resulted in political repercussions for the country in Lebanon. In October 2019, Iran found itself as one of the main targets of the massive protests that erupted in Lebanon. These demonstrations were driven by widespread grievances related to corruption and the government's inability to deliver essential services to the population. Large numbers of protestors also chanted slogans against Iran's interventions in Lebanon's internal affairs.[138] In response, Ayatollah Khamenei took a conciliatory approach, acknowledging that 'the people have justifiable demands, but they should know their demands can only be fulfilled within the legal structure and framework of their country'. At the same time, he accused the US of instigating the demonstrations against Iran.[139]

Massive demonstrations were reignited in April 2020, triggered by a mammoth explosion at Beirut's port which claimed the lives of two hundred people and inflicted economic damage estimated between $3.8 billion and $4.6 billion.[140] The mysterious explosion exacerbated the already dire economic conditions.[141] GDP plummeted from close to US$52 billion in 2019 to US$23.1 billion in 2021.[142] There were also severe shortages of fuel and electricity, along with frequent blackouts. To improve its image, Iran delivered a convoy of eighty tankers of free oil and diesel fuel to Hezbollah in 2021. However, this approach amounted to little more than a band-aid solution for an economy in desperate need of substantial foreign investment and major structural reforms.

As a result of deteriorating socioeconomic conditions, political gridlock, and the strain of 1.5 million Syrian and Palestinian refugees in a country with a population of 6 million, Lebanon has been teetering on the brink of becoming a 'failed state'.

Iran's Costly Intervention and Deterrence

Imam Musa Sadr, with limited assistance from the Shah's government, empowered the Shias, instilled a sense of pride, armed them, and established Amal in the mid-1970s to represent their collective interests. Building upon Sadr's pioneering groundwork, Ayatollah Khomeini continued to empower the Shias; he approved the creation of Hezbollah and expanded Iranian influence in Lebanon. This support for Hezbollah was not in response to any real threat from Lebanon or Israel. Rather, it was deeply rooted in Khomeini's commitment to pan-Shia principles and his anti-Israeli ideology. Consequently, he inevitably entangled Iran in the Israel–Palestine and Lebanon–Israel conflicts, transforming Iran and Israel from the uneasy allies they were during Mohammad Reza Shah's rule to the bitter enemies they became after the Islamic Republic was established. With remarkable speed, Hezbollah became a powerful militia in Lebanon during Khomeini's rule (1979–89). Other foreign players sought to create their own militia; Israel, for example, helped create the Army of South Lebanon. But no militia could compete with Hezbollah.

Under Khamenei's rule, the rationale for Iran's support for Hezbollah evolved, though its commitment to pan-Shiism remained unwavering. As Israel emerged as the primary ally of the United States in containing Iran, the most vocal opponent of its nuclear programme, and the leading advocate of harsh US sanctions on Iran, Hezbollah's strategic value as Tehran's key instrument of deterrence against Israel and the US substantially increased. At the same time, Hezbollah evolved to become the key player in Iran's Axis of Resistance and also emerged as an indispensable element in Lebanon's power structure. In the words of Rami Khouri, a few decades ago, Shias and Hezbollah resided in the 'basement of the power building in Lebanon, but now they have moved to its penthouse'.[143]

The Islamic Republic has also achieved a few other significant strategic objectives in Lebanon, although it long ago abandoned the naïve notion of establishing an Islamic republic there. Iran has expanded its power by creating a military and ideological sphere of influence in Lebanon.[144] Today, in collaboration with Hezbollah and Syria, Iran has compelled Lebanon to nullify the Israeli-proposed, US-supported peace treaty in the mid-1980s. Following two terrorist attacks targeting the headquarters of the US and French troops in Lebanon, both countries withdrew their troops.

However, the Islamic Republic has paid a heavy price for pursuit of its strategic goals. It has been harshly criticised by many Lebanese for encroaching upon their country's sovereignty by effectively turning Hezbollah into an armed quasi-state within the official Lebanese state. Its support for Hezbollah's activities heightened the determination of the

US to contain Iran and impose further sanctions, and generated tensions and conflicts with moderate Arab states.

Furthermore, Iran has incurred substantial economic costs for its involvement in Lebanon.[145] In 1985, the Iranian chargé d'affaires in Lebanon admitted that Iran had 'underwritten all the expenses of the families of martyrs in the south [Lebanon]. We will not disclose [the amount] until the victory of the revolution.'[146] Richard Norton, one of the most authoritative scholars of Lebanon, estimated that Iran provided approximately $100 million annually to Hezbollah in certain years in the 1980s,[147] while Mathew Levitt assessed Iran's financial support to be three times that amount.[148] By 2019, the US estimated that Iran was providing Hezbollah with 'upwards of $700 million' annually.[149] After the Hezbollah–Israel war in 2006, Iran reportedly provided financial support to 100,000 Lebanese people who had lost their homes for a year and reportedly spent millions to rebuild Lebanon.[150] Nasrallah openly acknowledged Hezbollah's financial reliance on Iran, stating in 2016 that 'Hezbollah's budget, its income, its expenses, everything it eats and drinks, its weapons and rockets, are from the Islamic Republic of Iran.'[151] Still, the Islamic Republic believes its investments in Hezbollah have yielded high dividends, as the organisation is a strategic asset that has diminished the regional threat against Iran. However, not allowing for a meaningful national debate on the wisdom and repercussions of Iran's policy towards Lebanon and Israel, the Islamic Republic has provoked the ire of many Iranians.

Iran's alliance with Syria and its heavy involvement in the Syrian civil war, as detailed in the next chapter, were primarily designed to protect Hezbollah in Lebanon.

Chapter 6
Iran's Enduring Alliance with Syria

During the initial phase of Syria's civil war in 2012, General Hossein Hamadani, commander of the IRGC forces in Syria, presented a roadmap to General Soleimani with the objective of preventing the imminent collapse of President Bashar al-Assad's regime, Iran's main Arab ally. Both generals believed that the armed opposition to Assad, supported by the Western powers and their regional allies, were gaining momentum. They saw the survival of the beleaguered president hinging upon a radical change in his war strategy and multifaceted support from Iran. Meeting the president at his palace in Damascus, Hamadani described Assad as despondent and hopeless, 'contemplating of leaving [Syria] for another country'.[1] Hamadani alleges that he persuaded a pessimistic Assad to persevere and adopt a 'hybrid war strategy' that incorporated both classical warfare tactics and asymmetric counterinsurgency methods – skills he had honed during the Iran–Iraq War. Amid the chorus of demands for 'Assad must go' from Arab countries and the West, and at a time when many observers were prematurely writing President Assad's obituary, why did a defiant Ayatollah Khamenei stand alone and unwavering in his support for Assad? This question becomes even more intriguing, given that Iran's engagement in the Syrian civil war was its most extensive and costly military expedition beyond its immediate borders in at least the last two centuries.

After the 1979 revolution, Iran, a non-Arab country with a Shia majority and a theocratic government, forged a political alliance with Syria, a secular Arab country with a Sunni majority that embraced nationalism and pan-Arabism. This seemingly strange alliance evolved into one the most enduring partnerships between two Islamic countries in the post-Second World War era. How did Iran expand its power in Syria while engaged in geostrategic rivalry with the US and Israel? What led Iran to form a tactical military alliance with Russia to ensure the survival of the Assad regime? And what price has Iran paid for its involvement in the Syrian civil war?

Mohammad Reza Shah and Syria

Iran became cautiously interested in Syria after its independence from France in 1946, swiftly establishing diplomatic relations.[2] Initially, bilateral relations were amicable, but they quickly became contentious. A major source of tension stemmed from their divergent foreign policy orientations. Mohammad Reza Shah criticised Syria for its close ties with the Soviets, embrace of pan-Arabism, and its short-lived union with Egypt between 1958 and 1961 when Gamal Abdel Nasser served as president. Moreover, Syria's refusal to recognise Israel and its pursuit of anti-Israel policies contrasted with Iran's friendly relations with the state. Tensions further heightened when the Ba'ath party staged a coup and took power in March 1963. The Shah regarded Ba'athism, a fusion of Arab nationalism and socialism, as repugnant, like pan-Arabism. Thereafter, bilateral relations became antagonistic, particularly after the Syrian prime minister Yusuf Zu'ayyin urged Iranian-Arabs to 'liberate' Khuzestan, which is home to Arab-Iranians.[3]

Bilateral relations gradually improved after the coup, orchestrated by Salah Jadid and Hafez Assad in 1966, in which Salah Jadid assumed power. The Shah welcomed the coup by this new generation of Syrian Ba'athists, partly because they strongly opposed the Iraqi Ba'ath party, an enemy of Iran. At the time, the primary goal of Iran's regional policy was to 'prevent Syria, Iraq, or Libya from joining forces in opposition to Iran'.[4] After Hafez Assad staged another coup in 1971, Iranian–Syrian relations improved, despite the Shah's expressed concern over Syria's decision to permit the Soviets to establish a naval base in Tartus. Assad astutely recognised that the Shah was emerging as a major player in the Middle East and consequently fostered friendly ties with him. In that spirit, he dispatched the prime minister, Abdul Halim Khaddam, to visit Tehran in 1973. As a gesture of goodwill, the Shah's government provided medical treatment in Tehran to twenty-one Syrians injured in the Yom Kippur War of 1973.[5]

A friendly chapter in bilateral relations opened when President Hafez Assad met with the Shah in Tehran in December 1975. Iran agreed to provide a $50 million grant and a $150 million loan to Syria for developmental projects.[6] The two leaders both had their own motives for this rapprochement. Assad, who harboured deep animosity towards Iraq, sought to pre-empt a potential alliance between Tehran and Baghdad against Damascus after the 1975 Algiers Accords had temporarily ended the simmering Iran–Iraq conflict. Moreover, he recognised that the Shah, with his close connections to the US and Israel, could potentially play a constructive role in Syria's future negotiations with Israel concerning the return of the Israeli-occupied Golan Heights to Syria. Maintaining cordial relations with Syria was a crucial step for the Shah to repair his tarnished image in the Arab world, where he was ostracised for his pro-Israel policies, and to consolidate his emerging leadership position in the Middle East.

Hafez Assad and Anti-Shah Islamists

Assad's proffered hand of friendship to the Shah was not entirely genuine. On the one hand, Iran and Syria maintained friendly diplomatic relations, but on the other, Assad was actively training anti-Shah dissidents in subversive activities in Syria. Imam Musa Sadr, who maintained close personal relations with Assad, and Mustafa Chamran transformed Syria and Lebanon into a haven for these aspiring Islamists. Ambassador Ardeshir Zahedi claimed that the Shah was aware of Syria providing logistical and financial support to Iranian dissidents, yet he argued Iran ignored it because Syria was 'never a big problem for Iran'.[7]

Many of the dissidents who received training in Syria later became influential figures in the Islamic Republic. Ali Jannati, a cleric who lived in Lebanon and Syria in the mid-1970s, received military training there and later became Iran's Minister of Culture and Islamic Guidance in 2013. He recalled how Imam Musa Sadr convinced Assad to grant residency permission to Iranian dissidents, allowing them to stay in Syria and travel freely to Lebanon for military training.[8] Seyyed Ahmad Avaei, who later commanded an IRGC unit, claimed that approximately 'twenty or so' Iranian activists underwent training at an exclusive military centre specifically designed for special operations. The centre was reportedly managed by Rafat Hafez, Hafez Assad's powerful younger brother.[9]

Marziyeh Hadidchi-Dabbagh (1939–2016), a founding member of the IRGC and the highest-ranking woman to ever command an IRGC unit, recounted that those Iranian dissidents had rented a two-bedroom house in Damascus behind the shrine of Hazrat Zeynab, the daughter of the first Shia imam, for 'around fifteen or sixteen activists'. This house eventually became the headquarters for pro-Khomeini activists in Syria.[10] When Ayatollah Khomeini moved to Paris before triumphantly returning to Iran, Hadidchi-Dabbagh was among the few who stayed in the ayatollah's private residence.

Seyyed Rahim Safavi was the Islamic Republic's highest-ranking official to have undergone military training in Syria and Lebanon. Imprisoned for his anti-Shah activities in Iran, he claimed to have escaped in the mid-1970s and found refuge in Syria, where he joined a small network of Islamist dissidents associated with Ayatollah Khomeini. His frequent travels between Syria and Lebanon provided him with essential training in guerrilla operations, demolition techniques, and effective use of explosives to destroy infrastructure, such as bridges and railways.[11] He returned to Esfahan, his birthplace, during the final days of the Pahlavi dynasty. He mobilised the revolutionaries, teaching them 'whatever I had learned about explosion and destruction in Syria and Lebanon'.[12] After the revolution, he joined the IRGC and subsequently fought in the Iran–Iraq War. He quickly climbed through the ranks and became the top IRGC commander in 1997. After serving in this position for a decade, he stepped down to become part of 'Khamenei's kitchen cabinet', as one of the Supreme Leader's top military and security advisors.

Assad increased his modest support for the Iranian dissidents as he sensed the impending likelihood of the Shah's downfall in mid-1978. In September of that year, Khomeini addressed a letter to Assad, appealing to him and fellow Islamic leaders to support the 'people's struggle against the Shah'.[13] Subsequently, Syria is said to have helped Iranian dissidents via its embassies.[14]

While Syria did provide some level of support to the anti-Shah Islamist dissidents, the Islamic Republic has exaggerated its importance to rationalise multifaceted assistance to Syria, especially throughout the Syrian civil war.

Khomeini's Tenuous Political Alliance with Syria

The same Hafez Assad who had developed friendly relations with the Shah later stood out as one of the world's first leaders to recognise the Islamic Revolution and establish close ties with the revolutionary regime. Tehran responded in kind, prioritising the improvement of bilateral relations as a cornerstone of its strategic pivot towards the Levant.[15] Gradually, the two countries formed an uneasy political alliance. The foundation of this alliance was the interplay of mutual perceptions of threat and the imperative to counterbalance regional adversaries. Both countries were drawn to each other by what Stephen Walt calls the 'balance of threat'.[16] Both Syria and Iran shared the goal of neutralising and mitigating the perceived threat emanating from Israel, Iraq, and the US. They also had their distinct reasons for forming an alliance.

Hafez Assad astutely foresaw the potential for the Islamic Revolution to reshape the landscape of Middle East. After condemning the Egyptian–Israeli peace treaty of 1979, he found himself isolated and vulnerable, no longer able to depend on the support from Egypt – the most powerful Arab country. A seasoned leader, Assad recognised that Iran could serve as a counterforce or spoiler against the peace treaty. He was so passionate about improving relations with Tehran that he reportedly sent a Qur'an to Khomeini. His vice president, Abdul Halim Khaddam, lauded the Islamic Revolution as 'one of the most important developments in our modern history'.[17]

For the Islamic Republic, an alliance with Syria was the crucial first step in expanding its influence in Lebanon and spreading its pro-Palestinian, anti-US, and anti-Israeli narratives across the Arab world.

However, with Iraq's invasion of Iran, strategic imperatives, more than ideology, started to mould Iran's deepening relationship with Syria.

Syrian Support in Iran's Hour of Need

During the Iran–Iraq War, Tehran bolstered its relations with Syria as a partnership capable of mitigating its international isolation and thwarting Iraq's efforts to forge a unified Arab front against Iran. This political alliance enabled Iran to establish a limited military presence in the Levant and mobilise Shia communities in Lebanon. Moreover, Syria emerged as Iran's primary Arab ally against Iraq.[18] In 1982, Syria shut off the oil pipeline from Iraq to the Mediterranean Sea, resulting in substantial loss of oil revenue to Iraq. The Islamic Republic reciprocated this favour generously by selling oil to Syria at discounted rates. Syria's support of Iran infuriated Saddam Hussein, who confided in his advisors during the waning days of the Iran–Iraq War that: 'I hope this day will never come, wherein I have to shake al-Assad's dirty hand, with the blood of Iraqis on it.'[19]

Syria also extended a lifeline to Iran for procuring weapons, selling the country limited quantities of arms, and facilitating acquisitions through international black markets at a crucial period when the US had imposed stringent arms sanctions on Iran. Tehran established two weapons procurement networks with Syria's assistance. One of them operated openly and legally. In 1982, Abdul Halim Khaddam visited Tehran, sealing a security agreement that enabled Iran to purchase weapons from Syria.[20] Syria sold Infantry Fighting Vehicles, Malyutka anti-tank guided missiles, and tanks.[21] The second weapons procurement network operated covertly and was overseen by Mohsen Rafiqdoust, one of the founders of the IRGC. He claimed that Iran obtained weapons from international black markets, subsequently transporting them to a secure warehouse that Assad had authorised for use by Iran at the Damascus airport. The acquired weapons were then secretly airlifted to Iran.[22]

In retrospect, the most significant Syrian contribution to Iran's efforts to achieve parity with Iraq was in the field of missile technology. In the early phases of the Iran–Iraq War, Iraq stunned Iran by striking the city of Dezful in south-western Iran with its Russian-made FROG-7 artillery rockets, resulting in the death of 70 people and injuries to over 300 civilians. Iraq's deadly attacks exposed Iran's vulnerability. A frantic Rafiqdoust reached out to Syria to purchase Syrian missiles.[23] However, Assad refused to sell missiles, maintaining that the sale would require Russian approval, which he thought he could not to obtain since Moscow was Iraq's main weapons supplier. Perhaps the real reason was Assad's fear that selling missiles would shift the trajectory of the war in Iran's favour and consequently anger his Arab friends.

However, Assad agreed to provide Iranians with basic training in missile technology in Syria.[24] Tehran welcomed this gesture, promptly dispatching thirteen IRGC members to Syria in November 1984. Led by a 21-year-old Hassan Tehrani Moghaddam (1959–2011), the team completed their training within three months.[25] Upon returning home, Tehrani Moghaddam spearheaded the building of the IRGC's 'New Missile Force'. He also established a research and development centre for missiles and oversaw the initiatives in 'reverse engineering' to produce missiles and rockets. Gradually, he earned the sobriquet 'Father of Iran's missile technology',[26] as missiles became a pivotal element of Iran's defence doctrine. In November 2011, Tehrani Moghaddam was killed in a mysterious explosion in an IRGC base. Iran accused Israel and the Mojahedin-e Khalq of carrying out the assassination.

Following the end of the Iran–Iraq War in 1989, the political alliance between Iran and Syria not only defied predictions of collapse, it grew stronger. Both countries continued to oppose Iraq, working collaboratively to keep it tamed and contained. In Lebanon, they also pursued similar anti-Israel and anti-US policies through helping Hezbollah and Amal.

Although the tenuous Iranian–Syrian political alliance endured during Hafez Assad's rule, it was not devoid of tension. The two partners did not always share common perspectives. In contrast to Iran, Syria had formal diplomatic relations with the US, although it had significant policy disagreements with Washington. Much to Tehran's chagrin, Assad also sided with the UAE in its dispute with Iran over the sovereignty of three small islands in the Persian Gulf. While both Iran and Syria condemned Iraq's invasion of Kuwait, Syrian troops participated in the American-led international coalition aimed at expelling Iraq from Kuwait in 1991. Iran, in contrast, maintained a position of active neutrality and denounced the deployment of the US troops. After the end of the Persian Gulf War, the US-sponsored Madrid Conference was held, co-chaired by the Soviet Union and the US. While Syria participated in that conference, Iran condemned it as a betrayal of the Palestinian cause. And, most importantly, Assad prevented Iran from political intervention in Syria while maintaining a delicate balance between the interests of Iran and Saudi Arabia, as well as other rich Persian Gulf countries.

Ultimately, despite efforts by the US and its regional allies to decouple Syria from Iran, the convergence of the two countries' interests prevailed, ensuring the flourishing of their political alliance.[27]

The Arab Spring Comes to the Mediterranean Shores

After the passing of Hafez Assad in June 2000, his inexperienced son, Bashar, assumed the presidency. During Bashar's rule, the alliance between Syria and Iran became deeper.[28] Three developments contributed to strengthening this alliance. The first factor was the US occupation of Iraq, which elevated the threat perception in Tehran and Damascus. Both countries feared that if the American military intervention succeeded in Iraq, the US might be tempted to destabilise or even attack them.[29] Therefore, they collaborated in turning Iraq into an intractable quagmire for the US. The second factor was the withdrawal of 18,000–20,000 Syrian troops from Lebanon in 2005. Subsequently, Syria had no option but to rely on Iran, Hezbollah, and Amal to maintain some influence in Lebanon.

The third and most significant development that elevated the level of cooperation between the two countries was the Syrian civil war. Although this has often not been emphasised enough, Syria's religious demography played an important role in bringing Assad into Tehran's orbit. Assad belongs to the Alawite sect, a small minority within Shiism, which is itself the largest minority in Islam. The Alawites, estimated to make up between 17 and 20 per cent of the population, are encircled by a vast Sunni majority, constituting about 80 per cent of the population. Over centuries, the Alawites, living in seclusion within the Sunni-dominated regions, developed what Leon Goldsmith refers to as 'sectarian insecurity' – a deep-seated fear of persecution and prosecution by the Sunni majority.[30] Until the 1920s, the Alawites were recognised as Nusayris or followers of Muhammad Ibn Nusayr al Bakri al Numayri (d. 883), who claimed to be the messiah of Shias but promptly became an outcast.[31] Ibn Taymiyya (1263–1328), a fundamentalist Sunni jurist claimed as an ideological ancestor by today's Sunni Islamists, including ISIS, denounced the Nusayrids and Shias alike as 'more heretical than the Jews and Christians'.[32] During the era of French rule, the Nusayrids established a semi-autonomous government (1920–36) and adopted the name Alawites. After the coup orchestrated by Hafez Assad in 1971, which brought the Alawites to power in Damascus, Ayatollah Hassan Mahdi Shirazi (1935–1980) and Imam Musa Sadr recognised the Alawites as a legitimate Shia sect, giving them Islamic legitimacy. Sadr declared that: 'The Alawis and the Shias are partners in distress, since they were persecuted like the Shias. We will not allow anyone to condemn this generous creed.'[33]

During the Syrian civil war, the blatantly anti-Alawite rhetoric used by some radical elements within the armed opposition to Assad reignited 'sectarian insecurity' among the Alawites. This unified their ranks, increased their support for Assad, and strengthened their bond with Iran.

Decoding Khamenei's Support for Assad

As the US was in the process of withdrawing all its combat troops from Iraq in 2011, the first flowers of the Arab Spring started to blossom.

Despotism appeared to be on the decline; a promising new era seemed to be dawning in the region. It all began in Tunisia, a former French colony, but it did not end well, as most people had hoped.[34]

Massive demonstrations erupted after Mohammad Bouazizi, a poor street vendor, set himself on fire on 17 December 2010. After years of harassment by the police, he had reached his breaking point: he was not going to let his cart of produce be confiscated again. His death unleashed the simmering rage of a population living under a long-running dictatorship. After a month of constant street protests, President Zine El Abidine Ben Ali, who had been in office for twenty-four years, was compelled to step down in January 2011.

Tunisia was the spark that lit a fire of grassroots protests for democracy and human dignity across the Arab world. Organised by people from all walks of life, popular protests led to the downfall of three long-serving and well-entrenched Arab dictators: Egypt's Hosni Mubarak, in power for thirty years; Muammar Gaddafi, who governed Libya for thirty-two years; and Ali Abdullah Saleh, who wielded authority over Yemen for twenty-two years. Bahrain, too, was shaken by tremendous protests organised by the Shia majority against the ruling Sunni dynasty of Al Khalifa. Fearing that the popular movement in Bahrain might quickly metastasise into the Shia-dominated regions of the Saudi kingdom, Riyadh militarily intervened, quelling the uprising.

The Islamic Republic initially celebrated these popular movements as the latest manifestation of the 'Islamic awakening', with the potential to free the Arab world from the grips of Western imperialism and pro-Western autocracies.[35] While Tehran hailed the protests in Tunisia, Egypt, Bahrain, and Yemen, it denounced NATO's military intervention in Libya, which led to the brutal killing of Gaddafi. Tehran also vehemently criticised Saudi Arabia for deploying troops to Bahrain to assist its Sunni bredren.

Iran's initial enthusiasm and support for the Arab Spring quickly dissipated when it reached Syria in January 2011.

The outbreak of large, peaceful uprisings against the Assad regime placed Tehran in a precarious position. Moderate voices advocated supporting the legitimate demands of the Syrian protestors, contending that it would be hypocritical to back and praise the popular uprisings everywhere else in the Arab world.[36] However, these voices were marginalised by hardliners even before the onset of the Syrian civil war. Consequently, Iran's deep state, in consultation with the Supreme National Security Council, devised Iran's strategy, reflective of the militarisation of Iran's regional policies during these years. Soleimani executed this strategy, often sidelining the Foreign Ministry and giving precedence to military considerations over diplomacy.

Throughout the civil war, no matter what twists it took, Ayatollah Khamenei consistently supported Assad, even as many observers prematurely celebrated Assad's imminent downfall.[37] The US State Department labelled Assad as a 'dead man walking'. Mohammad Riad al-Shaqfa, the leader of the Syrian Muslim Brotherhood, predicted during the early days of the uprising in Syria that Assad would fall 'in the next few months',[38] while Burhan Ghalioun, Chairman of the Syrian National Council, one of Syria's main opposition groups, confidently asserted that there was not even 'a 1% chance that Assad will survive'.[39] And when President Obama declared that 'Assad must go' as early as August 2011, Khamenei remained defiant, insisting that 'Assad must stay.'

During the Syrian civil war, the Islamic Republic pursued three overarching objectives: to protect the Assad regime against its enemies and strengthen its alliance with Syria under Assad family rule; to preserve the land bridge between Syria and Lebanon so as to facilitate the transfer of arms to Hezbollah in Lebanon; and to expand its own power while promoting the spread of Shiism where possible. As the civil war dragged on, Iran sought to establish a military foothold in Syria and the Mediterranean Sea, aiming to open a second front against Israel to complement the first one it had previously established in southern Lebanon. Iran was also committed to safeguarding Syria's territorial integrity, especially after the US deployed a small contingent of troops to Syria and began supporting the Syrian Kurds. Tehran expressed apprehension over the potential creation of an autonomous Kurdish entity in Syria, fearing it might align with Iraq's Kurds and galvanise separatist sentiments among Kurds within Iran. Foreign Minister Zarif warned that altering borders 'will be the beginning – if you believe [in religious texts] – of Armageddon'.[40]

Khamenei viewed the Syrian conflict as part of a conspiracy concocted by the US and Israel, aimed first at toppling Assad, then dismantling Hezbollah in Lebanon, and ultimately destabilising Iran. He bluntly stated that, 'If we couldn't stop those troublemakers in Syria, we [would have] had to stop them in Tehran, Fars, Khorasan, and Esfahan.'[41] For him, Syria served as a vital land bridge for transferring arms to Hezbollah, Iran's most valuable strategic asset.[42] Hassan Nasrallah went one step further, underscoring Syria's pivotal role as 'Iran's conduit to Palestine and Gaza', facilitating the transfer of armaments to militant groups.[43] Hojatolislam Mehdi Ta'eb, commander of the Ammar Headquarters tasked with countering the perceived 'soft warfare' waged by the West against Iran,[44] preposterously claimed that:

Syria is [our] thirty fifth province.... If the enemy attacks us and seeks to capture Khuzestan [Iran's oil- rich province] or capture Syria, our priority is to keep Syria, for if we keep Syria, we can recapture Khuzestan, but if we lose Syria, we cannot even protect Tehran.[45]

Tehran also feared that if the Assad regime were to be toppled, the US might install an anti-Iran regime in Damascus. The harsh reality was that Iran had no allies or friends among Assad's enemies, leaving the Islamic Republic with no viable choice but to align its fate with Assad's. The Syrian Muslim Brotherhood, with its strong commitment to Sunni Islam, opposed Iran. Following the 1979 revolution, this organisation denounced Tehran for aiming to re-establish 'the Shi'ite Safavid empire' to 'take over the Sunni world and turn it into a Shia world'.[46] Even Hamas, which was receiving generous support from Tehran, sided with the opposition to Assad and relocated its headquarters from Damascus to Qatar. Other figures opposing Assad were equally critical of Iran. Ghalioun stated that post-Assad Syria would sever its 'strategic military alliance' with Iran.[47] Abu Omar, an ISIS commander in Syria, insisted that all jihadists were united in considering Iran an enemy.[48] Meanwhile, the highly influential cleric Yusuf al Qaradawi accused Iran of 'seeking to disempower the Sunnis'.[49]

In the absence of any meaningful public discussion in Iran regarding the Syrian crisis, the Islamic Republic effectively utilised the mass media to carefully frame its policies towards the civil war, with Soleimani play-ing a major role.[50] He directly appealed to the people, reminding them of Iran's moral obligation to support Syria, a country that had extended a helping hand to Iran during the war with Iraq.[51] To rationalise Iranian intervention in Syria as a national security imperative, Soleimani went so far as to suggest that ISIS was founded with the aim of undermining Iran, not Syria.[52] As the civil war became more sectarian, he stressed that the people of faith had a religious obligation to protect the shrines of the revered Shia leaders in Damascus from the onslaughts by jihadists. Moreover, he connected Iran's involvement in Syria to Saudi Arabia's scheme to expel Iran from the Levant. He alleged that during the civil war, Saudi Crown Prince Mohammad bin Salman told Assad in Moscow that Syria's main problem was not ISIS but the 'connection with Iran and if you don't have that connection, everything [that is, the chaos] will be finished in Syria'.[53]

The Syrian Civil War: Assad Must Stay

While Iran primarily assisted the Syrian government militarily, it also provided diplomatic support. The first major international conference on the Syrian crisis, co-sponsored by the UN and the Arab League, was convened in Geneva in June 2012. Iran, Syria's most important ally, was not invited. This was a clear signal that the US and its allies were deter-mined to sideline Iran from any involvement in resolving the escalating crisis – a manifestation of the US containment strategy towards Iran. The conference, known as Geneva I, issued a communiqué that called for the establishment of a 'transitional government body with full execu-tive power' and the holding of free elections in Syria.[54] Both Syria and Iran rejected the communiqué, interpreting it as an attempt to oust President Assad. Six months later, in late 2012, Tehran submitted its own four-point peace proposal to the UN Secretary-General. This peace plan called for an immediate ceasefire, the provision of humanitarian aid to Syrians in distress, revising the Syrian constitution, and holding presi-dential and parliamentary elections to establish a government of national unity.[55] However, the proposal was dead on arrival. The opposition to

Assad, along with the US and its Arab allies, dismissed it as a last-ditch effort to save Assad from his imminent fall from power.

Inspired by the Arab Spring, peaceful demonstrations against the Assad regime began in January 2011, following the arrest of a few children in Daraa for writing anti-Assad graffiti. These demonstrations spread like wildfire, demanding democratic reforms. In response, Assad made some cosmetic reforms while intensifying his crackdown on the opposition. The protest movement took a violent turn after one hundred soldiers were killed in the old city of Jisr al Shughur near the Turkish borders in July 2011. The government blamed 'armed gangs' for the atrocity, while the opposition accused the government of killing the soldiers, who had allegedly refused to open fire on the protestors.[56] Subsequently, the peaceful protest movement gradually became more violent and ultimately evolved into a cataclysmic and sectarian civil war, drawing in foreign fighters. As early as February 2012, UN Secretary-General Ban Ki-Moon accurately captured the essence of the brewing conflict as a 'proxy war', in which 'the regional and international players [are] arming one side or the other'.[57] When the Syrian Free Army was established by Colonel Riad al-Assad and a handful of disgruntled officers from the Syrian army in July 2011, and subsequently received international support, it became evident that the simmering conflict between Assad and his enemies was unlikely to be resolved peacefully.

Even before the failure of Geneva I and Iran's own peace proposal, Tehran had concluded that the fate of Assad and its own future role in the Levant would be decided on the unforgiving battleground of Syria, rather than through negotiations at international conferences. Indeed, shortly after the eruption of peaceful protests against Assad, a situation room was established in Tehran under the direct supervision of Ayatollah Khamenei to monitor the unfolding events in Syria and formulate policy.[58]

Initially, the Iranian government publicly encouraged Assad to make concessions to the opposition and organise rallies to demonstrate his popularity. President Mahmoud Ahmadinejad even urged Assad to negotiate with the opposition. In a conciliatory message, he declared that Iran would support free elections and would accept the will of the Syrian people, regardless of the election outcome.[59]

While urging Assad to be accommodating to his opponents, the Islamic Republic utilised its resources and experience in crowd control and suppression, honed during Iran's 2009 Green Movement, to assist Syria. Prior to the Syrian uprising escalating into a full-blown civil war, Soleimani purportedly engaged in meetings with certain opponents of Assad, including representatives from the Muslim Brotherhood. His assessment was that these opponents were unequivocally intent on the removal of Assad from power. Furthermore, he perceived the crisis in Syria as emblematic of a new United States' 'regime change' strategy, executed through local proxies while being managed by the US covertly.[60] Therefore, Soleimani directed his efforts from the beginning towards providing military and security assistance to Damascus.

Supporting Syria militarily posed little challenge for Iran, as the two countries had discreetly established an extensive security channel for coordinating their activities over the course of decades. As early as 2005, they signed 'a mutual self-defence pact', with the aim of jointly neutralising threats from the US and Israel.[61] Although it was dismissed as insignificant at the time, the pact was instrumental in facilitating Tehran's growing military and naval presence in Syria.[62] After the pact, two Iranian warships docked at the Latakia port in 2011, establishing a modest presence in the Mediterranean Sea. Shortly before the civil war began, Israel and the US accused Iran of transporting sophisticated missiles to Syria to enhance its aerial detection capabilities.[63]

From the beginning of the Syrian uprising, Tehran and Washington accused each other of supporting and arming different sides of the conflict. The US accused Iran of providing multifaceted support to Assad's despotic government. Iran insisted that the US and its Western and Middle Eastern allies were generously arming and financially supporting Syrian opposition groups, including what Tehran alleged to be terrorist groups.[64] But it is undeniable that the US and its allies were directly intervening in the civil war, just as Iran was. Allegedly, Saudi Arabia, Turkey, the UAE, and Qatar were involved in a $1 billion clandestine CIA operation, called Timber Sycamore, to fund, train, and arm Assad's opponents in Jordan and Turkey.[65] The Saudis allegedly offered to pardon '1,239 inmates' and pay 'a monthly stipend' to them in exchange for their joining up to fight in the Syrian battlefields.[66]

Meanwhile, the Free Syrian Army (FSA), formed by defectors from the Syrian army, was supported by the US, Saudi Arabia, and Qatar. Its first commander, Colonel Riad al-Assad, was not shy about revealing his playbook, as early as September 2011, just seven months after the start of the Syrian uprising. He publicly declared that his goal was 'to carve out a slice of territory in northern Syria, secure international protection in the form of a no-fly zone, procure weapons from friendly countries' and then topple Assad.[67]

It's All About Hybrid Warfare

The Islamic Republic was initially hesitant to reveal the full extent of its military involvement in Syria, in order to avoid giving the US an excuse for potential military retribution or additional economic sanctions, and to shield itself from potential backlash by segments of the population opposed to its interventionist policy. Tehran acknowledged its military presence in Syria only when incontrovertible evidence was presented. Initially Tehran maintained it was playing a purely advisory role. By the second year of the civil war, General Mohammad Ali Jafari, IRGC commander, confirmed the presence of IRGC advisors in Syria, although he did not specify their number.[68] By 2013, Iran had reportedly deployed 4,000 troops in Syria,[69] gradually increasing the number to between 6,500 and 9,200 by 2016. This force included the Green Berets (Special Forces) of the regular army (*Artesh*) with expertise in asymmetric warfare.[70] One reliable route Iran used to airlift arms and personnel to Syria was through Iraq's airspace, despite the presence of US forces in that country. Secretary of Defense General Jim Mattis believed that 'Soleimani's greatest achievement may be persuading his proxies in the Iraqi government to allow Iran to use its airspace to fly men and ammunition to Damascus.'[71]

Generals Soleimani and Hamadani believed that the Syrian armed forces were too ill-equipped and poorly trained to succeed against irregular insurgents trained and funded by foreign powers.[72] They argued that Syria should adopt a hybrid warfare strategy, integrating both classical and asymmetric counterinsurgency methods.[73] Illustrating the inadequacy of the Syrian forces in countering insurgents, Soleimani joked that 'We tell Assad to send the police to the streets and suddenly he dispatches the army.'[74] Hamadani, who commanded the IRGC forces in Syria, claimed to have played a crucial role in persuading Assad to approve this shift in strategy. His narrative, which contains exaggerations, should be read with healthy scepticism.

Hamadani was an accomplished expert in the field of asymmetric warfare. Born into a family of humble origin in Abadan in 1951, he later moved to Tehran and joined the Imperial Army, where he received special training in guerrilla warfare. Following the revolution, he became a member of the IRGC and was assigned to serve in Iran's Kurdistan province. He participated in suppressing the Kurds' separatist uprising and later fought in the Iran–Iraq War. Through his dedication to the revolution and combat skills, he steadily advanced through the ranks. Ultimately he was appointed as the deputy commander of the IRGC in 2005. Hamadani was in Syria when the Arab Spring reached that country.

As the protest movement gained momentum, Hamadani found the Syrian government on the brink of collapse. Responding to the dire situation, he developed a 'strategic road map' aimed at saving the Assad regime. It comprised over one hundred initiatives for reforming Syrian military and political institutions.[75] He submitted the road map to Soleimani, who conditionally approved it and instructed him to share the document with Hezbollah's Nasrallah. 'If he [Nasrallah] agreed with it', Soleimani told Hamadani, 'you could then start your mission.' According to Hamadani, Khamenei had 'ordered that the grand strategies of the Axis of Resistance must be supervised by Seyyed Hassan Nasrallah'.[76] Upon reviewing the roadmap, Nasrallah recommended that Hamadani condense the document and focus exclusively on military issues, stressing that the Syrian government's primary concern was survival.[77]

Hamadani recalled that when he proposed his roadmap to Assad, the pessimistic president believed the game was over and was contemplating leaving Syria.[78] Nevertheless, he encouraged Assad to establish armed neighbourhood committees across Syria. He reminded the president that when Ayatollah Khomeini returned from exile to Iran in 1979, he established thousands of armed neighbourhood committees that became instrumental in consolidating the Islamic Republic. He urged Assad to emulate that model by opening the barracks and arming his civilian supporters.

Hamadani allegedly submitted his roadmap to Assad at a critical juncture, when the Syrian army was demoralised by defections, suffering from debilitating manpower shortages, and facing increasingly confident opposition forces.[79] These forces were estimated to include over 100,000 armed fighters, with at least 6,000 jihadists from groups such as ISIS and the al-Nusra Front, the Syrian branch of al-Qaeda.[80] Moreover, the city of Raqqa had fallen to the Syrian opposition, with both the democratic forces and terrorist groups establishing a foothold there.

Hamadani alleged that a reluctant Assad eventually agreed to one of his proposals and approved the plan to establish the Popular Committees.[81] These committees were trained for urban fighting and provided essential services to the areas the government had recaptured, allowing the regular armed forces to focus on the battlefields.[82] In 2020, an IRGC commander claimed that Hamadani had helped mobilised approximately 100,000 people to serve on the Popular Committees up till 2015, although this number seems highly inflated.[83] While these Popular Committees were important in maintaining Assad's grip on power, they were insufficient to defeat the Syrian opposition. Consequently, Tehran deepened its involvement by mobilising armed Shia fighters from Hezbollah.

Shia Internationalism and the Civil War

By 2013, Assad's armed opponents had gained a decisive advantage over the Syrian government, asserting control over a sizeable swath of Syrian territory. The government found itself increasingly isolated on the global stage. The economy languished. The country's infrastructure lay in ruins, and the government could no longer provide essential services to its citizens. Millions of people were internally displaced while millions more had become refugees in neighbouring countries. It was at that critical juncture that Iran changed the trajectory of the civil war by appealing to Shia internationalism.

Hezbollah was discreetly and tangentially involved in the Syrian civil war from its onset, fearing that publicly acknowledging the depth of its involvement could provoke retaliation by Syrian opposition forces and their Lebanese supporters.[84] However, after a deadly car blast in the Hezbollah-controlled district of Beirut in July 2013, Nasrallah changed course. He warned that if 'before the attacks we had 100 fighters in Syria, after these attacks we will have 2,000'.[85] This marked the beginning of Hezbollah's open and extensive intervention in Syria, all in collaboration with the IRGC.

The turning point came during the battle over the control of al Qusayr, a strategic town on Lebanon's border, in May–June 2013.[86] The al-Nusra Front (also known as an al-Qaeda affiliate in the Levant) had seized control of the town, effectively severing supply lines from Damascus to Homs, Syria's third most populous city, and to Latakia, the stronghold of the Alawites. To maintain its control, al-Nusra had constructed complex underground tunnels in the town, consisting of 'command rooms stocked with food, water and drugs; booby traps and mines; even cameras that monitored their attackers'. Al-Nusra admitted to learning these tactics from Hezbollah's operations against Israel.[87] However, all this preparation proved futile, as Hezbollah, supported by the Syrian army and the IRGC forces, engaged in direct combat with al-Nusra, ultimately defeating it, killing many of them and forcing many others to flee the region. Soleimani had reportedly planned and personally participated in the operation that resulted in the death of a dozen Hezbollah fighters and at least eight Iranians.[88] Randa Slim, a keen observer of Lebanese politics, considers this victory a decisive moment in the Syrian civil war because it provided 'a significant psychological boost to the beleaguered Assad's regime'.[89] The al-Nusra defeat demoralised terrorist groups and even the democratic opposition to Assad.

Who Did it?

While the Syrian-Hezbollah-IRGC forces were celebrating their victory in al Qusayr, sarin gas was deployed in Ghouta, a suburb of Damascus, amid the deadly battle between government forces and their opponents in August 2013. It was estimated that the heinous attack claimed the lives of over a thousand people, including hundreds of children.[90] It was the deadliest chemical assault since Iraq's use of chemical weapons against Iraqi Kurds and Iranian soldiers in Halabja in 1988. The US and Syrian opposition unequivocally denounced the Assad government for committing this atrocity. There was mounting pressure on Obama to authorise retaliatory missile strikes against Assad, who had crossed the 'red line' previously established by the president himself. On the other hand, Syria, Iran, and Russia contended that the attack was a 'false flag operation' carried out by elements within the Syrian opposition to divert attention from the pro-Assad forces' victory in the battle for al Qusayr and to establish a justification for direct US military involvement in the civil war. A few observers also voiced similar scepticism about Assad's alleged use of prohibited chemical weapons.[91]

Adding complexity to the situation was the report the president received from James Clapper, Director of National Intelligence. Clapper believed that the gas used in the attack was 'of a different composition than the Syrian army possessed'.[92] He believed that while the intelligence on Syria's use of sarin gas was 'robust', it 'was not a 'slam dunk'.[93] Rumours also circulated that a certain Ziyad Tariq Ahmed, most likely a pseudonym, from the al-Nusra Front was 'implicated in making and using sarin'.[94] In its investigation into the use of chemical weapons, the UN refrained from explicitly attributing blame to any specific party, confirming only the usage of banned chemicals.[95]

However, former American ambassador to Syria, Robert Ford, told me that 'based on his thorough review of the intercepted conversations among Syrian military officers, it was indisputably the Syrian government, rather than its opponents, that callously used chemical weapons against its own innocent people'.[96]

President Obama ultimately opted against retributory missile strikes. Instead, he brokered an agreement with Russia, backed by UN Security Council Resolution 2118, unanimously adopted in September 2013, to grant international inspectors the authority to dismantle Syrian chemical weapons. Obama proudly recalled that the day he 'decided not to enforce his red line and bomb Syria' as 'his liberation day', a clear departure from what he derisively labelled 'the Washington playbook'. In making this decision, he disregarded the recommendations from Secretary of State John Kerry, military leaders, and Washington's punditry.[97]

While Damascus and Tehran applauded Obama's decision, the Syrian opposition felt betrayed. The president was sharply criticised for 'his exaggerated fear' that a retaliatory strike on Syria might provoke Tehran and potentially derail the ongoing secret nuclear negotiations between the US and Iran.[98] The anticipation of a harsh reaction by Tehran might have factored into Obama's decision. However, a more pivotal factor in his decision was his conviction that the US should refrain from becoming implicated in another war in the Middle East. He had learned from Iraq and Afghanistan that while wars are easy to start, they are much harder to end. Ambassador Ford, who is no friend of the Syrian regime, echoed the same sentiment, stressing to me that the US had 'no vital national interests in Syria to engage in yet another war'.[99] Nevertheless, to appease his critics, Obama increased covert US support for the Syrian opposition.

Shadows of Doubt in Tehran

While the Obama administration was embroiled in internal disagreements on how to respond to the use of chemical weapons in Ghouta, the Islamic Republic grappled with its own internal dispute regarding who in Syria should bear responsibility and what actions Tehran must take in response. The Iranian government displayed exceptional sensitivity addressing this issue, given that Assad was its only Arab ally and that Iran had previously been the victim of Iraq's brutal chemical attacks. Even Ayatollah Khamenei, who had always been unequivocal in his stance about Syria, proceeded with unusual caution. He stated that, 'They started a controversy in the world that the Syrian government used a chemical bomb. I don't venture to judge who used it, but America, which claims that its red line is a chemical weapon, gave Saddam 500 of these bombs.'[100] As the ultimate 'Decider', he refused to change Iranian policy towards Syria or implicate Assad for using banned chemicals.

In contrast to Khamenei, Rafsanjani initially placed the blame squarely on Assad, albeit without explicitly naming him, but later had to modify his position under unbearable pressure. At first, he lamented that 'on one hand, the people of Syria are bombed with chemicals by their own government and, on the other hand, they expect [to be] bombed by Americans'.[101] His candid statement triggered a deluge of scathing criticisms from hardliners, who accused him of betraying Assad and undermining Iran's Syrian policy. The intensity of this vitriolic reaction was such that a besieged Rafsanjani claimed his words had been misconstrued. When the audio of his speech was circulated, his assertion that his voice had been 'doctored' proved utterly unconvincing.[102] In a face-saving move, he finally praised Syria as a bastion against Israel. However, this gesture came too late, as he was further marginalised, depriving Iran of his moderate voice at a time when its regional policies were veering towards radicalism.

The use of chemical weapons failed to alter the course of the civil war. Moreover, despite Iran's escalating military intervention, the balance of power did not shift in favour of the Assad regime. Tehran's next crucial move was the recruitment, training, arming, and deployment of Shias from Lebanon, Iraq, Afghanistan, and Pakistan to the Syrian battlefields, beginning in 2013.

Iraqi Asa'ib Ahl al-Haq and Kata'ib Hezbollah joined forces with fighters from the Zeynabiyoun and Fatemiyoun groups to fight in Syria's battlefields. The Fatemiyoun, the largest group deployed by the IRGC, primarily consisted of Shia Afghans. They were largely recruited from the ranks of 3.5 million Afghan refugees and migrants living in Iran.[103] Some members of the Fatemiyoun had previously fought alongside their Iranian brethren during the Iran–Iraq War in the 1980s.[104] In contrast, the much smaller Zeynabiyoun primarily consisted of Shias from Pakistan. Some members of these two organisations received traditional education in Iranian seminaries, particularly at Al Mostafa University, which was sanctioned by the United States.[105]

Trained by the IRGC, Zeynabiyoun and Fatemiyoun functioned as foot soldiers for the forces led by Iran in Syria. Tehran officially justified their deployment as necessary for protecting the sacred shrines of Hazrat Zeynab and Ruqayya in Damascus – who are, respectively, the daughter and granddaughter of Ali, the first Shia imam – from Jihadi attacks. Tehran hailed these fighters as 'defenders of the *haram* [shrine]'.[106] The Islamic Republic maintained that these two groups had voluntarily deployed to Syria, motivated by their religious conviction to combat anti-Shia jihadists and protect the holy shrines. Tehran acknowledged providing financial support to these groups and the families of those who were killed in Syria. However, most Western sources have characterised these groups as mercenaries who received a monthly stipend of $500 and were granted Iranian citizenship in exchange for their service in Syria.[107] They accused Iran of exploiting these fighters as 'cannon fodder',[108] or even as 'child soldiers', although others found no concrete evidence to support claims of coercion by Iran.[109] A more realistic assessment suggests that the Fatemiyoun and Zeynabiyoun were motivated by a combination of economic incentives provided by the Islamic Republic and genuine religious convictions. Estimates regarding the size of the deployment of these two groups vary significantly. Shuja Jamal estimated that between 2013 and 2019, 'as many as fifty thousand Afghans have fought in Syria'.[110] Foreign Minister Javad Zarif stated in 2020 that there were at one time 5,000 of these fighters.[111] The US State Department estimated, as of November 2020, that there were between 10,000 to 12,000 fighters in Syria.[112] While their actual number remains uncertain, the State Department's estimate appears to be more plausible.

Regardless of their numbers, the Fatemiyoun and Zeynabiyoun played a crucial role not only in Iran's military operations and consolidation of power but also in the reconstruction of war-torn regions in Syria. The precise number of Shia fighters who have returned to their home countries, and of those who have opted to settle in Syria, remain unknown. During the period from 2012 and 2016, 55 fighters from Pakistan, 255 from Afghanistan, 342 from Iran, and 878 from Lebanon lost their lives in Syria.[113]

Tehran and Moscow Join Hands

With the civil war showing no sign of abating, the UN-brokered Geneva II conference to end the Syrian civil war was held in February 2014. Initially, UN Secretary-General Ban Ki-Moon invited Iran to the conference. However, the opposition to Assad, spearheaded by Saudi Arabia and its Arab allies, vehemently objected to Iran's participation, with the intent of marginalising it in resolving the Syrian crisis. At the time, the US, engaged in secret nuclear negotiations with Tehran, attempted to find a compromise by proposing that Iranian participation be contingent on its acceptance of the terms outlined in the Geneva I communiqué, which Tehran had previously rejected. As expected, Iran declined this US proposal. Ultimately, Ban Ki-Moon rescinded the invitation to Tehran, and the conference proceeded.

Both Tehran and Damascus rejected the terms of the new communiqué. Tehran contended that it neither recognised Assad's legitimacy nor distinguished between the legitimate opposition to Assad and terrorists, stressing that there were over 11,000 terrorists with European citizenship fighting against Assad in Syria.[114] Deputy Foreign Minister Abbas Araqchi stated that, 'Everyone knows that without Iran the chances of a real solution to Syria are not that great.'[115] He was prescient: Geneva II, like Geneva I, faltered in its objectives. In a show of defiance against the backdrop of Geneva II, Assad held rigged presidential elections in June 2014, securing a decisive victory. A year later, in 2015, Iran submitted a refined version of its earlier peace plan to the UN. However, this proposal was also rejected by the Syrian opposition.[116]

With the utter failure of all diplomatic initiatives to halt the suffering in Syria, attention once again shifted to the battlefield.

By 2015, Tehran had grown increasingly alarmed. Despite its escalating military intervention in Syria, the Syrian government had failed to defeat its enemies, who had momentum and controlled a vast area of Syrian territory. Adding to Tehran's anxieties was the deepening, albeit mostly indirect, involvement of the US in Syria and its support for the Kurdish Syrian Democratic Forces (SDF), which held sway over some parts of northern Syria.[117] Furthermore, Saudi Arabia and Qatar continued their generous financial support and arming of their respective proxies. Turkey had also entered the fray, expanding its operations in Syria, and continuing to provide arms to its proxies, with the primary objective of undermining the Syrian Kurdish forces.

Most ominously, ISIS, al-Nusra, and some moderate opposition groups were rapidly advancing, consolidating their control over substantial portions of Syria. Since 2012, the opposition to Assad had held eastern

Aleppo, effectively establishing it as their de facto capital – a city that had once been a vital economic centre for Syria and was designated a UNESCO World Heritage site. In the summer of 2014, Al-Baghdadi, the declared leader of ISIS, relocated from Iraq to Syria, where his forces had captured Raqqa, a historic city that had once served as the temporary capital of the Abbasid dynasty. He subsequently declared Raqqa the capital of his newly established caliphate.[118] After capturing Mosul, Iraq's second largest city, in June 2014, ISIS, with its estimated 20,000 to 22,000 fighters, ruled over seven million Iraqis and Syrians.[119] In May 2015, a more confident ISIS seized control of Palmyra, another major Syrian city.

By mid-2015, Syria had essentially descended into a 'war of all against all', involving a complex array of indigenous, regional, and international actors, each seeking to advance its interests through various means. In that perilous era, Tehran forged a tactical military alliance with Russia, which received the full support from the Syrian government.[120] This was a contentious and sensitive decision, given Iran's historical mistrust of Russia. Over the past three centuries, no country has annexed more Iranian territory through sheer force than Russia. Furthermore, Russia's relentless imperialistic interventions in Iran's domestic politics in the modern era remain fresh in the collective memory of most Iranians.[121]

Who was the architect of this tactical Iranian–Russian military alliance and what were the reasons behind its formation? The initial narrative, supported by the IRGC and some Western sources, identified General Soleimani as the mastermind behind it. In this account, Soleimani visited Moscow in October 2015 to persuade a hesitant Putin to engage in military cooperation with Iran in Syria. Soleimani 'put the map of Syria on the table. The Russians were very alarmed, and felt the matters were in steep decline and that there were real dangers to the [Syrian] regime.' He reassured Putin that they still have valuable assets, and together they could turn the tide in favour of Assad's regime.[122] Mohammad Jafar Assadi, former commander of the IRGC advisors in Syria, recalled that during their '140-minute meeting' Soleimani reminded Putin that 'Syria is the last front or fortress of the East, and if we lose it, Western powers will have no respect for you.'[123]

Former foreign minister Zarif presents an entirely different narrative, suggesting that Tehran was deceived by Moscow into escalating its military intervention in Syria. He argues that the collaborative military efforts between Russia and Iran in Syria were a stratagem devised by Putin to sabotage the 2015 nuclear deal between Iran and six global powers, thwart any potential rapprochement between Iran and the US, and draw Tehran into Moscow's sphere of influence. He maintains that Putin had already decided to enter the war in Syria with his air force before he met with Soleimani in Moscow in October 2015.[124] Having learned from Russia's disastrous decision to deploy ground troops in Afghanistan in the 1980s, Putin's blueprint was to avoid repeating that blunder in Syria and minimise Russian casualties. Zarif contends that the Russian plan involved tasking the Syrian army and IRGC-led forces with the role of ground troops, bearing the brunt of the casualties, while the Russian air force provided support.

Regardless of who masterminded the Russian–Iranian tactical alliance, both parties shared common objectives, though each was driven by their distinct motivations for joining forces. Both countries staunchly opposed the US agenda of regime change in Syria and Western military intervention in the region. Both believed that the UN Security Council resolution was misused by Western powers to oust Muammar Gaddafi. They were also united in their determination to crush ISIS. After all, there were more Russians from Chechnya within ISIS ranks than any other country except Saudi Arabia.[125] For Iran, too, ISIS posed a grave security threat and had come too close to Iranian borders for comfort.

Furthermore, both countries recognised the significance of Syria as a strategic launching point for expanding their power in the Middle East. Iran understood that, given its own limited air power – even more limited than Syria's – the inevitable outcome of the civil war would be Assad's downfall and the unravelling of Iran's broader Levant strategy unless Russia's formidable aerial capabilities could be leveraged. Russia was eager to make its debut in the Middle East as a military power following the disintegration of the Soviet Union in 1991.[126] It sought to revive its long-standing military ties with Syria, dating back to the Cold War era, regain access to the Tartus naval base in the Mediterranean Sea (established in 1971 following the Soviet–Syrian agreement), and utilise the Hmeimim air base in Latakia as a hub for its military operations in Syria, as well as a strategic point in the broader region of the Middle East and North Africa.[127] In terms of Russian forces 'no more than 4,500 personnel were on the ground as of September 2016 and 3,000 by March 2018'.[128] Moreover, the Wagner Group and other Russian private military contractors were also involved in the Syrian war.[129]

Russia and Iran rationalised their intervention as counterterrorism operations. They dismissed the differentiation between democratic and terrorist factions within the Syrian opposition, treating them as if they were one and the same. Putin bluntly stated that, 'No one but President Assad's armed forces and Kurdish militias are truly fighting the Islamic State [ISIS] and other terrorist organisations in Syria', implying that all Assad opponents could potentially become legitimate targets for the Russian air force.[130] The divided nature of the Syrian opposition, coupled with occasional collaboration between the moderate opposition and terrorist organisations, provided Russia with justification to pursue a scorched-earth strategy of bombing the strongholds of all Assad's enemies. Statements from American officials provided some latitude for Russia to indiscriminately bomb the Syrian opposition. For instance, Secretary of State Hillary Clinton explicitly mentioned that the 'governments of Saudi Arabia and Qatar are providing clandestine financial and logistic support to ISIL [ISIS] and other radical Sunni groups'.[131] Secretary of State John Kerry also admitted 'Jaysh al-Islam', an active terrorist group in Syria, was supported by Saudi Arabia.[132] For Moscow and Tehran, the terrorist groups played a much more critical role in the civil war than the democratic and moderate opposition.

With the support of Iranian-led ground forces and the backing of the Russian air force, the balance of power quickly shifted in favour of Assad's regime. Consequently, the Syrian government achieved significant victories, reclaiming a sizeable portion of territory controlled by the opposition forces.

The Russian air campaign began in September 2015 by targeting Homs, a strategic province in western Syria, causing significant physical damage and inflicting heavy casualties on Assad's opposition. In March 2016, government troops took Palmyra, a historic city in the eastern Homs Governorate seized by ISIS in May 2015.[133] The biggest victory for the Assad regime came with the bloody battle of Aleppo in December

2016. The eastern part of Aleppo – one of the world's oldest cities – had fallen to anti-government forces in 2012 and became their de facto capital. After that defeat, the Assad government, controlling the western part, imposed a deadly and unfathomably destructive siege of the city, in the course of which it was accused by the opposition of using banned chemical weapons. Eventually, government forces, backed by the Russian air force and Iran-backed militias on the ground, recaptured Aleppo in 2016, compelling the opposition forces to evacuate the city. Samantha Power, former US ambassador to the UN, described the battle of Aleppo joining 'the ranks of those events in world history that define modern evil, that stain our conscience decades later – Halabja, Rwanda, Srebrenica and now Aleppo'.[134]

The collaboration between Russia and Iran extended to the use of Iranian air bases and air space by Russia for operations against the Syrian opposition. In August 2016, Russian bombers carried out attacks on ISIS and al-Nusra positions from the Nojeh air base in Hamadan, in mid-west Iran. This was the first instance since the 1979 revolution that Iran had granted permission to a foreign country to utilise one of its military facilities for combat purposes.[135] Missiles were also launched against Syrian opposition from the Russian warship in the Caspian Sea in northern Iran, which involved traversing Iranian air space. Parliamentarian Heshmatollah Falahatpisheh raised objections to the use of Iranian military bases, arguing it was a violation of the 1979 Iranian constitution.[136]

As the Syrian government made military advances on the battlefields, diplomatic discussions among Russia, Iran, and Turkey in 2017 culminated in the Astana peace process, running parallel to the UN-led talks in Geneva. The parties signed a memorandum to create four 'de-escalation zones' in Syria, to facilitate, among other things, access for humanitarian assistance for distressed civilians.[137] They also agreed to collaborate against any 'separatist agendas', a clear reference to the Syrian Kurdish groups who were supported by the US. Both Iran and Turkey remained wary of any movement towards autonomy by the Syrian Kurds, fearing that such developments might encourage Kurds within their own borders to pursue similar aspirations.

From the perspective of Moscow and Tehran, their tactical military alliance was remarkably successful, as both achieved their primary strategic objectives in Syria and subsequently improved their bilateral relations.

Geostrategic Rivalry with the US and Israel

Despite the advances made by the Syrian government on the front lines of the civil war after the Russian–Iranian tactical military alliance, Iran faced three major challenges: the continued threat posed by ISIS, the expanding role of the US in Syria, and Israel's military strikes against Iranian-led forces in Syria.

The threat posed by ISIS to Iran's national security became more tangible when the group managed to breach the country's security parameters to carry out attacks on two targets in Tehran in June 2017: the Majles and the shrine of Ayatollah Khomeini, both iconic symbols of the Islamic Revolution. These twin attacks resulted in the loss of eighteen lives and left over fifty others injured, revealing a dangerous breach of Iran's security parameters. Iran accused Saudi Arabia and the US of using ISIS as 'their proxy' to destabilise the country. It further claimed that the gunmen, the majority of whom were of Kurdish-Iranian descent, had previously fought alongside ISIS fighters in Raqqa in Syria and Mosul in Iraq. Ayatollah Khamenei quickly pledged that Iran would soon 'slap its enemies' for their terrorist activities. In retaliation, the IRGC launched six Zolfaghar ballistic missiles from Iranian soil, targeting ISIS's stronghold in the oil-rich Deir ez-Zor – the first instance of Iran launching ballistic missiles against terrorists in the Syrian conflict.[138] Iran claimed, 'a large number of terrorists were killed and weapons destroyed', although the claim was not independently verified. Following the missile strikes, Iran intensified its activities against ISIS. In November 2017, Tehran celebrated the liberation of Abu Kamal, a key ISIS stronghold on the Syrian border with Iraq. Syrian troops and forces under Soleimani's command fiercely battled ISIS fighters and successfully expelled them from the area. Indeed, Soleimani considered this a strategic triumph, as Abu Kamal was a vital region in his construction of the land bridge he had been building to expand Iranian power, stretching from Iranian territory through Iraq to Syria and Lebanon.

Iran became the first country to declare victory over ISIS immediately following the Abu Kamal operation. Soleimani penned a missive to Khamenei, proudly claiming that he had replaced the 'black flag of ISIS with the Syrian flag' in Abu Kamal. As usual, he denounced ISIS as a gang created by an 'American-Zionist' conspiracy to divide the Muslims, providing no supporting evidence.[139] He attributed this 'historic victory' to the guidance of ayatollahs Khamenei and Sistani. In response, Khamenei showered Soleimani with praise, commending him for 'eradicating this cancerous and fatal tumour [ISIS]'.[140]

However, the fall of Abu Kamal neither ended ISIS as an organisation nor halted its insurgency against the Syrian government. As Joshua Landis observed, however, it did mark 'the ultimate end of the territorial ambitions of Islamic State'.[141]

Iran's second challenge was the expanding presence of the US in Syria. Despite providing arms and training to various factions of the Syrian opposition throughout the civil war, the US had initially refrained from direct military intervention in Syria. However, by the middle of the 2010s, as the Russian air force entered the Syrian war theatre, President Obama changed the US policy of 'leading from behind'. He authorised increased air strikes against terrorists, accelerated the training and arming of the Kurdish SDF and other rebel groups, and, most significantly, deployed 2,000 US military personnel to Syria without the consent of the Syrian government. Syria, Russia, and Iran denounced the US presence as illegal. Ambassador Robert Ford told me that 'under international law, Iranian assistance to Syria and the presence of its forces and Russian forces were legally permissible, although perhaps ill-advised, as they were officially invited by the sovereign country of Syria, whereas the American military presence in Syria was not'.[142]

With certain adjustments, President Trump carried forward Obama's Syrian policy. Like Obama, Trump held the view that the US had no vital national interests in Syria. Consequently, he scaled down the number of US personnel from 2,000 to 400, a decision that ran contrary to the recommendations of his most senior national security advisors. Trump's goals included preventing the Assad government from regaining sovereignty over all of Syria, dismantling the strongholds held by ISIS and other terrorist groups, and providing support to the Syrian Kurds as a proxy force to maintain control over parts of north Syria. Trump also took a controversial step by authorising US-backed forces to seize the Conoco and Omar oil and gas fields in Syria, previously under ISIS control in Deir ez-Zor province. This action significantly reduced the likelihood of the Syrian government reclaiming these fields as long as US forces remained in the region, thereby depriving it of much-needed oil and gas revenues.

Trump's policy towards Syria, like Obama's, was driven in part by the goal of diminishing Iranian influence in the country. The resignation of Secretary of Defense General Mattis was triggered when Trump decided to decrease the number of US personnel in Syria. Mattis argued that the partial US withdrawal 'would, essentially, surrender Western influence in Syria to Russia and Iran'.[143] Secretary of State Rex Tillerson unequivocally stated that the US objective was 'to diminish Iran's influence' in Syria, which he described as 'a client state of Iran'.[144] To achieve this goal, alongside countering ISIS and weakening the Assad government, the US established two strongholds: one at the al-Tanf base in south-east Syria near the Iraqi and Jordanian border, and another in a northern Syrian enclave. To pressure Iran to leave Syria, the US reached out to Russia. In mid-2018, John Bolton, US National Security Advisor, claimed that 'the US, Israel, and Russia agreed that Iranian-backed troops must be removed from Syria'.[145] However, this outcome has not yet materialised.

The Islamic Republic's third significant challenge has been Israel's strong opposition to its military presence in Syria. As the civil war neared its conclusion, the Iranian-led forces opened a new war front against Israel in Syria. An Israeli expert captured the essence of Israel's policy towards Iran when he argued that Iran has built a 'double crescent, one is the regular Shia crescent' and the other 'around Israel, from Lebanon to Syria to Jordan to Gaza and to Yemen. Israel is seeking to destroy this in Syria, a point of convergence for the two crescents'.[146] As early as mid-2014, Israel had warned that Iran was creating a new Hezbollah in Syria, operating in close proximity to Israel's northern border[147] and engaging in low-intensity warfare against Israel.[148] To prevent a potential military confrontation, Moscow, which had fostered good relations both with Israel and Iran, reportedly brokered an informal agreement between the two countries. This agreement mandated that the Iran-led forces maintain a distance of 'at least 83 kilometres from the Israeli border and to station Russian military police near the Golan Heights' in Syria.[149]

Despite its strong opposition to Iran's military presence in Syria, Israel managed to avoid falling into the vortex of the Syrian civil war until around 2017. Up until then, a stubborn stalemate had prevailed in the civil war. As the possibility of Assad's and Iran's victory loomed, Israel changed course and escalated its attacks on Iranian forces in Syria.[150] Simultaneously, Tel Aviv intensified its cyber-attacks against Iranian nuclear facilities and conducted the assassination of Iranian nuclear scientists.

The confrontation between Israel and Iran reached a dangerous level in 2018 when an Israeli air strike against Iranian forces claimed the lives of seven IRGC forces in Syria.[151] Tehran was surprised by the Syrian air defence missile system's failure to intercept the Israeli attacks.[152] Mohammad Ali Sobhani, former director general of the Middle East department of the Ministry of Foreign Affairs, pointed out that Russia exercised control over Syrian airspace and deliberately chose not to interfere in Israeli airstrikes.[153] In retaliation, Iran launched multiple rockets at Israeli forces positioned along the Golan Heights border, inflicting limited damage.[154] Israel, undeterred, continued its offensive operations against Iranian-backed forces. Despite these attacks and counter-attacks, it appeared that both Israel and Iran had thus far carefully calibrated their military manoeuvres to prevent an all-out military confrontation.

Israel is committed to preventing Iran from establishing a military foothold in Syria. However, Iran has not been deterred by the military measures Israel has taken thus far. Tehran appears willing to accept limited casualties to maintain its military presence in Syria, which it views as an indispensable component of its Levant strategy.

Iran's Costly Intervention in Syria

The Iranian–Syrian political alliance, forged in the early days of the Islamic Revolution, has thrived and evolved into a strong partnership that was cemented during Syria's civil war. Today, Iran has achieved some of its top goals in Syria: President Assad has retained his grip on power, while Tehran has expanded its influence, helped weaken ISIS, established a modest military and naval presence in the Mediterranean country for the first time in Iran's modern history, and opened a new front against Israel, serving as a limited deterrence against Israel and the US. Additionally, the Islamic Republic has enlarged its religious footprint by establishing seventy Shia seminaries in Syria.[155]

However, Iranian power in Syria is often exaggerated. As early as 2013, former Syrian prime minister Riyad Hijab, claimed that 'Syria is occupied by the Iranian regime. The person who runs the country is not Bashar al-Assad but Qasem Soleimani.'[156] Shimon Shapira believed that Iran has won the civil war and 'is dominating Syria',[157] while David Lesch argued that Iran 'is taking over Syria', and that Russia 'will not actually provide a counterweight to Iran once the war is over'.[158]

The reality is that while Iran has established a sphere of influence in Syria, it cannot impose its hegemony or dictate its priorities on Assad. The two countries have cooperated when their strategic interests have converged. Several factors will constrain Iranian power. First, Russia maintains a significant military presence in Syria. While Moscow and Tehran both supported Assad, their ambitions for the future of Syria diverge. Crucially, Russia maintains friendly relations with all Arab countries and Israel. Second, the United States maintains a small contingent of forces in Syria, backing Syrian Kurds and other factions controlling parts of northern Syria, including key oil and gas fields. The US will leverage its power in Syria to contain Iran and limit its influence. Third, wealthy Arab nations, vital for Syria's economic recovery, oppose the expansion of Iranian power. And last, Israel's persistent aerial bombardment targeting Iranian military sites in Syria presents a major obstacle to Iran sustaining its military presence there.

Iran has paid an exorbitant price in blood and treasure to achieve its goals, raising concerns that its Syrian strategy has served its ideological interests much more than the country's national interests. Iran's support for the Assad government, in the face of humanitarian disaster and the atrocities of the civil war, has tarnished its reputation in the international community and strained its relationship with most Arab countries. From

March 2011 to March 2021, 306,887 civilians were killed in Syria, with the Syrian government, supported by Tehran, responsible for most of those deaths.[159] More than half of its population has been displaced, and its economy is in disarray. Iran's intervention has indeed contributed to the Syrian tragedy, as has the support from backers of the Syrian opposition.

The human and financial toll of Iranian involvement in the Syrian civil war has been substantial. It is estimated that by March 2016, 342 Iranian nationals, 878 Hezbollah combatants, and 311 fighters from Pakistan and Afghanistan had been killed in Syria.[160] The number of casualties certainly increased between 2016 and the end of the civil war.

Iran has also allocated substantial financial resources to the civil war, although its spending has often been exaggerated.[161] Heshmatollah Falahatpisheh, former chair of the Majles National Security Committee, estimated that Iran had spent between $20–$30 billion in the Syrian civil war up to 2020.[162] Staffan de Mistura, UN Special Envoy to Syria, provided a higher estimate, suggesting that Iran was spending $6 billion annually to support Assad.[163] At the same time, Iran's economic relations with Syria have been rather limited, insufficient to compensate for its considerable expenses. Before the start of the civil war in 2011, Iran's exports to Syria amounted to $516 million, and its imports from that country $29 million. By 2018, Iranian exports to Syria had plummeted to $29 million, while its imports were reduced to $1.3 million.[164] Religious tourism was a major source of Iran's contribution to the Syrian economy, with some 430,000 Iranian pilgrims visiting Shia shrines in Syria in 2009.[165]

To offset some of its expenses in Syria, Iran has attempted to position itself to capitalise on the economic opportunities arising from the reconstruction of Syria. General Rahim Safavi, one of the most ardent supporters of Syria, who received military training in that country in the 1970s, has stressed that the Iranian government 'should recover all the expenditures it incurred in Syria'. He further noted that Syria is willing to compensate for these expenses by allowing Iran to invest in its oil, gas, and sulphate mines.[166] The question remains: can Iran trust Assad in the post-civil war era?

However, Iran faces several obstacles in making substantial investments in Syria as long as its economy is burdened by US sanctions. Iran is also hindered by the Caesar Syria Civilian Protection Act, signed by Trump in 2019, which imposes sanctions on entities and individuals who profit from the Syrian conflict by engaging in reconstruction activities.[167] Furthermore, Iran must compete with Russia for investment opportunities.[168] Behrooz Bonyadi, a Majles deputy, has complained that Assad has given more concessions to Russia than to Iran.[169] Tehran will also have to compete with the wealthy Arab countries of the Persian Gulf that are gradually restoring diplomatic and economic relations with Damascus.

Iran has initiated several ambitious and potentially profitable economic plans, although it is unclear if they have commenced on the ground. In 2017, Syria granted Iran a leading role in a refinery project.[170] Tehran has reportedly agreed to build a new power plant in Latakia and a railway connecting Shalamcheh on the Iran–Iraq border to Basra in Iraq, which will then be extended to Syria, all within the framework of China's Belt and Road Initiative.[171] Tehran has also been in discussion about building 800,000 housing units in Syria.[172]

From Tehran's perspective, the strategic gains in Syria outweigh the economic costs incurred, even though it is unclear if Iran can trust Assad in the post-civil war period. However, Syria has become a bottomless pit, consuming Iran's resources with little hope of full recovery. In contrast, Iran's involvement in Yemen – the next destination in our journey – has required minimal expenditure but yielded limited gains for the Islamic Republic.

Chapter 7

Iran's Yemen Policy: Operating in the Grey Zone

On 14 September 2019, at the height of the civil war in Yemen, a barrage of missiles and drones struck two major Aramco oil facilities, Abqaiq and Khurais, in Saudi Arabia. These highly coordinated and unprecedented strikes, targeting the heart of Saudi Arabia's vast oil empire, struck the kingdom like an earthquake, with shockwaves reverberating throughout global oil markets.

The Houthis, officially known as Ansarallah, an insurgent group that has been the de facto government in North Yemen since 2014, claimed responsibility for these audacious strikes. Without delay, US Secretary of State Mike Pompeo dismissed the Houthis' statements and directly implicated Iran. In a harsh rebuttal, Iran's Foreign Minister Javad Zarif accused Pompeo of 'maximum deceit'. He vehemently denied Iran's involvement while affirming its firm political and ideological support for the Houthis.[1]

These attacks heralded the escalation of the civil war in Yemen, resulting in a humanitarian catastrophe in one of the world's poorest countries. According to a UN report, by the end of 2021, one child under the age of five was dying of malnutrition every nine minutes.[2]

Iran's involvement in Yemen – a country far from its border with no economic significance – may appear perplexing at first glance. However, a different picture begins to emerge once Iran's policies are analysed within the context of its geopolitical rivalry with Saudi Arabia, America's most important Arab ally, which has been the dominant foreign power in Yemen for decades.

Why and how has the Islamic Republic become involved in Yemen, particularly in its bloody civil war, and developed close relations with the Houthis? While Tehran's religious solidarity with the Ansarallah, adherents to a branch of Shia Islam, has influenced its policy towards Yemen, strategic imperatives have played a more significant role.

Mohammad Reza Shah and the Two Yemens

Persia's first encounter with Yemen took place under the Sassanid King Khosrow I (r. 531–579). At the request of a local leader, the king deployed 800 cavalrymen to Yemen to suppress a rebellion. They marched into Sana'a and installed a leader as the 'tributary vassal to Persia' in 570 – the year the Prophet Mohammad was born in Mecca, about 500 miles from Sana'a. However, when the Persians left, the vassal was killed. The Persians returned with 4,000 men and installed his son. They remained there for over a century, intermarrying with the local Arabs and became known as the Abna, or 'sons'.[3] After the rise of Islam, there was no major contact between Yemen and Persia for many centuries.

Iran also shares religious ties with Yemen, although they are not as deep-rooted as those with Lebanon and Iraq. While 30 to 40 per cent of Yemenis are Zaydi Shias, over 90 per cent of Iranians adhere to Twelver Shiism, the largest Shia denomination.[4] Zaydis follow Zayd ibn Ali (698–740) as the fifth imam, while Twelver Shias follow Mohammad Baqir as the fifth imam, as well as his descendants down to the twelfth imam.[5] Over centuries, these sects, both minorities within the Islamic community, developed distinct jurisprudence and eschatology.

The Zaydis established their first emirate in northern Iran along the Caspian Sea in Tabarestan in 864, which lasted for over half a century. A

Zaydi foothold was established in the Sa'dah region of northern Yemen around 897. His successors ruled over a sizeable portion of Yemen and parts of southern Saudi Arabia for centuries.[6]

The modern history of Yemen, like that of many other Arab countries, bears the indelible imprint of the British and Ottoman empires. In 1839, Britain seized control of the port city of Aden, thereby transforming the predominantly Sunni southern Yemen into a protectorate while overlooking the rest of the country. Their primary objective was to secure their maritime trade routes by imposing their authority over the strategic Bab al-Mandab Strait, which connects the Gulf of Aden to the Red Sea and was critical for the lucrative trade with the British colony of India. This subordinate status persisted until the British withdrew from the Persian Gulf and east of Suez in 1967. With the British withdrawal, leftist forces and the Front for the Liberation of Occupied South Yemen unified to establish a new republic. This republic, also known as the People's Democratic Republic of South Yemen, quickly evolved into the sole Marxist-Leninist country in the Middle East and the Arab world.

In contrast, the economically impoverished North Yemen, home to the Zaydis, preserved its independence until it succumbed to Ottoman rule following the capture of Sana'a in 1872. Ottoman colonial rule over the region came to an end with the collapse of the empire during the First World War. In 1918, a republic was established, which evolved into the Mutawakkilite kingdom – a Zaydi theocratic monarchy led by Imam Yahya Mohammad.

It was not until the early 1960s that Iran showed interest in North Yemen. This newfound interest had nothing to do with any sectarian sympathies towards the Zaydis. Instead, it was driven by strategic considerations, Iran's heightened threat perception, and the changing geopolitical dynamics in the Arabian Peninsula. Just a week after Mohammad al Badr assumed the title of Commander of the Faithful and Imam of the Mutawakkilite Kingdom, he was overthrown in a military coup orchestrated by Abdullah al-Sallal, along with other pro-Nasser officers. The coup makers abolished the monarchy and established a republic in September 1962, with al-Sallal as its first president. Imam Badr, however, refused to relinquish power and retreated to the mountains in northern

Yemen. With the support of the local tribes and others, he launched an insurgency against republican forces, leading to a civil war from 1962 to 1970. Mohammad Reza Shah, along with Saudi Arabia, Britain, Jordan, and the United States, supported the loyalists against the republican forces, backed directly by Egypt and indirectly by the Soviets.[7]

Iran's limited involvement in the civil war was largely driven by the Shah's efforts to undermine Nasser, whom the monarch perceived as the main source of instability in the Middle East. In a letter to President Johnson in January 1964, the Shah warned about 'the stockpiles of weapons of aggression in the possession of Egypt', delivered by the Soviet Union, that 'serve, overtly or under cover, as instruments of Egyptian intervention. Yemen, the Morocco–Algeria conflict, and the arming of Somalia for expansion are instances in point.'[8] The Shah's alarm was not unfounded: by 1966, Egypt had deployed over 70,000 troops in Yemen.[9] Moreover, the Shah, as the CIA noted, may have been tempted to 'take advantage of Egypt's defeat [in the 1967 war] to step up its clandestine aid to the Yemeni royalists'.[10]

In response to a request from an official Yemeni delegation visiting Tehran in 1963, the Shah approved limited military support for the royalists. At the same time, an unspecified number of Yemeni officers received training at a military academy in Tehran, while Yemeni tribesmen were trained in medical and combat fields and sabotage techniques.[11] Tehran dispatched trainers and advisors to the royalist camps in Yemen, airdropped material to resupply the besieged royalist troops, and transported heavy equipment through Saudi territory to Yemen.[12] Notably, even as other countries reduced their support for the royalists, the Shah remained committed. Britain's Neil Mclean travelled to Tehran to request additional military assistance for the royalists. Tehran delivered a shipment of military aid in October 1967, when it was 'the sole supplier of royalty force'.[13] Despite the extensive support the royalists received, the republicans eventually prevailed. Iran quickly recalibrated its policy by recognising the new government in North Yemen in September 1970.[14]

However, the end of the civil war and Iran's recognition of the new government did not mark the end of its involvement in the Arabian Peninsula.

Although Saudi Arabia and Iran, two pro-Western monarchies, were supporting the same side in the civil war in North Yemen, Riyadh expressed deep uneasiness over what it perceived as Iran's expansionist policy in the Arabian Peninsula, which Saudi Arabia considered to be its backyard. Saudi Arabia reluctantly tolerated the Shah's influence in the peninsula, constrained by its limited options in confronting a militarily stronger Iran. This underlying mistrust of Iran resurfaced during the communist-inspired insurgency in Oman's Dhofar province.

In 1972, Oman's ruler, Qaboos bin Said, met with the Shah in Tehran and requested military support to quell the rebellion in Dhofar. There is an uncanny historical echo here: two centuries earlier, at the request of Oman's ruler, Nader Shah (1688–1747) had dispatched a small expeditionary force to suppress a rebellion there, ultimately capturing Muscat in 1743. Mohammad Reza Shah also agreed to deploy a small expeditionary force to Dhofar to defeat the Marxist-Leninist Popular Front for the Liberation of Oman,[15] which was supported by approximately 300–400 South Yemeni troops, as well as by the Soviet Union, China, and Iraq.[16]

In the Presidential Daily Brief for President Nixon, we gain insights into the Shah's views about the potential presence of Western military powers in the region, his ambitions to dominate the Persian Gulf, and Saudi's anxieties regarding his support for Oman:

> The Shah interpreted the private arrangement [with Sultan Qaboos] as giving Iran the flexibility to oversee the movement of tankers not only in the strait [of Hormuz] but also in the Gulf of Oman, the Arabian Sea, and on toward the Bab el Mandeb.... The Sultan was wary of putting too much reliance on Iranian help, in part because he might thereby irritate king Faysal [of Saudi Arabia] who has long been suspicious that the Shah hopes to dominate the lower Persian Gulf.[17]

As the dominant power in the Persian Gulf, the Shah was unwilling to 'tolerate subversion' in the region[18] and believed that it should be free of influence of 'foreign military powers'.[19] Thus, he dispatched the largest expeditionary force in his 37-year rule to Oman. The military operation in Oman started in 1973 and ended in 1977. Iranian forces, estimated to have grown from '3,800 in 1975' to '25,000 in 1976', decisively defeated the communist rebels and reportedly suffered between 300 and 700 casualties.[20]

The four-year operation in Oman served Iran's national interests and strengthened its position as a major regional power. However, the Shah faced unwarranted criticism from Iranian leftists, some nationalists, and Islamists, who condemned the Shah for his 'imperialistic' intervention. In addition, certain Iranian dissidents supported the rebels, prompting the Shah to accuse them of treason.[21]

After Iran's victory in Dhofar, the Shah's relations remained cordial with North Yemen but strained with South Yemen. However, the Iranian revolution brought fundamental changes to Iran's relations with both Yemens.

Revolutionary Iran and the Houthi Movement

Iran's policy towards the two Yemens underwent a gradual shift following the Islamic Revolution, although neither was considered a priority for several years. The Yemen Arab Republic (North Yemen) was among the first countries to recognise the Islamic Republic and cultivate friendly relations with Tehran.[22] On behalf of President Ali Abdullah Saleh, a secular Zaydi politician, North Yemen's ambassador presented a Quran to Ayatollah Khomeini and conveyed his country's desire to improve relations with Iran. Communist South Yemen, whose troops had engaged Iranian forces in Dhofar in the mid-1970s, also established diplomatic relations with Tehran. In a goodwill gesture, Aden released the Iranian pilot it had captured during the Dhofar operation.[23] For a brief period, both Yemens maintained distant but friendly relations with Iran.

With the start of the Iran–Iraq War in September 1980, the Islamic Republic's relations with the two Yemens began to change. While neither Yemen openly supported Iran, North Yemen actively and directly aided Iraq. President Saleh deployed limited troops to Iraq to assist his Arab brethren.[24] There were reports of Saleh visiting Qasr-e Shirin, an Iranian city occupied by Iraq, to boost the morale of Iraqi troops.

Tehran knew of the presence of a small number of North Yemeni troops helping Iraq. Recently declassified CIA documents, however, unveil much more extensive involvement than previously acknowledged.[25] By 1982, North Yemen provided 'volunteers to aid Iraq in its war against Iran'.[26] However, by 1983, there were approximately two thousand Yemeni men serving in Iraq who were 'untrained militias recruited from the northern tribes'.[27] Over time, North Yemen gradually deployed its trained and professional troops to Iraq, with their number surpassing three thousand. In 1986 alone, North Yemen suffered 400 casualties. Besides paying wages to North Yemeni troops, President Saddam Hussein also gave 'at least $30 million directly to Sana'a for the use of its troops' in 1986 alone.[28]

Following the unification of the two Yemens in May 1990 and the conclusion of the Iran–Iraq War, Iran became more interested in Yemen, despite harbouring deep suspicions about Saleh, who had become the president of the new Republic of Yemen.

Following the Islamic Revolution in Iran, both Shia and Wahhabi radicalism flourished in the 1980s. The seizure of the Grand Mosque in Mecca, one of Islam's holiest sites, by anti-Saudi Islamists in November 1979, alerted Riyadh to the growing threat of Islamic radicalism. In response, the kingdom opted to disseminate its own conservative version of Wahhabism as a counterforce to Sunni and particularly Shia radicalism, allocating billions of dollars to build *madrassas* and Islamic centres worldwide. The Zaydi-dominated North Yemen, bordering the kingdom, became one of the battlegrounds for Saudi Arabia's Wahhabisation project. President Saleh, a Saudi ally, supported this ideological offensive.[29]

However, many Zaydis resisted this campaign.[30] Hossein Badr al-Din al-Houthi (1959–2004) was one of them. At the age of twenty-six, like many of his contemporaries, he was drawn to Iran's Islamic Revolution and decided to visit the country.[31] His fateful journey started in Syria, where he and his brother-in-law waited for a month to obtain a visa to travel to Iran during the Iran–Iraq War. Sparse information is available about their eighteen-day sojourn in Iran. They visited Qom, home to Iran's major Shia seminaries, and met with unidentified Iranian officials and clerics.[32] There is no evidence to suggest that they met with Ayatollah

Khomeini; Yemen, unlike Lebanon, was not a priority for Khomeini. Iranian sources, citing Hossein's brother-in-law, claim that Hossein's fervent support for the Islamic Republic prompted him to contemplate joining the Badr Brigade – an Iraqi militia force created and armed by the IRGC during the Iran–Iraq War.[33]

After returning home, Hossein Houthi became more politically active and served in parliament from 1993 to 1997. Simultaneously, he joined the Al Shabab al-Moumeneen, or the Believing Youth, a religious group with strong anti-imperialist proclivities dedicated to countering Saudi-financed Wahhabism.[34] Eventually, Hossein founded the Houthi movement, recruiting from the ranks of the Believing Youth in the impoverished Sa'dah governorate.

In 1994, as Hossein was mobilising the masses, Yemen descended into a civil war between President Saleh and the southern socialists, who accused him of monopolising power after the unification of the two Yemens. Saleh pressured Badr al-Din al-Houthi (1926–2010), Hossein's influential father, to join the government against the socialists. The senior Badr refused and instead went to Syria and from there to Iran.[35] The years he spent in Iran are even more poorly documented than his son's. His son, Hossein, allegedly revisited Iran and took his father back to Yemen in 1995.

Badr's refusal to collaborate with Saleh against the southern socialists was a foretaste of the emerging political feud between the Houthi movement and the Saleh government. Around that time in the 1990s, Iran cautiously began expanding its soft power in Yemen through investments in small developmental projects and increasing its 'spiritual' influence in Yemen, aligning with Hossein Houthi's efforts to empower the Zaydi community.[36] Iranian sources claimed that approximately 2,000 Yemenis converted to Twelver Shiism during this period. For a short time, there were no visa restrictions between the two countries, allowing a small number of Yemeni students to study in Iranian universities and Shia seminaries. Iran also shipped thousands of books to Yemen, along with Iranian films and Iranian-backed Arabic television channels, to disseminate the country's revolutionary message.[37]

At that time, Iran's limited activities in Yemen posed no serious threat to President Saleh's regime. In fact, to improve bilateral relations, President Saleh visited Iran and held a meeting with Ayatollah Khamenei in April 2000. Khamenei conveyed to his guest the importance of Islamic countries uniting to counter the American strategy of dividing the Islamic world, while Saleh emphasised that improving bilateral relations was essential for regional stability.[38] Three years later, in May 2003, President Khatami visited Yemen and met with Saleh. During his visit, he signed several agreements with Yemen, covering areas such as security and commerce. Iran also committed to providing more scholarships to Yemeni students, expanding cultural exchanges, and increasing its modest investments to improve Hodeidah's oil port anchorage.[39]

While Khatami refrained from meeting with any Zaydi clerics or members of the Houthi movement, presumably to avoid antagonising President Saleh, Hossein Houthi grew increasingly disillusioned with Saleh's persistent refusal to open the political process, halt the Saudi-funded proselytising among Zaydis, and ameliorate the deplorable economic conditions in the Sa'dah region. Meanwhile, Hossein expressed his vehement opposition to the US invasions of Afghanistan and Iraq, as well as its counterterrorism campaign in Yemen, which had resulted in the deaths of many terrorists and innocent civilians. The more alienated he became with Saleh's policies, the more radical he became. This radicalism manifested itself in his signature slogan of 'Death to America, Death to Israel, Curse the Jews, Victory to Islam' in 2002, which bore remarkable similarities to slogans chanted in Iran.[40] Against the backdrop of Hossein's radicalism and the increasing popularity of his movement, Saleh launched his war against Houthis. At that time, the Saleh government killed Hossein in cold blood, hoping to nip the nascent movement in the bud. But Saleh's expectations were about to be rudely disappointed.

Hossein Houthi's death elevated him to the status a martyr. Paradoxically, he became more dangerous to Saleh dead than alive. His death reinvigorated the Houthi movement, giving it a new lease on life. His brother, Abdul Malik Houthi, who succeeded him, unleashed an unrelenting asymmetric insurgency against the Saleh regime.

During the early phases of the Houthi insurgency, there was a discernible change in Saleh's stance towards Tehran. With support from Saudi

Arabia, he began consistently to accuse Iran of aiding and empowering the Houthi movement, progressively broadening the scope of his allegations. Although the United States publicly endorsed Saleh's allegations against Iran, newly declassified US documents reveal that, behind closed doors, it often disputed them. This inconsistency is understandable, as the United States was not opposed to Yemen undermining the Islamic Republic's reputation and at the same time was reluctant to jeopardise its friendly relationship with Saleh, who played a pivotal role in US counterinsurgency efforts against al-Qaeda.

Saleh's iron-fist policy towards the Houthis was ineffective and devoid of nuance, which only served to radicalise them further. He dismissed the Houthis as a dogmatic religious cult that needed to be forcefully eradicated. In contrast, Stephen Seche, American ambassador to Yemen, offered a nuanced and realistic assessment of the Houthis. He described the Houthis 'as a movement with religious undertones and politically addressable grievances rather than a radical, religiously motivated sect with which the ROYG [Republic of Yemen Government] cannot negotiate. Even their demands for greater religious freedom could be addressed through political means.'[41] Had Saleh heeded the ambassador's sage counsel, he might have been able to avert significant bloodshed and tamed the Houthi movement.[42]

Saleh, typical of authoritarian leaders, perceived compromise as a form of capitulation and instead sought to destroy the Houthis once and for all. In that spirit of arrogance and defiance, he did not even attempt to find a potential political solution to the simmering conflict, dismissing the suggestion to engage Ayatollah Sistani as a mediator. The vitriolic words of Mohammad al-Arifi a Saudi cleric, may have influenced Saleh's decision. The cleric dismissed Sistani, stating: 'They selected a sheikh who is a great sinner and infidel from a remote corner of Iraq, and said: We want this man to be the arbitrator between us.'[43]

While Saleh was suppressing the Houthis, his foreign minister delivered a letter on his behalf to Ayatollah Khamenei in 2007. In it, Saleh reiterated his desire to improve bilateral relations. Tehran was enthusiastic about the proposal, and Ali Akbar Velayati, Khamenei's top foreign policy advisor, urged Yemen to seek a peaceful solution to end bloody conflict with the Houthis.[44]

Just two months after this exchange of pleasantries between the two leaders, the Saleh regime began to portray Iran as the main instigator of the conflict in Yemen.[45] He portrayed the Houthis as an Iranian proxy, which they certainly were not, determined to create an Iranian-style theocracy in Yemen.[46] He seemed to have chosen to make Iran the scapegoat to divert blame from his failed strategy to defeat the Houthis. Moreover, as the American ambassador to Yemen observed, Saleh used the anti-Iran campaign 'to solidify U.S. military support against a common enemy', namely Iran.[47]

Gradually, Saleh became more fervent in his criticism of Iran to delegitimise the Houthi movement and to gain the support of the Arab countries opposed to Iranian advances in the Middle East. In 2007, Sana'a accused Iran of 'providing $100,000 every month to the Houthis', and recalled its ambassador from Tehran.[48] Both the Houthis and Tehran denied this allegation. In this instance, too, the American embassy maintained that Yemen 'does not make the case' for its allegations against Tehran,[49] asserting that there was 'little evidence' to support the claim Iran was engaged in Yemen.[50] Yemen also claimed that Tehran had crossed its 'red line' by converting Yemenis to Twelver Shi'ism, which had surely happened.

Yemen's relations with Iran further deteriorated when the Saleh regime launched Operation Scorched Earth in yet another offensive to eliminate the Houthis. Simultaneously, Saudi Arabia launched air strikes against the Houthis and imposed a partial blockade on Yemen's north Red Sea ports, seeking to create 'a buffer zone' and push the Houthis away from the Saudi border.[51] Yemeni analysts feared that Saudi Arabia's military intervention might provoke Iran's interference in Yemen.[52] It did not. However, in retaliation against the latest offensive, the Houthis intensified cross-border ambushes against the kingdom.[53] Saudi Arabia, much like Saleh, accused Iran of directing their 'proxy', the Houthis, to launch attacks on the Saudi border.[54] Iran rejected the allegation and condemned Saudi's military attack on the Houthis. The speaker of the Majles, Ali Larijani, said: 'I wonder how our Saudi brothers, who are Muslim, do such a thing as killing Muslims. If Saudis have rockets, why don't they use them against Israel instead of dropping them on poor innocent people?'[55]

As Operation Scorched Earth failed to subdue the Houthis, Yemen further excoriated Tehran, this time specifically lambasting Iran for arming the Houthis.[56] The US embassy in Yemen rejected this allegation as well. It reported to Washington: 'Most local political analysts report that the Houthis obtain their weapons from the Yemeni black market and even from the ROYG military itself.' The embassy quoted Yemeni officials saying that 'Iranians are not arming the Houthis. The weapons they use are Yemeni. Most actually come from fighters who fought against the socialists during the 1994 war and then sold them', and went on to say that the military in Yemen 'covers up its failure' by saying the weapons come from Iran.[57] The US embassy concluded that Iranian influence 'has thus far been limited to informal religious ties between Yemeni and Iranian scholars and negligible Iranian investment in the energy and development sectors'.[58]

The most unambiguous rejection of Yemen's alleged claim of Iranian intervention in its internal politics came from Secretary of State Hillary Clinton. Meeting with Yemen's Foreign Minister Abu Bakr al-Qirbi in January 2010, Clinton rejected the claim that 'the Houthi conflict in northern Yemen was fomented and supported by Iran', and encouraged a diplomatic solution to the conflict.[59]

While Iran consistently advocated for a negotiated settlement to the conflict in Yemen, it also provided diplomatic, moral, and possibly financial support to the Houthis. Both Yemen and Saudi Arabia were resolute in preventing Iran from assuming any mediating role in the conflict, fearing that this could open the door for its presence in the Arabian Peninsula. For instance, in December 2009, the Iranian Foreign Minister Manuchehr Mottaki offered to visit Sana'a to mediate between the Houthis and the government. Sana'a demanded that Iran must first condemn the Houthis for their insurgency, knowing Tehran would not do so.[60]

By the time the Arab Spring reached Yemen in 2011, Sana'a had successfully portrayed the Houthis as an Iranian proxy, despite their origins as an authentic home-grown movement. With the onset of the civil war, Tehran quickly seized the opportunity to expand its influence and reshape its relationship with the Houthis.

The Arab Spring in Yemen: 'A Divine Gift'

When the Arab Spring reached Yemen in early 2011, hundreds of thousands of people, including the Houthis and pro-democracy forces, took to the streets to topple President Saleh's dictatorial regime and establish a more transparent, accountable, and representative government. This political earthquake rattled the foundations of Saleh's fragile regime, presenting alluring opportunities for Iran and substantial risks for Saudi Arabia, Saleh's principal regional supporter.

Iran hailed the uprising in Yemen, just as it did those in Egypt, Bahrain, and Libya, as an Islamic, anti-Western popular movement. General Soleimani described it as 'a divine gift' bestowed upon Iran.[61] It was in that spirit that Iran made a major power play in Yemen.[62] Adapting its 'forward defence' strategy, Tehran began to expand its power in Yemen by forming an alliance with the Houthis, extending its strategic reach into the Arabian Peninsula, and becoming a thorn in Saudi Arabia's side while enhancing its deterrence capabilities against the kingdom. While the Iranian–Houthi partnership had a religious underpinning, it was also deeply entrenched in their joint opposition to Saudi Arabia's intervention in Yemen and their shared perception of a threat posed by the US.

Conversely, Riyadh was apprehensive about the potential strategic spillover of the Yemeni unrest into the kingdom. This anxiety was justified. In just a few tumultuous months, Saudi Arabia witnessed the overthrow of its allies in Egypt, Libya, and Tunisia due to unprecedented popular uprisings, while the kingdom found itself compelled to deploy troops to save its embattled ally in neighbouring Bahrain. What rendered the volatile situation in Yemen truly troubling was the limited range of options available to Riyadh. Kinetic intervention was exceedingly fraught with danger, carrying unpredictable consequences. The attempt to manage the conflict without direct military intervention, allowing various factions to engage in combat until Riyadh could align itself with the eventual victor, posed even greater risks. Remaining politically passive and accepting the outcome was no less than committing political suicide for Riyadh.

Therefore, Saudi Arabia, determined to preserve its hegemonic position in Yemen, and with support from the Gulf Cooperation Council

(GCC), developed the 'GCC Initiative'. This initiative, supported by the US and the UN, was designed to contain, control, and remotely manage the burgeoning protest movement in Yemen.[63] To placate protestors, it demanded the resignation of the besieged President Saleh, who had been described by Saudi Arabia as a 'weak leader' even before the start of the Arab Spring.[64] Cornered and devoid of appealing alternatives, Saleh resigned but retained leadership of his party. Moreover, he was granted immunity from prosecution, providing him with a pathway to potentially reclaim some of his lost power.[65] With Saleh ousted from power, Abd Rabbuh Mansur Hadi, the incumbent vice president, was selected as the interim president in February 2012 through the GCC Initiative.[66]

As anticipated, Tehran vehemently opposed the GCC Initiative because the Houthis were largely excluded from the deliberations about its future plans for Yemen. For Tehran, the initiative was a political stunt to rearrange the deck chairs on a sinking *Titanic*, effectively maintaining Yemen's existing power structure intact.

Sana'a Falls: Tehran's Fortunes Rise

The initial hope that Interim President Hadi could successfully reform the intractable political system dissipated quite quickly. In fact, when Hadi easily secured victory as the sole candidate in an engineered presidential election, it sent an unambiguous signal that the GCC Initiative was not designed fundamentally to change the existing power structure. Moreover, Hadi struggled to govern effectively a restless and impoverished country and maintain a semblance of domestic tranquillity. In contrast to Saleh, who had built a national support base during his three-decade reign, Hadi lacked both an independent source of popular backing and the requisite political skills to navigate the complex and unpredictable landscape of Yemen. He was essentially Saleh's political clone, but without any of his political gifts.

Hadi's foreign policy also closely mirrored Saleh's. He threw his support behind the US counterterrorism campaign and became increasingly dependent on Saudi Arabia's financial and military support. While

Hadi showed a willingness to engage with the Houthis, he was unwilling to share power with them, setting the stage for an inevitable clash.[67]

Sana'a fell to the Houthis on 21 September 2014 after days of widespread riots against high fuel costs and deteriorating socioeconomic conditions. In a last-ditch effort, Hadi made a belated pledge to establish a government of national unity – a step he should have taken upon assuming power. Meanwhile, the country was descending into chaos, and his grip on power was slipping away.

Just four months after the fall of Sana'a, on January 20, 2015, the Houthis stormed the presidential palace. They placed the president under house arrest and eventually forced his resignation. Subsequently, the Houthis established the Revolutionary Committee to run the country and formed 'Popular Committees' to patrol the streets – reminiscent of the neighbourhood committees formed by Iranian revolutionaries in 1979 to consolidate their power. After a month of house arrest, Hadi managed to escape to Aden in South Yemen, where he rescinded his earlier resignation and declared himself Yemen's legitimate president.

While the Houthis and Tehran extolled Hadi's overthrow as a manifestation of a popular revolution, he denounced it as a Houthi coup d'état. Yemen now descended into a classic civil war: both the Hadi government and the Houthis claimed sovereignty over Yemen. While Hadi was recognised as Yemen's legitimate president by the UN, US, Saudi Arabia, and many others, Iran stood alone in recognising the Houthi government.[68]

The fall of Sana'a was a turning point in Iran's relations with Yemen, driving it towards forging a political alliance with the Houthis. As pressure mounted from both the United States and Saudi Arabia, the Houthis gravitated towards closer ties with Tehran. Following Mansur Hadi's forced resignation, the Houthis released two members of Hezbollah and three IRGC personnel arrested from the crew of the *Jihan I* ship, which the US had seized in 2013 for allegedly carrying weapons to Yemen. Tehran rejected this allegation. When international airlines suspended their operations in Yemen in February 2015, Iran's Mahan and Yemenia airlines started fourteen direct flights per week between Sana'a and Tehran.[69] These flights were halted after two weeks when the US and its allies imposed an air and sea blockade on Yemen. Meanwhile, a high-ranking delegation of Houthis also visited Tehran and signed several agreements with Iran. Tehran committed to building a power plant, exporting oil to Yemen for one year, and assisting in the expansion of al Hodeidah port.[70] However, Tehran's alliance with the Houthis also carried inherent risks: in December 2014, the AQAP (al-Qaeda in the Arabian Peninsula), which opposed the Houthis, attempted to assassinate Iran's ambassador to Yemen. While the ambassador escaped unharmed, six people were killed, and a dozen others were wounded.[71]

Excluded from power due to the GCC Initiative, former President Saleh and the Houthis gravitated towards an informal yet uneasy alliance. This alliance played a more pivotal role in the Houthis' rise to power than their partnership with Tehran.[72] It was a marriage of convenience marked by mutual suspicion, with each anticipating betrayal at an opportune moment. Machiavellian to the core, Saleh may have underestimated the Houthis, believing he could outmanoeuvre and exploit the inexperienced group to restore his lost power. The Houthis could not forget or forgive Saleh's violent crackdown on their movement, recognised the imperative of utilising his extensive network of supporters to consolidate power. However, their mistrust of Saleh was so deep that they maintained 'separate lines of command and control at the operational level'.[73]

Tehran also regarded Saleh, who had assisted Saddam Hussein during the Iran–Iraq War and later emerged as an outspoken critic of Iran's involvement in Yemen, as a duplicitous and conniving politician. When ousted from power, Saleh proposed a 'strategic alliance with Tehran against the Arab coalition', which Iran swiftly rejected.[74] Nevertheless, Tehran tolerated Saleh as long as he sided with the Houthis against Mansur Hadi and was critical of Saudi Arabia.

The fragile alliance between the Houthis and Saleh shifted the trajectory of the conflict in the Houthis' favour. When their combined forces dissolved the parliament and advanced towards Aden, a panicked President Mansur Hadi once again fled, seeking refuge in Saudi Arabia, where he requested the kingdom's military intervention in Yemen. Ayatollah Khamenei questioned Hadi's legitimacy, disparaging him for resigning at a critical juncture and fleeing 'the country disguised in women's clothing'.[75]

Saudi Arabia's Military Intervention

In Riyadh, President Mansur Hadi received a warm welcome from Prince Mohammad bin Salman, the kingdom's de facto ruler, in March 2015. At the time, the young prince held the critical positions of defence minister, chief of the royal court, and deputy crown prince. With ambitions to ascend to the throne one day, the prince was eager to prove his visionary leadership by resolving the Yemen crisis. There seemed to have been a consensus among Saudi leadership that the Houthi insurgency could not be resolved through negotiation. Consequently, Mohammad bin Salman launched Operation Decisive Storm in March 2015. This kinetic intervention was designed to utilise overwhelming air power, along with the naval and air blockade of Yemen, to swiftly disrupt, disorient, and neutralise the Houthi–Saleh forces, reinstate President Mansur Hadi, and reassert Saudi dominance over Yemen. It did not take long for Saudi Arabia to realise that its military intervention could not produce the expected result of Houthi surrender. The war gave the Houthis a new sense of purpose, rallying their supporters to defend their country against foreign aggression.

The relentless Saudi aerial bombardment decimated much of Yemen's already depleted infrastructure, exacerbating widespread suffering across the nation. Amid widespread international condemnation for the indiscriminate bombings, Operation Decisive Storm was abruptly halted a mere month after its launch. However, this halt did not mean the end of the war. The Saudi-led coalition subsequently launched Operation Restoring Hope, with the goals of enabling increased humanitarian assistance to reach the besieged people of Yemen and repairing the kingdom's tarnished image. Even two years into the civil war, Mohammad bin Salman continued to believe that he could quickly defeat the Houthis 'in a few days', confidently stating that they would 'tire [themselves] out' and that 'time is in our favour'.[76] Time was not in his favour.

It is difficult to determine how much Saudi Arabia's perception of the threat emanating from Iran influenced Prince Mohammad's decision to intervene militarily in Yemen.[77] He publicly stated that Iran had aspirations to 'take over the Islamic world',[78] suggesting that Ayatollah

Khamenei was 'the new Hitler of the Middle East', who must not be appeased.[79] Riyadh harboured suspicions that Iran was supporting the Houthis to establish a Shia government in Yemen, which could potentially embolden Saudi Arabia's substantial Shia minority in the oil-rich provinces to destabilise the kingdom. Finally, Saudi Arabia was alarmed by Iran's favourable regional position. Following the US invasion of Iraq, the Saudi leadership seemed to have concluded that the region's strategic landscape had shifted in Iran's favour.[80] For the first time in centuries, Baghdad was under the control of a Tehran-friendly, Shia-dominated government. Assad, an Arab ally of Iran, remained in power in Syria, despite Riyadh's generous support for his opponents. And Hezbollah was a formidable player in Lebanon. Therefore, the kingdom was determined to prevent Iran from establishing a foothold in Yemen, which Riyadh deemed its security zone.

The Saudi military intervention in Yemen, backed by the US and Britain, proved insufficient to eradicate the Houthis. By 2017, Saudi Arabia had failed to achieve any of its major strategic goals in Yemen. However, the election of President Trump instilled a renewed sense of confidence in Riyadh to continue its failing strategy in Yemen. Trump not only backed Saudi Arabia's intervention but also resumed selling arms to the kingdom, which had been temporarily halted during the Obama administration. Furthermore, he was determined to reverse Iranian advances in the Middle East, a stance Prince Mohammad bin Salman welcomed. On 2 May 2017, the prince felt emboldened enough to threaten Iran openly, declaring that: 'We won't wait for the battle to be in Saudi Arabia. Instead, we will work so that the battle is for them in Iran, not in Saudi Arabia.'[81] Tehran took him in earnest and intensified its support of the Houthis.

Iran and the Civil War in Yemen

Iran has provided financial, political, diplomatic, and particularly military support to the Houthis during the civil war. Financial support appears to have been the least important ingredient of this assistance. Given the US sanctions imposed on Iran's financial institutions, it seems improbable that Tehran could have transferred substantial amounts of funds to the Houthis through conventional banking channels. It is plausible that the Islamic Republic could have funnelled limited cash to the Houthis through its charitable foundations, which operate independently of the Iranian state and are directly accountable to Ayatollah Khamenei. However, confirming such payments would require access to the official records of these foundations, a task that remains impossible at this time. A more likely channel of support for the Houthis, as the UN Panel of Experts concluded, is that 'the fuel was loaded from ports in the Islamic Republic of Iran under false documentation to avoid detection by inspections of the United Nations Verification and Inspection Mechanism.[82] In March 2018, Reza Heidari, an Iranian national, was convicted by a German court on charges related to the transfer of fuel to the Houthis.[83] The Houthis, of course, have their own revenue sources, including control of 'black markets' and 'the collection of illegal fees and levies' from sectors like oil and telecommunications.[84]

The Islamic Republic has not been shy in acknowledging its political support for the Houthis, considering it a religious and constitutional duty. The Houthis maintain an ambassador in Tehran, just as Iran does in Sana'a. While Tehran has been the Houthis' principal supporter, it has also been the most vocal critic of the Saudi-led operations in Yemen. Ayatollah Khamenei has denounced Saudi Arabia and the US for 'committing crimes and genocide', complaining that: 'If we say a few words, they say we are interfering, but when the Saudis bomb Yemen, that is not intervention.'[85]

Diplomatically, Tehran proposed a peace plan to end the carnage in Yemen. One month after Saudi Arabia began its military operations in Yemen, Foreign Minister Zarif presented a five-point ceasefire plan in March 2015. It called for an immediate halt to all military operations, unimpeded delivery of humanitarian aid to Yemen, 'resumption of Yemeni-led and Yemeni-owned national dialogue, with the participation of the representatives of all political parties, and establishment of an inclusive national unity government'.[86] Saudi Arabia and President Mansur Hadi rejected the peace proposal. In 2017, Iran submitted a modified iteration of the same proposal to the UN, which was ignored. Both Saudi Arabia and the US have effectively prevented Tehran from participating in major UN-sponsored fora related to Yemen, continuing the same policies they pursued towards Tehran during the civil wars in Lebanon and Syria.

Iran's Military Support

Military assistance to the Houthis is the most consequential component of Iran's strategy towards Yemen. The Islamic Republic's major challenge in delivering weapons to the Houthis pertains to UN Resolution 2216, passed in 2015, which explicitly prohibits the 'direct or indirect sale or transfer of arms to Houthis and Saleh'.[87] The resolution has put Tehran in a delicate predicament. On one hand, Iran did not want to leave the Houthis defenceless when Western powers were legally providing sophisticated arms to Saudi Arabia. On the other hand, Iran was determined to avoid being found in violation of the UN resolution, as that could have led to more sanctions being imposed on the country. Consequently, Tehran has frequently operated in a grey zone, clandestinely arming the Houthis while maintaining plausible deniability. This policy seems to have been relatively successful. The UN Panel of Experts on Yemen, appointed in 2014 to investigate the civil war, concluded in 2020 that while there is indisputable evidence of Iranian political and military support to the Houthis, 'the scale of such support is unknown'.[88] The panel also indicated that the Houthis may have procured weapons through 'well-established arms smuggling networks predating the conflict [the civil war]',[89] possibly from the Yemeni army. It stressed that the Houthis could have been importing 'high-value components, which are then integrated into locally assembled weapons systems, such as the extended-range unmanned aerial vehicles'.[90]

Iran began providing arms and ammunition to the Houthis with the onset of the Arab Spring, and possibly even earlier. Until 2011, the US embassy in Sana'a consistently rejected the allegation by the Yemeni government that Iran was providing military assistance to the Houthis. However, the US assessment changed following the Arab Spring, when it began accusing the IRGC of deploying advisors to Yemen, as well as arming the Houthis. In implementing its air and sea blockade of Yemen, the US and its allies intercepted and seized several fishing dhows and vessels that were suspected of delivering light arms and ammunition to the Houthis. Iran denied these allegations. The UN Panel of Experts confirmed that 2,064 of these weapons were 'linked to Iranian manufacture or origin', without directly implicating Iran for the arms transfer.[91] The IRGC was also accused of training the Houthis, though the sources of these claims were not identified. In 2014, an 'unidentified' senior Iranian official claimed that a 'few hundred' IRGC personnel had trained the Houthi fighters in Yemen.[92] Additionally, Iran was accused of 'training Houthi fighters in a small island off the Eritrean Coast'.[93] In 2016, both the US and the Hadi government claimed that 'a small number of Hezbollah operatives have been training Houthi rebels for some time'.[94] Tehran has vehemently rejected these allegations, insisting, unconvincingly that its role in Yemen is exclusively 'advisory' and asserting that Iran has neither a military base nor troops stationed there.[95]

Taking the War to Saudi Arabia

The civil war's trajectory changed when the Houthis–Saleh alliance deployed rockets, missiles, and unmanned aerial vehicles (drones), taking the war into Saudi Arabia's urban areas. They had access to 'extended-range' missile technology more advanced than the Scud-C and Hwasong-6 short-range ballistic missiles as early as 2015.[96] They acquired these missiles from the arsenal of the Yemeni government following its collapse in 2011. At this time, Saudi Arabia accused Iran of supplying missiles to the Houthis. In 2016, Saudi Arabia lodged a formal complaint with the UN, accusing Iran of violation of the UN Resolution 2216 by providing Zelzal-3 rockets to the Houthis. However, the UN Panel of Experts refuted this allegation, concluding that it 'has not seen sufficient evidence to confirm any direct large-scale supply of arms' from Iran to Yemen, 'although there are indicators that anti-tank guided weapons being supplied to the Houthi or Saleh forces are of Iranian manufacture'.[97] In a strongly worded letter to the UN Secretary-General, Tehran accused Saudi Arabia of committing atrocities, targeting '3,158 non-military sites' that included residential areas, mosques and schools between March 2015 and the end of August 2016.[98] Foreign Minister Zarif lambasted Saudi Arabia for trying to divert public attention from its bombing of Yemen 'to smithereens', killing thousands of innocent people.[99]

Less than a year after this diplomatic dispute at the UN, the Houthis launched a short-range ballistic missile at Riyadh international airport on 4 November 2017 – the anniversary of the attack on the American embassy in Tehran in 1979. Indeed, despite causing minimal damage and no casualties, the missile attack highlighted deficiencies in the king-dom's state-of-the-art air defence system. In response, Saudi Arabia promptly called the Houthi attack an 'act of war by Iran', alleging that Iran and Hezbollah had surreptitiously and illegally transported various components of the missile into Yemen, where they were assembled.[100] Merely a month after the Riyadh airport missile attack, in December 2017, the Houthis launched another short-range ballistic missile, this time targeting one of the palaces of King Salman. Although this missile attack caused even less damage compared to the previous one, the symbolism of targeting the king's palace was not lost on the Saudis. Riyadh mounted a vigorous response to these missile attacks. In ten days in December 2017, they conducted airstrikes that resulted in the death of 136 civilians in Yemen and inflicted substantial physical damage.[101]

Saudi Arabia claimed that its air defence had successfully intercepted the missiles aimed at Riyadh international airport. Nevertheless, inde-pendent experts concluded that the missile had struck close to its intended target and had not been brought down, revealing Saudi Arabia's vulnerabilities. The US also accused Iran of supplying missiles to the Houthis. US Ambassador Nikki R. Haley made a high-profile display of what she claimed were the remnants of the ballistic missiles used in the attacks in New York. She insisted that they were Iranian-made to divert attention from the deficiencies of the kingdom's air defence system. Some Defense Department officials, however, expressed doubt 'that the remnants on display validated Ms. Haley's claim'.[102]

This time, Saudi Arabia's allegation about Iran was accurate. The inves-tigation by the UN Panel of Experts determined that the Houthis lacked the technical expertise to domestically manufacture the missiles to attack Saudi Arabia.[103] For the first time, the panel determined that Iran was in non-compliance with UN Resolution 2216 by illegally supplying missiles to the Houthis. However, it did not directly implicate Iran in the execution of the attacks on Saudi Arabia. Contending that the Houthis had employed a modified version of ballistic missiles from their own inventory,[104] Tehran rejected the panel's findings, criticising it for refusing to disclose its sources and accusing it of political motivations.[105]

Ayatollah Khamenei called the UN allegation 'a lie', adding that, 'Yemen is surrounded. It is not possible to send them anything. If we could, instead of sending them one missile we would be sending them hundreds of missiles. But that is not possible.'[106] At the same time, Western sources continued accusing Iran of training the Houthis in irregular warfare and use of drones and missiles.[107]

Amid the ongoing debate regarding Iran's transfer of missiles and missile parts to the Houthis, former president Saleh met a brutal end. On 4 December 2017, a grenade struck his vehicle as he was trying to flee into Saudi-controlled territory. To ensure his death, a Houthi sniper shot him in the head. This marked the closing act of the relationship between the Houthis and Saleh, who had been both enemies and one-time allies. Before his death, Saleh had reportedly and unsuccessfully sought Iran's mediation with the Houthis, offering to help Iran expand its influence in southern Yemen.[108] An influential conservative newspaper with close ties to Ayatollah Khamenei editorialised that Saleh was a Saudi intelligence operative plotting a coup against the Houthis and got what was coming to him.[109] The Saudis, on the other hand, accused Iran of being responsible for the assassination.[110]

One of the key events in the civil war that profoundly impacted Riyadh's strategic calculations was the September 2019 attack on two major Saudi oil facilities in Abqaiq and Khurais by drones and missiles, some of which cost as little as $20,000 to build.[111] The kingdom's leadership was disorientated as its US-made sophisticated and expensive air defence system failed to protect the heart of its massive oil industry. This time, Riyadh's reaction to both the Houthis and Tehran was unexpectedly restrained.[112] Although the Houthis promptly claimed responsibility, Secretary of State Pompeo accused Iran of masterminding and executing the attacks, a charge Tehran vehemently denied. But the Saudi leadership was disappointed by the US reaction: despite its rhetorical denunciation of Tehran, Washington took no punitive measures against Iran. The UN Panel of Experts cleared the Houthis of responsibility and refrained from implicating Iran. Initially, UN Secretary-General Guterres confirmed that the United Nations 'is unable to independently corroborate that the cruise missiles and unmanned aerial vehicles used in these attacks are of Iranian origin'.[113] However, he later reversed his position, acknowledging that the drones and missiles 'were of Iranian origin', but stopped short of directly implicating Iran.[114]

In the court of Western public opinion, Iran was identified as the culprit for the attack on Saudi Arabia's vital oil facilities. Tehran was accused of training the Houthis in 'assembling, managing and repairing drones'.[115] Furthermore, it was reported that Iran had meticulously planned the missile attacks four months in advance as retaliation against the US for withdrawing from the nuclear deal. General Hossein Salami, IRGC commander, reportedly told a select group of the most senior military and intelligence officers that, 'It is time to take out our swords and teach them [the US] a lesson.' The attacks were reportedly authorised by Ayatollah Khamenei, 'but with strict conditions: Iranian forces must avoid hitting any civilians or Americans'.[116] But these assertions remain speculative.

Iran unconvincingly denied any involvement in the attacks on Saudi Arabia's oil facilities, using convoluted language to sow ambiguity regarding its precise role. Clearly, Tehran intended to strike a balance – demonstrating its power while avoiding responsibility for the attacks. On one hand, Rostam Qasemi, a senior IRGC official, stated that Houthis' missiles and drones used in the attacks were domestically manufactured in Yemen, 'with limited advisory and military assistance from Iran'.[117] On the other hand, the Iranian Foreign Ministry promptly refuted Qasemi's claim, stressing that Iran's support was strictly political and ideological.[118] Further complicating the situation, Brigadier General Abolfazl Shekarchi, a spokesperson of the Iranian armed forces, said, 'we provided them [Yemenis] with the experiences in technology in the defence sphere'.[119] Iran quickly moved into damage-control mode by clarifying that what Shekarchi actually meant was 'the capabilities of Yemeni Army and the Ansarallah [the Houthis] to design and manufacture missiles and UAVs [unmanned aerial vehicles] domestically'.[120]

Following the strikes on the oil facilities, additional missile attacks targeted the kingdom.[121] In 2021, Saudi Arabia reported a total of 430 missile and 851 drone attacks against the kingdom since 2015, killing 59 civilians.[122]

Iran and the Ceasefire of 2022

By 2018, 'Yemen, as a State, has all but ceased to exist.'[123] Saudi Arabia's extensive aerial bombardment of Yemen had failed to subdue the Houthi forces or restore Mansur Hadi. It had left the country in ruins, leading to an unprecedented man-made famine. The kingdom was accused of conducting a 'campaign of genocide' by a 'synchronized attack' on all aspects of life in Yemen, only possible with the complicity of the United States and United Kingdom.[124]

Numerous factors contributed to Saudi Arabia's inability to achieve its strategic objectives in Yemen. The major problem was that Saudi Arabia rushed into the conflict, in a state close to 'a panic with no end game in sight'. At the heart of its strategy was the flawed assumption that sheer air power, without deploying ground troops, could result in victory. This strategy was likely driven by concerns over potential high casualties for Saudi Arabia in Yemen and the risk of complicating Mohammad bin Salman's succession process. Furthermore, Riyadh relied on Yemeni forces loyal to President Mansur Hadi and proxy groups it funded.[125] However, controlling these forces remotely from Riyadh proved complicated and difficult. Adding to these challenges, Saudi Arabia initially hoped that its allies, such as Pakistan, Oman, and Egypt, would provide military assistance, but they did not.

Saudi Arabia also encountered inconsistent support from the United States, and at times, even criticism.[126] Nevertheless, both the US and Britain provided logistical and intelligence assistance for Saudi Arabia's military operations, while avoiding direct intervention in the civil war. Initially, President Obama voiced reservations about the wisdom of Saudi Arabia's military intervention in Yemen. As one US official recently remarked about the early phase of the civil war, 'We know we might be getting into a car with a drunk driver.'[127] However, neither the

US nor Britain were willing to halt their lucrative multi-billion-dollar arms sales of advanced weaponry to the kingdom. Furthermore, both countries, like Saudi Arabia, opposed Iran's backing of the Houthis and its military presence in the Arabian Peninsula. Therefore, despite their reservations, they supported Saudi Arabia's war efforts. Simultaneously, as the US and other global powers had signed a nuclear deal with Iran in 2015, the United States wisely attempted to strike a delicate balance between Iran and Saudi Arabia. This prompted President Obama to suggest that Iran and Saudi Arabia should learn to coexist harmoniously in the region. During Trump's presidency, there was a notable shift from Obama's policies towards the kingdom, as the US provided robust support for Saudi Arabia's war efforts. Around four months into Trump's presidency, King Salman surprised many by appointing his son, Mohammed bin Salman, as crown prince, thereby removing Mohammad bin Nayef, his nephew, from the position. Trump refrained from opposing this change in Saudi Arabia's domestic politics. In fact, he gave it his full support, significantly improving relations with the kingdom. However, under President Joe Biden, US–Saudi relations initially became somewhat strained, but later improved. During the presidential campaign, Biden pledged to isolate Saudi Arabia as a 'pariah' nation, citing its human rights atrocities, its involvement in the civil war in Yemen, and the murder of journalist Jamal Khashoggi. He also pledged to discontinue all American support for 'offensive operations' in Yemen. As president, however, he has continued arms sales to the kingdom, while pressuring the kingdom to agree to a ceasefire with the Houthis.[128]

Another factor that complicated Saudi Arabia's Yemen strategy was its disagreements with the UAE, its main regional supporter. The Saudi-backed forces were occasionally undermined by the Southern Transitional Council, a secessionist organisation consisting of several Yemeni groups that advocate separation of southern Yemen from the rest of the country and is often supported by the UAE. While the UAE was primarily interested in expanding its commercial and political influence over the region near the Bab al-Mandab Strait, Saudi Arabia, sharing long borders with Yemen, was deeply invested in the overall stability of the entire country. The UAE-backed separatist forces became so formidable that the UN Panel of Experts urged the UAE 'to refrain from taking actions that may undermine the sovereignty and territorial integrity of Yemen'.[129] Saudi Arabia ultimately brokered the Riyadh Agreement in 2019 between the UAE-aligned Southern Transitional Council and the Mansur Hadi government, ending their simmering dispute.[130] Subsequently, the UAE withdrew most of its modest military forces from Yemen. Iran and the Houthis, however, denounced the agreement as a sinister plot to place Yemen under the 'trusteeship' of Saudi Arabia.[131]

By 2022, it became abundantly clear that Saudi Arabia could neither break the stubborn stalemate between the warring factions in the civil war nor impose its will on Yemen. After seven years of a bloody and destructive civil war, Ansarallah/Houthis, the government of Yemen, and Saudi Arabia finally submitted to reality and accepted a ceasefire in April 2022, brokered by the UN Envoy Hans Grunberg. Following the ceasefire, Saudi Arabia pressured the ineffective Hadi to resign and established a Presidential Leadership Council to run South Yemen. Headed by Rashad al Alimi, a commander of the Yemen army, this council primarily comprised supporters of Saudi Arabia and the UAE, including the Southern Transitional Council and the Saudi-backed Aslah party.[132] Mohammad Abdelsalam, Ansarallah's chief negotiator, dismissed the removal of Mansur Hadi and the formation of the Presidential Council as nothing more than a 'reshuffling of mercenaries' backed by Saudi Arabia. Nevertheless, Iran supported the ceasefire. Ayatollah Khamenei offered some 'friendly' advice to the Saudis after the agreement: 'Why are you continuing a war you know you cannot win? Is there a possibility of the Saudis winning the war in Yemen? It is not possible.'[133]

The much-needed ceasefire resulted in a significant reduction in violence but did not end the civil war. In late 2022, Yemen's foreign affairs minister, Ahmed Awad bin Mubarak, publicly announced the government's intention to designate the Houthis as a terrorist organisation in response to their attacks in southern Yemen. Furthermore, the Presidential Council accused Iran of supplying the Houthis with suicide drones, an allegation Iran denied.[134] Soon after this announcement, the US Navy intercepted a fishing trawler carrying munitions and explosive materials in the Gulf of Oman in December 2022.[135] The US accused Iran of providing weapons and narcotics to Yemen as late as 2023.[136] Iran denied the allegation.

Iran–Saudi Rapprochement and Post-Ceasefire Yemen

After eight years of a devastating civil war, the Ansarallah/Houthis seem to have won but Yemen has lost, and its future is uncertain. The much-needed Iran–Saudi rapprochement has surely played a positive role in reducing violence in Yemen. Yemen has become a broken country, grappling with a humanitarian catastrophe. With the UN-sponsored ceasefire holding in Yemen, and Iran and Saudi Arabia resuming diplomatic relations in March 2023 – which were severed after the egregious burning of the Saudi consulate in Mashhad, Iran, in 2016 – there is now cautious optimism that peace could prevail in Yemen, and its much-needed reconstruction could begin.

Iran has achieved its top strategic objectives in Yemen: establishing a presence, albeit tenuous, in the country and assisting in the empowerment of the Houthis. Today, Iran exercises more power in Yemen than at any point in recent years. It has built deterrence and retaliatory capabilities against Saudi Arabia, helping to transform the civil war into a quagmire for the kingdom on its vulnerable southern flanks. Moreover, Iran has integrated the Houthis as new members of the Axis of Resistance it founded over two decades ago, solidifying its position as a regional power. The significance of this development was evident when, in response to the conflict in Gaza from 7 October 2023, the Houthis launched drone and missile attacks towards Israel to exert pressure for a ceasefire. Furthermore, they targeted cargo ships in the Red Sea, causing havoc in international commerce and diverting traffic away from the Suez Canal. In retaliation, the US and its allies conducted airstrikes against the Houthis and the US reinstated the Houthis as a designated terrorist entity.

Iran's support for the Houthis indirectly harmed the Iranian economy and escalated tensions with Saudi Arabia, many other Arab countries, and the United States, resulting in more Western sanctions against Iran. Ironically, the direct economic cost for Iran's intervention has been rather limited, substantially less than in Iraq, Syria, Lebanon and Gaza. Although there is no credible estimate of the expenditures associated with Iran's support for the Houthis, it is estimated that Iran has been spending 'only a few million dollars a year on the war', whereas Saudi Arabia was spending 'at least $5–6 billion a month'.[137]

Iran's power in Yemen is frequently exaggerated and its complex relationship with the Houthis often misconstrued. Tehran lacks the power to impose its will over the Houthis, let alone Yemen. Furthermore, the Houthis are not Iran's proxy and, as two Israeli experts observed, are not 'a tool for Iran's advancement'.[138] Nevertheless, Tehran shares some strategic goals with the Houthis, which explains why it has conveniently overlooked the atrocities committed by the Houthis, such as their blatant violation of human rights and acts of sexual violence against women.[139]

While Iran has been an important player in the civil war, it did not cause it. Iran capitalised on the opportunities that arose from that bloody conflict, which was exacerbated by sectarian divisions, regional disparities, tribal affiliation, and Saudi intervention. Much like other actors in the civil war, Iran tried to advance its own agenda.

Despite Iran's gains in Yemen, Tehran must recognise the constraints of its power. Once the civil war ends, Yemen will require the financial support of Saudi Arabia and its allies to rebuild its war-ravaged economy.[140] In that process, Saudi Arabia is poised to play a far more influential role in Yemen than Iran.

Iran's Yemen strategy is based on strategic patience and playing the long game, aiming to position itself as a force to be reckoned with in the critical Bab al-Mandab Strait. This would enable Iran to become a significant player in two of the world's most vital straits: Hormuz and Bab al-Mandab. Nearly one fifth of the world's oil and substantial amounts of seaborne trade pass through the Hormuz Strait, and a significant volume of oil, fuel, and goods from the Indian Ocean traverse Bab al-Mandab to reach the Mediterranean Sea via the Suez Canal; the security of these two vital maritime routes is thus crucial for the global economy. The importance of Iran's alliance with the Houthis became apparent in the role it played during the conflict between Israel and Hamas, which we will now explore.

Chapter 8

Iran's Evolving Relations with Hamas and the Palestine Islamic Jihad

On the morning of 7 October 2023, a day after the fifty-year anniversary of the Yom Kippur War, militants from the Izz al-Din Qassam Brigades, the armed wing of Hamas, breached the Gaza–Israel barrier and stormed Israeli towns, kibbutzim, and military centres by land, sea, and air. This operation, Al-Aqsa Flood, was allegedly masterminded by Yahya Sinwar, the leader of Hamas in the Gaza Strip since 2017. Buoyed by their unexpected initial military successes, Palestinian insurgents embarked on a violent spree through civilian areas, perpetuating indiscriminate and indefensible atrocities and acts of terrorism that resulted in the loss of 1,200 Israeli lives, including Israeli soldiers, women, and children, and the capture of over 250 hostages. This unprecedented operation inflicted more Jewish casualties than on any single day since the Holocaust. Former Israeli prime minister Ehud Barak described it as 'the worst event in the country's history since independence.'[1] The operation also revealed an embarrassing security lapse for Israel, a country renowned for its advanced intelligence capabilities. In retaliation, Israel launched a massive campaign of aerial bombardment, followed by a ground invasion, pummelling the Strip, and forcing the evacuation of the northern area of the Gaza Strip. Israel's declared objective was to destroy Hamas as a military force and prevent Gaza from launching strikes against it. At the time of writing, the death toll among Gazans, as estimated by the Gaza Health Ministry, stands at 33,137, with 12,000 of those being children. According to Israel's military, 13,000 militants have been killed. Gaza now lies in ruins, with 55 per cent of its buildings either damaged or destroyed. More than 1.7 million Gazans, constituting about 70 per cent of the population, have been displaced. Additionally, 90,000 Israelis from border communities, representing less than 1 per cent of the population, have also been displaced.[2]

In Tehran, Ayatollah Khamenei lauded the operation, affirming Iran's uncompromising opposition to Israel and its unwavering support for Hamas and the Palestinian cause, while former president Ebrahim Raisi stressed that supporting the Palestinian cause is both a constitutional and religious responsibility.[3] The Islamic Republic's policies towards the Palestinians and Israel mark a sea-change from the pro-Israel stance Iran maintained during the era of the Shah. What motivated revolutionary Iran to adopt an anti-Israel stance as one of the fundamental tenets of its foreign policy? Why did the Islamic Republic initially back the secular Palestinian Liberation Organisation (PLO), and later extend its support to the Palestine Islamic Jihad (PIJ) and Hamas, two Sunni militant organisations operating in Gaza?[4] And how does Iran justify its support for these organisations – both designated as foreign terrorist organisations by the United States – and has its policy effectively served its national interests? As elsewhere in the Middle East, Iran's policies here are intricately entwined with its strategic rivalry with the United States and Israel.

Mohammad Reza Shah's Uneasy Alliance with Israel

Persia has a long history with the Jewish people. The founder of the Achaemenid empire, Cyrus the Great, is venerated in the Hebrew scriptures for emancipating the Jews from captivity by the Babylonians.

He allowed the Jews to return to Jerusalem, rebuild their ruined temple, and freely practise their faith. While some of them returned to Jerusalem, others chose to remain in Iran. Since that time, Iran's Jewish community has made immense and valuable contributions to Iranian civilisation.

Cyrus's role exercised an outsized influence in the Jewish historical imagination, well into the twentieth century. In 1917, when Britain issued the Balfour Declaration, promising a 'national home for the Jewish people' in Palestine, Jews across Eastern Europe displayed 'pictures of Cyrus and of George V side by side'.[5] Zionists took the declaration as an agreement that Mandatory Palestine would eventually become the Jewish homeland.

Three decades later, in 1947, Iran played a role on a small UN committee responsible for recommending who should govern Palestine following the end of the British Mandate. Iran, with two other countries, advocated for a single binational and federated structure while the majority supported the creation of two separate Palestinian and Jewish states. A modified version of the proposal by the majority was adopted by the UN General Assembly in November 1947 (Resolution 181), leading to the establishment of Israel. Iran voted against that resolution and against Israel's admission to the UN (Resolution 273).[6]

The Iranian government's public stance and voting patterns within the UN diverged from the behind-the-scenes pro-Israel inclinations prevalent among its elites. In fact, Iran played a relatively important role in the early evolution of Israel. From the beginning, the Iranian government tried to play a delicate balancing act: fostering friendly relations with the newly established state, maintaining amicable relations with Arab countries staunchly opposed to the creation of Israel, and avoiding antagonising a sizeable portion of Iranians whose sympathies lay with the Palestinian cause. To appease its population, officials would sometimes make token anti-Israel statements, while privately engaging in diplomacy with Israel.

After Turkey fully recognised Israel, Iran became the second Muslim-majority country to de facto recognise Israel in March 1950. This important decision was allegedly influenced by a $400,000 bribe paid by pro-Israel forces to Prime Minister Mohammad Sa'ed Maraghei who remained cognisant of the formidable opposition to Israel from influential segments of Iranian society.[7] However, Maraghei enjoyed the backing of Mohammad Reza Shah, who, keen on establishing strategic ties with the United States, nurtured a cordial relationship with Israel.

The foundation of Iran's friendly relations with Israel was laid after the 1953 coup against Mosaddegh.[8] Both pro-US, Iran and Israel found common ground in their strategic interests and shared aversion to pan-Arabism and communism. The Shah moved cautiously from the outset, primarily due to his 'concern for the Islamic sensibilities of his subjects', as reported by the CIA.[9] In an effort to mitigate its regional isolation, Israel formulated the 'periphery doctrine' during Prime Minister David Ben-Gurion's tenure. This doctrine promoted forging alliances with non-Arab countries, notably Iran, Turkey, and Ethiopia. Among those, Iran was singled out as the 'jewel in the crown of the alliance of periphery'.[10]

The pivotal moment in their bilateral relations occurred with Israel's involvement in the creation of SAVAK, Iran's intelligence agency, in 1957. Although the US played a crucial role in the formation of SAVAK, General Mansur Qadar, a former Iranian ambassador and senior SAVAK official, believed that 'the American intelligence operations and methods were superficial and lacked depth. The Israelis, on the other hand, looked for and found the roots and therefore the sources that nourished the enemy and the danger it represented.'[11] Mossad, Israel's intelligence agency, facilitated training and exchanged intelligence with its Persian counterparts. Along with the United States, Israel enjoyed unparalleled access to Iran's top security and intelligence apparatus.

In July 1960, when the Shah was firmly ensconced on his throne, he publicly reaffirmed Iran's de facto recognition of Israel and highlighted his plan to expand bilateral ties. This audacious declaration elicited strong condemnation from Arab governments, particularly from President Nasser of Egypt.12 Nasser severed diplomatic relations with Iran, and Radio Cairo labelled Iran as 'a base for Western operations against the Arabs'.[13] In August 1960, a gathering of 150 clerics at Al-Azhar, the pre-eminent Sunni Islamic centre of learning, issued a call for Muslims to wage *jihad* against the Shah.[14]

Despite Nasser's attacks on the Shah, Iran's relations with Israel flourished in the 1960s and 1970s, evolving into what David Menashri, one of Israel's top scholars of modern Iran, described as 'an informal strategic alliance'.[15] After the Arabs' humiliating defeat by Israel in the June 1967 war, most 'Iranian officials were privately delighted by Nasser's humiliation', they 'still felt compelled to voice their public support for the 'legitimate rights' of the Arab people'.[16] The Shah's sympathies, too, lay 'with the Israelis', as he considered Nasser Iran's sworn enemy.[17] It was not surprising that while major Arab oil producers declined to sell oil to Israel, Iran, as noted by the CIA, emerged as:

Israel's chief supplier of crude oil until Israel began operating the Sinai oil fields following its conquest of the territory in the Six-Day War. After Israel returned the fields to Egypt under the Sinai II Agreements in 1975, Iran once again became the chief source of oil, supplying about 70 percent of Israel's recruitment until 1979.[18]

In return, Israel assisted Iran in the fields of 'water resources and agriculture',[19] and 'regularly sold armaments to Iran ... mainly small arms, mortars, and ammunition; provided engine overhaul and maintenance support for Iran's air force and army and extended technical support to Iran's infant defence industry'.[20] During the oil embargo imposed by the Arab oil producers on the United States in retaliation for its support of Israel during the Yom Kippur War of October 1973, the Shah continued to provide discounted oil to Israel. In the two decades preceding the revolution, the presence of Israeli contractors and military advisors in Iran was so substantial that a Hebrew-language school was opened in Tehran for Israeli children.[21]

Despite improving bilateral relations, the Shah, seeking to expand Iranian power, began to foster closer ties with Arab countries in the 1970s, while subtly distancing himself from specific Israeli policies.[22] In a way, Israel and Iran were becoming friendly rivals in the Middle East. Following Nasser's death in 1970 and the decline of pan-Arabism, the Shah strengthened ties with Egypt and other moderate Arab countries. This shift was driven by a significant change in the Middle East's geopolitical balance. As the most powerful indigenous force in the

Persian Gulf, the Shah expanded his influence across the broader Middle East.

However, two major developments caused a fissure between Tehran and Tel Aviv. First, to Israel's chagrin, the Shah signed the Algiers Accords with Iraq in 1975, ending decades of hostility between the two countries. As a result, he withdrew support for Iraqi Kurds, effectively ending the Mossad–SAVAK–CIA axis that had provided financial and military backing to Mullah Mostafa Barzani to undermine Baghdad (Chapter 3). Second, arguably the most significant shift in the Shah's policy pertained to the Arab states' conflict with Israel on the issue of Palestine. By mid-1975, according to a CIA memo, Tel Aviv had 'shown some uneasiness over the recent improvement in Iran's relations with Arab governments'.[23] According to the same memorandum, 'The Shah has traditionally tended to regard conflict between Israel and the Arabs as serving Iranian interest. It occupied the Arabs and gave Iran a freer hand to pursue its interests in the Persian Gulf.' However, the memorandum concluded:

> The Shah condemns Israeli occupation of Arab territory, calls for a return to the boundaries existing before the 1967 conflict, and does not accept the change in status of Jerusalem.... And he has stressed the theme that Israeli intransigence is the main impediment to a settlement.[24]

In 1975, Iran also voted in favour of UN General Assembly Resolution 3379, which labelled Zionism as a 'form of racism and racial discrimination'.[25] The Shah even publicly criticised the Jewish lobby in the United States.[26]

Despite these differences, Israel and Iran, two natural allies, maintained a robust relationship until 1979.[27] With the advent of the Islamic Revolution, Israel lost its most important regional ally.

Anti-Israel Discourse in the Clerical Establishment

Iranian Jews lived in peace in pre-revolutionary Iran, as the Shah's government pursued policies that were generally supportive of them.

However, anti-Israel, anti-Zionist, and at times anti-Semitic sentiments proliferated among both secular and particularly Islamic opponents of the Shah, similar to the simmering anti-Americanism. These anti-Israel proclivities intensified in the 1960s and 1970s when many present leaders of the Islamic Republic, nationalists and leftists who were based in Lebanon, Syria, and Iraq, forged ideological bonds with Palestinian militants.

In Iranian society, the reaction of the Shia clerical establishment to the founding of Israel was by far the most vehement. Shia clerics denounced Israel as an 'illegitimate' entity imposed by Western colonialism to divide Muslims. This opposition gained traction when Ayatollah Abolghasem Kashani (1882–1962) exerted pressure on Mosaddegh's popular government to revoke Iran's de facto recognition of Israel in 1952.[28] While Mosaddegh did not yield, he closed the Iranian consulate in Jerusalem in the early 1950s, citing 'budgetary constraints' as the official reason. Some Islamic Republic sources claim, unpersuasively, that the Mosaddegh government revoked Iran's de facto recognition of Israel.[29]

In the 1960s, Ayatollah Khomeini took up the mantle of anti-Israel politics. He consistently voiced his outrage about 'the Shah's cooperation with Israel' and accused Tel Aviv of 'helping to keep the Shah in power'.[30] Following the June Uprising of 1963, Khomeini's students at the Feyziyeh seminary in Qom presented a ten-point proposal to the government, which included the demand to 'eradicate Zionist and colonialist influence in Iran'.[31] Hashemi Rafsanjani, one of Khomeini's students, translated a book from Arabic to Persian about Palestine in the mid-1960s, dedicating it to 'More than one million displaced people [Palestinians] who, due to the crimes committed by colonialists and deceitful Zionists, were compelled to forsake all their possessions and currently [are] living in extreme poverty'.[32] SAVAK banned the book and imprisoned Rafsanjani. The opposition to Israel among pro-Khomeini clerics was so vocal that SAVAK warned them in the early 1960s, when Khomeini emerged as a major opposition figure to the Shah, not to discuss Israel from their pulpits.[33]

During his exile in Iraq from 1965 to 1978, Khomeini, recognising the fervent anti-Israel sentiments prevalent in the Arab world, grew increasingly vocal in his condemnation of Israel as he cultivated new relationships with the Palestinian resistance. In 1967, he penned an open letter to Prime Minister Amir Abbas Hoveyda, delivering a stern warning against forging 'an alliance of brotherhood with Israel, this enemy of Islam and the Muslims who has displaced more than a million helpless Muslims!'[34] A year later, he issued a ruling that it would be permissible for the faithful to allocate part of their religious tax to the Palestinian mujahedin.[35] Meanwhile, Khomeini's followers built a small anti-Shah and anti-Israel network in Lebanon, collaborating with militant Palestinians.

Anti-Israel sentiments were not limited to Islamist factions. Anti-imperialism and anti-Zionism were hallmarks of leftist and secular nationalists. This hostile attitude towards Israel found its way into Iran's literary circles, particularly after the June 1967 war, through figures like Ali Shariati, recognised as the intellectual architect of the Islamic Revolution, and Jalal Al-e Ahmad, who visited Israel in 1963 and wrote a book that was complimentary about the kibbutzim.[36] In March 1978, a group of prominent nationalist and Islamic-nationalist dissidents, including figures such as Karim Sanjabi, the leader of the National Front, wrote a letter to the UN Secretary-General, vehemently condemning the presence of Israeli troops in Lebanon and demanding their immediate and unconditional withdrawal.[37]

Shortly before the revolution, Khomeini's opposition to Israel was displayed on the global stage. In response to a letter from Yasser Arafat, leader of the Palestine Liberation Organization (PLO), Khomeini expressed gratitude for Arafat's support and reaffirmed his staunch opposition against Israel. He even accused 'Israeli soldiers' of assisting the Shah to quash the revolutionary movement, despite a lack of supporting evidence.[38] Tel Aviv was aware of Khomeini's animosity towards it. Its ambassador to Iran, Uri Lubrani, asked his American counterpart to urge the Shah's opponents to cease making anti-Semitic comments, or risk tarnishing their global image.[39] The message had no impact on Khomeini and his followers. In late 1978, while in Paris, Khomeini unequivocally declared that after the revolution, Iran would sever all ties with Israel. He proved to be true to his word.

The Islamic Republic's Fleeting Honeymoon with Arafat

As soon as Khomeini returned to Iran in February 1979, he broke off relations with Israel. Even before cementing anti-Americanism as the fundamental tenet of Iran's foreign policy, he laid down an anti-Israel and pro-Palestine policy as a foundation. This shift was motivated more by Khomeini's commitment to pan-Islamism than safeguarding Iran's national interests. It reflected the sentiment of a country deeply immersed in the fever of revolutionary idealism and at war with the prevailing global order. This paradigm change was perhaps designed to 'legitimize Iran's Islamic leadership in a matter that historically had been infused with Arab nationalism and widely supported by Arab leaders'.[40] Khomeini's objective was to Islamise the Palestinian cause while advocating for the eradication of the state of Israel.[41]

Yasser Arafat, leader of PLO, became the first foreign leader to visit Iran in February 1979, less than three weeks after Khomeini's triumphant return to his homeland. Iranian revolutionaries, enamoured of the Palestinian cause, warmly welcomed Arafat as a hero. Iranian revolutionaries would likely have treated Arafat with far less fanfare and admiration if they had been aware that in 1969, the Shah, in his efforts to cultivate favour with the Arab world, had generously provided Arafat with a $500,000 gift, and that Arafat had referred to the Shah as '*akhi*' or brother.[42]

In Tehran, Arafat declared, 'a new era has begun between Iran and Palestine'.[43] In a highly publicised move, the key to the Israeli embassy in Tehran was handed over to Arafat, and the street where it was located was renamed Palestine Street. Arafat was also granted an audience with Ayatollah Khomeini. Much to Arafat's satisfaction, Khomeini denounced the Camp David Accords between Egypt and Israel, labelling them a 'crime against the Muslims'.[44]

Beneath the veneer of unity, hidden tensions were simmering between Iran and the PLO. For one thing, the PLO was not under Khomeini's thumb, and he resented it. For another, Khomeini didn't hesitate to emphasise that the path to liberating Palestine demanded an unwavering commitment to Islamic principles. This emphasis implicitly challenged Arafat's secular ideology, illuminating why Khomeini and Arafat 'just didn't hit it off well'.[45] To Islamise the Palestinian conflict with Israel, Khomeini called the day he urged all Muslims to express solidarity with Palestinians Quds Day – the Arabic title for Jerusalem – and set the date as the last Friday of Ramadan.[46]

Khomeini and the PLO initially formed a marriage of convenience based on their mutual hostility towards Israel. However, their disagreements widened over time. Despite this gradual estrangement, they never formally parted ways.

The limits of the PLO's influence in Iran and Iran's sway over the PLO became evident in the first two years of the revolution. In August 1980, the CIA reported that Khomeini had invited the PLO to assist in training the IRGC, but it 'apparently played little role in the formation of the Guards because many Iranian officials, including regular military officers, feared that the Palestinians would gain too much influence in the Iranian military'.[47] Arafat also dispatched a delegation to Tehran to mediate the release of American hostages, hoping to repair the PLO's tainted image in the US. However, the PLO delegation left Tehran, 'extremely offended and disappointed by the cool treatment' they received.[48]

The PLO's stance on the Iran–Iraq War further strained its relationship with Tehran. In contrast to Syria, which supported Iran, the PLO initially maintained neutrality. Arafat 'hoped to mediate the differences between the two sides and travelled to both capitals in the early days of the war, but his mission failed, leading to strains with both sides', the CIA reported.[49] Following this unsuccessful endeavour, the PLO increasingly leaned towards Baghdad, its major financial supporter. The disagreements between the two sides again came to light, this time at the Non-Aligned Movement conference in Harare, Zimbabwe, in September 1986. During the meeting, Arafat implored Iran to end the war, emphasising its detrimental impact on the Palestinian cause with the statement 'enough is enough'. He presented a peace proposal that avoided identifying Iraq as the instigator of the war, directly clashing with Iran's key precondition for peace talks. In response, President Khamenei, who attended the meeting, harshly criticised Arafat: 'It was expected that in his [Arafat's] speech yesterday morning, he would talk about the successes achieved by the Palestinian nation in fighting against the aggression of the Zionist regime, rather than encouraging others [Iraq] to support the aggression [against Iran].'[50]

Iran's policy towards the PLO was intrinsically intertwined with its complex interactions with Israel. Despite his anti-Israel policy, Khomeini wisely refrained from direct military confrontation with Israel. When Israel invaded Lebanon in 1982 amid the Iran–Iraq War, there were reckless calls from militant Iranians to dispatch troops to Lebanon to fight Israel. Acutely aware of the military disparity between Iran and Israel, Khomeini dismissed this call to action.[51] Nevertheless, he approved the establishment of Hezbollah in 1982 to combat Israel in Lebanon.

For its part, Israel, uncertain about the fate of Iran's infant revolution, adopted a wait-and-see approach towards Tehran. It has been suggested that Tel Aviv was discreetly exploring the possibility of re-establishing some form of relations with the Islamic Republic. Israel seemed to believe that revolutionary idealism would eventually give way to pragmatism, ultimately prompting Tehran to temper its overt belligerence and establish some form of relationship with Tel Aviv.[52] Certainly, this prevailing attitude of guarded optimism did not wield as much influence over Israel's policy towards Iran as did its strategic calculus. In the initial phases of the Iran–Iraq War, according to Tel Aviv University's Institute for National Security Studies, Israel secretly sold $500 million worth of spare parts to Iran from 1981 to 1983 – a claim denied by Tehran.[53] Tel Aviv's decision was rooted in its assumption that a militarily formidable Iraq prevailing over Iran posed a more immediate threat to Israeli national security interests than a militarily weakened Iran. However, as the conflict dragged on, and the prospect of an Iraqi defeat grew more palpable, both the United States and Israel adjusted their strategies to thwart Iran from achieving an outright victory.

Iran and the Islamisation of Palestinian Politics

During the seven-year interregnum between 1988 and 1995, three events reshaped the strategic landscape of the Middle East and altered

Iran's relations with Israel, the PLO, and militant Palestinian organisations. This transformation commenced in December 1988 amid the first Intifada, when Arafat recognised Israel, renounced armed struggle, condemned terrorism, and actively engaged in the new US-sponsored peace process. This major change unfolded against the backdrop of the collapse of the Soviet Union and the end of the Cold War in 1991, as well as Iraq's decisive defeat in the Persian Gulf War in the same year.[54]

One of the earliest manifestations of the emerging unipolar world dominated by the United States was the signing of the Oslo Accord by Israel's Prime Minister Yitzhak Rabin and PLO Chairman Arafat in 1993, followed by the signing of the Oslo II Accords in 1995 by Israel and the PLO. Together, these historic accords set in motion a phased and peaceful process aimed at achieving a two-state solution, involving the establishment of limited self-governance by the Palestinian Authority in the West Bank and the Gaza Strip, with the eventual goal of creating a Palestinian state living in peace and harmony alongside Israel. Through these accords, Israel also recognised the PLO as the representative of the Palestinian people.

Tehran denounced the Oslo Accords as treasonous to the Palestinian cause. As a result, there was a shift in perception towards Arafat, who was once revered in Tehran as an icon of the Palestinian struggle, now becoming a pariah. At the same time, the geopolitical calculus between Iran and Israel underwent a shift starting in the 1990s. While Israel welcomed the destruction of much of the military capabilities of its arch-enemy Iraq, it also grew apprehensive because a debilitated Iraq after the Persian Gulf War could no longer serve as a counterbalance to Iran. Moreover, Israel had abandoned the delusion that moderate elements would prevail in Iran's power struggle.[55] Having signed two peace treaties – with Egypt in 1979 and Jordan in 1994 – Israel began to improve relations with Arab countries while undermining and demonising the Islamic Republic, which Tel Aviv seemed to perceive as a rising and dangerous rival.[56] In 1992, Israeli Foreign Minister Shimon Peres warned that 'Iran is the greatest threat and greatest problem in the Middle East, because it seeks the nuclear option while holding a highly dangerous stance of extreme religious militancy.'[57]

Years later, Ahmadinejad's Holocaust denial and egregious call for Israel's eradication provided Israel with another powerful narrative to portray Iran as the major source of regional instability. This effectively sidelined the Israel–Palestine conflict and diverted attention away from Israel's contentious settlements in the Occupied Territories, and created the conditions for Israel to improve relations with many Arab countries. These seismic developments in the first half of the 1990s auspiciously removed major threats for Iran from its north (the Soviet Union) and west (Iraq), allowing the country to reallocate its precious resources to fortify its regional position. In this new environment, Tehran emerged as a vocal critic of the Oslo Accords and Israel. For Ayatollah Khamenei, opposing Israel and supporting the Palestinians was not just an ideological imperative, as it was under Khomeini's rule. It also became a necessity to expand Iranian power abroad and establish deterrence against Israel by securing strategic depth along its vulnerable borders in Lebanon, Syria and the Gaza Strip.[58] The Islamic Republic began to portray Israel as a major security threat collaborating with the US to undermine its sovereignty and prosperity. Tehran then used the Oslo Accords as an instrument to gradually Islamise the Palestinian cause by arming Palestinian Islamists and opening a new front against Israel among Palestinians in the Gaza Strip in harmony with its call for the destruction of Israel.

As a result of the changes in Israel's and Iran's calculations, and in the wake of the US invasions of Afghanistan in 2001 and Iraq in 2003, the two countries entered a 'shadow war', opting to avoid direct kinetic confrontation by largely waging their battles in other countries and often in grey areas. This phase of Iran–Israel encounters coincided with the rise of General Soleimani as the architect and implementer of Iran's regional strategies, including its connection to Hamas and the PIJ.

Iran and the Founding of the Palestine Islamic Jihad

When Arafat made history by recognising Israel in 1988, President Khamenei was a few months away from succeeding Ayatollah Khomeini as Iran's Supreme Leader.[59] He took a dim view of Arafat's efforts towards peace, stating: 'Yasser Arafat is no longer interested in fighting. His current stance mirrors Anwar Sadat's position a decade ago, emphasising negotiation with Israel, reconciliation with the United States, and ending the struggle against Israel.'[60] As the Supreme Leader, Khamenei's attitude towards Arafat and Israel grew increasingly hostile. In 2014, nearly a decade after Arafat's death, Khamenei reflected on his life, asserting:

> They couldn't tolerate even someone as accommodating toward the Zionists as Yasser Arafat. They besieged him, humiliated him, poisoned him, and destroyed him. It is not like that if you don't show power to the Zionists, they will show mercy on you. Absolutely not. The only remedy that exists before the demise of this regime is for the Palestinians to confront it with power; if they deal forcefully, there is a possibility that this wolf-like regime might give in.[61]

To bolster alternatives to Arafat, Khamenei increased Iranian support for the Islamisation of Palestinian politics well before Arafat's death. This served his overarching agenda of promoting resistance as a model of fighting Israel and the West, and expanding Iranian regional power.[62] While some Israeli experts suggest that Tehran's ultimate objective is 'to utilize the Palestinian narrative as leverage its attempts to achieve regional hegemony and maintain its leadership in the Muslim world', attributing such grand ambitions to Iran's Palestine policy oversimplifies the real dynamics motivating Iran and exaggerates its actual capabilities.[63]

The Islamisation of Palestinian politics began with the establishment of the Palestine Islamic Jihad (PIJ) in 1981 and Hamas in 1987 in Gaza.[64] The process accelerated after the signing of the Oslo Accords in 1993 and 1995. In fact, it is their utter disdain for the Oslo Accords that has cemented the bonds between the two Sunni organisations of the PIJ and Hamas and Tehran. While there is no evidence to suggest that Tehran played any role in the creation of either organisation, it did support and influence their evolution, particularly following the eruption of the Palestinian Intifada against Israel in 1987.

The PIJ was founded in the Gaza Strip by Fathi Shaqaqi and the cleric Abd al Aziz Awda in 1981.[65] However, Shaqaqi played a bigger role than Awda in expanding the organisation.[66] He was born in a refugee camp in Gaza in 1951. After completing his undergraduate studies in the West Bank, he went to Egypt, where he obtained a medical degree in the mid-1970s. Like many in his generation, he was initially drawn to the ideas of Hassan al-Banna, who founded the Muslim Brotherhood in 1928. A pioneering Islamic thinker, al-Banna believed in countering Western colonialism through an Islamic revival. After joining the Muslim Brotherhood, young Shaqaqi quickly grew disillusioned with what he perceived as its political quietism and excessive focus on providing social services to the needy.

Shaqaqi's political philosophy was also influenced by Ayatollah Khomeini's writings on the intricate relationship between Islam and governance, as well as by the triumph of Iran's Islamic Revolution. Using the pseudonym Fathi Abdulaziz, Shaqaqi authored a pamphlet titled *Imam Khomeini: The Alternative Islamic Solution*. This pamphlet, published in Egypt shortly after Iran's revolution, marked the first Arabic publication to delve into Khomeini's worldview. Khomeini epitomised what Shaqaqi sought to emulate: a leader who mobilised millions of people under the banner of Islam to overthrow a well-fortified and armed regime.[67]

Shaqaqi argued that Palestine should hold a central position in the Islamic discourse, serving as a force to unify the Islamic *ummah* and transcend the Shia–Sunni divide – a sentiment that resonated with Tehran.[68]

Upon returning to Gaza from Egypt, Shaqaqi founded the PIJ. He felt that the Muslim Brotherhood, having neglected the plight of Palestinians still living under Israeli occupation, had lost its mantle of leadership. He also found the existing major Palestinian groups, particularly the PLO, dominated by secular nationalists and socialists, to be inadequate. He believed that the PIJ symbolised the future of the Palestinian struggle because it synthesised the liberation of Palestine with the revitalisation of Islam.

It did not take long for Shaqaqi to embrace armed struggle, establish-ing a small underground group called Saraya al-Quds Brigades, or al-Quds Brigades, as the military wing of the PIJ. Shaqaqi's confrontations with Israeli security forces resulted in frequent interrogations and periods of incarceration. In 1987 he was released from prison and was deported by Israel to Lebanon, where his fate took a new turn. In Lebanon he reportedly met with Hezbollah operatives and forged ties with Tehran. Iranian sources have disclosed no information about the nature of these contacts. He eventually went to Syria where, under President Hafez Assad's protection, he expanded the scope of PIJ activities.

In the same year that Shaqaqi was deported to Lebanon, six PIJ prisoners managed to escape from an Israeli jail in Gaza, leading to confrontations between Israeli security forces and Palestinians. These clashes sparked the first Intifada in 1987, a popular uprising in the West Bank and Gaza opposing Israel's occupation and advocating for the establishment of an independent Palestinian state, which captured global headlines.

In 1988, Shaqaqi embarked on a fateful journey to Tehran to meet with the top decision makers of the Islamic Republic, leading to enduring relations between the PIJ and the Islamic Republic. Most importantly, he was granted a brief audience with Ayatollah Khomeini, shortly prior to Khomeini's death in June 1989. Khomeini, sadly, urged Shaqaqi to persist in the armed struggle against Israel, emphasising that: 'Jews immigrating to Palestine are different from Jews in other countries. Jews in Palestine, regardless of their characteristics, whether armed or unarmed, governmental, or non-governmental, are all considered usurpers and enemies.'[69] In other words, Palestinian militants must consider all Israelis to be legitimate targets of their violence. Robert Fisk claimed, without providing the source, that Iran 'pledged millions of dollars for the Palestinian resistance' following that meeting.[70] While the Islamic Republic has not officially disclosed the exact extent of its financial support for the PIJ, it is widely acknowledged that it has been one of the primary sources of funding for the organisation.

Tehran favoured Shaqaqi over Arafat, despite Arafat's towering stature and popularity, because Shaqaqi was a committed Islamist with close ideological ties to the Islamic Republic, rather than a secularist.

Additionally, Tehran welcomed Shaqaqi's policy of neutrality during the Iran–Iraq War, which stood in stark contrast to Arafat's support for Iraq. And, unlike the PLO, which relied on financial support from pro-Western Arab countries Tehran despised, the PIJ had limited support from the Arab countries, making it more susceptible to Tehran's influence.

Shortly after his initial visit, Shaqaqi returned to Tehran to attend Ayatollah Khomeini's funeral and reiterated his unwavering support for Khamenei.[71] In October 1991, coinciding with the US-sponsored Madrid Conference to revive the Arab–Israeli peace process, the Islamic Republic organised a parallel conference in Tehran in opposition to it. Once again, Shaqaqi, representing the PIJ, along with other militant Palestinian groups, participated. With the signing of the Oslo Accords, Shaqaqi, along with a few other militant organisations, formed an informal coalition against the accords and the principle of a two-state solution.

The PIJ intensified its activities against Israel and the Oslo Accords. On 22 January 1995, it carried out one of its first suicide attacks: the Beit Lid massacre, killing twenty-one IDF soldiers at a bus stop as they waited to go on their weekend leave. Less than four months later, another PIJ militant rammed his car into a bus full of soldiers heading to Kfar Darom and detonated a bomb, killing seven soldiers and one American civilian. The PIJ's declaration of war on Israel was unmistakable, and Israel stood prepared to respond in kind. By way of retribution, Israel's Kidon, a department within Mossad, tracked Shaqaqi down in Malta on his way back from Libya. On 26 October 1995, Shaqaqi was killed outside the Diplomat Hotel in Malta.[72] Islamic Jihad confirmed his death and vowed vengeance a few days later.

To honour the fallen leader, Ayatollah Khamenei condemned Israel for the assassination of Shaqaqi and praised him as 'one of those who followed the path of Iran's great Islamic revolution and the universal movement of Imam Khomeini and stood firm and defiant until the very end'.[73] Shaqaqi's death did not dampen relations between the PIJ and Tehran; the ideological affinity was too strong. In fact, Shaqaqi's successor, Ramadan Abdullah Shallah, improved them.

Shallah reportedly stated that the PIJ is another fruit of the 'Ayatollah Khomeini's fructuous tree'.[74] This close relationship, however, was not without tension, as the PIJ appeared determined to assert its independence and maintain some distance from Tehran. In the 2010s, much to Tehran's displeasure, the PIJ adopted a neutral stance during the Syrian civil war. Moreover, the PIJ declined to denounce Saudi Arabia's military intervention in Yemen against Ansarallah, an ally of Iran. In response, Tehran provided temporary and limited support to the Sabireen movement, founded in 2014 as a breakaway group from the PIJ, composed of purported converts to Shiism, and led by Hisham Salem.[75] The group was effectively dissolved in 2019 after Hamas arrested Salem. Despite these minor disputes, the PIJ has remained Iran's most trusted partner in Palestine, even though it lacks the massive popular support Hamas enjoys.

Reaching Out to Hamas

While Tehran was establishing close ties with the PIJ, it also cultivated a friendly relationship with Hamas, or Harakat al-Muqawama al-Islamiyya, the Islamic Resistance Movement, a militant organisation founded by Sheikh Ahmed Yassin in late 1987 during the first Intifada against the Israeli occupation. Hamas emerged mostly from the ranks of the Gaza branch of the Muslim Brotherhood. The Brotherhood initially advocated non-violent means against Israeli occupation and allocated much of its resources to providing charitable services for Palestinians. However, the PIJ's popularity among Palestinians, especially the youth, undeniably played a role in the decision to establish Hamas and later to form the Izz al-Din Qassam Brigades as its armed wing. The Brigades was named after the legendary Syrian militant and imam who opposed the British occupation of Palestine, making a doomed last stand in 1935 when he was surrounded by the British police near the hills of Jenin. As with the establishment of the PIJ, Tehran played no role in founding Hamas. Tehran only began providing financial and military support to Hamas years after its founding.[76]

Ayatollah Khamenei had ideological motivations for supporting Hamas that predate the Islamic Revolution. Long before Hamas emerged from the ranks of the Gaza branch of the Muslim Brotherhood,

Khamenei, then a young member of a small network of pro-Khomeini clerics opposing the Shah's regime in the 1960s, was drawn to the ideology and worldview embraced by the Muslim Brotherhood. Fascinated by literary pursuits, the young Khamenei translated a couple of books from Arabic, including *The Future of This Religion*, written by Sayyid Ibrahim Husayn Qutb (1906–1966), the chief theorist of the Muslim Brotherhood in the 1950s and 1960s. Qutb's writings marked a radical and violent phase in the evolution of the Muslim Brotherhood. Praised and condemned as one of the founders of modern Sunni Jihadism, Qutb, a prolific writer, denounced the West for keeping the Muslim world underdeveloped and corrupt, spreading decadence, materialism, and hedonism.[77] His solution for the salvation of the Islamic world was a return to the ways of the early days of Islam. Qutb was eventually convicted of plotting to assassinate the Egyptian president Gamal Abdel Nasser and was hanged in 1966. However, his ideas continue to resonate in the Islamic world.

Khamenei was incarcerated by SAVAK in the mid-1960s for his political activities and for the translation of one of Qutb's short books from Arabic into Persian, which was banned in Iran. During his defence testimony, Khamenei praised Qutb as an exceptional and inspirational Muslim thinker and an astute interpreter of the holy Quran. He harshly criticised SAVAK for banning the publication of a book that he claimed vehemently opposed colonialism and communism, and called for unity among all Muslims to safeguard their independence. He accused the prosecutor and SAVAK agents of censoring the book without bothering to read it and learn from its rich contents.[78]

Thirty-two years after his incarceration by SAVAK, Khamenei, in his capacity as Iran's Supreme Leader, met with Sheikh Ahmed Yassin, the founder and spiritual leader of Hamas, in Tehran in May 1998. In many ways, when it came to Palestine, the two leaders were ideological soulmates. Hamas's official charter, written in 1988, called for the destruction of Israel, which Khameini welcomed.[79] Khamenei praised the quadriplegic and blind sheikh and his followers as 'the real representatives of the Palestinian's Islamic resistance', adding that 'those who have tried to humiliate Palestine have no right to speak in the name of the greatness of Palestine', an unambiguous reference to the PLO and Arafat. Both leaders condemned the Nakba (catastrophe), meaning the forced expulsion of hundreds of thousands of Palestinians in 1948 by Israel. Many of these Palestinians ended up as refugees in neighbouring countries, with very few rights, or packed into Gaza, one of the most densely populated places on earth. Yassin agreed with Khamenei, asserting that 'Palestine belongs to all Muslims, and we will continue our struggle until the liberation of the Quds.'[80] The two leaders also rejected the Oslo Accords, agreed on the agenda to promote the Islamisation of Palestinian politics, and embraced armed resistance against Israel as a strategic choice.[81] Following this meeting, preparations were made to open an office for Hamas in Tehran.[82]

Hamas began to carry out its military operations against Israel starting in 1989 – when it abducted two Israeli soldiers. As of 2023, the CIA estimated that, in addition to Hamas's security forces, the Izz ad-Din Qassam Brigades have 20,000 to 25,000 fighters, while other sources have reported up to 40,000 fighters.[83] The evidence overwhelmingly suggests that Tehran provides financial and military assistance to both the PIJ and Hamas, although the extent remains ambiguous. But what's in it for Iran? What does it get from funding, arming, and training Sunni organisations in Palestine?

Dispute and Reconciliation with Hamas

While Iran was actively fostering closer relationships with Hamas and the PIJ, Israeli and American sources claimed in 2002 that Tehran had established a new alliance with the PLO through Russian mediation. The seizure of a shipment of 50 tons of allegedly Iranian-supplied weapons aboard the *Karine A* freighter, supposedly destined for the Palestinian Authority, was viewed as apparent evidence of this alliance. Tel Aviv accused Tehran of trying 'to create another base, besides its base in Lebanon' against Israel.[84] Both the Palestinian Authority and Tehran denied these allegations, with Tehran emphasising it 'had had no military relations with Arafat'.[85] Within a week of the seizure, President George W. Bush labelled Iran as a member of 'the Axis of Evil', effectively ending the unprecedented cooperation between revolutionary Iran and the US that started with toppling the Taliban in Afghanistan. Given the evident lack of trust between Tehran and Arafat, it seems improbable that the weapons shipping was part of Iran's new 'alliance' with Arafat. However, Iran was certainly seeking to create a presence in Gaza, not through Arafat's PLO, but through arming Hamas and the PIJ.

As early as 2008, Israeli experts warned that Hamas had become both an 'agent' of Tehran and an 'Iranian satellite' in Gaza.[86] However, Tehran's relationship with Hamas has been more intricate and contentious than assumed. Hamas has persistently sought to maintain its independence from Tehran.[87] Its policy during the Syrian civil war exemplifies the fractious nature of its relationship with Tehran.

From 2011 to 2017, during Iran's extensive and costly involvement in the tumultuous Syrian civil war, relations between Iran and Hamas remained strained. In Bashar Assad's hour of need, Hamas abandoned him and expressed support for his armed opposition, despite Assad having granted the group political sanctuary and freedom to operate from Damascus for years. In February 2012, Hamas relocated its headquarters from Damascus in Syria to Doha in Qatar, signalling its new policy towards the developing Syrian civil war. But Hamas wasn't acting out of a long-standing principle; rather, it was making rushed and opportunistic geopolitical calculations. At that time, Assad's regime appeared to be teetering on the edge of collapse, with the Syrian Muslim Brotherhood, a sister organisation of Hamas, waiting in the wings to take its place. Moreover, Hamas hoped to expand relations with the affluent Arab countries of the Persian Gulf.

The Arab Spring upheaval in Egypt was perhaps the principal reason behind Hamas's decision to distance itself from Assad's regime. On 11 February 2011, President Hosni Mubarak announced his resignation, after weeks of protests across Egypt. The Egyptian Muslim Brotherhood, officially outlawed since the time of Gamal Abdel Nasser, albeit tacitly tolerated, could now openly run in parliamentary elections under its own banner. Hamas's optimism about its alignment with Egypt was further reinforced when Mohammad Morsi, leader of the Muslim Brotherhood, won the presidential elections in Egypt in June 2012, sparking a political earthquake throughout the Arab world. In power, Morsi cultivated close ties with Hamas. One of his major achievements was brokering a ceasefire in a week-long armed conflict between Hamas and Israel in November 2012. Ismail Haniyeh, who led the Hamas government in Gaza at the time, travelled to Cairo and declared at a mosque, 'I salute all people of the Arab Spring, or Islamic winter, and I salute the heroic people of Syria who are striving for freedom, democracy and reform.'[88] Hamas's support for the Syrian opposition to Assad could not have been delivered more explicitly. It was also a stinging rebuke to the Islamic Republic.

Following the relocation of Hamas's headquarters in 2012, its deputy foreign minister Ghazi Hamad called relations with Iran 'no good at all' and acknowledged that 'there are disagreements, tensions, both within the political wing of Hamas – some who want to reach out to Saudi Arabia, others not – and the military wing, who want the weapons that Iran can bring.'[89] For years, Hamas was beset by a schism, with radical members of the Qassam Brigades pitted against the more accommodating political faction tasked with navigating international politics. Compounding this division were the political disagreements between Haniyeh and Khaled Mashal, the leader of Hamas outside the Gaza Strip who played a pivotal role in the relocation of Hamas's headquarters. Mashal leaned towards closer ties with Qatar and other Gulf countries, and favoured closer collaboration with Mahmoud Abbas, President of the Palestinian Authority, which Tehran opposed.[90] Tehran consistently sided with the armed wing of Hamas and with Haniyeh, even amid the disagreements with Hamas during the Syrian civil war.[91] It was not surprising, therefore, that Haniyeh visited Iran and met with Ayatollah Khamenei in February 2012 to appease Tehran and bolster the strained relationship.[92] Although Tehran never severed its relations with Hamas and always maintained its close ties with the Qassam Brigades,[93] tensions escalated further when Hamas declined to condemn Saudi Arabia for its military intervention in Yemen against the Houthis, whom Tehran supported during the Yemeni civil war.[94]

Hamas faced a dilemma: supporting Tehran would antagonise the Saudi kingdom and potentially jeopardise, even sever, its financial support from wealthy Persian Gulf countries. In both the Syrian and Yemeni contexts, Hamas's policy towards Tehran and the Arab world mirrored Arafat's stance. Both the PLO and Hamas tended to align with their Sunni Arab counterparts when faced with a choice between them and Iran. The Islamic Republic certainly recognised this stark reality but hesitated to publicly admit it or recalibrate its policy.

It did not take long for Hamas to realise that it had bet on the wrong horse in aligning itself with Egypt's Muslim Brotherhood and supporting Assad's opponents. Not only did its manoeuvre fail to strengthen Hamas's regional position, but it also seriously undermined its relations with Tehran. The epiphany came after the overthrow of President Morsi in a coup orchestrated by General Abdel Fattah el-Sisi in July 2013. Hamas had now lost its most powerful backer and its ideological sibling in the Arab world. Furthermore, by the mid-2010s, Hamas began to recalibrate its policy as it became increasingly clear that Assad was unlikely to lose the civil war and might even emerge victorious. Hamas, therefore, made a dramatic about-turn and reached out to Tehran again. Haniyeh visited Tehran in September 2015 and met with Ayatollah Khamenei, who warned him about infiltration 'by those who seek to compromise with Israel' – an unusually direct criticism from Khamenei who typically treated Hamas with kid gloves.[95]

Iran reconciled with Hamas after significant changes occurred in the highest echelons of that organisation's leadership. To Iran's satisfaction, Ismail Haniyeh assumed the role of head of Hamas's political bureau outside of Gaza, replacing Khaled Mashal. More importantly, Yahya Sinwar became Hamas Chief in Gaza. Sinwar always maintained close relations with the IRGC and was deeply involved in security-related issues.[96] He was born in 1962 in the Khan Younes refugee camp in Gaza and joined Hamas at a young age.[97] He was one of the first to join the Izz ad-Din Qassam Brigades, quickly becoming close to Mohammed Deif, its chief military strategist and leader. Sinwar helped to create Hamas's secret police, which was responsible for assassinating collaborators with Israel. After serving in an Israeli jail for more than two decades, he was released in a prisoner swap in 2011 and quickly emerged as one of the most powerful Hamas leaders.

In August 2017, Sinwar announced that, 'After years of tension due to the Syrian Civil War, the Hamas movement improved its relations with Iran, and today Iran is the biggest supporter of the Hamas movement.'[98] He declared that Iran had become 'the largest backer financially and militarily' of the Izz al-Din Qassam Brigades, describing this support as strategic.[99] A high-level Palestinian delegation, including Hamas representatives, also visited Tehran to attend President Hassan Rouhani's inauguration and sought to 'turn a new page'. Haniyeh met with Khamenei again in June 2021.[100] As a gesture of contrition, Hamas praised President Assad for giving them freedom of action when they operated from Damascus.[101] He 'appreciated and thanked the Islamic Republic of Iran for helping the Palestinian resistance with money and weapons'.[102] In June 2022, Hamas and Syria restored ties.

Relations between Hamas and Tehran have remained robust to this day. Even before Sinwar's 2017 announcement of improved Hamas–Tehran relations, Soleimani was providing multifaceted aid to Hamas. However, amidst this support, the critical question of how Tehran's backing of Hamas served Iranian national interests was often overlooked by the Islamic Republic.

Soleimani and the Arming of Hamas and PIJ

Hezbollah leader Hassan Nasrallah recalled that it was General Soleimani who formulated Iran's policy towards Hamas, integrating it into the Axis of Resistance, arming it, and providing it with financial support.[103] According to Nathan Sales, the ambassador-at-large and coordinator for counterterrorism at the State Department, Iranian funding for Hamas and other Palestinian groups reached its height at approximately $100 million annually in 2018. He also noted that Iranian support for 'other terrorists … comes close to one billion dollars' annually.[104] However, the precise amount and method by which Tehran transfers funds to Hamas remain unclear. At least in one case, Mahmood Zahar, one of the founders of Hamas, recounted that during his visit to Tehran in 2009, Soleimani provided him with $2 million in cash to support Hamas.[105]

Tehran has faced significant obstacles in supplying arms to Gaza due to Israel's stringent blockade and sophisticated surveillance capabilities. While Israel consistently accuses Iran of being the primary arms supplier for Hamas, Tehran refutes these claims, asserting that it has only provided technological expertise to Hamas. However, there is compelling evidence that Iran has secretly supplied weapons and technological expertise to Hamas through different channels. In 2021, Hamas acquired 'Fajr-3 and Fajr-5 rockets from Iran'.[106] However, Hamas also has its own sources for arms procurement and has domestically produced rockets 'with ranges of almost 100 miles, technically putting most of Israel within range'.[107] Concurrently, Hamas has also engaged in weapons smuggling through various channels, including transporting pieces through tunnels under the Egypt–Gaza border.[108] During the 2008–9 war between Israel and Hamas, the Palestinian Information Center claimed that Hamas, with assistance from Mohammad al-Zawari and his Tunisian team, had domestically produced thirty drones, called Aba'bill, that were used during the conflict.[109]

No one exerted a more significant influence on shaping Iran's Levant policy and its relationship with militant Palestinian organisations than Qasem Soleimani. The Islamic Republic only began to disclose some of Soleimani's ideas and involvement in Palestinian politics after his assassination in 2020. At that juncture, Ayatollah Khamenei stated that the US plan was to:

> keep the Palestinians in a weak state so that they don't dare [to fight]. This man [Soleimani] filled the hands of the Palestinians. He did something that a small area, like the Gaza Strip, stands tall against the Zionist regime.... These were done by Haj Qasem Soleimani. He made them able to stand, to be able to resist. This is what our Palestinian brothers have repeatedly told me.[110]

Indeed, it was Soleimani who, despite the estrangement between Hamas and Tehran during the early stages of the Syrian civil war, played the crucial role in keeping Hamas within the Iran-led Axis of Resistance.

Soleimani viewed the liberation of Palestine as a fundamental aspect of his vision to bolster Iranian regional influence, propagate Islam, establish deterrence against the US and Israel, and encircle Israel. He portrayed his anti-Israel and pro-Palestine stance as both a religious duty and a strategic necessity. He consistently emphasised that Iranian support for Palestine was rooted not in self-interest or the promotion of the country's national interests, but rather in an unwavering commitment to Islamic principles.[111]

Soleimani had no tolerance for Iranians critical of the Islamic Republic's costly intervention in the Levant. In 2017, he remarked:

> A few years ago [during the Green Movement protests] some people chanted the slogan of 'No Gaza, no Lebanon, I give my life for Iran.' I ask you, where are they now? They will not hold any political position and will not be allowed to play any role in the country's political decision-making.[112]

After Iran signed the nuclear deal with the six global powers in 2015, Soleimani reassured Hamas and other militant Palestinian groups that Iranian support for Palestine remained unshakeable. He told them that, 'I can say unequivocally that Mohammad Javad Zarif, our country's Foreign Minister, had a specific and clear mission, which was the nuclear issue, and he was not authorised to discuss any other issues.'[113] Sinwar recalled that after Trump pledged to move the US embassy to Jerusalem, Soleimani called the commanders of Qassam Brigades and Quds Brigades, affirming that 'Iran, the Pasdaran, and the Quds Force will allocate all its resources in defence of Quds as the capital of Palestine, and that there are no preconditions for this support.'[114]

As a military leader and strategist, Soleimani believed that the destiny of Palestine would not be determined at the negotiating table but on the battlefield. Consequently, he fostered much stronger ties with the Izz al-Din al-Qassam Brigades and Quds Brigades, rather than focusing on the political wings of the organisations. Like the PIJ, which strengthened its ties with Iran when Shaqaqi was expelled to Lebanon by Israel in the late 1980s, Hamas developed closer relations with Iran when one of its leaders, Khaled Mashal, was expelled from Jordan in 1999 and relocated to Damascus, where he met with the Quds Force. After Sheikh Yassin was assassinated by Israeli security forces in March 2004, Hamas, desperate for military and security assistance, moved closer to Tehran.

Iran's military relationship with Hamas took a giant leap forward after Israel unilaterally withdrew its forces from the Gaza Strip in August

2005, ending thirty-eight years of occupation and paving the way for legislative council elections in Gaza in March 2006, monitored by President Jimmy Carter. Hamas won that election, securing 76 out of 132 seats in the legislative council. Subsequently, Carter futilely urged the international community to recognise Hamas.[115] Tehran welcomed Hamas's victory and was pleased when a power-sharing plan between Fatah, the most powerful group within the PLO, and Hamas failed to materialise, leading to a bloody feud among Palestinians. Haniyeh, who led Hamas, rejected the order by Palestinian Authority President Mahmoud Abbas to step down as prime minister in Gaza in June 2007 and continued to rule.

For the first time, Hamas, with support from the PIJ, assumed a leadership role in Gaza, independent of the Palestinian Authority, which Tehran deemed as mere collaborators with Israel and the US. In response to what they perceived as a Hamas coup d'état, Israel, with Egypt's consent, implemented a comprehensive air, sea, and land blockade on Gaza. With Hamas governing Gaza and the Palestinian Authority in control of the West Bank, the Palestinian movement became divided both ideologically and geographically. Consequently, it became significantly weaker, and lacked the necessary cohesion to present a unified vision for negotiations with or confronting Israel.

Within Israel, some voices welcomed the division within the Palestinian movement, viewing it as an opportunity to hinder the realisation of a two-state solution and expand Israeli settlements in the Occupied Territories. Among them was Benjamin Netanyahu, who returned as prime minister in 2009 for his second term. He quietly undermined the foundational principle of the Oslo Accords, which entailed land for peace.[116] He is suspected of believing that 'maintaining separation between the PA [Palestinian Authority] in the West Bank and Hamas in Gaza will prevent the establishment of a Palestinian State'.[117] Therefore, he developed a nuanced and complex policy towards Hamas. He maintained close security cooperation with the PA in the West Bank and turned it into 'Israel's de facto policing and social services subcontractors'.[118] Simultaneously, he urged Qatar, an affluent Persian Gulf emirate, to fund Gaza's Hamas government, which he hoped to keep in check by occasional raids and invasions.[119] Former prime minister Barak recalled in 2024 that: 'Six times in the past twelve years he [Netanyahu] has rejected plans proposed by the heads of Israel's secret security agency, known as Shabak, to eliminate the Hamas leadership.'[120] Yossi Kuperwasser, a former head of research for Israel's intelligence, succinctly explained Israel's strategy: to keep Hamas 'strong enough to rule Gaza, but weak enough to be deterred by Israel'.[121]

However, many in Israel did not fully anticipate the ripple effects: the evolving situation in Gaza created an enticing environment for Iran to enhance its influence by intensifying its military ties with Hamas and the PIJ. This loose alliance reached a level that posed a significant challenge to Israel, as starkly evidenced in the events of October 2023.

Since 2006, Hamas and Israel have been engaged in three wars. Tehran has militarily backed Hamas and the PIJ in all of them. Its impact, however, was most visible in the 2008 and 2023 wars. Tehran has consistently refrained from supplying Hamas and the PIJ with its most advanced weapons and technologies. This policy was carefully crafted to reduce the substantial military disparity between Hamas and the PIJ and the superior Israeli forces, effectively positioning them as a significant challenge but not an imminent or serious threat. This strategic calibration was designed to avoid any escalation that could provoke Israel into a direct military confrontation with Iran.[122] It also is an integral component of Iran's broader shadow war against Israel, and its plan to establish three fronts in southern Lebanon, Syria, and Gaza against Israel.

The first major war between Hamas, supported by the PIJ, and Israel began in 2008, when Hamas launched rockets into Israel, prompting an Israeli ground invasion. Labelled Operation Cast Lead by Israel and the Gaza Massacre by Palestinians, the invasion lasted twenty-two days, from 27 December 2008 to 18 January 2009, before a ceasefire was reached. According to the UN, the war resulted in the death of between 1,387 to 1,417 Palestinians and 13 Israelis. Tens of thousands of homes were destroyed in Gaza, leaving thousands of Palestinians without access to running water or electricity. The UN report held that Hamas and other armed groups had used civilian areas as human shields, accusing them of launching 'rockets and missiles toward Israel'. It also criticised Israel for 'deliberate attacks against the civilian population'.[123] In a display of solidarity with Hamas, Hezbollah launched rockets and missiles on Israel for three days, sparking Israeli retaliation.

When a ceasefire was finally established between Israel and Hamas, Ayatollah Khamenei hailed it as a triumph for the Palestinian resistance and a miraculous achievement, despite the staggering physical damage and human toll. In March 2009, the Islamic Republic organised a conference in Tehran in solidarity with Gaza as a symbol of resistance against Israel. The Majles also designated the day of the ceasefire, 18 January, as 'Gaza Day' in the country's official calendar.[124] Ramadan Shalah, PIJ leader, visited Tehran and thanked Khamenei profusely, saying: 'On behalf of the Palestinian people and the resistance forces, I appreciate and thank Your Excellency and the great nation of Iran for the comprehensive support ... the victory of the Gaza war is actually the victory of the Iranian nation.'[125] Tehran declined to disclose specifics regarding the nature of its support.

After Soleimani's assassination in 2020, Tehran provided some details about his role in the 22-day war of 2008–9. In February 2012, Khamenei had acknowledged Iran's role in the conflict without specifically mentioning Soleimani's name. He said: 'We intervened in those events against Israel. Its result was the victory of the 33-day war [Hezbollah–Israel war of 2006] and the 22-day war.'[126] Nine years after Khamenei made that statement, Osama Hamdan, a senior Hamas representative in Lebanon, was quoted saying that 'Martyr Soleimani was with us every moment of this battle', and transferred the Russian-made Cornet missiles to Gaza. He asserted that in Soleimani's 'presence, the Cornet missiles were modified' and 'we established several missile-producing facilities in Gaza'.[127] Iranian Minister of Cultural Heritage, Handicrafts and Tourism Ezzatollah Zarghami who previously oversaw the IRGC's missile programme, affirmed on 22 November 2023 that he personally delivered missiles to Hezbollah and Hamas. 'We are not afraid of [these actions], nor do we conceal them,' he declared. Zarghami further disclosed that he conducted missile training sessions inside the tunnels Hamas had built.[128]

Ahmad Abdalhadi, a Hamas official in Lebanon, recalled that Soleimani 'visited Gaza several times, and from the very beginning participated in designing and drawing [our] defensive map. And this is no secret, and the enemy knows all of this. However, what they know is much less than what they don't know.'[129] Abdalhadi also claimed that 'the idea of building underground tunnels' in Gaza came from Soleimani and Imad Mughniyeh, leading to more than 360 kilometres of tunnels being built.[130] It was also reported that Soleimani had facilitated the transfer of advanced technology to Hezbollah for the construction of extensive underground tunnels designed to withstand chemical attacks. The tunnels provide shelter for fighters for extended periods, up to four months.[131]

Ziyad al-Nakhaleh, PIJ Secretary General, praised Soleimani for taking:

> a strategic step by arming us with missiles and weapons, which was more like a miracle.... Soleimani was personally involved. He travelled to several countries and made these transfers possible through planning. The weapons Commander Soleimani gave Gaza were the same missiles with which we bombed Tel Aviv.[132]

Following the 2008–9 war, a discernible pattern of conflict emerged: Palestinian militants would launch rockets and missiles at Israel, typically causing limited physical damage and few casualties. In response, Israel would retaliate with precision aerial and naval bombardments, often followed by ground incursions, resulting in substantial casualties and infrastructure damage. The introduction of the US-funded Iron Dome air defence system in 2011–12 proved pivotal and somewhat changed this pattern. This system, engineered to intercept and neutralise short-range rockets and missiles, significantly curtailed the effectiveness of attacks by Hamas and the PIJ.

This pattern of warfare between Israel and Hamas was also evident in Operation Protective Edge, a conflict which broke out on 8 July 2014. In the ensuing seven weeks, 67 Israelis and 2,251 Palestinians were killed, including 1,462 Palestinian civilians, of whom 299 [were] women and 551 children, and 11,231 Palestinians were injured.[133] While the UN Secretary-General described Israel's blockade of Gaza as 'a continuing collective penalty against the population in Gaza', the United Nations report also concluded that 'Palestinian armed groups fired 4,881 rockets and 1,753 mortars towards Israel, killing six civilians and injuring as many as 1,600 people, including 270 children.'[134] Having allegedly intercepted a ship stocked with weapons from Iran and Syria destined for Hamas and other militant groups, Prime Minister Netanyahu declared that 'the entire operation [the 2014 war] ... was organized by Iran', though he provided no evidence to support this assertion.[135] And, as expected, Iran dismissed the charge.

We witnessed this pattern of warfare once again during the fifteen days of fighting in the Gaza Strip in 2021. Thirteen Israelis and at least 243 Palestinians were killed. Israel accused Hezbollah, Hamas and the IRGC of coordinating their activities through a joint military operation in Beirut. While Tehran denied the charges, Sinwar was quoted in Israeli newspapers as confirming 'full coordination between the resistance in Lebanon and resistance in Gaza' without specifying details.[136]

From 2009 to 2023, the intermittent wars between Israel and Hamas inflicted grave losses on both sides, particularly on Gaza and the Palestinians. Yet, these pale in comparison to the event of October 2023.

Hamas's October Surprise Attack on Israel and Iran's Response

When news of Hamas's incursion into Israel broke in October 2023, Ayatollah Khamenei swiftly praised Hamas for shattering Israel's perception of military invincibility. He gleefully declared that Israel 'has suffered a military and intelligence defeat that cannot be overcome. The Zionist regime's intelligence agencies failed to anticipate the operation, and its army was asleep and not ready, taking them a day or two to regroup.'[137] However, when reports surfaced regarding Iran's possible direct involvement in the operation, he repeatedly and unequivocally denied any prior knowledge or participation by Tehran.[138]

In his first public declaration, President Joe Biden denounced Hamas for committing 'atrocities that recall the worst ravages of ISIS, unleashing pure unadulterated evil upon the world', but did not mention Iran as a culprit.[139] However, the *Wall Street Journal* claimed that the IRGC 'had worked with Hamas' since August 2023 to plan the October incursion and had given the green light to Hamas to carry out the operation five days before the attack.[140] A few days after the publication of this report, Secretary of State Blinken reaffirmed what Biden had indicated earlier but left the door open for future reopening of the case: 'We haven't seen direct evidence that Iran participated in or helped plan the attack. That doesn't mean that it didn't; we just don't have the evidence to show it.'[141] Clearly, Washington exhibited prudence at a volatile moment by withholding accusations against Tehran unless solid intelligence regarding its involvement was presented.

Unlike Washington's measured approach, Tel Aviv oscillated between direct accusations and insinuations regarding Iran's involvement in the Hamas operation. This calculated ambiguity not only kept Tehran uncertain about Israel's intentions but also left open the potential for its future retaliatory military action against Iran. Lior Haiat, the spokesman for Israel's Foreign Ministry, bluntly stated that Tehran is 'without a doubt ... behind the scenes' of this war against Israel.[142] Prime Minister Netanyahu asserted that 'Iran supports Hamas ... provides over 90% of Hamas's budget. It finances, it organises, it directs, it guides. I cannot tell you for certain that in this specific operation, at this particular moment, they were involved in the micro-planning.' He added, 'there is no Hamas without Iran. And no Hezbollah either.'[143] The reality is, Iran has not been the main financial backer of Hamas in Gaza. It is reported that 'between 2012 and 2021, Qatar provided $1.49 billion in financial aid to support various projects for Palestinian civilians in Gaza', all of which was fully coordinated with Israel, the United States, and the UN.[144] Moreover, Israel never attempted to turn off the source of Hamas funding.[145] Israel agreed to this arrangement under the 'flawed assumption that Hamas was neither interested [in] nor capable of a large-scale attack'. However, since money is fungible, Hamas could have diverted some of these funds for military operations.[146]

Meanwhile, Iranian officials and media unabashedly proclaimed Iran's steady support for Palestinians, often without providing specific details, while deflecting any blame for brutalities committed by Hamas. They insisted that the 7 October attack was planned and executed by Palestinians themselves. However, their messaging often remained deliberately convoluted, leaving ambiguity about Iran's potential involvement.[147] On one occasion, IRGC spokesman Ramazan Sharif linked the

7 October attack to retaliation for Soleimani's 2020 assassination, a claim promptly rejected by Hamas.[148] In cryptic language, Mohammad Kosari, a Majles representative, hinted that Mohammad Zeif (Deif), one of the alleged architects of October 2023 operation, had collaborated with Qasem Soleimani on numerous operations, though he provided no specific cases. He went on to claim that 'the preparation for this operation [October 2023] was not made in one or two days, but several years ago. The Axis of Resistance has been able to completely fill the hands of Hamas and Islamic Jihad in Gaza, and therefore Hamas has carried out this operation with great capability.'[149] Kosari did not, however, suggest that Iran was behind the October operation. Deif's close relationship with Soleimani is well established. Deif, the mysterious commander of the Qassam Brigades, was born Mohammad Masri in Khan Yunis refugee camp in Gaza and adopted the name Deif when he joined the first Intifada. He was arrested by Israel in 1989.[150] After Israel killed Deif's daughter and wife in 2014, Soleimani wrote a letter to him, hailing him as a 'living martyr', the highest accolade within the Axis of Resistance. He assured Deif that, 'despite all the pressure' Iran 'will not abandon you. Victory is near.'[151]

Tehran not only praised Hamas for its October incursion but also issued a stern warning to Israel against any potential invasion of Gaza.[152] Moreover, while Iran had no desire to escalate the Gaza conflict into a regional conflagration and adhered to its long-standing policy of avoiding direct kinetic confrontation with Israel, it also underscored its inability to control members of the Axis of Resistance from launching attacks against Israel and the United States in the event of a Gaza invasion. After Israel launched its ground invasion on 27 October 2023, the Axis of Resistance entered the fray, targeting American bases in Iraq and Syria. They vowed to continue their operations until Israel agrees to a ceasefire. Concurrently, Hezbollah launched missile attacks on Israel from southern Lebanon, starting 8 October, 2023. and the Houthis attacked commercial vessels in the Red Sea, seeking to disrupt international shipping.[153] The Axis was demonstrating its capability to launch a multi-front and coordinated attack against its enemies.

In January 2024, during a missile attack by the Axis of Resistance, three American service members lost their lives at Tower 22 outpost in Jordan, near the Syrian border. In retaliation, the United States targeted the Iraqi and Syrian militias, resulting in the deaths of sixteen Iraqis, including civilians, and eighteen Syrians.[154] Amidst the escalating attacks by the Axis of Resistance and Israel's refusal to agree to a ceasefire, Iran and the US reportedly convened secret meetings to avert the conflict from spiralling into a regional war. Subsequently, the assaults by Iraqi and Syrian militias diminished, while the Houthis persisted with their attacks, albeit with less intensity.[155]

Iran and Israel: Moving Towards a Regional War?

Despite efforts by the US and Iran to prevent the escalation of the Gaza conflict, Tel Aviv appeared inclined to expand the theatre of the war to include Hezbollah and ultimately Iran, anticipating full support from the United States. In that vein, in December 2023, Israel killed General Razi Mousavi, a senior IRGC advisor in Syria, with precision missiles at his home in Damascus. Tel Aviv accused Mousavi of 'coordinating the military alliance between Iran and Syria and arming Iranian-backed militias, including Hezbollah'.[156] Iran condemned the attack and vowed retaliation, pointing out that Mousavi held a diplomatic passport and was serving in Syria at the invitation of its government.[157]

Israel's assault on the top leadership of the Quds Force continued. On 1 April 2024, Israeli missiles struck Iran's consulate in Damascus, located adjacent to its embassy. The attack demolished the compound and killed General Mohammad Reza Zahedi and two other senior IRGC officers, along with ten others. Commander Zahedi was the highest-ranking Iranian military official killed since the assassination of General Soleimani in 2020. Tel Aviv levelled accusations against Zahedi, alleging he orchestrated 'Iranian efforts to smuggle arms to Palestinian terrorists' and planned future deadly attacks on Israel. Tel Aviv's message was clear and resolute: it would relentlessly target the architects of the so-called 'Iranian octopus'.[158]

Tehran was stunned by the direct assault on its consulate, which it considered as an inviolable extension of its sovereign territory. Ayatollah Khamenei pledged to exact revenge for the deaths of Iranian officers, declaring, 'We will make them regret this crime and similar acts, with the help of God.'[159] Hardliners demanded a robust response, questioning the wisdom of Iran's 'strategic patience' and its failure to retaliate in the face of Israel's repeated assaults inside Iranian territory, as well as in Syria and Lebanon. They argued that this passivity had only emboldened Israel to intensify its attacks in both frequency and lethality.

While Washington publicly urged Tehran and Tel Aviv to exercise restraint, cautioning that retaliatory measures could escalate into a full-scale war potentially engulfing the entire region, it also emphatically stated that it would defend Israel against any Iranian actions. After nearly two weeks of extensive deliberations, Ayatollah Khomeini ultimately authorised the IRGC to conduct Operation True Promise, a high-stakes retaliatory strike from Iranian territory against Israel on 13 April 2024. This marked the first time Iran had carried out strikes inside Israeli territory. This unprecedented, coordinated assault on a nuclear-armed country involved '120 ballistic missiles, 170 drones, and more than 30 cruise missiles, lasting five hours'.[160] It was perhaps the largest coordinated drone attack ever, perhaps utilising the swarming tactic that allows a group of drones to operate in unison, with capabilities to rapidly change direction or mission, a tactic Israel previously implemented on a smaller scale against Hamas in 2021.[161]

It remains uncertain whether Israel miscalculated by not anticipating any response from Tehran following the killing of Zahedi. Even if Israel did foresee a reaction, it is unlikely they expected such a bold, intense, direct, and dramatic response originating from Iranian soil. Ultimately, Iran aimed to establish a new deterrence dynamic with Israel.

In all military confrontations, accurate damage assessments are initially challenging and tend to unfold gradually. Israel, with direct assistance from the United States, Britain, France, and Jordan, asserted that its multilayered air defence system intercepted 99 per cent of the incoming Iranian projectiles, with only one fatality reported. Conversely,

Tehran contended that its operation was successful, as its inexpensive drones and missiles managed to penetrate the multilayered and highly expensive Israeli air defence system, revealing its vulnerabilities and weaknesses. Air raid sirens were sounded in 720 locations in Israel, and explosions were heard in cities across the country.[162] General Salami, commander of the IRGC, boasted that the operation against Israel exceeded his expectations, emphasising that:

> We conducted a limited operation, which was commensurate with the extent of the Zionist regime's wickedness. It was within our capacity to launch a more extensive operation, but we confined it to targeting those capabilities of the Zionist regime that were employed in the attack on our embassy.[163]

Salami clearly articulated Iran's new strategy of reciprocal retaliation: if attacked by Israel, Iran will retaliate. Tehran maintained that it intentionally designed the operation not to inflict serious damage to avoid provoking a full-scale war, a claim rejected by Israel. Tehran also claimed it struck and damaged two regions in Israel with significant military facilities. According to the United States, 'five ballistic missiles evaded air defences and impacted on Israeli territory'.[164] While both the United States and Israel portrayed the Iranian operation as a military failure, Ayatollah Khamenei presented his own narrative:

> The focus on the number of missiles fired or hitting their target, emphasised by the opposing side, is peripheral. The primary concern lies in the demonstration of the Iranian resolve and the power of its armed forces on the international stage – a development that has provoked the ire of our adversaries.[165]

The Iranian missile and drone attack, broadcast globally on television, posed a predicament for Israel. Since its establishment in 1948, Israel, surrounded by hostile countries, had adhered to a defence strategy that involves retaliating to violent attacks with even greater force, thereby establishing a deterrent against further aggression. However, with Washington's public commitment to defend Israel while explicitly stating it would not engage in any Israeli-led offensive operations against Iran, the question arose: would Israel maintain its traditional defence doctrine in its response to Iran? The dilemma for Israel was further compounded because Tehran insisted that any Israeli retaliation would be met with a response significantly larger and more damaging than the initial attack. Additionally, Tehran warned the US that supporting Israeli retaliation could lead to attacks by the Axis of Resistance and Iran on its bases in the region.

Following a week of deliberations, Israel executed a retaliatory strike against the Isfahan region of Iran on 19 April 2024, an area recognised for its major military and nuclear facilities. While both sides acknowledged that the strike did not result in any fatalities, they presented conflicting reports on the extent of the damage. The US confirmed that an Israeli missile successfully reached its intended target in Isfahan. Conversely, Iran disputed the effectiveness of the attack, alleging that 'Israel only made a failed and humiliating attempt to deploy quadcopters [drones]', which were shot down.[166] This incident echoed a similar attack on 28 January 2023, when Israeli suicide drones were reported to have struck a military facility in the same region.[167] Additionally, there were unsubstantiated claims that the strike had significantly impaired Iran's principal air defence systems in Isfahan, which Iran swiftly denied.

Faltering Deterrence or a New Deterrence Mechanism?

Following the Islamic Revolution, Iran's policies towards Israel and the Palestinians transformed dramatically, without any thorough public discourse on the implications for its national interests. General Soleimani unequivocally articulated the ideological underpinnings behind Iran's unwavering backing of the Palestinian cause, stating:

> As you know, some people say that we support Palestine because of our interests. But this has not been true since the onset of the Islamic revolution, and it still is not because we are not ready to negotiate or come to an agreement with the United States and others about the question of Palestine.[168]

He unambiguously stated that Iran's policy towards Palestine does not necessarily align with or advance its national interests.

The Islamic Republic's ideological commitment to the Palestinian cause remains deeply intertwined with its regional strategy and rivalries, often adversely impacting its national interests. Currently, anti-Israeli rhetoric and actions constitute a central tenet of the Islamic Republic's identity and ethos, while anti-Iran policies form a foundational pillar of Israel's Middle East strategy.

Iran has consistently used Hamas as a key element of its policy towards Palestine. Despite relying on Iranian financial and military support, Hamas has not acted strictly as an Iranian proxy and has occasionally acted against Iranian interests for its own advantage, notably during the Syrian and Yemeni civil wars. Overall, both Hamas and the PIJ have derived greater benefits from their association with Iran than Iran has from them. Still, given that anti-Israeli sentiment has been deeply embedded in the Islamic Republic's identity, a significant shift in its stance is unlikely in the near term.

Nor is the Islamic Republic likely to cease its support for Hamas.[169] Tehran appears convinced that Israel will not succeed in destroying Hamas. Should Hamas be eliminated, Iran would likely arm other organisations poised to take its place. For Tehran, as long as Israel continues its occupation of the Palestinian territories, Palestinian militancy will flourish, affording Iran opportunities to pursue its policies.

As of this writing, it appears that both Iran and Israel meticulously orchestrated their retaliatory operations to prevent the conflict from escalating into a regional war. This cautious strategy indicates the emergence of new deterrence dynamics and an intensifying rivalry between the two nations. In this precarious new phase, the decades-long shadow war between Iran and Israel could easily metamorphose into direct kinetic confrontations, potentially undermining the national interests of both countries. For Tehran, a critical question arises: is it willing to engage in a war against Israel driven more by its ideological commitment to the Palestinian cause than by its national interests? The Islamic Republic might be prepared to accept this risk, but whether the Iranian populace shares this willingness remains questionable. The Islamic Republic has yet to adequately explain how its policies towards Israel have served Iran's national interest.

Conclusion

Iranian Regional Policies at a Perilous Crossroads

> The nation which indulges towards another an habitual
> hatred or an habitual fondness is in some degree a slave.
> It is a slave to its animosity or to its affection, either of
> which is sufficient to lead it astray from its duty and its interest.
> — President George Washington's Farewell Address, 1796.

Iran's rise as an anti-American power in Iraq, Syria, Lebanon, Yemen, and, to a much lesser extent, in the Gaza Strip, stands out as one the most consequential developments in the Middle East since the Second World War, slightly tilting the balance of power in the region in its favour. Despite relentless efforts by the United States to contain it, Iran has successfully expanded its regional power and emerged as a quintessential revisionist power, seeking to change the US-dominated regional order for its benefit. Its armed forces are ranked as the seventeenth most powerful in the world, with highly advanced missile and drone capabilities.[1] It has also emerged as 'a large-scale exporter of low-cost, high-tech weapons'.[2] Additionally, Iran appears to have effectively positioned itself as a threshold nuclear power, with the necessary infrastructure, expertise, and capability to rapidly develop a nuclear bomb should it make the political decision to do so.

The asymmetric military actions of the Iran-led Axis of Resistance against the United States and Israel, following Israel's incursion into the Gaza Strip in late 2023, are the latest manifestations of the new landscape Iran has helped shape in the Middle East. For years, Tehran has been striving to emulate NATO's model of alliance formation by establishing the Axis of Resistance. However, the differences between the two are vast. NATO is an alliance among democratic states that typically operates within the confines of an international system, whereas the Axis is an Islamic-based alliance comprising like-minded non-state and state actors that often defy international norms. The key point is that the US and Israel no longer face opposition from individual states or fragmented actors. Instead they confront the Islamic Republic and the Axis of Resistance, which can operate in a coordinated and synchronised manner from multiple fronts across the Middle East.

This power shift resulting from Iran's rise has emerged after over four decades of US–Iran cold war, driven by conflicting geopolitical and geostrategic interests. Today, as emphasised by CIA Director William Burns, Washington must contend with Iran.[3] After all, Iran stands at the nexus of the most daunting challenges facing the US in the Middle East, from terrorism and weapons proliferation to energy security, and the Israeli–Palestinian conflict.

Iran's rise may seem sudden, but it has been gradual and deliberate. This process began in the 1970s, during Mohammad Reza Shah's reign, and accelerated after the revolution. What a CIA report surmised about Mohammad Reza Shah's foreign policy is equally applicable to ayatollahs Khomeini and Khamenei: 'The Shah is heir to a traditional Persian sense of isolation in largely hostile environment.... At the same time, this historical perception increases the Shah's determination to build Iran's power so that it can [go] do it alone if necessary.'[4] Although Mohammad Reza Shah and the ayatollahs Khomeini and Khamenei spoke different political languages and used distinct strategies, their goal was to make Iran a major power; they wanted to establish Iran as a major player in an inhospitable, unpredictable, and strategically important region of the world. The Shah forged an alliance with the US based on a bandwagon strategy to secure his throne at home and expand power abroad in the name of advancing Iranian national interests. In contrast, the Islamic Republic has employed a counterbalancing strategy, championing anti-Americanism wrapped in an Islamic guise, to solidify its rule domestically and extend its regional influence. Iran's foreign policy, therefore, is not merely a matter of regime ideology; it is also shaped by the dynamics of its immediate neighbourhood, its relationships with global powers, and its historical memory of being both victim and victor in imperial power struggles. The continuing potency of these forces suggests that a future Iranian state will pursue many similar goals in the region, regardless of the ideology it professes or its institutional configuration.

Mohammad Reza Shah expanded Iran's regional power and built deterrence against perceived foreign threats, namely Soviet communism and pan-Arabism. In the 1960s, he helped to empower the marginalised Shias in Lebanon as a counterforce against pan-Arabism while providing military assistance to anti-Abdel Nasser loyalists in the North Yemen civil war. In the 1970s, he cultivated friendly relations with Syria and provided financial support. He was instrumental in forming the Tehran–Washington–Tel Aviv Axis by clandestinely arming Iraqi Kurds as a proxy to undermine Iraq. And he deployed troops to Oman, successfully quelling a communist rebellion in the Dhofar province. With US backing, he emerged as the dominant indigenous power in the Persian Gulf in the 1970s and one of the most, if not the most, influential leaders in the Middle East.

Even though the Islamic Republic dismantled the alliances established by Pahlavi Iran, it nonetheless maintained a focus on expanding power, now setting its sights beyond the Persian Gulf, on the Levant and the Arabian Peninsula. Contrary to the Islamic Republic's claims, Iran's regional policy is not entirely defensive. Nor is it purely offensive, as its adversaries assert. Instead, it incorporates both defensive and offensive elements. The reigning ayatollahs have excelled in mobilising religious sentiments and sensibilities to build power, both at home and further afield. They are not mad mullahs, ready to sacrifice their interests for the sake of eternal glory in martyrdom. They are much more Machiavellian than their frequently apocalyptic rhetoric implies.

Iran's Rise in Two Strokes

Iran's rise in the Middle East was neither accidental nor merely a matter of being in the right place at the right time, poised to exploit the chaos created by the failed or failing states in the Middle East to advance its interests. It has been a four-decade-long, dangerous, risky, and expensive endeavour that has unfolded in two phases: pre-take-off and take-off.

The first phase began with the Islamic Revolution, which fundamentally changed Iranian foreign policy and provided the Islamic Republic with the will and energy to export its revolution to the Arab Middle East. Tehran forged a new political alliance with Syria and helped establish Hezbollah in Lebanon. It was, however, the eight-year war with Iraq that reshaped the Iranian state, laid the military foundation of its ascendancy, and transformed the IRGC into a disciplined military force. In contrast to Iran's Imperial Army, whose senior leaders often received their education in Western military colleges, the IRGC is a home-grown force, created and sustained by men who honed their skills in the art of warfare on unforgiving battlefields. 'Strategic necessity', as Gray observed, 'is the mother of military invention.'[5] Iran did not conjure up a knock-out military innovation during the war.[6] However, to level the playing field with Iraqi forces, who enjoyed military superiority, Iran made advancements in two critical areas: asymmetric and hybrid warfare, and the establishment of a secret regional network that evolved into the Axis of Resistance.

By the turn of the new century, the Islamic Republic's regional power had seemingly peaked. Iraq, Iran's enemy, was emasculated after the 1990–91 Persian Gulf War, while Tehran's alliance with Damascus remained robust. Hezbollah had ventured into Lebanon's electoral arena, while maintaining its military autonomy and establishing a state within a state, and helping Iran in establishing strategic depth against Israel from southern Lebanon. Tehran also had developed ideological ties with the Houthis and security relationships withPalestinian militants in Gaza.

Without a monumental change in the region's landscape, these relationships represented the best Iran could hope to maintain – a standing that would deter rivals from attempting to weaken it. The American invasion of Iraq brought about that change, marking the take-off phase of Iran's rise, with Khamenei and Soleimani responsible for its management. Ambassador Crocker pointed out that Khamenei is 'even more effective than his predecessor was, or the Shah of Iran's regime, in projecting power through the region'.[7] It was under Khamenei's leadership that Iran's rise took place. Inadvertently, the US invasion served as a catalyst that cleared the path for Iran to reach the summit of its influence. In this complex process no one handed anything to Iran: at great risk of provoking harsh American military retribution, Iran intervened in Iraq to achieve its goals. In a single stroke, the US eliminated Saddam Hussein, the strongest counterweight to Iranian power expansion. Tehran then capitalised on a series of blunders committed by the US and helped to transform Iraq into a Shi'a-dominated country, a friend, and a significant trading partner. Iran both supported the US-backed state formation in Iraq and contributed to making Iraq a quagmire for the US by arming anti-US militias. It further expanded its power by deploying fighters and advisors to combat ISIS.

With Iraq neutralised, Iran became involved in conflicts in Lebanon, Syria, Yemen, and Gaza. Even before the Israel–Hezbollah War in 2006, Iran had expanded its strategic depth by opening a front against Israel in Lebanon. Tel Aviv was taken aback by how Soleimani had transformed Hezbollah into an effective hybrid fighting force. For the first time, an Arab force – Hezbollah – did not lose to the superior Israeli military, although the damage to Hezbollah and Lebanon in the 2006 war was staggering. With the conclusion of the war, a tenuous deterrence emerged between Hezbollah, which was Lebanon's most powerful force, and Israel, and, by extension, between Iran and Israel. This deterrence endured until Iranian missiles struck inside Israel in April 2024.

In the Syrian civil war, the Quds Force became deeply involved and rescued President Assad from the brink of defeat – Iran's most extensive and expansive military expedition outside its immediate neighbourhood in centuries. Tehran formed a multinational Shia force, forged an alliance with Russia in 2015, fought ISIS and Assad's opponents, established a modest military presence in Syria and a naval presence in the Mediterranean Sea, and opened a second front against Israel. At the same time, Iran became entangled in the civil war in Yemen, allying with the Houthis, who quickly joined the Axis of Resistance against the

Saudi-backed forces. Thereafter, Iran extended its influence into the Arabian Peninsula and created a quagmire for its rival Saudi Arabia on its southern flank. If Tehran's long game in Yemen bears fruit, it will be a key player around the Strait of Hormuz and the Bab-al-Mandab Strait, two of the world's most critical choke points. The mullahs have now become tried-and-true Machiavellians. And if these engagements didn't suffice, Tehran simultaneously escalated its transfers of arms and technology to Hamas and the PIJ, integrating these two Sunni organisations into its Axis of Resistance and intensifying its 'shadow war' with Israel.

Iran's extensive military involvement in multiple conflicts has produced a battle-hardened, hybrid armed force with deep familiarity with the Middle East's fault lines. It has also driven the expansion of a relatively self-sufficient military-industrial complex. During the Iran–Iraq War, when faced with a militarily superior Iraq and a crippling US arms embargo, Iran was compelled to develop this complex to manufacture weapons and reverse-engineer missiles. Over time, the complex has evolved to produce advanced drones, missiles, and other weaponry. Today, this complex is not only the chief supplier of arms and ammunition to the Axis of Resistance but also the backbone of Iran's armed forces.

By the end of the second decade of the new century, the stars seemed to align for Iran in the region, as it had successfully navigated a complex geopolitical landscape, positioning itself as a major regional power. However, the assassination of General Soleimani in January 2020 dealt a significant blow to Iranian regional policies, as the Islamic Republic lost its most charismatic and effective military leader and strategist, and its master network builder. Since his death, Iranian power has plateaued and with Israel's wars on Hamas and Hezbollah, it has suffered a major setback.

A Sustainable Rise and Effective Deterrence?

As the Islamic Republic commemorates its forty-fifth anniversary, it wields more power in the Middle East than at any point in Iran's recent history, all while protecting Iran's political independence and territorial integrity. This accomplishment is no small feat. However, Iran's rise is unsustainable, and its deterrence strategy has been only partially effective, even creating new strategic threats for the country. The precarious situation Iran faces today results from several factors: the militarised nature of its power and its failure to build robust economic ties, reliance on non-state actors, the US containment strategy, and, perhaps most importantly, brewing domestic turmoil.

We must resist the temptation to exaggerate Iran's power. Iran is not the new superpower of the Middle East.[8] It has been unable to impose its hegemony over Iraq, Syria, Lebanon, Yemen, and Gaza, and has only established spheres of influence. The Islamic Republic has behaved more like a spoiler power: it possesses enough assets to achieve some goals, albeit at exorbitant costs, while either preventing the US from achieving its objectives or substantially raising the costs for Washington to do so. Its limited power is largely manifested through its influence over non-state actors within the Axis of Resistance and, to a lesser degree, through its security and military relationships with other states, primarily with Syria and secondarily with Iraq.[9] Relying on non-state actors, who can attack US forces while providing Iran with plausible deniability, is unsustainable and continues to generate dangerous tensions in a global order where states remain the central and defining force. Despite receiving generous support from Tehran, Hamas's refusal to support Syria and Iran during the Syrian civil war exemplifies this dynamic. No state can be expected to endure armed non-state actors funded by foreign powers indefinitely, and Iran itself would surely not tolerate such a scenario. Tehran would be well-advised to incentivise its non-state partners and proxies to integrate into the state apparatuses of the countries where they operate.

Except for Iraq, the Islamic Republic has also failed to complement its military and security relationships with mutually beneficial economic ties. In 2021, Iran's total exports to Iraq reached $6.1 billion, while imports from Iraq amounted to $1.1 billion.[10] In contrast, its combined exports and imports to Lebanon, Syria, and Yemen totalled approximately $412 million.[11] (Iran has no economic relationship with Gaza.)

Against this backdrop, Iranian military expenditures have been remarkably high for a country under economic sanctions. Given Tehran's opacity regarding its expenses, we can only cautiously estimate its allocations to its allies for certain years, which should provide us with a better understanding of the costs associated with Iran's interventions in the region.[12] The damage of the Iran–Iraq War totalled $1 trillion, with Iran's share comfortably exceeding half of that amount. In 2019, Iran contributed an estimated $700 million to Hezbollah, in 2018 Iran gave $100 million to Hamas and the PIJ, $36 million to support the anti-US Shia militias in Iraq, and 'several millions' to the Houthis. Most importantly, Iran spent between $20 billion and $30 billion in the Syrian civil war from 2011 to 2020. Tehran has attempted to offset some of its expenses, particularly in Syria, but has faced significant obstacles bypassing US sanctions and competing with affluent Persian Gulf countries and Russia. The Islamic Republic claims, correctly, that its expenditures constitute a small percentage of its gross domestic product, significantly less than those of Saudi Arabia and Israel. Nevertheless, these costs have further burdened an already struggling economy.[13]

More than its reliance on non-state actors and lack of economic ties to its allies, Iranian power is primarily constrained by the United States' containment strategy, even in the few countries where it has been most visible and effective. Iraq has cultivated strategic relations with the US, the Lebanese government maintains close ties with Washington, and the US supports Syrian Kurds with a small contingent of military forces in Syria, pressuring President Assad to distance himself from Tehran. In Yemen, the combined efforts of the United States, Britain, and Saudi Arabia persist in restraining Iranian influence. Meanwhile, in Gaza, Israel is determined to destroy or significantly diminish the military and operational capabilities of Hamas and PIJ.

Significantly, the power disparity between the US and Iran has eroded the effectiveness of Iran's deterrence strategy, while introducing new threats for Tehran. The US has refrained from launching military strikes on Iran's nuclear and military facilities, partly due to Iran's missile and drone capabilities, as well as its leadership of the Axis of Resistance. While avoiding direct acts of war might seem insignificant, in the context of long-standing hostilities and regional instability, it represents a notable success for Iran's deterrence strategy. However, this hasn't prevented the US from undermining Iran through other means, such as imposing stringent sanctions, launching cyber-attacks on critical nuclear and military infrastructure, and supporting dissident groups opposed to the Islamic Republic.

Israel shares the US's reluctance to launch direct military attacks on Iran, largely because of Iran's deterrence strategy. Israel, like the US, has undermined Iran through various means. It has been a key advocate for increased US sanctions on Iran and the termination of the JCPOA by the US, and has led efforts to form anti-Iran coalitions with several Arab countries. Israel has reportedly assassinated several of Iran's nuclear scientists, stolen its nuclear secrets, committed acts of industrial sabotage, and repeatedly targeted its facilities and personnel in Syria and Lebanon. Moreover, Israel has established its own strategic depth against Iran. It has developed close military and intelligence ties with the Kurdistan Regional Government in Iraq and the Republic of Azerbaijan on Iran's northern border. Through the Abraham Accords, Israel has also gained a foothold in the Persian Gulf with normalised relations with Bahrain and the UAE, and potentially Saudi Arabia.

Finally, the sustainability of Iran's ascent is highly questionable, as it has gradually lost the delicate balance between its ambitions and capabilities, leaving the country increasingly vulnerable to foreign interference. Today, Iran finds itself entangled in a cold war with the US, pursuing the unrealistic goal of pushing the US out of the Middle East. It is also engaged in a regional rivalry with the much richer Saudi Arabia and a 'shadow war' with Israel, which could easily escalate into a kinetic confrontation. Iran would be well-advised to abandon the illusion of destroying Israel.

As Iran's deterrence strategy appears to be failing to adequately thwart its threat, it might be compelled to build a nuclear bomb. In May 2024, former foreign minister Kamal Kharazi, one of Ayatollah Khamenei's top foreign policy advisors, openly suggested that if its existence is threatened, Iran could 'change its nuclear doctrine'.[14]

Iran's National Interest and its Regional Policies

Despite differing definitions of national interest, there is broad agreement that it encompasses a state's ability to protect its sovereignty, enhance its international power, safeguard territorial integrity and the security of its people, advance its ideological and cultural values, and ultimately improve its citizens' well-being and prosperity. National interest should be analysed as a balance of multiple factors, rather than by overstressing any single variable at the expense of others.

Since 1979, Iran has not lost any territory, even during its war with Iraq, marking the first time in over three centuries that it has not ceded any land in a war. Despite the invasions of its neighbours, Iraq and Afghanistan, and the pervasive chaos in the Middle East, Iran has remained unified, sovereign, and relatively stable, while substantially expanding its power. It played an important role in weakening ISIS in Iraq and Syria, mitigating a severe regional threat. These developments have undoubtedly served Iranian national interests.

At the same time, Iran's cold war with the United States, some aspects of its regional policies, and its entanglement in civil and sectarian conflicts have been costly, triggering additional Western sanctions on an already heavily sanctioned nation. These sanctions have led to economic downturns and a lower standard of living for Iranian citizens, clearly undermining national interests. Although the Islamic Republic has often used Islam as a tool to advance its agenda, it generally operates based on a cost–benefit analysis. However, the impulse to advance its ideological preferences often takes precedence over Iranian national interests, as is evident in Iran's policies towards Israel and the Palestinians. What is most urgent is for the Islamic Republic to find a balance between its religious priorities and Iran's national interests.

The dire economic situation in Iran today has led to widespread alienation, hopelessness, anger, mistrust of the government, and unprecedented migration, including some of its best and brightest. The detrimental impact of US sanctions in perpetuating this situation, coupled with systemic corruption and mismanagement, is undeniable.[15] As long as the United States can effectively prevent Iran from participating fully in the global economic system, as it has for decades, Iran – a country rich in natural resources and even richer in human resources – cannot fulfil its economic potential. This, in turn, will continue to alienate its population and potentially destabilise the country. Iran's 'pivot' towards Russia and China offers no remedy for the existing condition. The United States has effectively made it exceptionally diffi-cult and costly for Iran to economically benefit from its rich natural resources. Despite having the world's second-largest natural gas reserves, Iran has been unable to play the major role it should in the global natural gas market, potentially losing billions of dollars. Under Mohammad Reza Shah, Iran was among the world's top exporters of crude oil and perhaps the most influential force in the Organization of Petroleum Exporting Countries (OPEC). Today, it has lost this respected position in OPEC and the global oil markets. Moreover, Iran has been unable to engage in any major developmental projects, either domesti-cally or regionally, or attract significant foreign investment. US opposi-tion has delayed the completion of the Pakistan–Iran peace gas pipeline and hindered the recent Indian project to build a terminal in Chabahar on the Gulf of Oman. Historically a centre of the Silk Road, Iran has gradually been losing its preeminent position in the developing regional trade corridors.

One thing has been clear for decades: Iran cannot win its cold war with the United States, a conflict it should not have started that has now ossified into a rigid anti-Americanism at the expense of Iranians' quality of life. Today, unless both the United States and Iran find ways to tacti-cally cooperate when their interests converge, and gradually develop mechanisms to manage their disputes, their cold war could, intention-ally or unintentionally, escalate into a hot war. As long as the animosity and cold war between Iran and the US persist, stability will remain elusive in the Middle East. However, powerful constituencies in both the US and Iran oppose any rapprochement. In the United States, hardliners consider any move to reconciliation with Iran as appeasement of an inherently hostile power. In Iran, any significant softening of attitude to the US risks delegitimising the regime among its core supporters: for them, it's an existential gamble.

All Foreign Policy is Local

Expanding power abroad without legitimacy or popular support at home is unsustainable. When the revolution broke out in 1979, the Shah was at the height of his power in the Middle East and had effectively countered major foreign threats. At the same time, Iranians enjoyed one of the highest standards of living in the region. However, the Shah's autocracy had alienated many Iranians. His rule may have been unchallenged by foreign powers, but he was unequipped to face the rebellion from within. Thus, Mohammad Reza Shah lost his Peacock Throne when he was strong abroad but vulnerable at home.

Today, the greatest threat to the sustainability of Iran's rise comes from within. As the product of a popular revolution, the Islamic Republic initially had a cohesive, large, and heterogeneous governing elite, enjoying widespread popular support. However, irreconcilable factional disputes within the elite, coupled with the Islamic Republic's repressive political and social policies, fractured elite cohesion and rendered it more homogeneous, with substantially less popular backing and with hardliners in charge of all major commands of powers.

Today, the Islamic Republic has become increasingly disconnected from the lives of ordinary Iranians. The state is heading in an unsustainable direction, while a defiant and creative civil society moves in the opposite direction, as if they live in two different worlds. Exacerbating these tensions is the sensitive issue of succession for the 85-year-old Ayatollah Khamenei. This has intensified the fierce rivalry between factions, each pushing for their own candidate to succeed Khamenei. Once again, Iran has become restless.

One of the manifestations of this restlessness was the 2009 Green Movement, when people took to the streets en masse to protest the results of the disputed presidential election. These demonstrations were unprecedented in two respects: they were arguably the largest protest movement in the Islamic Republic within the past three decades, and they marked the first instance where protestors specifically targeted Iranian regional policies in their slogans. Protestors were chanting, 'Neither Gaza, nor Lebanon, I sacrifice my life for Iran', an unambiguous rejection of Iran's policies towards Hezbollah and militant Palestinian organisations. After this movement was violently suppressed, nearly a decade passed before Iranians took to the streets again.

While withdrawing from Iran's nuclear deal, President Trump implemented his 'maximum pressure' campaign and imposed crippling sanctions. As a result, Iran's GDP per capita (at current US$) collapsed from $5,758.6 in 2017 to $2,746.4 in 2020 – a decrease of approximately 52.3 per cent in just three years.[16] Clearly, mismanagement and corruption, alongside US sanctions, precipitated this drastic decline. During those three years, there were several large protest movements. In 2017–18, protests over worsening economic conditions erupted in the city of Mashhad, and then spread to many major cities in Iran, resulting in the death of twenty-two protestors. In 2019, larger protests occurred in major cities across the country in response to the government's unexpected and huge hike in gas prices. Over three hundred people lost their lives during these protests, known as 'Bloody November', in opposition to this reckless decision.

Economic conditions weren't the only cause of discontent. Many Iranian women were no longer willing to endure mandatory hijab and repressive dress codes. In September 2022, when Mahsa Amini, a 22-year-old Kurdish woman, was killed while in the custody of the Guidance Patrol for wearing 'inadequate' hijab, their simmering rage reached a boiling point. Thousands of women started ripping off and even burning their headscarves in the streets. The Woman, Life, Freedom movement had begun.

For over six months, Iranians from all walks of life demonstrated in cities large and small across the country, calling for gender equality and freedom, denouncing Ayatollah Khamenei, and demanding the revolutionary overthrow of the Islamic Republic. This was the most serious and radical challenge to the Islamic Republic since the Green Movement. These protests reportedly resulted in the deaths of at least 500 people, predominantly young, and the incarceration of over 22,000 protestors.

Even though the protests have died down for the moment, the Woman, Life, Freedom movement achieved much and could reignite in a different form in the near future. It has left a powerful legacy, as Iran's vibrant young population has irrevocably changed the political discourse about hijab, gender equality, and the future of the Islamic Republic itself.[17] A new era has dawned, as Iran's younger generations come of political age. They do not remember the Shah, or the Islamic Revolution that overthrew him, so their sympathies don't lie with the revolution's current torchbearers.

Even if the Islamic Republic reforms key aspects of its regional policy and pursues a less confrontational and interventionist policy, Tehran must urgently address essential domestic issues. These include meeting the demands of its restless youth, improving the desperate economic conditions, ending its repression of personal freedoms, granting civil liberties, and promoting free and competitive elections. If the Islamic Republic fails to adequately address these critical imperatives, its extraordinary and costly rise could be reduced to a mere footnote in Iran's long history, with the Republic's very survival hanging precariously in the balance. Projecting power abroad is difficult, but maintaining it is even more challenging.

Acknowledgements

This book is a labour of love – the culmination of over a decade of research, writing, teaching, participation in conferences, public speaking, and several hundred interviews with national and international media outlets about Iranian foreign and security policies. A circle of family members, colleagues, students, and friends made invaluable contributions to the completion of this book.

First and foremost, I would like to express my deepest gratitude to my wife, Ramak. She read the entire book several times, providing insightful and substantive suggestions. She did considerable amount of research, identifying and analysing Persian-language sources. Her realism and unique understanding of life under the Islamic Republic and Iranian culture softened the rough edges of my observations in this book. I cannot envision completing this project without her boundless kindness, love, unwavering support and encouragement, and enduring patience with my idiosyncratic writing habits.

My sister, Farzaneh Milani, an accomplished author and a pioneer in the field of Iranian women's studies, persistently and kindly encouraged me for years to write this book. She read the introduction and made insightful suggestions. My oldest brother, Hassan Milani, an engineer by training, a successful businessman and a quiet philanthropist, has been a pillar of support and encouragement throughout my life. And my older brother, Abbas Milani, one of the most distinguished political historians of his generation, continues to inspire me with his prolific and creative scholarship. My good friend, Randy Borum, critiqued and improved the initial book proposal. And Elizabeth Ricketts edited the first short draft of this manuscript.

I am thankful to several research assistants at the University of South Florida's Center for Strategic & Diplomatic Studies for their invaluable assistance. Arman Mahmoudian, now Dr Mahmoudian, did a superb job of collecting Persian-language sources on Iran's regional policies. He is a gifted young scholar in his own right. The talented Sina Azodi, now Dr Azodi, was most helpful in finding American archival sources. And Arman Mohammadi helped at the beginning of this project.

I am grateful to the late Professor Roy Mottahedeh of Harvard University for his support of my academic endeavours and for connecting me with Novin Doostdar, of Oneworld Publications, whom I first met many years ago at Oxford. Novin's professionalism helped make the process of completing this project considerably less arduous.

I was lucky to work with an outstanding team at Oneworld Publications. Two anonymous external reviewers read the initial manuscript and enriched it with their criticisms and sound suggestions. Rida Vaquas, content editor, was most discerning and creative in reviewing the manuscript. Her probing questions, criticisms, and suggestions substantially improved the quality of this book. I could not have asked to work with a more professional copy editor than Sophie Richmond. Her meticulous attention to detail, expert revisions, and patience with my numerous changes greatly enhanced the readability and quality of this work. My gratitude also goes to Laura McFarlane, Production and Editorial Manager, Ben Summers, the art director, and Paul Nash, Head of Production.

I owe a debt of gratitude to the following prominent Iranian and American experts and diplomats I interviewed about Iranian domestic and foreign policies: Mehdi Bazargan, former Iranian prime minister; Ardeshir Zahedi, former Iranian foreign minister; Hojatolislam Mohammad Mousavi Khoeiniha, the 'spiritual advisor' of the students who stormed and occupied the US embassy in Tehran in 1979; L. Bruce Laingen, former American chargé d'affaires in Iran; Chris Hill, former US ambassador to Iraq; Robert Ford, former US ambassador to Syria; Ryan Crocker, former US ambassador to Iraq; retired General Frank McKenzie, former commander of US Central Command; Randa Slim, an expert from the Middle East Institute in Washington; and, Rami G. Khouri, from the American University of Lebanon. I am equally grateful to those who have asked for anonymity.

On a personal note, I wish to express my gratitude to my three accomplished daughters, Shayda, Doniya, and Ava, for their endless love and support. During the Covid-19 pandemic, when I struggled with the anxiety of the new era, they each encouraged me in their own unique way to channel all my energy into completing this project. In fact, I completed much of the writing of this book during those trying times. In that phase, Max Linder, my son-in-law, or *shah damad* as I call him, read parts of the manuscript and made constructive suggestions. I am also grateful to Aaron Henricks for reading the introduction, offering insightful comments, and assisting me in selecting the title of the book.

My good friends in Tampa, Florida, consistently supported me during the writing of this book. Specifically, I am grateful to Azita Eskandari and Saied Shayes for their friendship, and for being excellent travel companions when I needed a distraction from my writing.

Finally, if there is any merit to this book, the credit should go to the individuals mentioned. However, I take full responsibility for all its shortcomings.

New York, 4 July 2024

Select Bibliography

Abedi, Mahan. *Iran Resurgent: The Rise and Rise of the Shia State*. Hurst & Co., 2019.

Abrahamian, Ervand. *Oil Crisis in Iran: From Nationalism to Coup d'état*. Cambridge University Press, 2021.

Abisaab, Rula. *Converting Persia: Religion and Power in the Safavid Empire*. London: I.B. Tauris, 2004.

Adib-Moghaddam, Afshin. *What is Iran? Domestic Politics and International Relations in Five Musical Pieces*. Cambridge University Press, 2021.

Afrasiabi, Kaveh and Nader Entessar. *Trump and Iran: From Containment to Confrontation*. Lexington, 2019.

Ajami, Fouad. *The Vanished Imam: Musa al Sadr and the Shia of Lebanon*. Cornell University Press, 2012.

Akbarzadeh, Shahram and Dara Conduit, eds. *Iran in the World: President Rouhani's Foreign Policy*. Palgrave Macmillan, 2016.

Akbarzadeh, Shahram, William Gourlay, and Anoushirvan Ehteshami, 'Iranian Proxies in the Syrian Conflict: Tehran's "Forward Defense" in Action', *Journal of Strategic Studies*, Vol. 46, Issue 3, 2023, pp. 683–706.

Alavi, Seyyed Ali. *Iran and Palestine: Past, Present, Future*. Routledge, 2011.

Alfoneh, Ali. *Iran Unveiled: How the Revolutionary Guards is Turning Theocracy into Military Dictatorship*. American Enterprise Institute, 2013.

Alvandi, Roham. *Nixon, Kissinger, and the Shah: The United States and Iran in the Cold War*. Oxford University Press, 2014.

Amanat, Abbas. *Iran: A Modern History*. Yale University Press, 2017.

Amirabdollahian, Hossein. *Sobh-e Sham* [Morning in Damascus], prepared by Mohammad Mohsen Mos'hafi. Tehran, Sooreh-mehr 2020.

Ansari, Ali. *Modern Iran Since 1921: The Pahlavis and After*. Pearson Education, 2003.

Ayatollahi Tabaar, Mohammad, 'Causes of the US Hostage Crisis in Iran: The Untold Account of the Communist Threat', *Security Studies*, Vol. 26, Issue 4, 2017, pp. 665–97.

Azani, Eitan. *Hezbollah: The Story of the Party of God*. Springer, 2011.

Azizi, Arash. *The Shadow Commander: Soleimani, the U.S., and Iran's Global Ambitions*. Oneworld, 2020.

Azizi, Hamidreza, 'The Concept of "Forward Defense": How Has the Syrian Crisis Shaped the Evolution of Iran's Military Strategy?', Geneva Center for Security Policy, February 2021.

Baconi, Tareq. *Hamas Contained: A History of Palestinian Resistance*. Stanford University Press, 2022.

Bajoghli, Narges. *Iran Reframed: Anxieties of Power in the Islamic Republic*. Stanford University Press, 2019.

Bajoghli, Narges, Vali Nasr, and Djavad Salehi-Isfahani. *How Sanctions Work: Iran and the Impact of Economic Warfare*. Stanford University Press, 2024.

Barzegar, Kayhan and Masoud Rezaei, 'Ayatollah Khamenei's Strategic Thinking', *Discourse: An Iranian Quarterly*, Vol. 11, No. 3, Winter 2017, pp. 27–54.

Bill, James. *The Eagle and the Lion: The Tragedy of American Iranian Relations*. Yale University Press, 1988.

Blanford, Nicholas. *Warriors of God: Inside Hezbollah's Thirty-year Struggle against Israel*. Random House, 2011.

Blight, James, Janet Lang, Malcolm Byrne, and John Tirman. *Becoming Enemies: US–Iran Relations and the Iran–Iraq War, 1979–1988*. Rowman & Littlefield, 2012.

Boroujerdi, Mehrzad and Kourosh Rahimkhani. *Postrevolutionary Iran: A Political Handbook*. Syracuse University Press, 2018.

Braden, Evan. *On the Hegemon's Shadow: Leading States and the Rise of Regional Powers*. Cornell University Press, 2016.

Brandt, Marieke *Tribes and Politics in Yemen: A History of the Houthi Conflict*. Oxford University Press, 2024.

Chamran, Mostafa. *Lebanon* (His Letters and Recollections from Lebanon). Tehran, 1984.

Chehabi, H.E. *Distant Relations: Iran and Lebanon in the Last 500 Years*. I.B. Tauris, 2007.

Chubin, Shahram. *Iran and Iraq at War*. Routledge, 2019.

Clark, Victoria. *Yemen: Dancing on the Heads of Snakes*. Yale University Press, 2010.

Cockburn, Patrick. *Muqtada: Muqtada al-Sadr, the Shia Revival, and the Struggle for Iraq*. Scribner, 2008.

Cooper, Andrew Scott. *The Fall of Heaven: The Pahlavis and the Final Days of Imperial Iran*. Henry Holt & Co., 2016.

Crist, David. *The Twilight War: The Secret History of America's Thirty-year Conflict with Iran*. Penguin Books, 2012.

Crooke, Alastair. *Resistance: The Essence of the Islamist Revolution*. Pluto Press, 2009.

Day, Stephen. *Regionalism and Rebellion Yemen: A Troubled National Union*. Cambridge University Press, 2012.

Doroodian, Mohammad. *Aqaz ta Payan* [The Beginning Until the End]. Center for the Study and Research of War, No date.

Ehteshami, Anoush. *Iran: Stuck in Transition*. Routledge, 2017.

Ehteshami, Anoush and R. Hinnebusch. *Syria and Iran: Middle Powers in a Penetrated Regional System*. Routledge, 1997.

Eisenstadt, Michael, 'Iran's Grey Zone Strategy: Cornerstone of Its Asymmetric Way of War', Washington Institute for Near East Policy, May 19, 2021.

—— *The Strategic Culture of the Islamic Republic of Iran*. Marine Corps University Middle East Studies Monograph No. 1, August 2011.

Entessar, Nader, 'Israel and Iran's National Security', *Journal of South Asian and Middle Eastern Studies*, Vol. 27, No. 4, Summer 2004.

Esfandiary, Diana and Ariane Tabatabai, 'Iran's ISIS Policy', *International Affairs*, Vol. 1, 2015, pp. 1–15.

Fantappie, Maria and Vali Nasr, 'The War that Remade the Middle East: How Washington Can Stabilize a Transformed Region', *Foreign Affairs*, November 20, 2023.

Feldman, Noah. *The Arab Winter: A Tragedy*. Princeton University Press, 2020.

Felter, Jospeh and Brian Fishman, 'Iranian Strategy in Iraq: Politics and Other Means', Counterterrorism Center, West Point, October 2008.

Fromkin, David. *A Peace to End All Peace: The Fall of the Ottoman Empire and the Creation of the Modern Middle East*. Henry Holt & Co., 1989.

Fuller, Graham. *The Center of the Universe: The Geopolitics of Iran*. Westview Press/Rand Corporation, 1991.

Gasiorowski, Mark and Malcolm Byne, eds. *Mohammad Mosaddeq and the 1953 Coup in Iran*. Syracuse University Press, 2004.

Ghazvinian, John. *America and Iran: A History*. Alfred A. Knopf, 2021.

Goldsmith, Leon. *Cycle of Fear: Syria's Alawites in War and Peace*. Hurst & Co., 2015.

Goodarzi, Jubin. *Syria and Iran: Diplomatic Alliance and Power Politics in the Middle East*. Tauris Academic Books, 2006.

Gray, Colin. *Irregular Enemies and the Essence of Strategy: Can the American Way of War Adapt?* US Army War College Press, March 2006.

Hadian, Nasser and Shani Hormozi, 'Iran's New Security Environment Imperatives: Counter Containment or Engagement with the US', *Iranian Review*, Vol. 1, No. 4, Winter 2011, pp. 13–35.

Hamadani, Hossein. *Payam-e Mahiha* [The Message of the Fish], with Gul Ali Babaee. Sa'eqe, 2016.

Hamilton, Robert, Chris Miller, and Aaron Stein, 'Russia Intervention in Syria: Historical and Geostrategic Context', Foreign Policy Research Institute, September 2020.

Hamzeh, Ahmad Nizar. *In the Path of Hizbullah*. Syracuse University Press, 2004.

Harr, Scott, 'Trans-rational: Iran's Transitional Strategy for Dominance and Why it Cannot Survive Great Power Competition', *Military Review*, March–April 2020, pp. 77–84.

Hashemi Nader and Danny Postal. *The Syria Dilemma*. MIT Press, 2013.

Hatina, Meir. *Islam and Salvation in Palestine: The Islamic Jihad Movement*. Syracuse University Press, 2001.

Hill, Christropher. *Outpost: Life on the Frontlines of American Diplomacy: A Memoir*. Simon & Schuster, 2014.

Hiltermann, Joost. *A Poisonous Affair: America, Iraq, and the Gassing of Halabja*. Cambridge University Press, 2007.

Hunter, Shirin. *Iran's Foreign Policy in the Post-Soviet Era: Resisting the New International Order*. Praeger, 2010.

—— 'Iran's Pragmatic Regional Policy', *Journal of International Affairs*, Vol. 26. No. 2, Spring 2003, pp. 133–47.

Jabar, Faleh. *The Shiite Movement in Iraq*. Saqi Books, 2003.

Johnson, David. *Hard Fighting: Israel in Lebanon and Gaza*. Rand Corporation, 2011.

Jones, Seth, 'Containing Iran: Understanding Iran's Power and Exploiting its Vulnerabilities', Center for Strategic and International Studies, January 2020.

Juneau, Thomas, 'How War in Yemen Transformed the Iran–Houthi Partnership', *Studies in Conflict and Terrorism*, July 30, 2021.

—— *Squandered Opportunity: Neoclassical Realism and Iranian Foreign Policy*. Stanford University Press, 2015.

Juneau, Thomas and Sam Razavi, eds. *Iranian Foreign Policy Since 2001: Alone in the World*. Routledge, 2013.

Kadhim, Abbas. *Reclaiming Iraq: The 1920 Revolution and the Founding of the Modern State*. University of Texas Press, 2012.

Kaye, Dalia Dassa, Ali Reza Nader and Parisa Roshan. *Israel and Iran: A Dangerous Rivalry*. Rand, 2011.

Kaye, Dalia Dassa and Sanam Vakil, 'The Limits of Cooperation between Israel and the Arab States', *Foreign Affairs*, April 26, 2024.

Landis, Joshua, 'The Syrian Uprising 2011: Why the Assad Regime is Likely to Survive to 2013', *Middle East Policy*, Vol. XIX, No. 1, Spring 2012, pp. 72–84.

Leffler, Melvyn. *Confronting Saddam Hussein: George W. Bush and the Invasion of Iraq*. Oxford University Press, 2023.

Legrenzi, Matteo and Fred Lawson, 'Iran and Its Neighbors since 2003: New Dilemmas', *Middle East Policy*, Vol. 21, No. 4, 2014, pp. 105–11.

Lesch, David. *Syria: The Fall of the House of Assad*. Yale University Press, 2011.

Lim, Kevjn. *Power, Perception and Politics in the Making of Iranian Grand Strategy*. Palgrave Macmillan, 2022.

Limbert, John. *Negotiating with Iran: Wrestling the Ghosts of History*. United States Institute of Peace, 2009.

Litvak, Meir, 'The Islamization of the Palestinian–Israeli Conflict: The Case of Hamas', *Middle Eastern Studies*, Vol. 14, No. 1, January 1998, pp. 148–63.

Maloney, Suzanne. *The Iranian Revolution at Forty*. Brookings, 2020.

Ma'oz, Moshe and Avner Yaniv, eds. *Syria under Assad*. Croom Helm, 1986.

McKenzie, Kenneth. *The Melting Point: High Command and War in the 21st Century*. Naval Institute Press, 2024.

Mearsheimer, John. *Conventional Deterrence*. Cornell University Press, 1983.

Menashri, David, 'Israeli Relations with Iran: The Pahlavi Period', *Encyclopedia Iranica*.

—— 'Iran, Israel and the Middle East Conflict', *Israel Affairs*, Vol. 12, Issue 2, 2006, pp. 107–22.

Mesbahi, Mohiaddin, 'Free and Confined: Iran and the International System', *Iranian Review of Foreign Affairs*, Vol. 2, No. 5, Spring 2011, pp. 9–34.

Milani, Abbas. *Shah*. Palgrave, 2011.

—— *The Myth of the Great Satan: A New Look at America's Relation with Iran*. Hoover Institution Press, 2010.

Milani, Mohsen, 'Iran and Russia's Uncomfortable Alliance: Their Cooperation in Syria in Context', *Foreign Affairs*, August 31, 2016.

—— 'Iran's Game in Yemen: Why Tehran Isn't to Blame for the Civil War', *Foreign Affairs*, April 19, 2015.

—— 'Why Tehran Won't Abandon Assad(ism)', *Washington Quarterly*, December 2013, pp. 79–98.

—— 'Tehran's Take: Iran's Policy toward the U.S.', *Foreign Affairs*, Vol. 88, No. 4, July–August 2009, pp. 42–62.

—— 'Iran's Relations with Iraq: 1921–79', *Encyclopedia Iranica*. Columbia University, 2006, pp. 564–72.

—— 'Iran's Ambivalent World Role', in *Comparative Foreign Policy*, ed. by Steven Hook, Prentice Hall, 2002, pp. 219–44.

—— *The Making of Iran's Islamic Revolution*. Westview Press, 1994.

Mohseni, Payam and Hussein Kalout, 'Iran's Axis of Resistance Rises: How It's Forging a New Middle East', *Foreign Affairs*, January 24, 2017.

Monshipouri, Mahmood. *In the Shadow of Mistrust: The Geopolitics and Diplomacy of US–Iran Relations*. Oxford University Press, 2022.

Mottahedeh, Roy. *The Mantle of the Prophet: Religion and Politics in Iran*. Pantheon Books, 1985.

Mousavian, Seyyed Hossein and Mohammad Reza Chitsazian, 'Iran's Foreign Policy in the Middle East: A Grand Strategy', *Middle East Policy*, Vol. 27, Issue 3, Fall 2020, pp. 99–144.

Murray, Williamson and Kevin Woods. *The Iran–Iraq War: A Military and Strategic History*. Cambridge University Press.

Nasr, Vali. *The Shia Revival: How Conflict within Islam Will Shape the Future*. W.W. Norton, 2016.

—— 'Regional Implications of Shi'a Revival in Iraq', *Washington Quarterly*, Vol. 27, No. 3, Summer 2002, pp. 7–24.

Nejat, Seyyed Ali, 'Iran's Foreign Policy and the New Developments in the Middle East', *Journal of Politics* (in Persian), Vol. 1, No. 4, Winter 2015.

Norton, Richard. *Hezbollah: A Short History*. Princeton University Press, 2007.

—— *Amal and the Shi'a: Struggle for the Soul of Lebanon*. University of Texas Press, 1987.

Osiewicz, Przemyslaw. *Foreign Policy of the Islamic Republic of Iran: Between Ideology and Pragmatism*. Routledge, 2021.

Ostovar, Afshon. *Vanguard of the Imam: Religion, Politics, and Iran's Revolutionary Guards*. Oxford University Press, 2016.

Pahlavi, Mohmmad Reza Shah. *Answer to History*. Stein & Day, 1980.

Pape, Robert. *Dying to Win: The Strategic Logic of Suicide Terrorism*. Random House, 2005.

Parsi, Trita. *Losing an Enemy: Obama, Iran, and the Triumph of Diplomacy*. Yale University Press, 2017.

—— *Treacherous Alliance: The Secret Dealings of Israel, Iran, and the United States*. Yale University Press, 2007.

Perthes, Volker, 'Ambition and Fear: Iran's Foreign Policy and Nuclear Programme', *Survival*, Vol. 52, No. 3, June–July 2010, pp. 95–114.

Pollack, Kenneth. *Unthinkable: Iran, the Bomb, and American Strategy*. Simon & Schuster, 2013.

Rafiqdoust, Mohsen (with Saeed Alaeyun). *Baraye Tarikh Meegooyam: Khaterat e Moshen Rafiqdoust* [I Say it for History: Mohsen Rafiqdoust's Memoirs], Vols 1–3. Entesharat-e Sourey-e Mehr, 2013.

Ramazani, R.K. *Independence without Freedom: Iran's Foreign Policy.* University of Virginia Press, 2013.

—— *The Foreign Policy of Iran: A Developing Nation in World Affairs.* University Press of Virginia, 1966.

Razoux, Pierre. *The Iran–Iraq War*, trans. by Nicholas Elliot. The Belknap Press of Harvard University Press, 2015.

Reisinezhad, Arash. *The Shah of Iran, the Iraqi Kurds, and the Lebanese Shia.* Palgrave Macmillan, 2019.

Riedel, Bruce. *America and the Yemens: A Complex and Tragic Encounter.* Brookings Institution Press, 2023.

Rose, Gideon, ed. *Iran and the Bomb: Solving the Persian Puzzle.* Council on Foreign Relations, 2012.

Roshandel, Jalil, 'Iran's Foreign and Security Policies: How the Decision-making Process Evolved', *Security Dialogue*, Vol. 31, Issue 1, 2000. pp. 105–17.

Sadjadpour, Karim. *Reading Khamenei: The World View of Iran's Most Powerful Leader.* Carnegie Endowment for International Peace, 2009.

Safavi, Seyyed Rahim, prepared by Majid Najafpour. *Az Jonoob-e Lebanon ta Jonoob-e Iran* [From South of Lebanon to South of Iran]. Markaz-e Asnad-e Enqelab-e Islami, 2009.

Saikal, Amin. *Iran Rising: The Survival and Future of the Islamic Republic.* Princeton University Press, 2009.

Samii, Abbas William, 'A Stable Structure on Shifting Sands: Assessing the Hizbullah–Iran–Syria Relationship', *Middle East Journal*, Vol. 62, No. 1, Winter 2008, pp. 32–53.

Samuel, Annie Tracy. *The Unfinished History of the Iran–Iraq War: Faith, Firepower, and Iran's Revolutionary Guards.* University of Tennessee Press, 2023.

Sariolghalam, Mahmood, 'Prospects of Change in Iranian Foreign Policy', Carnegie Endowment for International Peace, February 20, 2018.

Seale, Patrick. *The Struggle for Syria.* Yale University Press, 1987.

Seliktar, Ofira and Farhad Rezaei. *Iran, Revolution and Proxy Wars*, Palgrave Macmillan, 2019.

Shawcross, William. *The Shah's Last Ride: The Fate of an Ally.* Simon & Schuster, 1988.

Sick, Gary, 'Iran's Quest for Superpower Status', *Foreign Affairs*, Vol. 65, No. 4, 1987.

—— *All Fall Down: America's Tragic Encounter with Iran.* Random House, 1985.

Simon, Steven. *Grand Delusion: The Rise and Fall of American Ambitions in the Middle East*. Penguin Books, 2023.

Skare, Erik. *A History of Palestinian Islamic Jihad: Faith, Awareness, and Revolution in the Middle East*. Cambridge University Press, 2021.

Slavin, Barbara. *Bitter Friends, Bosom Enemies: Iran, the U.S., and the Twisted Path to Confrontation*. St. Martin's Griffin, 2009.

Smith, Thomas, 'The Gaza Wars, 2008–2014: Human Rights Agency and Advocacy', in Thomas Smith, *Human Rights and War through Civilian Eyes*. University of Pennsylvania Press, 2017, pp. 108–48.

Steinberg, Guido. *The 'Axis of Resistance': Iran's Expansion in the Middle East Is Hitting a Wall*. SWP Research Paper 2021RP/6, Stiftung Wissenschaft Politik, August 2021.

Tabatabai, Ariane, *No Conquest, No Defeat: Iran's National Security Strategy*. Oxford University Press, 2020.

—— 'Syria Changed the Iranian Way of War', *Foreign Affairs*, August 16, 2019.

Tabrizi, Aniseh and Raffaelo Pantucci, eds. *Understanding Iran's Role in the Syrian Conflict*. Occasional Paper, Royal United Services Institute, August 2016.

Takeyh, Ray. *The Last Shah: America, Iran, and the Fall of the Pahlavi Dynasty*. Yale University Press, 2021.

Talhamy, Yvette, 'The Syrian Muslim Brothers and the Syrian–Iranian Relationship', *Middle East Journal*, Vol. 63, No. 4, October 22, 2009, pp. 561–80.

Terrill, Andrew, 'Iranian Involvement in Yemen', *Orbis*, Vol. 58, No. 3, Summer 2014, pp. 429–40.

Zahedi, Ardeshir. *Khaterat-e Ardeshir Zahedi* [The Memoirs of Ardeshir Zahadi], 3 vol. Ibex Publishers, 2020.

Uskowi, Nader. *Temperature Rising: Iran's Revolutionary Guards and Wars in the Middle East*. Rowman & Littlefield, 2019.

Vaez, Ali, 'Why the War in Gaza Makes a Nuclear Iran More Likely: The Conflict Has Empowered Tehran – but Also Fueled Its Sense of Vulnerability', *Foreign Affairs*, January 25, 2024.

Vatanka, Alex. *The Battle of the Ayatollahs in Iran*. I.B. Tauris, 2021.

—— 'Iran's Yemen Play: What Tehran Wants – and What it Doesn't', *Foreign Affairs*, March 4, 2015.

Woodward, Bob. *Veil: The Secret Wars of the CIA: 1981–1987*. Simon & Schuster, 1987.

Wright, Robin. *The Last Great Revolution: Turmoil and Transformation in Iran*. Vintage, 2001.

Zarif, Mohammad Javad and Zarif, M.J., 'An Insider's View of Iran's Foreign Policy: Negotiation from Strength', *Foreign Policy Journal* (in Persian), Vol. 32, No. 4, 2019. http://fp.ipisjournals.ir/article_34884.html.

Notes

Introduction: The Riddle of Iran's Rise

1 Minutes after killing Soleimani, the United States launched another drone strike, targeting Abdulreza Shahlaei, an IRGC commander, in Yemen. He survived the attack.

2 'Remarks by President Trump on the Killing of Qasem Soleimani', January 3, 2020. https://trumpwhitehouse.archives.gov/briefings-statements/remarks-president-trump-killing-qasem-soleimani/?utm_source=link.

3 The State Department designated as a 'Foreign Terrorist Organization' (FTO) the Islamic Revolutionary Guard Corps (IRGC) in its entirety, including the Qods Force in April 2019. https://2017-2021.state.gov/designation-of-the-islamic-revolutionary-guard-corps/#:~:text=In%202017%2C%20the%20 Department%20of%20the%20Treasury%20designated,number%20of%20 terrorist%20groups%2C%20including%20Hizballah%20and%20Hamas.

4 Personal interview with General Kenneth F. McKenzie, Tampa, Florida, October 17, 2022.

5 Henry Kissinger, 'Opening Statement before the Senate Armed Services Committee', January 25, 2018, pp. 3–4. https://www.armed-services.senate.gov/imo/media/doc/Kissinger_01-25-18.pdf.

6 Samuel Huntington, 'The Lonely Superpower', *Foreign Affairs*, March/April 1999.

7 Braden discusses the complexities associated with the rise of regional powers and the corresponding reactions from the United States. Evan Braden, *On the Hegemon's Shadow: Leading States and the Rise of Regional Powers*. Cornell University Press, 2016.

8 Kenneth Waltz, *Man, the State, and War: A Theoretical Analysis*. Columbia University Press, 1959, pp. 235–39.

9 Unless otherwise noted, all translations from Persian-language sources are the author's own.

10 John Stuart Mill, *On Liberty*. Cambridge University Press, 2011, p. 67.

1 Pax Americana in Iran and Roots of Anti-Americanism

1 Charles T. Cross, 'Inspection Memorandum', Tehran, Documents from the U.S. Espionage Den, Vol. 62, July 1978, No. 11, p. 24. The book is one of 63 volumes of documents that were shredded by US personnel when the American embassy was attacked in Tehran, then pieced together by the hostage takers.

2 In this chapter, I have used information from my following two pieces: 'Iran's Ambivalent World Role', in *Comparative Foreign Policy: Adaptation Strategies of the Great and Emerging Powers*, ed. by Steven W. Hook. Prentice Hall, 2002, pp. 219–44; and 'Pre-revolutionary Iran and Great Power Rivalry', in *Great Power Competition*, ed. by Adib Farhadi and Anthony J. Masys. Springer, 2021, pp. 155–78.

3 Touraj Daryaee, ed., *Oxford Handbook of Iranian History*. Oxford University Press, 2012, p. 244.

4 Abbas Amanat, *Iran: A Modern History*. Yale University Press, 2017, p. 433.

5 Arvand Abrahamian, *The Coup 1953, the CIA, and the Roots of Modern U.S.–Iranian Relations*. The New Press, 2015, pp. 26–7.

6 For details, see Cyrus Ghani, *Iran and the Rise of Reza Shah: From Qajar Collapse to Pahlavi Power*. I.B. Tauris, 1998; and Mehran Kamrava, *A Dynastic History of Iran: From the Qajars to the Pahlavis*. Cambridge University Press, 2022.

7 See Chelsi Mueller, 'Anglo-Iranian Treaty Negotiations: Reza Shah, Teymurtash and the British Government, 1927–32', *Iranian Studies*, Vol. 49, Issue 4, July 2016, pp. 577–92. For a critical analysis of the new the oil agreement, see Mohammad Gholi Majd, *Great Britain and Reza Shah: The Plunder of Iran, 1921–1941*. University of Florida Press, 2001. And for a more balanced analysis of the oil agreement, see Manuchir Farmanfarmaian and Roxane Farmanfarmaian, *Blood and Oil*. The Modern Library, 1997, pp. 85–131.

8 For a good discussion of US–Iran relations, see Mahmood Monshipouri, *In the Shadow of Mistrust: The Geopolitics and Diplomacy of US–Iran Relations*. Oxford University Press, 2022, and John Ghazvinian, *America and Iran: A History*. Alfred A. Knopf, 2021.

9 Shaul Bakhash, *The Fall of Reza Shah: The Abdication, Exile, and Death of Modern's Iran's Founder*. I.B. Tauris, 2021, pp. 25–44 and 59–69.

10 For the most authoritative study of the life and times of Mohammad Reza Shah, see Abbas Milani, *Shah*. Palgrave, 2011.

11 For details, see Louise Fawcett, *Iran and the Cold War: The Azerbaijan Crisis*. Cambridge University Press, 1992.

12 Reza Aslan, *An American Martyr in Persia: The Epic Life and Tragic Death of Howard Baskerville*. W.W. Norton, 2022.

13 Fakhreddin Azimi, *Iran: The Crisis of Democracy: From the Exile of Reza Shah to the Fall of Musaddiq*. I.B. Tauris, 2009.

14 For an excellent account of Mosaddegh's legacy, see Christopher de Bellaigue, *Patriot of Persia: Muhammad Mossadegh and a Tragic Anglo-American Coup*. HarperCollins, 2012.

15 On the coup, see Mark J. Gasiorowski and Malcom Byrne, eds, *Mohammad Mosaddegh and the 1953 Coup in Iran*. Syracuse University Press, 2004; Stephen Kinzer, *All the Shah's Men: An American Coup and the Roots of Middle East Terror*. John Wiley and Sons, 2003. In 2000, *The New York Times* published pdf files of a secret CIA report about the coup: 'Clandestine Service History, Overthrow of Premier Mosaddeq of Iran, November 1952–August 1953'. http://www.nytimes.com/library/world/mideast/041600 iran-cia-index.html. For a different perspective, see Abbas Milani, *The Myth of the Great Satan: A New Look at America's Relations with Iran*. Hoover Institution Press, 2010.

16 Yonah Alexander and Allen Nanes, *The United States and Iran: A Documentary History*. University Publications of America, 1980, pp. 264–312.

17 Afsaneh Najmabadi, *Land Reform and Social Change in Iran*. University of Utah Press, 1987.

18 'Imam Khomeini's Biography', Khamenei.ir. https://english.khamenei.ir/news/2116/Imam-Khomeini-s-Biography, and Baqer Moin, *Khomeini: Life of the Ayatollah*. I.B. Tauris, 2009.

19 Ruhollah Khomeini, *Kashfal Asrar* [Secret Unveiled]. Tehran, n.d., p. 185.

20 For details, see Mohsen Milani, *The Making of Iran's Islamic Revolution*. Westview Press, 1994, 2nd edn, pp. 47–55.

21 Central Intelligence Agency, Foreign Assessment Center, 'Islam in Iran', August 1979. NLC-25-43-7-2-bm. Released September 5, 2005. His actions and declarations, however, negated this alleged conciliatory message to Washington.

22 Ruhollah Khomeini, *Islam and Revolution: Writings and Declaration of Imam Khomeini*. Translated and annotated by Hamid Algar. Mizan, 1981, pp. 178–82. For Ayatollah Khomeini's speech about the passage of the 'capitulation laws', see Khomeini portal. http://en.imam-khomeini.ir/en/n38665/Imam-Khomeini-s-speech-about-Capitulation-Law.

23 James Bill, *The Eagle and the Lion: The Tragedy of American Iranian Relations*. Yale University Press, 1988, p. 254.

24 National Security Council, 'National Security Memorandum 92', November 7, 1970. https://www.nixonlibrary.gov/sites/default/files/virtuallibrary/documents/nsdm/nsdm_092.pdf SINA.

25 Bill, *The Eagle and the Lion*, pp. 183–26.

26 Michael Clare, *American Arms Superpower*. University of Texas Press, 1984, p. 78.

27 The quote is by representative Gerry Studds. See ibid., p. 89.

28 Barry Rubin, 'Iran: The Rise of a Regional Power', *Middle East Review of International Affairs*, Vol. 10, No. 3, September 2006, pp. 142–51.

29 Central Intelligence Agency, 'Briefing Papers for Visit of General Nematollah Nasiri', April 28, 1975, https://www.cia.gov/readingroom/docs/CIA-RDP85T00353R000100270011-5.pdf.

30 Mohammad Reza Pahlavi, *Be Su-ye Tamaddon-e Bozorg* [Towards the Great Civilisation]. Tehran, 1974.

31 Bill, *The Eagle and the Lion*, p. 204.

32 Central Intelligence Agency, 'National Intelligence Bulletin', November 7, 1974. https://www.cia.gov/readingroom/docs/CIA-RDP79T00975A027100010034-2.pdf.

33 'Simon Quoted as Calling the Shah of Iran "a Nut"', *The New York Times*, July 16, 1974. https://www.nytimes.com/1974/07/16/archives/simon-quoted-as-calling-the-shah-of-iran-a-nut.html.

34 Quoted in George C. Wilson, 'Gen. George Brown Dies', *Washington Post*, December 6, 1978.

35 Jimmy Carter, *Keeping Faith*. New York, 1983, p. 143.

36 Mehdi Bazargan, *Enqelab dar dou Harekat* [Revolution in Two Strokes]. Tehran, 1984, p. 26.

37 For details, see Mohsen Milani, *The Making of Iran's Islamic Revolution*, pp. 115–18.

38 Central Intelligence Agency, 'Briefing Papers for Visit of General Nematollah Nasiri', April 28, 1976. https://www.cia.gov/readingroom/docs/CIA-RDP85T00353R000100270011-5.pdf.

2 Revolutionary Iran's Regional Policy: Anti-Americanism on Steroids

1 Bazargan, *Enqelab dar Dou Hareket* [Revolution in Two Strokes], pp. 37–40.

2 Milani, *The Making of Iran's Islamic Revolution*, pp. 125–33.

3 Kambiz Fattahi, 'Ayatollah Khomeini's Secret Letter to Carter', BBC Persian, November 4, 2015. The article contains the Khomeini's message in English. I am grateful to Dr Sina Azodi for sharing this document with me. https://www.bbc.com/persian/iran/2015/11/151103_u01-khomeini-carter-secret-message.

4 For details, see Ebrahim Yazdi, *Barresiy-e Safar-e Huyser be Iran* [Review of Huyser's Trip to Iran]. Tehran, 1984.

5 On the importance of independence in Iranian foreign policy, see. R.K. Ramazani, *Independence without Freedom: Iran's Foreign Policy*. University of Virginia Press, 2013.

6 David Rockefeller and Henry Kissinger pressured President Carter to admit the Shah to the US. See Carter, *Keeping Faith*, p. 454. See also William J. Daugherty, 'Jimmy Carter and the 1979 Decision to Admit the Shah to the US'. https://americandiplomacy.web.unc.edu/2003/04/jimmy-carter-and-the-1979-decision-to-admit-the-shah-into-the-united-states/. Daugherty was held captive as a hostage in Tehran.

7 Quoted in Hamilton Jordan, *Crisis: The Last Years of Carter Presidency*. Newsweek, 1982, p. 5.

8 Bruce Laingen, *Yellow Ribbons: The Secret Journal of Bruce Laingen*. Brassey's, 1992, p. 10.

9 For details see, Mohsen Milani, 'Hostage Crisis (The Tehran Hostage Crisis of 1979)', *Encyclopedia Iranica*, Vol. 6. Columbia University, 2004, pp. 522–35. I have used information and sources from this article in this section.

10 Carter, *Keeping Faith*, p. 466.

11 Personal interview with Seyed Mohammad Mousavi Khoeiniha, June 1993, Tehran, Iran, as quoted in Milani, 'Hostage Crisis'.

12 Tabaar has argued that the hostage crisis was a pre-emptive act by the Islamists to outbid the leftists' anti-American activities. Mohammad Ayatollahi Tabaar, 'Causes of the US Hostage Crisis in Iran: The Untold Account of the Communist Threat', *Security Studies*, Vol. 26, Issue 4, 2017, pp. 665–97.

13 Paul Ryan, *The Iranian Rescue Mission: Why It Failed*. Stanford University Press, 1985, p. 60.

14 On the destructive role played by the leftists and the Tudeh party during Bazargan's rule and during in the hostage crisis, see Mohsen Milani, 'Harvest of Shame: Tudeh and the Bazargan government', *Middle East Studies*, Vol. 29, No. 2, April 1993, pp. 307–20.

15 Laingen, *Yellow Ribbons*, p. 10.

16 Personal interview with Ambassador Bruce Laingen, Tampa, Florida, November 23, 1998.

17 Mehdi Bazargan, *Shura-ye Enqelab Va Doulat-e Movaghat* [The Council of Revolution and the Transitional Government]. Tehran, 1983.

18 On the IRGC, see Afshon Ostovar, *Vanguard of the Imam: Religion, Politics, and Iran's Revolutionary Guards*. Oxford University Press, 2016; Ali Alfoneh, *Iran Unveiled: How the Revolutionary Guards is Turning Theocracy into Military Dictatorship*. American Enterprise Institute, 2013; and Ray Takeyh, *Guardians of the Revolution: Iran and the World in the Age of the Ayatollahs*. Oxford University Press, 2016.

19 Personal interview with Mehdi Bazargan, June 14, 1992, Tehran, Iran.

20 For Mousavi's letter, see Parsine.com, April 26, 2012, http:www.parsine.com/fa/news/60911/1367.

21 'The Release of a Sensitive Audio File about Soleimani and Russia's Sabotage of the JCPOA', BBC Persian, April 25, 2021. https://www.bbc.com/persian/iran-56878595.

22 Former Prime Minister Jafar Sharif Imami recalled that every detail about Iranian foreign policy and the armed forces had to be reported to the Shah and approved by him. He indicated that the Shah did not trust anyone's judgement and did not believe in consulting with others. See *Iranian Oral History*, Harvard University, interview with Jafar Sharif Imami, Tape Number 4, Side 2, starting at 20 minutes into the interview.

23 See Jalil Roshandel, 'Historical Analysis of Iran's Foreign Policy and Its Main Approaches During the 14th Century (sh)', Iran Academia University, 2022. https://iranacademia.com/icci-2022/historical-analysis-of-irans-foreign-policy-and-its-main-approaches-during-the-14th-centurysh/?lang=en.

Also see his 'Iran's Foreign and Security Policies: How the Decision-making Process Evolved', *Security Dialogue*, Vol. 31, Issue 1, 2000. pp. 105–17.

24 For an American perspective on Iran's regional objectives, see US Defense Department, *Unclassified, Annual Report on Military Power of Iran*, US Defense Department, April 2012, Fall update, Executive Summary. https://fas.org/man/eprint/dod_iran_2010.pdf and '2023 Annual Threat Assessment of the US Intelligence Community', pp. 15–18. https://www.dni.gov/files/ODNI/documents/assessments/ATA-2023-Unclassified-Report.pdf.

25 Official Translation of the Constitution of the Islamic Republic of Iran. https://www.refworld.org/docid/3ae6b56710.html. For a good discussion of the constitution, see Asghar Schirazi, *The Constitution of Iran: Politics and the State in the Islamic Republic*. I.B. Tauris, 1997.

26 'Statement for the Record General Michael "Erik" Kurilla Commander, US Central Command before the House Armed Services Committee on the Posture of US Central Command', March 7, 2024. https://www.centcom.mil/ABOUT-US/POSTURE-STATEMENT/.

27 R.K. Ramazani, *The Gulf Cooperation Council: Record and Analysis*. University Press of Virginia, 1988.

28 For an excellent discussion of Iran's national security strategy, see Ariane Tabatabai, *No Conquest, No Defeat: Iran's National Security Strategy*. Hurst, 2020. See also Kevjn Lim, *Power, Perception and Politics in the Making of Iranian Grand Strategy*. Palgrave Macmillan, 2022; and Amin Saikal, *Iran Rising: The Survival and Future of the Islamic Republic*. Princeton University Press, 2009.

29 President Ali Khamenei's speech at the UN General Assembly, September 1987. Khamenei portal. https://english.khamenei.ir/news/1413/Leader-s-Speech-at-UN-General-Assembly.

30 On Ayatollah Khamenei's strategic thinking, see the well-researched article in Persian by Keyhan Barzegar and Masoud Rezaei, 'Ayatollah Khamenei's Strategic Thinking', *Discourse: An Iranian Quarterly*, Vol. 11, No. 3, Winter 2017, pp. 27–54. See also 'Iran's Foreign and Defense Policies', Congressional Research Service, January 11, 2021, pp. 9–12. https://sgp.fas.org/crs/mideast/R44017.pdf.

31 As quoted in Barzegar and Rezaei, 'Ayatollah Khamenei's Strategic Thinking'.

32 Fars News, March 10, 2022, http://fna.ir/79a44.

33 For a short and perceptive piece on this network, see Michael Axworthy, 'The Shia Rising', *New Statesman*, February–March 23, 2018. See also Afshon Ostovar, 'The Grand Strategy of Militant Clients: Iran's Way of War', *Security Studies*, Vol. 28, No. 1, 2019, pp. 159–88. https://www-tandfonline-com.ezproxy.lib.usf.edu/doi/pdf/10.1080/09636412.2018.1508862?needAccess=true.

34 'Talking with Commander Nazeri: A Narrative about the Formation of Asymmetric Forces within the IRGC' (in Persian), Sharq, May 11, 2016.

35 Mohiaddin Mesbahi, 'Free and Confined: Iran and the International System', *Iranian Review of Foreign Affairs*, Vol. 2, No. 5, Spring 2011, p. 23.

36 On deterrence, see John Mearsheimer, *Conventional Deterrence*. Cornell University Press, 1983; and Kevin Chilton and Greg Weaver, 'Waging Deterrence in the Twenty-first Century', *Strategic Studies Quarterly*, Spring 2009, pp. 31–42. https://www.law.upenn.edu/live/files/1363-waging-deterrence-in-the-21st-century-chilton.

37 For more details on the Axis of Resistance, see the thoughtful piece by Guido Steinberg, 'The "Axis of Resistance": Iran's Expansion in the Middle East Is Hitting a Wall', *Stiftung Wissenschaft Politik*, August 2021. https://www.swp-berlin.org/en/publication/irans-expansion-in-the-middle-east-is-hitting-a-wall; Ali Soufan, 'Qasem Soleimani and Iran's Unique Regional Strategy', *CTCS Sentinel*, November 2018, Vol. 11, Issue 10, pp. 1–13. https://ctc.usma.edu/wp-content/uploads/2018/11/CTC-SENTINEL-112018.pdf; and Seth G. Jones, *War by Proxy: Iran's Growing Footprint in the Middle East*, Center for Strategic and International Studies, March 2019.

38 For an analysis that acknowledges the conceptual flaw of categorising these groups as mere proxies, see Diane Zorri, Houman Sadri, and David Ellis, *Iranian Proxy Groups in Iraq, Syria, and Yemen: A Principal–Agent Comparative Analysis*. JSOU Report 20-5. JSOU Press, 2020.

39 For an excellent and nuanced analysis of Iran's regional network, see *Iran's Networks of Influence in the Middle East, Strategic Dossier*, International Institute for Strategic Studies (IISS), 2019. https://www.iiss.org/publications/strategic-dossiers/iran-dossier.

40 Stephen Walt, 'Alliance Formation and the Balance of World Power', *International Security*, Vol. 9, No. 4, Spring 1985, pp. 3–43.

41 On soft balancing see, Robert A, Pape, 'Soft Balancing against the US', *International Security*, Vol. 30, No. 1, 2005, pp. 7–45.

42 For a perceptive analysis of Iran's strategic thinking and role of threat perception in formulation of policy, see J. Mathew McInnis, 'Iran's Strategic Thinking: Origins and Evolution', American Enterprise Institute, May 2015.

43 On the importance of threat perception in international affairs, see Robert Jervis, *Perception and Misperception in International Politics*. Princeton University Press, 1976, pp. 58–113.

44 Melvyn Leffler, *Confronting Saddam Hussein: George W. Bush and the Invasion of Iraq*. Oxford University Press, 2023. For the rejection of one of Leffler's main contentions, see David Corn, 'The Iraq Invasion 20 Years Later: It was Indeed a Big Lie that Launched the Catastrophic War', *Mother Jones*, March 2023. https://www.motherjones.com/politics/2023/03/

the-iraq-invasion-20-years-later-it-was-indeed-a-big-lie-that-launched-the-catastrophic-war/.

45 For a perceptive analysis of the role of fear in Iranian foreign policy, see Volker Perthes, 'Ambition and Fear: Iran's Foreign Policy and Nuclear Programme', *Survival*, Vol. 52, No. 3, June-July 2010, pp. 95–114.

46 Personal interview with Mehdi Bazargan, June 13, 1992, Tehran, Iran.

47 See Norman Podhoretz, 'The Case for Bombing Iran', *Commentary Magazine*, May 6, 2007; Mathew Kroenig, 'Time to Attack Iran: Why a Strike Is the Least Bad Option', *Foreign Affairs*, January–February 2013. https://www.foreignaffairs.com/articles/middle-east/2012-01-01/time-attack-iran; Rachel Benaim and Lazar Berman, 'Sheldon Adelson Calls on US to Nuke Iranian desert', *The Times of Israel*, October 24, 2013. https://www.timesofisrael.com/sheldon-adelson-calls-on-us-to-nuke-iranian-desert/.

48 'Fact Sheet – US Military Bases and Facilities Middle East', American SecurityProject.https://www.americansecurityproject.org/fact-sheet-us-military-bases-and-facilities-in-the-middle-east/.

49 For Tehran's assessment of its security environment in the first decade of the new century, see Naser Hadian and Shani Hormozi, 'Iran's New Security Environment Imperatives: Counter Containment or Engagement with the US', *Iranian Review*, Vol. 1, No. 4, Winter 2011, pp. 13-35. For an American perspective, see Shahram Chubin, Bayman et al., *Iran's Security Policy*, Rand, 2011. https://books.google.com/books?hl=en&lr=&id=c_K0-LEwJaAC&oi=fnd&pg=PR3&dq=iran%27s+syrian+policy&ots=9ZRnGpmrBU&sig=q6ok7McWU7qvMBoKnMTU341e-ok#v=onepage&q=iran's%20syrian%20policy&f=false.

50 As quoted by Barzegar and Rezaei, 'Ayatollah Khamenei's Strategic Thinking', p. 32.

51 For Iran's policy towards the US, see Mohsen Milani, 'Tehran's Take: Iran's Policy toward the U.S.', *Foreign Affairs*, 88, 4, July–August 2009, pp. 42–62.

52 On Iranian foreign policy see, Shahram Akbarzadeh and Dara Conduit, eds, *Iran in the World: President Rouhani's Foreign Policy*. Palgrave Macmillan, 2016; and Thomas Juneau and Sam Razavi, eds, *Iranian Foreign Policy Since 2001: Alone in the World*, Routledge, 2013.

53 For the impact of Iran's internal politics on its foreign policy, see Meir Litvak, 'Internal Political Struggles in Iran and their Impact on Foreign Policy', in *Iran in a Changing Strategic Environment*, Meir Litvak, Emily Landau, and Ephraim Kam, eds. Institute for National Security Studies,Tel Aviv, Israel, No. 173, March 2018, pp. 65–78.

54 See Mahmood Sariolghalam 'Prospects of Change in Iranian Foreign Policy', Carnegie Endowment for International Peace, February 20, 2018. https://

carnegieendowment.org/2018/02/20/prospects-for-change-in-iranian-foreign-policy-pub-75569.

55 See Shirin Hunter, 'Iran's Pragmatic Regional Policy', *Journal of International Affairs*, Vol. 26, No. 2, Spring 2003, pp. 133–47, and David Menashri, 'Iran's Regional Policy: Between Radicalism and Pragmaticism', *Journal of International Affairs*, Vol. 60, Issue 2, Summer 2007, pp. 153–67.

56 As early as 1983, a CIA report identified Rafsanjani and Khamenei as potential rivals. Central Intelligence Agency, Directorate of Intelligence, 'Khamenei and Rafsanjani: Rivals for Power in Iran', December 26, 1983. https://www.cia.gov/library/readingroom/docs/CIA-RDP84S00927 R000200110004-7.pdf.

57 Directorate of Intelligence, 'Iranian Factionalism: Implications for the United States', November 14, 1986. https://www.cia.gov/library/reading-room/docs/CIA-RDP91B00874R000200040002-5.pdf.

58 For details, see Mohsen Milani, 'Iran's Persian Gulf Policy in the Post-Saddam Era', in *Contemporary Iran: Economy, Society, and Politics*, ed. by Ali Gheissari. Oxford University Press, 2009, pp. 349–66.

59 Anthony Lake, 'Confronting Backlash States', *Foreign Affairs*, March/April 1994.

60 'The Full Text of the Letter of the IRGC Commanders to Khatami', *Aftab News*, June 11, 2005. https://aftabnews.ir/0001UA.

61 'Rafsanjani's Full Letter to Ayatollah Khamenei', BBC Persian, July 9, 2009. https://www.bbc.com/persian/iran/2009/06/090609_op_ir88_hashemi_khamenei_letter.

62 James B. Steinberg, Michael E. O'Hanlon, and Susan E. Rice, *The New National Security Strategy and Preemption*, Brookings Policy Briefing Series, December 21, 2002. https://www.brookings.edu/research/the-new-national-security-strategy-and-preemption/.

63 'Mike Pompeo Speech: What Are the 12 Demands Given to Iran?', Al Jazeera, May 21, 2018. https://www.AlJazeera.com/news/2018/5/21/mike-pompeo-speech-what-are-the-12-demands-given-to-iran.

3 Iraq–Iran War: Laying the Foundation for Iran's Rise

1 Saddam Hussein made this statement in his meeting with the National Command and the Revolutionary Command Council on September 16, 1980. See Williamson Murray and Kevin Woods, *The Iran–Iraq War: A Military and Strategic History*. Cambridge University Press, 2014, pp. 48–9.

This book contains a wealth of primary documents on Iraq, captured by the US after its invasion.

2 E.J. Keall, 'Ayvan-e Kesra', Iranicaonline. https://www.iranicaonline.org/articles/ayvan-e-kesra-palace-of-kosrow-at-ctesiphon.

3 Mohsen Milani, 'Iran's Relations with Iraq: 1921–79', *Encyclopedia Iranica*. Columbia University, 2006, pp. 564–72. I have incorporated some information from this article in this section.

4 Central Intelligence Agency, *The World Factbook*, 2022. https://www.cia.gov/the-world-factbook/about/archives/2022/countries/iraq/.

5 For an excellent account of the founding of Iraq, see Abbas Kadhim, *Reclaiming Iraq: The 1920 Revolution and the Founding of the Modern State.* University of Texas Press, 2012.

6 Masoud Kuhestanizhad, *Chaleshha va ta'amolat-e Iran va Eraq dar Nimeh-ye nakhost-e Sadeh-ye bistom* [Challenges and Interactions of Iran and Iraq in the first Half of the Twentieth Century]. Iran's Foreign Ministry, 2005, p. 57.

7 Faisal, the son of the Guardian of the Two Holy Places in Mecca, was chosen by Winston Churchill to reward his family for their collaboration with the British against the Ottomans. Initially installed as the King of Syria, Faisal was later removed by France. For details see, David Fromkin, *A Peace to End All Peace: The Fall of the Ottoman Empire and the Creation of the Modern Middle East.* Henry Holt, 1989, pp. 502–7.

8 Daniel Yergin, *The Prize: The Epic Quest for Oil, Money, and Power.* Simon & Schuster, pp. 138–47, and 158.

9 Ghani, *Iran and the Rise of Reza Shah*, pp.333–8.

10 Reza Shah chronicled details of his expedition to Khuzestan. See Reza Pahlavi, *Safarnameh-ye Khuzestan* [Khuzestan Travelogue]. Tehran, 1972.

11 R.K. Ramazani, *The Foreign Policy of Iran: A Developing Nation in World Affairs.* University Press of Virginia, 1966, pp. 260–61.

12 Special National Intelligence Estimate, SNIE 34–58, Washington, DC, August 26, 1958. https://history.state.gov/historicaldocuments/frus1958-60v12/d249.

13 John P. Glennon, ed., *Foreign Relations of the United States, 1955–1957, Near East Region; Iran; Iraq,* Vol. 12. Department of State, 1991, p. 585.

14 'Telegram From the Embassy in Iran to the Department of State', Tehran, August 14, 1958. https://history.state.gov/historicaldocuments/frus1958-60v12/d247.

15 Nezaam Ali Dehnavi, 'Rawabet-e Iran va Iraq dar 'asr-e Hokoomat-e Abd-al-Karim Qasem', *Fasl-name-ye Rawabet-e Khareji-e Iran*, May 19, 2004, pp. 41–72, esp. 54–64.

16 Ardeshir Zahedi, *Khaterat-e Ardeshir Zahedi* [The Memoirs of Ardeshir Zahadi], Vol. 3. Ibex Publishers, 2020, pp. 103–5. The ambitious general was assassinated by a SAVAK agent in Iraq in August 1971.

17 Nina D. Howland, ed., *Foreign Relations of the United States, 1964–1968, Iran*, Vol. XXII. Washington, DC, 1999, pp. 7–8.

18 Ibid., pp. 7–8.

19 Assadollah Alam, *The Shah and I: The Confidential Diary of Iran's Royal Court, 1969–1977*. I.B. Tauris, 1992, pp. 82 and 176.

20 Central Intelligence Agency, 'Briefing Papers for Visit of General Nematollah Nasiri', April 28, 1976, https://www.cia.gov/readingroom/docs/CIA-RDP85 T00353R000100270011-5.pdf.

21 Ibid., pp. 82, 176.

22 Abdolreza H. Mahdavi, *Siasat-e Khareji-e Iran, dourun-e Pahlavi* [Iranian Foreign Policy Under the Pahlavis]. Tehran, 1996, pp. 357–8.

23 Arash Reisinezhad, *The Shah of Iran, the Iraqi Kurds, and the Lebanese Shia*. Palgrave, 2019, pp. 211–88. This is one of the finest books on the Shah's foreign policy, including his effective use of non-state actors or proxies.

24 Barzani served as defence minister in the Kurdish Republic of Mahabad in 1945. The Soviet-backed republic was crushed by the Iranian government.

25 The head of Mossad's operations in Iraqi Kurdistan, Eliezer Tsafrir, allegedly made the statement about Barzani. See Trita Parsi's excellent book, *Treacherous Alliance: The Secret Dealings of Israel, Iran, and the United States*. Yale University Press, 2007, p. 53.

26 Directorate of Intelligence, 'Israel and Iran: The Ties that Bind', October 7, 1985. https://www.cia.gov/readingroom/docs/CIA-RDP85 T01058R000506980002-7.pdf.

27 Central Intelligence Agency, 'The Implications of the Iran–Iraq Agreement', an Interagency Memorandum produced under the auspices of the National Intelligence Officer for the Middle East, April 1975, p. 2. https://www.cia.gov/readingroom/docs/CIA-RDP79R01142A000500050002-7.pdf.

28 Roham Alvandi, *Nixon, Kissinger, and the Shah: The United States and Iran in the Cold War*. Oxford University Press, 2014, p. 103. Alvandi offers an insightful analysis of the Shah's relationship with the Kurds and the US.

29 Central Intelligence Agency, 'The Implications of the Iran–Iraq Agreement', Interagency Memorandum produced under the auspices of the National Intelligence Officer for the Middle East, April 1975, p. 3. https://www.cia.gov/readingroom/docs/CIA-RDP79R01142A000500050002-7.pdf.

30 Ali Bigdeli, 'Qarardad-e 1975 Iran va Eraq' [The 1975 Iran–Iraq Agreement], *Fasl-nama-ye Ravabet-e Khareji-ye Iran*, May 19, 2004, pp. 143–56.

31 Central Intelligence Agency, *National Intelligence Bulletin*, March 7, 1975, p. 8. See https://www.cia.gov/readingroom/docs/CIA-RDP79T00975 A027500010012-3.pdf.

32 Central Intelligence Agency, 'The Implications of the Iran–Iraq Agreement', an Interagency Memorandum produced under the auspices of the National Intelligence Officer for the Middle East, April 1975, p. 4. https://www.cia. gov/readingroom/docs/CIA-RDP79R01142A000500050002-7.pdf.

33 Zahedi writes that 'in those years [around 1975], the Israelis were unhappy about the resolution of Iran Iraq conflict'. Ibid., Vol. 3, p. 99. He told the Shah that the Israelis and Americans didn't mind 'adding fuel to the conflicts we had with Iraq', p. 107.

34 Office of the Historian, Department of State, 279. 'Telegram from the Embassy in Iran to the Department of State', Tehran, March 13, 1975. https:// history.state.gov/historicaldocuments/frus1969-76v27/d279.

35 Ibid., p. 4.

36 Office of the Historian, Department of State, '278. Backchannel Message from the President's Deputy Assistant for National Security Affairs (Scowcroft) to Secretary of State Kissinger'. Washington, DC, March 10, 1975. https://history.state.gov/historicaldocuments/frus1969-76v27/d278.

37 Iran Oral History Project, Harvard University, interview with Isa Pejman, 1983. For the transcript of the interview, see: https://iiif.lib.harvard.edu/ manifests/view/drs:2898228$22i.

38 US Department of State, '284. Telegram from the Embassy in Iran to the Department of State, Tehran, March 25, 1975: Iran–Iraq Accord: Analysis of Iranian Perspective', by Richard Helms, US Ambassador. https://history. state.gov/historicaldocuments/frus1969-76v27/d284.

39 The Shah recalled that he spoke at length with Saddam Hussein in Algeria and that the two leaders 'agreed to bury our differences and succeeded in ending the misunderstandings which colonialist influences had maintained between us'. Mohammad Reza Pahlavi, *Answer to History*. Stein and Day, 1980, p. 133.

40 Murray and Woods, *The Iran–Iraq War*, p. 23.

41 Office of the Historian, Department of State, 275. 'Backchannel Message from the Ambassador to Iran [Helms] to the President's Deputy Assistant for National Security Affairs (Scowcroft)', March 8, 1975. https://history. state.gov/historicaldocuments/frus1969-76v27/d275.

42 Central Intelligence Agency, 'The President's Daily Brief', November 14, 1974. https://www.cia.gov/readingroom/docs/DOC_0006007868.pdf.

43 Office of the Historian, Department of State, 271. 'Telegram from the Interests Section in Baghdad to the Department of State', Baghdad, February 1, 1975. https://history.state.gov/historicaldocuments/frus1969-76v27/d271t.

44 Chad Nelson, 'Revolution and War: Saddam's Decision to Invade Iran', *Middle East Journal*, Vol. 72, No. 2, Spring 2018, p. 256. https://brightspot-cdn.byu.edu/fd/de/1caa93b14ef8ac3cacd77b40e45f/nelson-revolution-and-war.pdf.

45 I have used some information and sources for this chapter from Mohsen Milani, 'Iran's Policy toward the Persian Gulf', in *Contemporary Iran: Economy, Society and Politics*, ed. by A. Gheissari. Oxford University Press, 2009, pp. 349–66.

46 Directorate of Intelligence, Central Intelligence Agency, 'Iran–Iraq: Determining Who Started the Iran–Iraq War', November 25, 1987. https://www.cia.gov/readingroom/docs/CIA-RDP90T00114R000700730002-0.pdf.

47 See Kanan Makiya, *Republic of Fear: The Politics of Modern Iraq*. University of California Press, 1998.

48 National Foreign Assessment Center, 'Iran–Iraq: Deteriorating Relations: An Intelligence Memorandum', November 1979, p. 2. https://www.cia.gov/readingroom/docs/CIA-RDP81B00401R000500100030-5.pdf.

49 For details of the coup, see Mark Gasiorowski, 'The Nuzih Plot and Iranian Politics', *International Journal of Middle East Studies*, Vol. 34, No. 4, November 2002, pp. 645–66. For the Islamic Republic's version of the coup, see Khomeini portal. http://en.imam-khomeini.ir/en/n26731/Nojeh_coup_plot_in_1980_displayed_western_animosity_towards_Islamic_Revolution.

50 Claudia Wright, 'Religion and Strategy in the Iraq–Iran War', *Third World Quarterly*, Vol. 7, No. 4, October 1985, p. 844.

51 Foreign Assessment Center, 'The Iran–Iraq War, Military Performance and Prospects', December 1980. https://www.cia.gov/readingroom/docs/CIA-RDP81B00401R000500030002-5.pdf.

52 Bruce Riedel, 'What Iran's Revolution Meant for Iraq', Brookings, January 24, 2019, p. 4. https://www.brookings.edu/blog/order-from-chaos/2019/01/24/what-irans-revolution-meant-for-iraq/.

53 Pierre Razoux, *The Iran–Iraq War*, translated by Nicholas Elliot. The Belknap Press of Harvard University Press, 2015, p. 70. Razoux claims that King Khalid tried to persuade Saddam not to invade Iran but failed.

54 Nikola Schahgaldian and Gina Barkhordarian, *The Iranian Military under the Islamic Republic*. Rand Corporation, 1987, pp. 19–20.

55 Pollack argues that Saddam Hussein's primary motive for invading Iran was to seize the oil in Khuzestan. Kenneth Pollack, 'The Oil Thief of Baghdad:

Understanding Saddam's Motives for Invading Iran', *Middle East Journal*, Vol. 76, No. 4, Spring 2023, pp. 507–30.

56 Foreign Assessment Center, 'The Iran–Iraq War, Military Performance and Prospects', December 1980. https://www.cia.gov/readingroom/docs/CIA-RDP81B00401R000500030002-5.pdf.

57 Central Intelligence Agency, 'Memorandum: Some Implications of Renewed US Arms Deliveries to Iran', November 2, 1980.

58 Foreign Assessment Center, 'The Iran–Iraq War, Military Performance and Prospects', December 1980. https://www.cia.gov/readingroom/docs/CIA-RDP81B00401R000500030002-5.pdf.

59 For his version of the events, see Abol Hassan Bani Sadr, *My Turn to Speak*. Brassey's, 1989, pp. 1–21, 73–83, and 105–15.

60 For details, see Mohammad Sohrabi, Amrollah Ashrafi, and Morteza Karimi, 'Anatomy of Political Parties and Groups in Iraq and Their Implications on the Relations between Iran and Iraq', *Fasl Nameh Elmi-e Motaleat Ravabet-e Beynolmellal*, March 4, 1995. Also see, Hanna Batatu, 'Shi'i Organizations in Iraq: Al-Da'wah al-Islamiyah and al-Mujahidin', in *Shi'ism and Social Protest*, ed. by J.R.I. Cole and N. Keddie. Yale University Press, 1986, pp. 179–200.

61 Augustus R. Norton, *Hezbollah: A Short History*. Princeton University Press, 2007, pp. 70–71.

62 Human Rights Watch, *Judging Dujail: The First Trial Before the Iraqi High Tribunal*, November 2009. https://www.hrw.org/reports/iraq1106webw cover.pdf.

63 Sohrabi et al., 'Anatomy of Political Parties and Groups in Iraq', p. 11.

64 Mahan Abedin, 'The Supreme Council for the Islamic Revolution in Iraq (SCIRI)', *Middle East Intelligence Bulletin*, October 2003.

65 'Why Did the Senior Officials Decide to Continue the War', Tasnim, May 29, 2019. https://tn.ai/2018213.

66 Ayatollah Khamenei's website, September 17, 1986. https://farsi.khamenei. ir/speech-content?id=12531.

67 'Why Wasn't the War Ended after Khorramshar?', *Tarikh-e Irani*, May 24, 2019. http://tarikhirani.ir/fa/news/5855.

68 Ruhollah Khomeini, 'Message to the Nation and Army of Iraq', Khomeini portal, July 14, 1982. http://www.imam-khomeini.ir/fa/C207_43791/.

69 Central Intelligence Agency, Special Analysis, July 24, 1982. 'Iran–Iraq: Military Strengths and Weakness'. https://www.cia.gov/readingroom/docs/ CIA-RDP84B00049R001102740016-5.pdf.

70 Mohammad Doroodian, *Aqaz Ta Payan* [The Beginning Until the End], Center for the Study and Research of War, no date, p. 89.

71 Javed Ali, 'Chemical Weapons and the Iran–Iraq War: A Case Study in Noncompliance', *Nonproliferation Review*, Spring 2001, p. 48. https://www. nonproliferation.org/wp-content/uploads/npr/81ali.pdf.

72 UNSCR, Resolution 552, June 1, 1984, http://unscr.com/en/resolutions/552.

73 Ronald O'Rourke, 'The Tanker War', *Proceedings* (US Naval Institute), Vol. 114/5/1,023. From 1981 to 1988, there were 451 hits on ships, 283 by Iraq and 168 by Iran.

74 Lee Allen Zatarain, *America's First Clash with Iran: The Tanker War, 1987–88*. Casemate, 2013.

75 Central Intelligence Agency, 'Memorandum: Iran–Iraq War: The Military Situation', August 28, 1984. https://www.cia.gov/readingroom/docs/ CIA-RDP85T00287R001302000001-7.pdf.

76 Doroodian, *Aqaz Ta Payan*, p. 119.

77 Bruce Riedel, 'What Iran's Revolution Meant for Iraq', p. 4.

78 'Shaking Hands with Saddam Hussein: The U.S. Tilts toward Iraq, 1980–1984', National Security Archive Electronic Briefing Book, No. 82, edited by Joyce Battle, February 25, 2003. https://nsarchive2.gwu.edu/NSAEBB/ NSAEBB82/. For US policy towards the war, see James Blight, Janet Lang, Malcolm Byrne, and John Tirman, *Becoming Enemies: US–Iran Relations and the Iran–Iraq War, 1979–1988*. Rowman & Littlefield, 2012.

79 Ronald Reagan Presidential Library and Museum, NSDD Digitalized Reference Copies, National Security Decision Directive 139, 'Measures to Improve U.S. Posture and Readiness to Respond to Developments in the Iran–Iraq War', Washington, DC, April 5, 1984. https://www.reaganlibrary. gov/public/archives/reference/scanned-nsdds/nsdd139.pdf.

80 On the US policy and position on the use of chemical weapons, see David M. Walker, '"An Agonizing Death": 1980s U.S. Policy on Iraqi Chemical Weapons during the Iran–Iraq War', *Journal of the Middle East and Africa*, Vol. 8, No. 2, 2017, pp. 175–96. See also Richard Russell, 'Iraq's Chemical Weapons Legacy', *Middle East Journal*, Vol. 59, No. 2, Spring 2005, pp. 187–208 and Joost Hillerman, *A Poisonous Affair: America, Iraq, and the Gassing of Halabja*. Cambridge University Press, 2007.

81 Memorandum to Mr Robert C. McFarlane, The White House: 'US Policy Towards the Iran–Iraq War: Status Report on NSDD-114', December 19, 1983. See https://www.cia.gov/readingroom/docs/CIA-RDP85M00363 R000400740033-5.pdf.

82 United States Department of State, 'Iraqi Use of Chemical Weapons', From Jonathan Howe and Richard Murphy to Lawrence S. Eagleburger, November 21, 1983. https://nsarchive2.gwu.edu/NSAEBB/NSAEBB82/ iraq25.pdf. Obtained from Digital National Security Archive, Joyce Battles, editor. See also Michael Brill, Wilson Center, March 31, 2022. https://www.

wilsoncenter.org/blog-post/part-ii-we-attacked-them-chemical-weapons-
and-they-attacked-us-chemical-weapons-iraqi#:~:text=In%20February%
201984%2C%20an%20Iraqi,offered%20the%20rationalization%20that%20
Iraq's.

83 United States Department of State, 'Iraqi Warning re. Iranian Offensive',
February 1984. https://nsarchive2.gwu.edu/NSAEBB/NSAEBB82/iraq41.
pdf. Obtained from Digital National Security Archive, Joyce Battles, editor.

84 Department of State, December 1983. Obtained from 'Shaking Hands with
Saddam Hussein', ed. Joyce Battle. https://nsarchive2.gwu.edu/NSAEBB/
NSAEBB82/.   Joyce's   article: https://nsarchive2.gwu.edu/NSAEBB/
NSAEBB82/iraq31.pdf.

85 Shane Harris and Mathew Aid, 'Exclusive: CIA Files Prove America Helped
Saddam as He Gassed Iran', *Foreign Policy*, August 26, 2013. https://foreign-
policy.com/2013/08/26/exclusive-cia-files-prove-america-helped-saddam-
as-he-gassed-iran/#.

86 Gary Sick, *All Fall Down*. Penguin Books, 1986. Also see Seymour Hersh,
'The Iran Pipeline, a Hidden Chapter', *The New York Times*, December 8,
1991.

87 Trita Parsi, *Treacherous Alliance*, p. 95.

88 Directorate of Intelligence, 'Israel and Iran: The Ties that Bind', October 7,
1985. https://www.cia.gov/readingroom/docs/CIA-RDP85T01058
R000506980002-7.pdf.

89 Directorate of Intelligence, Central Intelligence Agency, 'Intelligence
Assessment: Iran–Iraq: Buying Weapons for War', May 1984. https://www.
cia.gov/readingroom/docs/CIA-RDP85T00283R000500120005-5.pdf.

90 For details, see Malcolm Byrne and Peter Kornbluh, *The Iran–Contra
Affair: The Making of a Scandal, 1983–1988*. Chadwyck-Healey, 1990,
pp. 213–14.

91 *Hope and Anxiety: Ayatollah Hashemi Rafsanjani's Memoir, 1984–85*. Diary
of June 24, 1985, pp. 94–6. www.shifteshab.com.

92 Theodore Draper, *A Very Thin Line: The Iran–Contra Affairs*. Hill & Wang,
1991, p. 169. See also *The Tower Commission Report: The Full Text of the
President's Special Review Board*. Bantam Books, Times Books, 1987, p. 29.
https://archive.org/details/towercommissionoounit/page/n1/mode/
2up?q=100.

93 Doroodian, *Aqaz ta Payan*, p. 166. For a somewhat different IRGC interpre-
tation of the McFarlane trip to Tehran, see Mehdi Ansari, 'Majeray-e
McFarlane' [The McFarlane Affair]. Center for the Study and Research of
War, 2005.

94 Doroodian, *Aqaz ta Payan*, p. 166.

95 See *The Tower Commission Report*, pp. III-18.

96 Razoux, *The Iran–Iraq War*, p. 384.

97 For a good discussion of the case of Mehdi Hashemi, see Ulrich Von Schwerin, 'Mehdi Hashemi and the Iran–Contra Affair', *British Journal of Middle Eastern Studies*, Vol. 42, No. 4, 2014, pp. 520–37. For his background, see Mehrzad Boroujerdi and Kourosh Rahimkhani, *Postrevolutionary Iran: A Political Handbook*. Syracuse University Press, 2018, p. 20.

98 Directorate of Intelligence, Central Intelligence Agency, 'After Al Faw: Implications and Options for Iraq and Iran', March 12, 1986. https://www.cia.gov/readingroom/docs/CIA-RDP86T01017R000202020001-4.pdf.

99 Director of Central Intelligence, Special National Intelligence Estimate, 'Is Iraq Losing the War?', April 1986. https://www.cia.gov/readingroom/docs/CIA-RDP90R00961R000300060003-9.pdf.

100 Directorate of Intelligence, Central Intelligence Agency, National Intelligence Council: 'NIC Outlook: The Implications of a Possible Iranian Victory over Iraq', March 1986. https://www.cia.gov/readingroom/docs/CIA-RDP90R00038R000500590001-6.pdf.

101 'Hossein Alaei in the Café News', Khabaronline, February 8, 2011. khabaronline.ir/x36LJ.

102 Doroodian, *Aqaz Ta Payan*, p. 137.

103 Directorate of Intelligence, Central Intelligence Agency, 'Iranian National Security Policy: Growing Pragmatism and Effectiveness', March 25, 1987. https://www.cia.gov/readingroom/docs/CIA-RDP90T00114R000600900001-3.pdf.

104 Ronald Reagan Presidential Library and Museum, NSDD Digitalized Reference Copies, National Security Directive 114, 'US Policy Toward the Iran–Iraq War', November 26, 1983. https://www.reaganlibrary.gov/public/archives/reference/scanned-nsdds/nsdd114.pdf.

105 Michael H. Armacost, Under Secretary of State for Political Affairs, 'U.S. Policy in the Persian Gulf and Kuwaiti Reflagging', presented before the Senate Foreign Relations Committee, June 16, 1987.

106 House Joint Resolution 216, 100th Congress, *Overview of the Situation in the Persian Gulf: Hearing before the Committee on Foreign Affairs*, Washington, DC, 1987, p. 301. https://www.congress.gov/bill/100th-congress/house-joint-resolution/216. From Milani, 'Iran's Policy toward the Persian Gulf', p. 365.

107 David Crist, *The Twilight War: The Secret History of America's Thirty-year Conflict with Iran*. Penguin, 2012, pp. 296–9. This is the most authoritative account of the history of US conflict with Iran during the war from an American perspective.

108 Dwight Jon Zimmerman, 'Operations Prime Chance and Praying Mantis: USSOCOM's First Test of Fire', *Defense Media Matters*, June 27, 2013.

https://www.defensemedianetwork.com/stories/ussocoms-first-test-of-fire-operations-prime-chance-and-praying-mantis/.

109 Shane and Aid, 'Exclusive: CIA Files Prove America Helped Saddam as He Gassed Iran'.

110 Crist, *The Twilight War*, p. 338.

111 *Aparat*, 'The Words of Ayatollah Hashemi and Hassan Rouhani about the Fall of Faw', Video, no date. https://www.aparat.com/v/p42p9kv.

112 Crist, *The Twilight War*, p. 338.

113 '"Chemical Ali" Admits Ordered Kurd Villages Cleared', Reuters, January 28, 2007. https://www.reuters.com/article/us-iraq-trial-chemical-ali-admits-ordered-kurd-villages-cleared-idUSPAR85001420070128.

114 'A Televised Presentation of the Letter of Mohsen Rezaei at the End of the War', BBC Persian, September 30, 2014. https://www.bbc.com/persian/iran/2014/09/140930_l39_mohsen_rezaei_secret_letter_war.

115 'Imam Khomeini: Accepting the Resolution is More Deadly for me than Drinking a Cup of Poison', Jamaran News, July 18, 2010. https://tinyurl.com/2frcfuhs. For Khomeini's secret letter to the most senior officials of the country about why he decided to declare a ceasefire, see Baztab, September 29, 2006. http:/www/baztab/com/print/php?id=49451.

116 The letter was released by Rafsanjani and was published by Mehr News, September 29, 2006. https://www.mehrnews.com/news/386966/.

117 'Publication of Hashemi Rafsanjani's Memoirs about Khomeini's Decision to Step Down from the Leadership by Accepting the Resolution', BBC Persian, January 4, 2023.

118 Hashemi Rafsanjani, *The End of Defending and the Start of Reconstruction*, July 21, 1988, p. 221. Tehran did not respond to this proposal.

119 On the Mojahedin-e Khalq, see Ervand Abrahamian, *The Iranian Mojahedin*. Yale University Press, 1989.

120 Hossein Alaei, 'The Monafeqin Attack on Iran and the Morsad Operation', Khabaronline, July 17, 2022. khabaronline.ir/xj5yT. This is a detailed account of the last days of the war written by a high-ranking IRGC official.

121 'Rezaei: We Should Not Have Entered Iraq after the Conquest of Khorramshahr. Hashemi: The Imam Ordered It', *Tarikh-e Irani*, September 27, 2016. http://tarikhirani.ir/fa/news/5608.

122 Patrick Brogan, 'Iraq', in *The Fighting Never Stopped*. Vintage Books, 1990, p. 263.

123 Richard Stone, 'Seeking Answers for Iran's Chemical Weapons Victims – Before Time Runs Out', *Science Magazine*, January 4, 2018.

124 Kamran Mofid, *The Economic Consequences of the Gulf War*. Routledge, 1990, p. 45.

125 For details, see the analysis of the war's impact on the IRGC by Annie Tracy Samue, *The Unfinished History of the Iran–Iraq War: Faith, Firepower, and Iran's Revolutionary Guards*. University of Tennessee Press, 2023.

126 Memorandum to Mr Robert C. McFarlane, 'US Policy toward the Iraq–Iran War', December 19, 1983. https://www.cia.gov/readingroom/docs/CIA-RDP85M00363R000400740033-5.pdf.

127 I have used some information and sources from my article, Mohsen Milani, 'Iran's Active Neutrality during the Kuwaiti Crisis: Causes and Consequences', *New Political Science*, Summer 1992, pp. 41–60.

128 Central Intelligence Agency: 'Intelligence Assessment: Iraq's Air Force: Improving Capabilities, Ineffective Strategy', October 1987. https://www.cia.gov/readingroom/docs/CIA-RDP88T00096R000700910001-5.pdf.

129 Directorate of Intelligence, Central Intelligence Agency, 'A Negotiated End to the Iran–Iraq War: A Speculative Look at the Implications for the Middle East and US Interests', August 5, 1988. The document indicates that Saddam Hussein had 'no intention of repaying more than $35 billion in aid given by the Gulf Arabs since the war began'. https://www.cia.gov/readingroom/docs/CIA-RDP05-00761R000101070001-5.pdf.

130 'Report to the Secretary-General on Humanitarian Needs in Kuwait and Iraq', prepared by Matti Athisaari, March 20, 1991. https://www.un.org/depts/oip/background/reports/s22366.pdf.

131 Saddeq Mostofi, 'Letters Exchanged between Two Enemies', BBC Persian, July 9, 2017. https://www.bbc.com/persian/iran-38554970.

132 Ibid.

4 Invading Iraq: America's Unintended Strategic Gift to Iran

1 For details, see Mohsen Milani, 'Iran's Policy Towards Afghanistan', *Middle East Journal*, Vol. 60, No. 2, Spring 2006, pp. 235–56.

2 Mohsen Aminzadeh, 'Diplomasee-ye Dourey-e Khatami ta Ahmadinejad [Iranian Diplomacy from Khatami to Ahmadinejad]', Shargonline, 2005. Shargonline.ir/spe/spe/archives/2005_327_23_28_Print.php.

3 James Risen, *State of War: The Secret History of the CIA and the Bush Administration*. Free Press, 2006, p. 215.

4 See Mohsen Milani, 'Iran's Policy toward Post-Saddam Iraq', in *Iraq, its Neighbors and the United States*, ed. by P. Marr et al. United States Institute of Peace Press, 2011, pp. 67–92. I have used information and sources from this book chapter that covers Iran's policies until 2011.

5 *Jomhouri-e Eslami*, April 11, 2002.

6 For a good discussion of Iran's policy towards Iraq in the first two years after the US invasion, see Kamran Taremi, 'Iranian Foreign Policy Towards Occupied Iraq, 2003–05', *Middle East Policy*, Vol. 12, No. 4, Winter 2005, pp. 28–47.

7 Ken Adelman. 'Cakewalk in Iraq', *Washington Post*, February 13, 2002. https://www.washingtonpost.com/archive/opinions/2002/02/13/cakewalk-in-iraq/cf09301c-c6c4-4f2e-8268-7c93017f5e93/.

8 Norton, *Hezbollah*, p. 119.

9 See Ayoub Mennati and Nasser Hadian, 'The Islamic Republic of Iran's Foreign Policy Towards Iraq from the Perspective of Balance of Threat Theory, 2003–2018', *Jame'e Shenasi-e Jahan-e Islam*, Vol. 7, Fall/Winter 2009, pp. 139–64.

10 Council on Foreign Relations, 'Gaddis: Bush Pre-emption Doctrine the Most Dramatic Policy Shift Since Cold War', February 10, 2004. https://www.cfr.org/interview/gaddis-bush-pre-emption-doctrine-most-dramatic-policy-shift-cold-war.

11 National Intelligence Council, 'Iran: Nuclear Intentions and Capabilities, National Intelligence Estimate', November 2007. www.dni.gov/press_releases/20071203_release.pdf.

12 Barbara Slavin, *Mullahs, Money, and Militias: How Iran Exerts Its Influence in the Middle East*, Special Report 206. United States Institute of Peace, June 2008.

13 Gideon Rose, 'Why America Invented Ahmad Chalabi', *The New York Times*, November 5, 2015. https://www.nytimes.com/2015/11/05/opinion/why-america-invented-ahmad-chalabi.html.

14 Dana Priest and Robin Wright, 'Iraq Spy Service Planned by U.S. to Stem Attacks', *Washington Post*, December 11, 2003.https://www.washingtonpost.com/archive/politics/2003/12/11/iraq-spy-service-planned-by-us-to-stem-attacks/4fab9e87-4c52-4234-b93d-b47ffc2f9b53/.

15 I have used information from the following sources on Iran's policy towards Iraq: Kayhan Barzegar, 'Iran's Foreign Policy Strategy after Saddam', *Washington Quarterly*, Vol. 33. Issue 1, 2010, pp.173–89; Joseph Felter and Brian Fishman, *Iranian Strategy in Iraq: Politics and Other Means*, Counterterrorism Center, West Point, October 2008. This is a well-researched piece. https://apps.dtic.mil/sti/citations/ADA488417; and Kenneth Katzman, 'Iran's Influence in Iraq', CRS Report for Congress, September 29, 2006. https://www.everycrsreport.com/files/20060929_RS22323_ce031e2710f-76c848500b217e967dc2838920a69.pdf.

16 For Sadr's biography, see Patrick Cockburn, *Muqtada: Muqtada al-Sadr, the Shia Revival, and the Struggle for Iraq*. Scribner, 2008.

17 Nathalie Miria Schmidhauser, 'A Balancing Act: The Sadrist Movement between Nationalist Rhetoric and Sectarian Politics', *International Journal of Contemporary Iraqi Studies*, Vol. 7, No. 2, June 2013, pp. 109–29.

18 'PM Maliki Recounts His June 7–9 Visit To Tehran', Cable: 08BAGHDAD1784, June 14, 2009, Secret. https://wikileaks.org/plusd/cables/08BAGHDAD 1784_a.html.

19 Anthony Cordesman and Jose Ramos, 'Sadr and the Mahdi Army: Evolution, Capabilities, and a New Direction', Center for Strategic and International Studies, August 4, 2008.

20 'Revisiting History', Shafaqna, May 24, 2018. https://fa.shafaqna.com/news/429815/.

21 *Comprehensive Report of the Special Advisor to the DCI on Iraq's WMD* (Duelfer Report). http://www-personal.umich.edu/~graceyor/govdocs/duelfer.html.

22 Personal interview with Ambassador Chris Hill, Tampa, Florida, December 22, 2022.

23 Esther Pan, 'Iraq: Madrid Donor Conference', Council on Foreign Relations, February 2, 2005. https://www.cfr.org/backgrounder/iraq-madrid-donor-conference.

24 'Final Text of President Talabani's Letter to PM Jafari', Cable: 05BAGHDAD2472, June 12, 2005. https://wikileaks.org/plusd/cables/05 BAGHDAD2472_a.html.

25 'Navigating the Rift between the U.S. and Iran – Rubaie on the UIA's Balancing Act', July 19, 2005. https://wikileaks.org/plusd/cables/05 BAGHDAD3001_a.html.

26 Edward Wong, 'Beleaguered Premier Warns U.S. to Stop Interfering in Iraq's Politics', *The New York Times*, March 30, 2006.

27 'PM Maliki: Strengthened Center or Emerging Strongman?' Cable: 09BAGHDAD379 (Under Crocker), February 13, 2009. https://wikileaks.org/plusd/cables/09BAGHDAD379_a.html.

28 Personal interview with Ambassador Chris Hill, Tampa, Florida, December 22, 2022.

29 Najim Abed Al-Jabouri and Sterling Jenson, 'The Iraqi and AQI Roles in the Sunni Awakening', *Prisim*, Vol. 2, No. 1, December 2010, p. 5.

30 'Zarqawi Letter: February 2004, Coalition Provisional Authority. English translation of terrorist Musab al-Zarqawi letter obtained by United States Government in Iraq'. https://2001-2009.state.gov/p/nea/rls/31694.htm.

31 'Iraq Forces Attack Iranian PMOI Rebels at Camp Ashraf', BBC, April 8, 2011. https://www.bbc.com/news/world-middle-east-13011469.

32 https://www.state.gov/foreign-terrorist-organizations/.

33 Ernesto Londono, 'At Least 52 Iranian Exiles Killed in Iraqi Camp', *Washington Post*, September 3, 2013. https://www.washingtonpost.com/world/national-security/at-least-52-iranian-exiles-executed-in-iraqi-camp-un-says/2013/09/03/4eab81fa-14e5-11e3-a100-66fa8fd9a50c_story.html.

34 Jeremiah Goulka, Lydia Hansell, et al., *The Mujahedin-e Khalq in Iraq: A Policy Conundrum*. Rand, 2009. https://www.rand.org/content/dam/rand/pubs/monographs/2009/RAND_MG871.pdf.

35 'PM Maliki Recounts his June 7–9 Visit to Tehran', 08BAGHDAD1784, June 14, 2008. https://wikileaks.org/plusd/cables/08BAGHDAD1784_a.html.

36 Ibid.

37 'Iraq–Iran Diplomacy a Sign of Iranian Influence or Iraqi Resolve?', 09BAGHDAD289, Robert Ford, February 4, 2009. https://wikileaks.org/plusd/cables/09BAGHDAD289_a.html.

38 James A. Baker and Lee H. Hamilton, co-chairs, *The Iraq Study Group Report*. Vintage Books, 2006, pp. xv and 50–53.

39 Author's interview with Ambassador Ryan Crocker, August 26, 2021.

40 Patrick Cockburn, 'The Botched US Raid that Led to the Hostage Crisis', *Independent*, April 3, 2007. https://web.archive.org/web/20070406172103/http://news.independent.co.uk/world/middle_east/article2414760.

41 Department of State Archive, 'On-the-Record Briefing with U.S. Ambassador to Iraq Ryan C. Crocker on His Meeting with Iranian Officials', May 28, 2007. https://2001-2009.state.gov/p/nea/rls/rm/2007/86961.htm. Ambassador Crocker believed that Sadr did not control all the elements of the Jaysh al-Mahdi but Iran did.

42 'Iran Managing the Post-Basrah Backlash', 08BAHHDAD1262, Ambassador Ryan C. Crocker, April 23, 2008. https://wikileaks.org/plusd/cables/08BAGHDAD1262_a.html.

43 Marisa Cochrane, 'March 2003–May 31, 2008: The Battle for Basra', *Iraq Report* 9, Institute for the Study of War and Weekly Standard, May 2008, p. 9. See https://understandingwar.org/sites/default/files/reports/Iraq%20Report%209.pdf.

44 'Sadr's Hadi al-Amri on Basrah Crackdown and Talks in Tehran', 08BAGHDAD1033, April 3, 2008. https://wikileaks.org/plusd/cables/08BAGHDAD1033_a.html.

45 Babak Rahimi, 'The Mumahidun: Muqtada Al-Sadr's New Militia', *Terrorism Monitor*, Vol. 6, Issue 17, September 4, 2008, p. 1.

46 'Basra Intelligence Chief on Local and Foreign Threats', 09BASRAH49, September 10, 2009. Confidential. https://wikileaks.org/plusd/cables/09BASRAH49_a.html.

47 'Iraq: Make It a Strong Partner in Dealing with Iran', 09BAGHDAD575, Robert Ford, March 5, 2009. See https://wikileaks.org/plusd/cables/09BAGHDAD575_a.html.

48 Ryan N. Mannina, 'How the 2011 US Troop Withdrawal from Iraq Led to the Rise of ISIS', *Small Wars Journal*, December 23, 2018. https://smallwarsjournal.com/jrnl/art/how-2011-us-troop-withdrawal-iraq-led-rise-isis#_edn7.

49 'PM Maliki: Strengthened Center or Emerging Strongman?' 09BAGHDAD379, Ambassador Robert Crocker, February 13, 2009. https://wikileaks.org/plusd/cables/09BAGHDAD379_a.html.

50 Radio Farda, August 16, 2021. https://www.radiofarda.com/a/02-safavi-on-khamenei-maliki/26861938.html.

51 Diana Esfandiary and Ariane Tabatabai, 'Iran's ISIS Policy', *International Affairs*, Vol. 1, 2015, pp. 1–15.

52 Hesther Saul, 'President Obama Claims Rise of ISIS is "Unintended Consequence" of George Bush's Invasion in Iraq', *Independent*, March 18, 2015. https://www.independent.co.uk/news/world/middle-east/president-obama-claims-rise-of-isis-is-unintended-consequence-of-george-w-bush-s-invasion-in-iraq-10115243.html.

53 Mannina, 'How the 2011 US Troop Withdrawal from Iraq Led to the Rise of ISIS'.

54 Anthony Dworkin, 'Beyond Good and Evil: Why Europe Should Bring ISIS Foreign Fighters Home', Policy Brief, European Council on Foreign Relations, October 21, 2019. https://ecfr.eu/wp-content/uploads/beyond_good_and_evil_why_europe_should_bring_isis_foreign_fighters_home.pdf.

55 'Commander Soleimani's Role in the Liberation of Mosul', Taghrib News, July 10, 2017. https://www.taghribnews.com/fa/note/274497./

56 As quoted in Shahram Akbarzadeh, 'Iran and Daesh: The Case of a Reluctant Shia Power', *Middle East Policy*, Vol. 22, No. 3, Fall 2015, p. 54.

57 As quoted in ibid., p. 46. Originally from Tasnim, October 13, 2014. http://tnews.ir/news/2DFD31724384.html.

58 Mohammad Javad Zarif, 'A Message from Tehran', *The New York Times*, April 20, 2015. https://www.nytimes.com/2015/04/20/opinion/mohammad-javad-zarif-a-message-from-iran.html.

59 Abbas Kadhim and Luay Al Khatteeb, 'What Do You Know about Sistani's Fatwa?', *Huffington Post*, July 10, 2014. https://www.huffpost.com/entry/what-do-you-know-about-si_b_5576244.

60 Hezbollah was highly critical of Berri for collaborating too closely with the United States.

61 *Donya-ye Eqtesad*, August 29, 2020. https://donya-e-eqtesad.com/fa/tiny/news-3725774.

62 'New Revelations about Commander Soleimani's Fight against ISIS', *ILNA*, October 30, 2014. https://www.ilna.ir/fa/tiny/news-218895.

63 For details, see Nader Uskowi, *Temperature Rising: Iran's Revolutionary Guards and Wars in the Middle East*. Rowman & Littlefield, 2019.

64 'David Petraeus on Soleimani', *NPR*, January 5, 2020. https://www.npr.org/2020/01/05/793722592/david-petraeus-on-soleimani.

65 For details, see *Iran's Networks of Influence in the Middle East, Strategic Dossier*, International Institute for Strategic Studies (IISS), 2019. https://www.iiss.org/publications/strategic-dossiers/iran-dossier.

66 'The Untold Aspects of Haj Qasem Soleimani's Role in Iraq', Jamaran News, July 24, 2020. https://tinyurl.com/6vp6feem.

67 F. Nadimi, 'Iran's Expanding Military Role in Iraq'. Washington Institute for Near East Policy, September 8, 2014. http://www.washingtoninstitute.org/policy-analysis/view/irans-expanding-military-role-in-iraq.

68 'Interview with Mazad Khemas', Tasnim, January 6, 2020. Khemas was the representative of Iraq's Supreme Islamic Council in Iran. https://tn.ai/2175293.

69 Masoud Asadollahi, 'He Thought Strategically and Acted Tactically', Khamenei portal, January 9, 2021. http://www.jamejamalborz.ir/Home/NewsInfo/40852.

70 Jamaran News (2020).

71 Soleimani was reportedly involved in political issues as well. MP Qassim Daoud reported to the American Embassy that 'Soleimani offered him money to support his campaign, which he said he declined in favor of taking a small rug.' See 'De-Ba'athification Fallout: INA Asks Ambassador to Reassert U.S. Opposition to Ba'ath'. 10BAGHDAD304, US Embassy in Baghdad, Ambassador Christopher Hill, February 5, 2010. https://wikileaks.org/plusd/cables/10BAGHDAD304_a.html.

72 *Donya-ye Eqtesad*, August 29, 2020.

73 Ali Alfoneh 'Iran-backed Popular Mobilization Forces Preparing for Post-Islamic State Iraq', Middle East Institute, August 3, 2017. https://www.mei.edu/publications/iran-backed-popular-mobilization-forces-preparing-post-islamic-state-iraq.

74 Marisa Cochrane Sullivan, 'Iran's Hard Power Influence in Iraq', *Critical Threats*, April 10, 2009. https://www.criticalthreats.org/analysis/irans-hard-power-influence-in-iraq.

75 Kenneth Pollack, 'Iraq: Understanding the ISIS Offensive Against the Kurds', Brookings, August 11, 2014. See https://www.brookings.edu/articles/iraq-understanding-the-isis-offensive-against-the-kurds/.

76 https://www.khabaronline.ir/news/1339497/.

77 Ali Akbar Dareini, 'Iran General Helped Iraq's Kurds Battle IS Group', Associated Press, September 24, 2014. https://apnews.com/article/f3ee9f207f394c87a06412c03372a757.

78 'An Official of the Kurdistan Region of Iraq: Iran Was the First Country That Supported Us Against ISIS', December 30, 2024. isna.ir/x8PQgS.

79 'Barzani's Letter to Hassan Rouhani: Appreciation and Thanks for Iran's Support', Mehr News, August 11, 2014. mehrnews.com/xqXLT.

80 'Iran Sent Soldiers to Fight in Iraq', Al Jazeera, August 23, 2014. https://www.Al Jazeera.com/news/2014/8/23/iran-sent-soldiers-to-fight-in-iraq.

81 Bill Roggio, 'US Airstrikes in Amerli Supported Deadly Shia Terror Group', *Long War Journal*, September 2, 2014.

82 Galip Delay, 'After the Kurdish Independence Referendum', *Foreign Affairs*, October 2, 2017. https://www.foreignaffairs.com/articles/middle-east/2017-10-02/after-kurdish-independence-referendum.

83 'Details of Commander Soleimani's Negotiations with Barzani', Etemadonline, October 26, 2017. https://www.etemadonline.com/fa/tiny/news-143969.

84 Ardeshir Pashang, 'Analysis of the Islamic Republic of Iran's Relations with Iraq's Kurdish Region' (in Persian), International Peace Studies Center, Tehran, January 12, 2011.

85 'Le Figaro: Israel's Mossad Recruiting Iranian Dissidents to Work Against Tehran Regime', *Haaretz*, January 11, 2012. https://www.haaretz.com/1.5163229.

86 'Iranian General Reportedly Played Key Role in Swift Takeover of Iraq's Kirkuk', Radio Free Europe, October 21, 2017. https://www.rferl.org/a/iranian-general-irgc-commander-soleimani-reportedly-played-key-role-swift-takeover-iraqs-kirkuk-kurdish-parties-puk-kdp/28807424.html.

87 Mohsen Milani, 'What Detente Looks Like: The United States and Iran Join Forces Against ISIS', *Foreign Affairs*, August 27, 2014.

88 Carole Morello, 'Tillerson Tells Iranian Militias in Iraq to "Go Home"', *Washington Post*, October 22, 2017.

89 Congressional Research Service, 'Iran's Revolutionary Guard Named a Terrorist Organization', April 9, 2019. https://crsreports.congress.gov/product/pdf/IN/IN11093.

90 'Analysis of Adel Abdul Mahdi's Visit to Iran', Mehr News, July 22, 2019. mehrnews.com/xPKyQ.

91 US Department of Defense, 'Iran Shoots Down U.S. Global Hawk Operating in International Airspace', June 20, 2019. https://www.defense.gov/News/News-Stories/Article/Article/1882497/iran-shoots-down-us-global-hawk-operating-in-international-airspace/.

92 Michael R. Gordon, 'Rocket Attack in Iraq Kills U.S. Contractor, Wounds Four U.S. Troops', December 28, 2019. https://www.wsj.com/articles/rocket-attack-in-iraq-kills-u-s-contractor-wounds-four-u-s-troops-11577492632.

93 'The Islamic Revolutionary Corps' Declaration on the Martyrdom of Commander Soleimani', Sharq, January 3, 2020. mshrgh.ir/1025984.

94 'The Leader of the Islamic Revolution's Declaration on the Killing of Commander Soleimani', Foreign Ministry, Iran, January 3, 2020. https://mfa.gov.ir/files/Pdf/0570636-newsExportec2eb24f6d0e476bbb16ec67ae9 5c9a7.pdf.

95 'Commander Hajizadeh: The American Command Center in Ein al-Asad was Destroyed: 5,000 Americans Would Have Been Killed if it Responded', Tasnim, January 9, 2020. https://tn.ai/2178606.

96 'Commander Salami: After Haj Qasem's Martyrdom, We Were in an Unknown Psychological Atmosphere with America', Kabarnegaran-e Javan, January 12, 2020. http://www.yjc.ir/ooUEkE.

97 Personal interview with General Frank McKenzie, Tampa, Florida, October 17, 2022.

98 Radio Farda, April 21, 2021. https://web.archive.org/web/20210426192005/ https://www.radiofarda.com/a/iran-zarif-qasem-soleimani-attack/ 31222159.html.

99 'A Representative of the Supreme Parliament of Iraq Revealed: Behind the Curtain of the Resignation of Adel Abdul Mahdi', Jamaran News, December 29, 2019. https://www.jamaran.news/fa/tiny/news-1319038.

100 Renad Mansour and Christine van den Toon, 'The 2018 Iraqi Federal Elections: A Population in Transition?', LSE Middle East Center. July 2018. https://eprints.lse.ac.uk/89698/7/MEC_Iraqi-elections_Report_2018.pdf. In the 2018 national elections, Iran's traditional allies, the ISCI, al Dawa, and the pro-Iran PMU militias did well.

101 'Iraq's Al-Kazemi Government: Real Change or a Temporary Settlement?', Arab Center for Research & Policy Studies, May 13, 2020. https://www. dohainstitute.org/en/PoliticalStudies/Pages/The-Formation-of-Al-Kazemi-Government-in-Iraq.aspx.

102 'Al-Mahdi's Allegation Regarding Martyr Soleimani's Terror', Araya News, December 13, 2020. https://www.aryanews.com/news/20.

103 'Adel Abdul Mahdi: The Agreement between Iran and Saudi Arabia Was the Result of the Blessing of Martyr Soleimani', Tasnim, February 20, 2023. https://tn.ai/2867958.

104 'Kadhimi in Tehran', BBC Persian, September 12, 2021. https://www.bbc. com/persian/iran-58535633.

105 'Iraqi Prime Minister's Request to Iran and America: Do not Settle Scores in Iraq', Hamshahrionline, August 29, 2020. hamshahrionline.ir/ x7cYk.

106 'Limiting Iran's Energy Exports to Iraq is the Result of al Kazemi's Trip to America', Niroghahian, August 29, 2020. https://nirogahian.ir/?p= 31406.

107 'Sadr Becomes First Iraqi Shi'ite Leader to Urge Assad to Step Down', Reuters, April 9, 2017. https://www.reuters.com/article/us-mideast-crisis-iraq-syria-sadr/sadr-becomes-first-iraqi-shiite-leader-to-urge-assad-to-step-down-idUSKBN17B070.

108 'Increasing the Trend of Divergence among Iraqi Shiites: Reasons and Considerations for Iran', Center for Strategic Studies. https://risstudies. org/%D8%A7%D9%81%D8%B2%D8%A7%DB%8C%D8%B4-%D8%B1%D9%88%D9%86%D8%AF-%D9%88%D8%A7%DA%AF%D8 %B1%D8%A7%DB%8C%DB%8C-%D8%AF%D8%B1-%D8%B4%DB%8 C%D8%B9%DB%8C%D8%A7%D9%86-%D8%B9%D8%B1%D8% A7%D9%82%D8%9B-%D8%AF%D9%84/.

109 Neta C. Crawford, 'Blood and Treasure', Watson Institute, Brown University, March 15, 2023. https://watson.brown.edu/costsofwar/files/ cow/imce/papers/2023/Costs%20of%2020%20Years%20of%20Iraq%20 War%20Crawford%2015%20March%202023%20final%203.21.2023.pdf.

110 Ibid.

111 NBC News, March 20, 2023. https://www.nbcnews.com/meet-the-press/ meetthepressblog/iraq-war-numbers-rcna75762.

112 Kyle Rempfer, "'Iran Killed More US Troops in Iraq than Previously Known", Pentagon Says', *Military Times*, April 4, 2019. https://www.militarytimes.com/news/your-military/2019/04/04/iran-killed-more-us-troops-in-iraq-than-previously-known-pentagon-says/.

113 Observatory of Economic Complexity (OEC). https://oec.world/en/ profile/bilateral-country/irn/partner/irq.

5 Iran's Power Play in Lebanon

1 As quoted in Andrew Chadwick, 'The 2006 Lebanon War', *Small Wars Journal*, November 20, 2012. https://smallwarsjournal.com/jrnl/art/ the-2006-lebanon-war-a-short-history.

2 'The Story of Commander Soleimani's First Meeting with Seyyed Hassan Nasrallah', *Donya-e Eqtesad*, February 14, 2020. https://donya-e-eqtesad. com/fa/tiny/news-3625594.

3 Lenny Ben-David, 'Soleimani Statue Put Up in Lebanon's "Iran Garden"', *The Times of Israel*, March 5, 2020. http://blogs.timesofisrael.com/ soleimani-statue-put-up-in-lebanons-iran-garden/.

4   Norton, *Hezbollah*, p. 140.

5   As quoted in Mathew Levitt, 'Hezbollah: Financing Terror through Criminal Enterprise', Washington Institute for Near East Policy, May 25, 2005. https://www.washingtoninstitute.org/policy-analysis/hezbollah-financing-terror-through-criminal-enterprise.

6   The Achaemenids imported cedar wood from the Levant, which they controlled, to build their palaces. Richard Frye, *The Heritage of Persia*. World Publishing Company, 1963, p. 121. The image of the cedar tree is now superimposed on the Lebanese flag.

7   Rula J. Abisaab, *Converting Persia: Religion and Power in the Safavid Empire*. I.B. Tauris, 2004, pp. 302–14.

8   Houchang Chehabi and Majid Tafreshi, 'Musa Sadr and Iran', in *Distant Relations: Iran and Lebanon in the Last 500 Years*, ed. by H.E. Chehabi. I.B. Tauris, 2007, pp. 137–61. This book is an excellent source on Iran–Lebanon relations.

9   Zahedi, *Khaterat-e Ardeshir Zahedi* [Memoirs of Zahedi], Vol. 3, p. 145.

10 Foreign Relations of the United States, Department of State, 'Telegram from the Embassy in Iran to the Department of State', Tehran, August 14, 1958. https://history.state.gov/historicaldocuments/frus1958-60v12/d247.

11 Foreign Relations of the United States, Department of State, 'Memorandum of Conversation', Washington, DC, July 1, 1958, 3–3:46 p.m. https://history.state.gov/historicaldocuments/frus1958-60v12/d242.

12 Foreign Relations of the United States, Department of State, 'Intelligence Memorandum: The Arab Threat to Iran', No. 1355/66, Washington, DC, May 21, 1966. https://history.state.gov/historicaldocuments/frus1964-68v22/d139.

13 R.K. Ramazani, *Revolutionary Iran: Challenges and Response in the Middle East*. Johns Hopkins University Press, 1986, p. 149.

14 Foreign Relations of the United States, Department of State, 'Briefing Notes by Director of Central Intelligence Dulles', Washington, DC, July 14, 1958. https://history.state.gov/historicaldocuments/frus1958-60v12/d110.

15 For details, see Abbas Samii, 'The Shah's Lebanon Policy: The Role of SAVAK', *Middle Eastern Studies*, Vol. 33, No. 1, January 1997.

16 As quoted in Reisinezhad, *The Shah of Iran, the Iraqi Kurds, and the Lebanese Shia*, p. 1.

17 On Sadr's life, see Fouad Ajami, *The Vanished Imam: Musa al-Sadr and the Shi'a of Lebanon*. Cornell University Press, 1986.

18 Bakhtiyar, an ambitious man, was later exiled by the Shah due to suspicions that he was planning a coup against the Pahlavis. When Bakhtiyar visited

Lebanon in the late 1960s, Lebanon declined the Shah's request to extradite him to Iran. The incident created the only major political crisis between Iran and Lebanon before the Islamic Revolution in Iran. Zahedi writes that Lebanon was pressured by Iraq and Egypt not to extradite the general. Bakhtiyar was later assassinated by SAVAK agents in Iraq in 1973. Zahedi, *Khaterat-e Ardeshir Zahedi* [Memoirs of Ardeshir Zahedi], Vol. 3, p. 148.

19 As quoted in Reisinezhad, p. 100, footnote 149.

20 Mostafa Chamran, *Lebanon* [His letters and Recollections from Lebanon]. Tehran, 1984, p. 50.

21 Sadeq Tabatabaei, 'Khaterat-e Siyasi-Ejtemaei' [Socio-political Memoirs], as quoted in Khomeini's portal. http://www.imam-khomeini.ir/fa/c13_155741/.

22 Sheikh Mostafa Messri, 'How Amal Was Formed', Hawzeh News, June 13, 2012. https://hawzahnews.com/x4qbG. For an excellent account of Amal's formation and evolution, see Richard Norton, *Amal and the Shi'a: Struggle for the Soul of Lebanon*. University of Texas Press, 1987.

23 Norton, *Hezbollah*, p. 22.

24 For the Islamic Republic's view on why Sadr decided to wage armed struggle, see 'When and Why Imam Moussa Sadr Took Up Arms', *Holdy Defense News*, August 5, 2014. https://dnws.ir/0006OZ.

25 Quoted in Yossi Melman, 'Our Allies, the Iranian People', *Haaretz*, May 29, 2016. https://www.haaretz.com/1.4934249.

26 Zahedi, Vol. 3, p. 148.

27 Author's telephone interview with former ambassador Zahedi, August 23, 2020.

28 Gholamreza Nejati, ed., *Khaterat-e Mohandes Mehdi Bazargan: Sixty Years of Service and Resistance* [Bazargan's Memoirs], Vol. II. Reca Publisher, 1998, p. 176. It was Mehdi Bazargan who recommended that Sadr invite Chamran to Lebanon.

29 Ibid., pp. 176–83. These statements were made by Ebrahim Yazdi. For the most authoritative book on the Liberation Movement, see H.E. Chehabi, *Iranian Politics and Religious Modernism: The Liberation Movement of Iran Under the Shah and Khomeini*. Cornell University Press, 1990.

30 Nejati, ed., *Khaterat-e Mohandes Mehdi Bazargan* [Bazargan's Memoirs], Vol. 3, pp. 176–7.

31 Reisinezhad, *The Shah of Iran*, p. 194.

32 Andrew Scott Cooper, *The Fall of Heaven: The Pahlavis and the Final Days of Imperial Iran*. Henry Holt, 2016, p. 332.

33 As quoted in Houchang Chehabi and Majid Tafreshi, 'Musa Sadr and Iran', in *Distant Relations*, ed. H.E. Chehabi, p. 160.

34 Human Rights Watch, 'Lebanon: Gaddafi Son Wrongfully Held for 8 Years', January 16, 2024. https://www.hrw.org/news/2024/01/16/lebanon-gaddafi-

son-wrongfully-held-8-years; 'Why is Hanibal Gaddafi on a Hunger Strike in a Lebanese Prison?', Al Jazeera, January 8, 2023.

35 Scott Cooper, *The Fall of Heaven*, p. 294.
36 Rula J. Abisaab, 'Sayyid Musa al-Sadr, the Lebanese State, and the Left', *Journal of Shiʻa Islamic Studies*, Vol. III, No. 2, Spring 2015, p. 114.
37 Central Intelligence Agency, National Foreign Assessment Center, 'The Amal Movement in Lebanon', November 20, 1981. https://www.cia.gov/library/readingroom/docs/CIA-RDP83M00914R000300020014-6.pdf.
38 For a good analysis of the conditions that led to the creation of Hezbollah, see Eitan Azani, *Hezbollah: The Story of the Party of God*. Springer, 2011, pp. 75–108.
39 'How Seyyed Hassan Nasrallah Met Imam Khomeini', Center for the Documents of the Islamic Revolution, August 13, 2006. https://irdc.ir/fa/news/5704/.
40 'Imam Khomeini's Decree on Seyyed Hassan Nasrallah', Political Studies and Research Institute, August 13, 2006. https://psri.ir/?id=ovc412pm.
41 For details, see Zeʻev Schiff and Ehud Yarʼari, *Israel's Lebanon War*, ed. and trans. by Ina Friedman. Simon & Schuster, 1985.
42 As quoted in Alyssa Fetini, 'A Brief History of Hizballah', *Time*, June 8, 2009. http://content.time.com/time/world/article/0,8599,1903301,00.html.
43 Ramazani, *Revolutionary Iran*, p. 181.
44 'Haj Ahmad Chose Hezbollah's Name', Mashregh News, December 5, 2015. mshrgh.ir/504229.
45 'How the Core of Hezbollah Was Formed Under IRGC Supervision', Holy Defense News, August 14, 2014. https://dnws.ir/0006Y6.
46 Besides the sources cited in this chapter, I have benefited from the following books on Hezbollah: Nasr, Vali, *The Shia Revival: How Conflicts within Islam Will Shape the Future*. W.W. Norton, 2006; Mathew Levitt, *Hezbollah: The Global Footprint of Lebanon's Party of God*. Georgetown University Press, 2013; Alastair Crooke, *Resistance: The Essence of the Islamist Revolution*. Pluto Press, 2009; Eitan Azani, *Hezbollah: The Story of the Party of God*. Palgrave Macmillan, 2009; Nicholas Blandford, *Warriors of God: Inside Hezbollah's Thirty-year Struggle Against Israel*. Random House, 2011; and Ahmad Nizar Hamzeh, *In the Path of Hizbullah*. Syracuse University Press, 2004.
47 For details of this horrendous massacre, see Thomas Friedman, *From Beirut to Jerusalem*. Farrar, Straus and Giroux, 1989, pp. 76–105.
48 'Haj Ahmad Chose Hezbollah's Name', Mashregh News, December 5, 2015. mshrgh.ir/504229.
49 'Imam Said: I Take No Responsibility for This', Imam Khomeini portal, April 16, 2014. http://www.imam-khomeini.ir/fa/NewsPrint.aspx?ID=22207.

50 Ibid.
51 Mohsen Rezaei, Commander of the IRGC, rejected the claim that Khomeini opposed sending troops to Lebanon. 'Imam Khomeini Did Not Oppose Sending Troops to Lebanon', Tasnim, July 4, 2016.
52 Hossein Bastani, 'The Islamic Republic's Unspoken Aspects of the Case of Ahmad Motevaselian', BBC Persian, July 7, 2020. https://www.bbc.com/persian/iran-features-53320271.
53 'How the Nucleus of Hezbollah Formed under the Supervision of the IRGC', Holy Defense News, June 24, 2024. https://dnws.ir/0006Y6.
54 'What You Need to Know about Hezbollah', Jahan News, January 25, 2014. https://www.jahannews.com/phototitr/339704/%d8%a2%d9%86%da%86%d9%87-%d8%af%d8%b1%d8%a8%d8%a7%d8%b1%d9%87-%d8%ad%d8%b2%d8%a8-%d8%a7%d9%84%d9%84%d9%87-%d9%84%d8%a8%d9%86%d8%a7%d9%86-%d8%a8%d8%a7%db%8c%d8%af-%d8%a8%d8%af%d8%a7%d9%86%db%8c%d8%af
55 'How the Core of Hezbollah Was Formed Under IRGC Supervision', Holy Defense News, August 14, 2014. https://dnws.ir/0006Y6.
56 'Haj Ahmad Chose Hezbollah's Name', Mashregh News, December 5, 2015. mshrgh.ir/504229.
57 Hamzeh, In the Path of Hizbullah, p. 32.
58 Ahmad Motevaselian, born in Yazd in 1954, came from a lower middle-class family and was arrested by SAVAK and tortured. See 'The Biography of Ahmad Motevaselian'. https://tinyurl.com/uf7suxem.
59 Abbas William Samii, 'A Stable Structure on Shifting Sands: Assessing the Hizbullah–Iran–Syria Relationship', Middle East Journal, Vol. 62, No. 1, Winter 2008, pp. 32–53.
60 Blandford, Warriors of God, p. 42.
61 'The Formation of Lebanon's Hezbollah as Told by Iran's Defense Minister', Holy Defense News, May 23, 2016. https://dnws.ir/000Lmt.
62 'The Narrative of the Iranian Commander about Seyyed Hassan Nasrallah's Involvement in Hezbollah', Tabnak, December 19, 2014. https://www.tabnak.ir/fa/news/459580/.
63 For a thorough analysis of Iran–Hezbollah relations, see Paul J. Tompkins Jr., Guillermo Pinczuk, and Theodore Plettner, Unconventional Warfare Case Study: The Relationship between Iran and Lebanese Hizbollah. United States Army Special Operations Command, January 2017. ttps://www.soc.mil/ARIS/books/pdf/_ARIS_Iran-Hiz_Jan2017.pdf.
64 To Director of Central Intelligence, 'Iranian Involvement with Terrorism in Lebanon', June 26, 1985, by DDI Working Group on TWA Hijacking. https://www.cia.gov/library/readingroom/docs/CIA-RDP85T01058R000406550001-6.pdf.

65 George. P. Shultz, 'Memorandum to the President, Our Strategy on Lebanon and the Middle East', October 13, 1983. https://www.cia.gov/library/readingroom/docs/CIA-RDP85M00363R000400680020-6.pdf.

66 For the initial CIA reaction, see *National Intelligence Daily*, November 13, 1982. https://www.cia.gov/library/readingroom/docs/CIA-RDP84T00301 R000600010060-5.pdf. Twenty years later, Israel reinvestigated the case. See Emanuel Fabian, 'Israel Reopens Probe into Deadly 1982 Blast', *The Times of Israel*, November 18, 2022. https://www.timesofisrael.com/israel-reopens-probe-into-deadly-1982-blast-at-army-headquarters-during-lebanon-war/.

67 For the initial CIA reaction, see *National Intelligence Daily*, November 5, 1983. ttps://www.cia.gov/library/readingroom/docs/CIA-RDP85T01094 R000500010094-8.pdf. The actual number of casualties, according to Israeli sources, was 28 Israeli and 32 Lebanese. Anna Ahonheim, 'Israel to Reopen Investigation into Deadly Tyre Disaster, 40 Years Later', *Jerusalem Post*, November 18, 2022. https://www.jpost.com/middle-east/article-722786.

68 The US and French troops were components of the Multinational Force in Lebanon, which was deployed in 1982 to restore order in the country and avert violent clashes between Israeli and Lebanese forces.

69 From National Intelligence Council to the Director of Central Intelligence, 'Retaliation for Beirut Bombing', by Graham Fuller, National Intelligence Officer for NESA, October 28, 1983. https://www.cia.gov/library/readingroom/docs/CIA-RDP88B00443R001404090006-1.pdf.

70 Imam Khomeini portal, December 7, 1983. http://www.imam-khomeini.ir/fa/c14_13169/.

71 Reagan Addresses Lebanon and Grenada. https://www.c-span.org/video/?67921-1/reagan-address-lebanon-grenada.

72 David E. Johnson, *Hard Fighting: Israel in Lebanon and Gaza*. Rand Corporation, 2011, p. 11. https://www.rand.org/pubs/monographs/MG1085.html/.

73 Alastair Crooke, *Resistance: The Essence of Islamist Revolution*. Pluto Press, 2009.

74 Central Intelligence Agency, 'The Rising Tide of Shia Radicalism: An Intelligence Assessment', September 11, 1985, pp. 2–5 and p. 9. https://www.cia.gov/library/readingroom/docs/CIA-RDP86T00587R000400440002-6.pdf.

75 'Interview with Hossein Sheikholeslam', Center for the Documents of the Islamic Revolution, March 9, 2020. https://irdc.ir/fa/print/5663.

76 Mehr News, December 3, 2004. mehrnews.com/x39zP. This article pertains to the opening of a new section at the Behesht-e Zahra cemetery in Tehran, dedicated to those who lost their lives in 'martyrdom operations'.

77 Israeli Brig. Gen. Shimon Shapira accuses Hossein Dehghan, a high-rank-
    ing IRGC officer, of masterminding the 1983 attacks. He also writes that
    Imad Mughniyeh supervised the operations. See Shimon Shapira, 'Iran's
    New Defense Minister: Behind the 1983 Attack on the U.S. Marine Corps
    Barracks in Beirut', Jerusalem Center for Public Affairs, November 13, 2013.
    https://jcpa.org/irans-new-defense-minister-behind-the-1983-attack-
    on-the-u-s-marine-corps-barracks-in-beirut/.

78 Bob Woodward, *Veil: The Secret Wars of the CIA, 1981–1987.* Simon &
    Schuster, 1987, pp. 396–8. The Saudis contributed $3 million to the opera-
    tion. Israel reported that Iran's embassy in Damascus financed the two
    attacks on US and French troops and identified thirteen individuals who
    operationalised them.

79 Bob Woodward and Charles Babcock, 'Anti-Terrorist Unit Blamed in Beirut
    Bombing', *Washington Post*, May 12, 1985. Reprinted in the *Los Angeles
    Times*. https://www.latimes.com/archives/la-xpm-1985-05-12-mn-18480-
    story.html.

80 Director of Central Intelligence, 'Evidence of State Involvement in Hijacking',
    DDI Working Group on TWA Hijacking, June 24, 1985. https://www.cia.
    gov/library/readingroom/docs/CIA-RDP87T00434R000300240061-2.
    pdfarine.

81 Directorate of Intelligence, 'Amal and Hezbollah: The Line Between Politics
    and Terrorism', August 16, 1985. https://www.cia.gov/library/readingroom/
    docs/CIA-RDP85T01058R000506780001-0.pdf; 'The Hijacking of TWA
    847 – Further Thoughts', June 21, 1985. https://www.cia.gov/library/readin-
    groom/docs/CIA-RDP89T01156R000100060015-1.pdf.

82 Director of Central Intelligence, 'Evidence of State Involvement in Hijacking',
    DDI Working Group on TWA Hijacking, June 24, 1985. https://www.cia.
    gov/library/readingroom/docs/CIA-RDP87T00434R000300240061-2.
    pdfarine.

83 To Director of Central Intelligence, from DDI Working Group on TWA
    Hijacking. June 24, 1985. https://www.cia.gov/library/readingroom/docs/
    CIA-RDP87T00434R000300240061-2.pdf.

84 Ali Akbar Hashemi Rafsanjani, *Hopes and Worries: Ayatollah Hashemi
    Rafsanjani's Memoir in 1364* [1985], with Sara Lahoti, June 24, 1985,
    pp. 94–6. www.shiftshab.com.

85 To Director of Central Intelligence, from DDI Working Group on TWA
    Hijacking. June 24, 1985. https://www.cia.gov/library/readingroom/docs/
    CIA-RDP87T00434R000300240061-2.pdf.

86 Naiem Qasem, 'The War of Camps', Rasekhoon, January 15, 2013. https://
    rasekhoon.net/article/show/662432.

87 Rafsanjani, *Hopes and Worries*, p. 95.

88 Central Intelligence Agency, Top Secret, February 22, 1988. https://www.cia.gov/library/readingroom/docs/DOC_0000522257.pdf.

89 'Joint Declaration by Amal Movement and Lebanon's Hezbollah after the Allegiance to the Leader of the Revolution', Khameini.ir, July 23, 1989. https://farsi.khamenei.ir/news-content?id=12135.

90 Directorate of Intelligence, 'Lebanon: Iranian and Syrian Influence with the Hostage Captors', January 30, 1987. https://www.cia.gov/library/readingroom/docs/CIA-RDP90G01359R000500030003-9.pdf.

91 'Interview with Hossein Sheikholeslam', Center for the Documents of the Islamic Revolution, March 9, 2020. https://irdc.ir/fa/print/5663.

92 Ibid.

93 For the Taif agreement, see: https://peacemaker.un.org/sites/peacemaker.un.org/files/LB_891022_Taif%20Accords.pdf. The agreement created a new power-sharing formula that diminished the power of Maronites and increased the power of Sunnis and, to a lesser degree, Shias. Also see Joseph Buhout, 'The Unravelling of Lebanon's Taif Agreement: Limits of Sect-based Power Sharing', Carnegie Endowment for International Peace, May 16, 2006. https://carnegieendowment.org/2016/05/16/unraveling-of-lebanon-s-taif-agreement-limits-of-sect-based-power-sharing-pub-63571.

94 Ahmad Nizar Hamzeh, 'Lebanon's Islamists and Local Politics: A New Reality', Third World Quarterly, Vol. 21, No. 5, 2000, p. 750.

95 Telephone interview with Randa Slim, September 15, 2021.

96 Ronen Bergman, 'Mossad Sheds Light on Argentina Terrorist Attacks in 1990s', The New York Times, July 22, 2022. https://www.nytimes.com/2022/07/22/world/middleeast/argentina-mossad-hezbollah-bombings.html.

97 Jeffrey Goldberg, 'In the Party of God', The New Yorker, October 6, 2002. https://www.newyorker.com/magazine/2002/10/14/in-the-party-of-god.

98 Gal Lutt, 'Israel's Security Zone in Lebanon: A Tragedy?', Middle East Forum, September 2000, pp. 13–20. https://www.meforum.org/70/israels-security-zone-in-lebanon-a-tragedy.

99 United Nations Security Council, Resolution 1559, September 2, 2004. http://unscr.com/en/resolutions/doc/1559.

100 Hezbollah justified its operations as self-defence, asserting that Israel was occupying a fifteen-square mile border region known as the Shebaa Farms, a claim disputed by Israel.

101 Matt M. Matthews, 'We Were Caught Unprepared: The 2006 Hezbollah–Israel War', The Long War Series, Occasional Paper 26, US Army Combined Arms Center, 2008, p. 19. This is an excellent account of the war.

102 'The Story of Commander Soleimani's First Meeting with Hassan Nasrallah' [Interview with Hassan Nasrallah], Donya-e Eqtesad, February 13, 1990. https://donya-e-eqtesad.com/fa/tiny/news-3625594.

103 'The Untold Stories of the 33-day War According to Commander Soleimani', Khamenei.ir, October 1, 2019. https://farsi.khamenei.ir/others-dialog?id=43598.

104 Ibid.

105 'The Details of the Conversation of the "Seyyed of Resistance" [Nasrallah] with Al-Mayadeen Network', IRIB News Agency, December 28, 2020, p. 25. https://www.iribnews.ir/00CS5a.

106 Matthews, 'We Were Caught Unprepared', p. 61.

107 Ibid., p. 37.

108 Khamenei.ir, October 1,2019.

109 Nicholas Blanford, 'A Rare Trip through Hizbullah's Secret Tunnel Network', Christian Science Monitor, May 11, 2007. https://www.csmonitor.com/2007/0511/p01s02-wome.html.

110 Yaakav Katz, 'IDF Declassifies Intelligence on Hizbullah's Southern Lebanon Deployment', Jane's Defense Weekly, July 9, 2010, as quoted in Johnson, Hard Fighting, p. 49.

111 Amos Harel, 'Hezbollah Missiles Strikes Navy Warship; Four Killed', Haaretz, July 16, 2006. https://www.haaretz.com/2006-07-16/ty-article/hezbollah-missile-strikes-navy-warship-four-killed/0000017f-dc8f-db5a-a57f-dcefb5c80000.

112 Norton, Hezbollah, p. 136.

113 Matthews, 'We Were Caught Unprepared', p. 38. This statement was made by an Israeli admiral.

114 Khamenei.ir, October 1, 2019.

115 Jay Mouawad and Steven Erlanger, 'Israel Strikes Back after Rockets Kill 8 in Haifa', The New York Times, July 16, 2006. https://www.nytimes.com/2006/07/16/world/middleeast/16cnd-mideast.html.

116 'The Untold Stories of the 33-Day War According to Commander Soleimani', Khamenei.ir, 2019.

117 Seymour M. Hersh. 'The Next War: Is a Damaged Administration Less Likely to Attack Iran, or More?' The New Yorker, November 27, 2006. https://www.newyorker.com/magazine/2006/11/27/the-next-act.

118 'Rice Sees Bombs as Birth Pangs', Al Jazeera, July 22, 2006. https://www.AlJazeera.com/news/2006/7/22/rice-sees-bombs-as-birth-pangs.

119 Avi Kober, 'The Israel Defense Forces in the Second Lebanon War: Why the Poor Performance?', Journal of Strategic Studies, Vol. 31, No. 1, 2008, p. 23. https://doi.org/10.1080/01402390701785211.

120 Johnson, Hard Fighting, p. 49.

121 Yaakav Katz, 'IDF Declassifies Intelligence on Hizbullah's Southern Lebanon Deployment', Jane's Defense Weekly, July 9, 2010, as quoted in Johnson, Hard Fighting, p. 49.

122 Johnson, *Hard Fighting*, p. 49.

123 Ibid.

124 Johnson, *Hard Fighting*, pp. 47 and 49.

125 United Nations Security Council, Resolution 1701 (2006). https://peace maker.un.org/sites/peacemaker.un.org/files/IL-LB_060814_SCR1701. pdf.

126 'The Meeting of the Speaker of the Lebanese Parliament and a Delegation of Amal and Hezbollah Leaders with the Leader of the Revolution', Khamenei.ir, November 14, 2006. https://farsi.khamenei.ir/news-content? id=1447.

127 'Factbox: Costs of War and Recovery in Lebanon and Israel', Reuters, August 9. 2007. https://www.reuters.com/article/us-lebanon-war-cost/ factbox-costs-of-war-and-recovery-in-lebanon-and-israel-idUSL082257 1220070709.

128 Ibid.

129 As quoted in Matt Mathews, 'We Were Caught Unprepared', p. 38.

130 Marvin Kalb and Carol Saivetz, 'The Israeli-Hezbollah war of 2006: The Media as a Weapon in Asymmetrical Conflict', Brookings, 2007. https:// www.brookings.edu/wp-content/uploads/2012/04/2007islamforum_ israel-hezb-war.pdf.

131 Alastair Crooke and Mark Perry, 'How Hezbollah Defeated Israel: Winning the Intelligence War, Part I', *Asia Times*, October 12, 2006; Alastair Crooke and Mark Perry, 'How Hezbollah Defeated Israel: Winning the Ground War, Part II', *Asia Times*, October 13, 2006.

132 The English Summary of the Winograd Commission Report. https:// www.nytimes.com/2008/01/30/world/middleeast/31winograd-web. html.

133 Ladane Nasseri, 'Iran Willing to Give Military Aid to Lebanese Army, Vahidi Says', Bloomberg, August 25, 2010. https://www.bloomberg.com/ news/articles/2010-08-25/iran-willing-to-give-military-aid-to-lebanese- army-defense-minister-says?embedded-checkout=true.

134 Neil MacFarquhar, 'Iran is Seeking Lebanon Stake as Syria Totters', *The New York Times*, May 24, 2012. https://www.nytimes.com/2012/05/25/ world/middleeast/with-syria-in-turmoil-iran-seeks-deeper-partner-in- lebanon.html.

135 Morteza Abdolhosseini, 'Iran: Lebanon's Fiftieth Trading Partner', *Farhikhtegan*. https://farhikhtegandaily.com/news/44197/.

136 Trading Economics (data from the World Bank). https://oec.world/en/ profile/bilateral-country/lbn/partner/irn.

137 Ibid.

138 Kasra Aarabi, 'Iran's Regional Influence Campaign is Starting to Flop', *Foreign Policy*, December 11, 2019. https://foreignpolicy.com/2019/12/11/collapse-iranian-shiism-iraq-lebanon/.

139 'The West is Looking for the Model of "Statelessness" in Iraq and Lebanon', Khamenei.ir, November 1, 2019. https://farsi.khamenei.ir/others-note?id=43870.

140 'The World Bank in Lebanon', World Bank Group. November 2, 2022. https://www.worldbank.org/en/country/lebanon/overview#1.

141 Kelly Kimbal, 'In 2021, Lebanon Suffered While the World Looked On', *Foreign Policy*, December 26, 2021. https://foreignpolicy.com/2021/12/26/lebanon-economic-crisis-politics-covid-2021/.

142 'The World Bank in Lebanon', World Bank Group.

143 Telephone interview with Rami Khouri, August 11, 2020.

144 'The Rising Tide of Shia Radicalism: An Intelligence Assessment', September 11, 1985, pp. 2–5. https://www.cia.gov/library/readingroom/docs/CIA-RDP86T00587R000400440002-6.pdf.

145 Judith Harik, 'Hizballah's Public and Social Services and Iran', in *Distant Relations: Iran and Lebanon in the Last 500 Years*, ed. H.E. Chehabi. I.B. Tauris., 2006, p. 275.

146 Ramazani, *Revolutionary Iran*, p. 186.

147 Norton, *Hezbollah*, p. 110.

148 Mathew Levitt, *Hezbollah: The Global Footprint of the Party of God*, p. 12.

149 Department of the Treasury, Under Secretary Sigal Mandelker Speech before the Foundation for the Defense of Democracies, June 5, 2018. https://home.treasury.gov/news/press-releases/sm0406.

150 'The Details of the Conversation of the "Seyyed of Resistance" [Nasrallah] with Al-Mayadeen Network', IRIB News Agency, December 28, 2020, pp. 25–6. https://www.iribnews.ir/00CS5a. Nasrallah claimed that Soleimani was personally in charge of providing this huge financial support.

151 'Hezbollah Brushes off US Sanctions, says Money Comes via Iran', Yahoo News, June 24, 2016. https://www.yahoo.com/news/hezbollah-brushes-off-us-sanctions-says-money-comes-175216620.html, and Abdulamir Navabi and Sajad Aspari, 'Describing the Threats in the Region Against the Islamic Republic and the Role of Lebanon's Hezbollah in Mitigating these National Security Threats', *Journal of Political and International Studies*, Vol. 5, No. 17, Winter 2014.

6 Iran's Enduring Alliance with Syria

1 Hossein Hamadani, *Payam-e Mahiha* [The Message of the Fish], with Gul Ali Babaee. Sa'eqe, 2016, p. 448.

2 I have used much information and sources in this chapter from Mohsen Milani, 'Why Tehran Won't Abandon Assad(ism)', *Washington Quarterly*, December 2013, pp. 79–98.

3 Jubin Goodarzi, *Syria and Iran: Diplomatic Alliance and Power Politics in the Middle East.* Tauris Academic Books, 2006, p. 15. This is the best book on Pahlavi Iran's relations with Syria.

4 Zahedi, *Khaterat-e Ardeshir Zahedi* [Memoirs of Ardeshir Zahedi], Vol. 3, p. 150.

5 Iranian embassy in Damascus, Syria, 'The Islamic Republic of Iran's Relations with Syria'. https://web.archive.org/web/20100526124036/http:/www.mfa.gov.ir/cms/cms/damascus/fa/CulturalPart/Ravabet.html.

6 Ibid.

7 Zahedi, *Khaterat-e Ardeshir Zahedi* [Memoirs of Ardeshir Zahedi], Vol. 3, p. 150.

8 'What Was Imam Khomeini's Important Message to Imam Musa Sadr?', Center for Documents of the Islamic Revolution, excerpts from Ali Janati's memoirs, September 2, 2019. https://www.irdc.ir/fa/news/5160/%D9%BE%DB%8C%D8%BA%D8%A7%D9%85-%D9%85%D9%87%D9%85-%D8%A7%D9%85%D8%A7%D9%85-%D8%AE%D9%85%DB%8C%D9%86%DB%8C-%D8%A8%D9%87-%D8%A7%D9%85%D8%A7%D9%85-%D9%85%D9%88%D8%B3%DB%8C-%D8%B5%D8%AF%D8%B1-%DA%86%D9%87-%D8%A8%D9%88%D8%AF.

9 'Helping Activists of the Islamic Movement against the Pahlavi Regime', *Farhikhtegan Daily*, June 11, 2017. http://fdn.ir/7089.

10 *Hadidchi-Dabbagh's Memoirs.* Imam Khomeini portal, www.imam-khomeini.ir/fa/bookPrint.aspx?ID=87423&ppage, p. 83.

11 Memoirs of Seyyed Rahim Safavi, prepared by Majid Najafpour, *Az Jonoob-e Lebanon ta Jonoob-e Iran* [From South of Lebanon to South of Iran]. Markaz-e Asnad-e Enqelab Islami, 2009, pp. 100–6. See also, 'The Impact of Syrian Aid on the Victory of the Islamic Revolution: The Transfer of Training from Syrian Camps to Isfahan Revolutionaries on the Eve of the Islamic Revolution Victory', Islamic Revolution Document Center, no date.

12 Safavi (2009), pp. 123–4.

13 'What Was Imam Khomeini's Important Message to Imam Musa Sadr?', Center for Documents of the Islamic Revolution, September 2, 2019. http://www.imam-khomeini.ir/fa/n3082/.

14 Tasnim, December 13, 2015. https://tn.ai/941583. The article provides no documentation to prove the assertion.

15 I have benefited from the following sources. Yair Hirschfeld, 'The Odd Couple: Ba'athist Syria and Khomeini's Iran', in Moshe Ma'oz and Avner Yaniv, eds, *Syria under Assad*. Croom Helm, 1986; Yosef Olmert, 'Iranian–Syrian Relations: Between Islam and Realpolitik', in David Menashri, ed., *The Iranian Revolution and the Muslim World*. Westview, 1990; Christin Marschall, 'Syria–Iran: A Strategic Alliance, 1979–1991', *Orient*, Vol. 33, No. 3, September 1992; and Shireen T. Hunter, 'Iran and Syria: From Hostility to Limited Alliance', in Hooshang Amirahmadi and Nader Entessar, eds, *Iran and the Arab World*. St Martin's Press, 1993.

16 Stephen Walt, 'Alliance Formation and the Balance of World Power', *International Security*, Vol. 9, No. 4, Spring 1985, pp. 3–43.

17 'Abdul Halim Khaddam: From Vice President of Syria to Exile in Paris', *Asharq al-Awsat*, April 1, 2020. https://english.aawsat.com/home/article/2210646/exclusive-abdul-halim-khaddam-vice-president-syria-exile-paris.

18 Elie Chalala, 'Syria's Support of Iran in the Gulf War', *Journal of Arab Affairs*, Vol. 7, No. 2, Fall 1988.

19 Sh-SHTP-a-001-023, Saddam Hussein and Ba'ath Party Members Discussing the Iran–Iraq War, March 6, 1987. Quoted in Murray and Woods, *The Iran–Iraq War*, p. 289.

20 'The Timeline of Eight Years of Holy Defense'. https://tinyurl.com/7e9f8f8w.

21 'Syria's Arms Transfer to Iran', Stockholm International Peace Research Institute Database, 1980–88. https://www.sipri.org/databases/armstransfers.

22 Mohsen Rafiqdoust (with Saeed Alaeyun), *Baraye Tarikh Meegooyam Khaterat e Moshen Rafiqdoust* [I Say it for History: Mohsen Rafiqdoust's Memoirs], Vol. 1. Entesharat-e Sourey-e Mehr, 2012, pp. 91–2.

23 For the chronology of the development of Iranian missile programme, see https://www.iranwatch.org/our-publications/weapon-program-background-report/iran-missile-milestones-1985-2020.

24 Rafiqdoust, *Baraye Tarikh Meegooyam*, Vol. 1, p. 285.

25 'The Biography of Hassan Tehrani Moghaddam', Hamsharionline, February 19, 2013. hamshahrionline.ir/x3KMx.

26 'The Story of the 2 Rockets that Shahid Tehrani Moghaddam Did Not Allow to be Launched', Tansim, November 23, 2018. https://tn.ai/18742633.

27 For an analysis of the convergence and divergence of interests between Tehran and Damascus, see Fred Lawson, 'Syria's Relations with Iran:

Managing the Dilemmas of Alliance', *Middle East Journal*, Vol. 61. No. 1, Winter 2007, pp. 29–47.

28 On the Iranian Syrian relationship, see Anoush Ehteshami and R. Hinnebusch, *Syria and Iran: Middle Powers in a Penetrated Regional System*. Routledge, 1997; and Hussein J. Agha and Ahmad S. Khalidi, *Syria and Iran: Rivalry and Cooperation*. Pinter, 1995.

29 Akan Malici and Allison L. Buckner, 'Empathizing with Rouge Leaders: Mahmoud Ahmadinejad and Bashar al-Assad', *Journal of Peace Research*, Vol. 45, No. 6, 2008, pp. 783–800. They argue that presidents Ahmadinejad and Assad 'perceived US actions towards their countries as highly hostile and threatening'.

30 Leon Goldsmith, *Cycle of Fear: Syria's Alawites in War and Peace*. Hurst, 2015, pp. 22–30 and 35.

31 Yvette Talhamy, 'The Syrian Muslim Brothers and the Syrian–Iranian Relationship', *Middle East Journal*, Vol. 63, No. 4, October 22, 2009, p. 176, and Yvette Talhamy, '"The Fatwas" and the Nusayri/Alawis of Syria', *Middle Eastern Studies*, Vol. 46, No. 2, March 2020, pp. 175–94.

32 Goldsmith, *Cycle of Fear*, p. 35.

33 Talhamy, '"The Fatwas" and the Nusayri/Alawis of Syria', p. 190.

34 For a sobering and perceptive analysis of why the Arab Spring failed, see Noah Feldman, *The Arab Winter: A Tragedy*, Princeton University Press, 2020.

35 'Khamenei: Arab Revolts Sign of "Islamic Awakening"', Radio Free Europe/Radio Liberty, February 4, 2011. https://www.rferl.org/a/iran_khamenei_islamic_awakening/2297319.html.

36 On the similarities and differences between Iran's Green Movement and the Arab Spring see Charles Kurzman, 'The Arab Spring: Ideals of the Iranian Green Movement, Methods of the Iranian Revolution', *International Journal of Middle East Studies*, Vol. 44, No. 1, 2012, pp. 162–5.

37 I have benefited from the following sources on Iran's policy towards the Syrian civil war: Thomas Juneau, 'Iran's Costly Intervention in Syria: A Pyrrhic Victory', *Mediterranean Politics*, Vol. 25, No. 1, 2000, pp. 26–44; Aniseh Tabrizi, Raffaelo Pantucci, et al., *Understanding Iran's Role in the Syrian Conflict*. Occasional Paper, Royal United Services Institute, August 2016. https://www.rusi.org/explore-our-research/publications/occasional-papers/understanding-irans-role-syrian-conflict; and Geneive Abdo, 'How Iran Keeps Assad in Power in Syria', *Foreign Affairs*, August 25, 2011. https://www.foreignaffairs.com/articles/iran/2011-08-25/how-iran-keeps-assad-power-syria.

38 Joshua Landis, 'The Syrian Uprising 2011: Why the Assad Regime is Likely to Survive to 2013', *Middle East Policy*, Vol. XIX, No. 1, Spring 2012,

pp. 72–84. Landis was among the few experts who believed that Assad was likely to survive the civil war.

39 'Syria Opposition Leader Interview Transcript; "Stop the Killing Machine"', *Wall Street Journal*, December 2, 2011. https://search-proquest-com. ezproxy.lib.usf.edu/wallstreetjournal/docview/907127644/5FA1B4A8ABC F4B43PQ/1?accountid=14745.

40 Rob Taylor, 'Iran Warns of Possible "Armageddon" If Syria Can't Be Held Together', *Wall Street Journal*, March 15, 2016.

41 'If the Troublemakers Were Not Stopped in Syria, We Should Have Stopped Them in Tehran, Khorasan and Isfahan', Fars News, January 5, 2017. https://www.farsnews.ir/news/13951016000570/%D8%A7. Amirali Hajizadeh, Commander of the IRGC Air Force, echoed this sentiment. 'We Would Have Witnessed Suicidal Operations in Our Own Cities', Mezan News, January 5, 2017. https://www.mizanonline.com/fa/news/263519/.

42 See Ehud Yaari, 'Iran's Ambitions in the Levant', *Foreign Affairs*, May 1, 2017. https://www.foreignaffairs.com/ articles/iran/2017-05-01/irans-ambitions-levant.

43 'The Details of the Conversation of the "Seyyed of Resistance" [Nasrallah] with Al-Mayadeen Network', IRIB News Agency, December 28, 2020, pp. 25–26. https://www.iribnews.ir/00CS5a.

44 Raz Zimmt, 'The "Ammar Headquarters" and the Challenges of the Iranian Political System', Alliance Center for Iranian Studies, Tel Aviv University, February 5, 2012. https://en-humanities.tau.ac.il/iranian/publications/irans_pulse/2012-5.

45 'Syria is Iran's 35th Province', *Asr-e Iran*, February 14, 2013. asriran.com/00152w.

46 Talhamy, 'The Syrian Muslim Brothers and the Syrian–Iranian Relationship', p. 572.

47 'Syria Opposition Leader Interview Transcript; "Stop the Killing Machine"', *Wall Street Journal*, December 2, 2011.

48 Anne Barnard and Eric Schmitt, 'As Fighters Flood Syria, Fears of a New Extremist Haven', *The New York Times*, August 8, 2013. http://www.nytimes.com/2013/08/09/world/middleeast/as-foreign-fighters-flood-syria-fears-of-a-new-extremist-haven.html?smid=tw-share&_r=0&pagewanted=print.

49 Geneive Abdo, 'Why Sunni–Shia Conflict is Worsening', *CNN*, June 7, 2013. https://edition.cnn.com/2013/06/07/opinion/abdo-shia-sunni-tension/index.html.

50 The US Department of the Treasury identified Soleimani as the person responsible for overseeing the Quds Force officers who plotted to assassinate Saudi Arabia's ambassador to the US.

51 'Soleimani's Speech at the First Anniversary of Hamadani's Death', ISNA, October 5, 2016. https://www.isna.ir/news/95071409366/.

52 'Qasem Soleimani: ISIS Was Formed to Undermine Iran, Not Syria', *Radio Farda*, October 6, 2016. https://www.radiofarda.com/a/02-solimani-syria-iran-policy/28034371.html.

53 As quoted in Payam Mohseni and Hussein Kalout, 'Iran's Axis of Resistance Rises: How It's Forging a New Middle East', *Foreign Affairs*, January 24, 2017. https://www.foreignaffairs.com/iran/irans-axis-resistance-rises.

54 The United Nation, General Assembly and Security Council, July 6, 2012. https://peacemaker.un.org/sites/peacemaker.un.org/files/SY_120630_Final%20Communique%20of%20the%20Action%20Group%20for%20Syria.pdf.

55 Hossein Amirabdollahian, *Sobh-e Sham* [Morning in Damascus], prepared by Mohammad Mohsen Mos'hafi. Soremehr, 2020, pp. 62–4.

56 'Syria Vows Retaliation over "Deadly Ambush"', Al Jazeera, June 7, 2011. https://www.AlJazeera.com/news/2011/6/7/syria-vows-retaliation-over-deadly-ambush.

57 'Iran Accused of Setting Up Pro-Assad Militias', Al Jazeera, August 15, 2012. https://www.Al Jazeera.com/news/2012/8/15/iran-accused-of-setting-up-pro-assad-militias.

58 The statement was made by Hassan Nasrallah, 'The Details of the Conversation of the "Seyyed of Resistance" [Nasrallah] with Al-Mayadeen Network', IRIB News Agency, December 28, 2020, p. 21. https://www.irib-news.ir/ooCS5a.

59 'Ahmadinejad: Iran Supports the Will of the Vote of the Syrian People, Regardless of What the Result Will Be', Khabaronline, August 15, 2012. khabaronline.ir/x42vX.

60 IRIB News Agency, December 28, 2020, pp. 19–21. https://www.iribnews.ir/ooCS5a.

61 Ewen MacAskill, 'Iran and Syria Confront US with Defense Pact', *Guardian*, February 17, 2005. https://www.theguardian.com/world/2005/feb/17/usa.syria.

62 Bilal Y. Saab, 'Syria and Iran Revive an Old Ghost with Defense Pact', Brookings, July 4, 2006. https://www.brookings.edu/opinions/syria-and-iran-revive-an-old-ghost-with-defense-pact/.

63 Charles Levinson, 'Iran Arms Syria with Radar – System Could Help Tehran Dodge Israeli Strike; Blow to U.S. Strategy on Damascus', *Wall Street Journal*, June 30, 2010.

64 Mohammad Ali Shahrivari, Esmail Shafiee, and Nafiseh Vaez, 'An Analysis of the Policies of the Islamic Republic of Iran and Saudi Arabia towards Syria' (in Persian), *Journal of Foreign Policy Studies in the Islamic World*, Vol. 5, No. 20, Winter 2016, pp. 99–127.

65 Mark Mazzetti, Adam Goldman, and Michael Schmidt, 'Behind the Sudden Death of a $1 Billion Secret C.I.A. War in Syria', *The New York Times*, August 2, 2017. https://www.nytimes.com/2017/08/02/world/middleeast/cia-syria-rebel-arm-train-trump.html.

66 Michael Winter, 'Saudis Sent Death-row Inmates to fight Syria', *USA Today*, January 21, 2013. The Saudis stopped the programme when it was publicised. https://www.usatoday.com/story/news/world/2013/01/21/saudi-inmates-fight-syria-commute-death-sentences/1852629/.

67 Liz Sly, 'In Syria, Defectors Form Dissident Army in Sign Uprising May be Entering New Phase', *Washington Post*, September 25, 2011. https://www.washingtonpost.com/world/middle-east/in-syria-defectors-form-dissident-army-in-sign-uprising-may-be-entering-new-phase/2011/09/24/gIQAKef8wK_story.html.

68 'Jafari: We Will Not Preemptively Attack. If You Do Not Stop Israel, We Will Reconsider Our Nuclear Commitments', ISNA, September 16, 2012. https://www.isna.ir/news/0000178343/.

69 Robert Fisk, 'Iran to Send 4,000 Troops to Aid President Assad Forces in Syria', *Independent*, June 16, 2013. It became hard for Iran to deny the presence of its military forces when Assad agreed to release 2,130 prisoners in exchange for the release of the 48 incarcerated Iranians captured by the rebels in 2013. See, 'Syrian Rebels Free 48 Iranians', Radio Free Europe/Radio Liberty, January 9, 2013.

70 Ken Hawrey and Alice Naghshineh, 'Translation: The Deployment of Aretesh Special Forces to Syria', *Critical Threats*, April 11, 2016. https://www.criticalthreats.org/print/ana_576a8ccd446a7.

71 As Quoted in Dexter Filkins, 'The Shadow Commander', *The New Yorker*, September 23, 2013, p. 4.

72 'General Soleimani: If Syria had One Hemmat and Kharazi, It Would Not Be in the Situation It Is Today', ISNA, February 28, 2013. https://www.isna.ir/news/91121006864/. As quoted in a good piece by Will Fulton, Joseph Holliday, and Sam Wyer, 'Iranian Strategy in Syria', Institute for the Study of War and AEI's Critical Threats Project, May 2013, p. 13. http://www.understandingwar.org/sites/default/files/IranianStrategyinSyria-1MAY.pdf.

73 See the good piece by Ariane Tabatabai, 'Syria Changed the Iranian Way of War', *Foreign Affairs*, August 16, 2019. https://www.foreignaffairs.com/articles/syria/2019-08-16/syria-changed-iranian-way-war.

74 Quoted in Fulton et al., 'Iranian Strategy in Syria', p. 13.

75 Hamadani,(2006), pp. 443–4.

76 Ibid., p. 434.

77 Ibid., p. 445.

78 Ibid., p. 448.

79 For the list of the Syrian opposition groups, see Joseph Holliday, 'Syria's Armed Opposition', Institute for the Study of War, March 2012.

80 Anne Barnard and Eric Schmitt, 'As Fighters Flood Syria, Fears of a New Extremist Haven', *The New York Times*, August 8, 2013.

81 Karen DeYoung and Joby Warrick, 'Iran and Hezbollah Build Militia Networks in Syria in Event that Assad Falls', *Washington Post*, February 10, 2013.

82 Nicholas Heras, 'The Counter-insurgency Role of Syria's "Popular Committees"', *Jamestown Foundation: Terrorism Monitor*, Vol. 11, No. 9, May 2, 2013.

83 'The Complementary Role of Martyrs Soleimani and Hamdani in the Final Victory of the Axis of Resistance', IRIB News Agency, January 11, 2020. https://www.iribnews.ir/00AzBr.

84 Marisa Sullivan, 'Hezbollah in Syria', Institute for the Study of War, April 2014. https://www.jstor.org/stable/pdf/resrep07896.pdf?refreqid=excelsior%3Ab87c1b3b2236011eefea190e89761ec1.

85 Anne Barnard, 'Car Bombing Injures Dozens in Hezbollah Section of Beirut', *The New York Times*, July 10, 2013. https://search-proquestcom.ezproxy.lib.usf.edu/nytimes/docview/1398953410/fulltext/2FB553B8C9C940AFPQ/2?accountid=14745.

86 For a solid analysis of this critical war, see Nicholas Blanford, 'The Battle for Qusayr: How the Syrian Regime and Hizb Allah Tipped the Balance', *CTC Sentinel* (Combating Terrorism Center at West Point), Vol. 6, Issue 8. https://ctc.westpoint.edu/the-battle-for-qusayr-how-the-syrian-regime-and-hizb-allah-tipped-the-balance/.

87 Jennifer Cafarella, 'Jabhat al-Nusra in Syria: An Islamic Emirate for Al-Qaeda', Institute for the Study of War, December 2014. http://www.understandingwar.org/sites/default/files/JN%20Final.pdf. 'In Syrian Victory, Hezbollah Risks Broader Fight', *The New York Times*, June 5, 2013. https://search-proquest-com.ezproxy.lib.usf.edu/nytimes/docview/2214943466/4E1F73CC0F4B4BECPQ/6?accountid=14745.

88 Filkins, 'The Shadow Commander', 2013, p. 4. John Maguire, a former CIA officer, is the source.

89 Telephone interview with Randa Slim, September 15, 2021.

90 'Timeline of Syrian Chemical Weapons Activity, 2012–2020', Arms Control Association, May 2020. https://www.armscontrol.org/factsheets/Timeline-of-Syrian-Chemical-Weapons-Activity.

91 Günther Meyer, 'Is Assad to Blame for the Chemical Weapons Attack in Syria?', *DW*, June 4, 2017. https://www.dw.com/en/is-assad-to-blame-for-the-chemical-weapons-attack-in-syria/a-38330217.

92 Ibid.

93 Jeffrey Goldberg, 'The Obama Doctrine: The U.S. President Talks through his Hardest Decisions about America's Role in the World', *The Atlantic*, April2016.https://www.theatlantic.com/magazine/archive/2016/04/the-obama-doctrine/471525/.

94 Seymour M. Hersh, 'Whose Sarin?', *London Review of Books*, Vol. 35, No. 4, December 19, 2013. https://www.lrb.co.uk/the-paper/v35/n24/seymour-m.-hersh/whose-sarin.

95 '"Clear and Convincing" Evidence of Chemical Weapons Use in Syria, UN Team Reports', *UN News*, September 16, 2013. https://news.un.org/en/story/2013/09/449052-clear-and-convincing-evidence-chemical-weapons-use-syria-un-team-reports.

96 Personal interview with Ambassador Robert Ford, October 2, 2022. On Ford's personal view about the Syrian crisis, see Robert Ford, 'The Syrian Civil War: A New Stage, but Is It the Final One?', Middle East Institute, April 2019. https://www.mei.edu/sites/default/files/2019-04/Ford_The_Syrian_Civil_War.pdf.

97 Goldberg, 'The Obama Doctrine'.

98 Hisham Melhem, 'How Obama's Syrian Chemical Weapons Deal Fell Apart: A Tale of Syrian Deception, Russian Duplicity, and American Dithering', *The Atlantic*, April 10, 2017. https://www.theatlantic.com/international/archive/2017/04/how-obamas-chemical-weapons-deal-fell-apart/522549/.

99 Personal interview with Ambassador Robert Ford, October 2, 2022.

100 'The Leader of the Revolution: We Have No Animosity Against the American People; We Oppose Arrogance', Iranian Diplomacy, November 20, 2013. http://www.irdiplomacy.ir/fa/news/1924815/.

101 'Release of the Audio file of Hashemi Rafsanjani's Words', Rajanews, August 22, 2012. https://www.rajanews.com/news/149584. For the actual video, see 'Iranian Expediency Council Chairman Rafsanjani: Syrians Were Bombed with Chemicals by Their Own Government', MEMRI, September 2013. https://www.memri.org/tv/iranian-expediency-council-chairman-rafsanjani-syrians-were-bombed-chemicals-their-own-government.

102 'Hashemi Said that the Voice is Fake; I Did Not Accuse the Syrian government of [using] Chemical Weapons', *Hamshahrionline*, September 4, 2013. hamshahrionline.ir/x3XJp.

103 The UN Refugee Agency, 'Iran Becomes the Second Largest Refugee Hosting Country as Forced Displacement Hits New Record High Globally', https://www.unhcr.org/ir/2023/06/14/iran-becomes-the-second-largest-refugee-hosting-country-as-forced-displacement-hits-new-record-high-globally/.

104 'How was the Fatemiyoun Brigade Formed?', *Kayhan*, May 30, 2015. https://kayhan.ir/oooByQ.

105 Frud Bezhan, 'Top U.S. Envoy Says New Sanctions Against Iran Coming "Until the End" of Trump Administration', Radio Free Europe, December 22, 2020. https://www.rferl.org/a/iran-u-s-sanctions-religious-seminaries-network-al-mustafa/31014153.html.

106 'Everything We Need to Know about the Fatemiyoun and Zeynabiyoun', Holy Defense News, July 28, 2020. https://dnws.ir/ooii7t.

107 Farnaz Fassihi, 'Iran Pays Afghans to Fight for Assad; Offers Them $500 Stipend, Residency Benefits', *Wall Street Journal*, May 15, 2014.

108 Ali Alfoneh and Michael Eisenstadt, 'Iranian Casualties in Syria and the Logic of Intervention', Washington Institute for Near East Policy, Washington, DC, March 11, 2016. https://www.washingtoninstitute.org/policy-analysis/iranian-casualties-syria-and-strategic-logic-intervention. See also: 'Iran Sending Thousands of Afghans to Fight in Syria', Human Rights Watch, January 29, 2016. https://www.hrw.org/news/2016/01/29/iran-sending-thousands-afghans-fight-syria.

109 Ahmad Shuja Jamal, *The Fatemiyoun Army: Reintegration into Afghan Society*, US Institute of Peace, Washington, DC, 2019, pp. 5 and 8. https://www.jstor.org/stable/pdf/resrep20233.pdf?refreqid=excelsior%3Af93cdfe307567391e2bdd12d0beofd6c.

110 Ibid., p. 3.

111 Summary of Zarif's interview, December 23, 2020. BBC Persian, https://www.bbc.com/persian/iran-55409057.

112 Ibid.

113 Alfoneh and Eisenstadt, 'Iranian Casualties in Syria and the Logic of Intervention'.

114 Ali Akbar Velayati, 'Velayati's narrative of Iran's Influence in the Region: Denial of the Syrian Government Worsens the Situation', February 4, 2014. https://velayati.ir/fa/news/844/.

115 'What is the Geneva II Conference on Syria?', BBC News, June 24, 2014. https://www.bbc.com/news/world-middle-east-24628442.

116 Amirabdollahian, (2020), pp. 47–9.

117 Mark Mazzetti and Matt Apuzzo, 'U.S. Relies Heavily on Saudi Money to Support Syrian Rebels', *The New York Times*, January 23, 2016.

118 Nate Rosenblatt and David Kilcullen, *How Raqqa Became the Capital of ISIS: A Proxy Warfare Case Study*, Joint Project by New American and Arizona State University, July 2019, p. 9. https://d1y8sb8igg2f8e.cloudfront.net/documents/How_Raqqa_Became_the_Capital_of_ISIS_2019-07-26_134456.pdf.

119 Witness Statement of The Honorable Brett H. McGurk, Special Presidential Envoy for the Global Coalition to Counter ISIS, Testimony Before the Senate Foreign Relations Committee on 'Global Efforts to Defeat ISIS', June 28, 2016. https://www.foreign.senate.gov/imo/media/doc/062816_McGurk_Testimony.pdf.

120 For a good discussion of the Iranian–Russian cooperation, see Nicole Grajewski, 'The Evolution of Russian and Iranian Cooperation in Syria', Center for Strategic and International Studies, November 17, 2021. https://www.csis.org/analysis/evolution-russian-and-iranian-cooperation-syria.

121 Mohsen Milani, 'Iran and Russia's Uncomfortable Alliance: Their Cooperation in Syria in Context', *Foreign Affairs*, August 31, 2016. https://www.foreignaffairs.com/articles/iran/2016-08-31/iran-and-russias-uncomfortable-alliance.

122 Laila Bassam and Tom Perry, 'How Iranian General Plotted Out Syrian Assault in Moscow', Reuters, October 6, 2015. http://www.reuters.com/article/us-mideast-crisis-syria-soleimaniinsigh-idUSKCN0S02BV20151006.

123 'The Story of Putin's 140-minute Meeting with General Soleimani', *Jahan News*, July 15, 2019. https://www.jahannews.com/news/694357.

124 'The Publication of Zarif's Audio File about Soleimani and Russia's Sabotage of the JCPOA', BBC Persian, April 25, 2021. https://www.bbc.com/persian/iran-56878595.

125 'Islamic State and the Crisis in Iraq and Syria in Maps', BBC News, March 28, 2018. https://www.bbc.co.uk/news/world-middle-east-27838034.

126 For a good analysis of the nature and consequences of the Russian interventions in Syria, see Robert Hamilton, Chris Miller, and Aaron Stein, *Russia's Intervention in Syria: Historical and Geopolitical Context*, Foreign Policy Research Institute, September 2020. https://www.fpri.org/wp-content/uploads/2020/09/report-1-hamilton-stein-miller.pdf.

127 Anton Mardasov, 'How Russia Made Hemeimeem Air Base Its African Hub', Middle East Institute, May 28, 2020. https://www.mei.edu/publications/how-russia-made-hemeimeem-air-base-its-african-hub.

128 Samuel Charap, Elina Treyger, and Edward Geis, 'Understanding Russia's Intervention in Syria', October 31, 2019, p. 10. https://www.rand.org/content/dam/rand/pubs/research_reports/RR3100/RR3180/RAND_RR3180.pdf.

129 Sergey Sukhankin, 'Russian PMCs in the Syrian Civil War: From Slavonic Corps to Wagner Group and Beyond', Jamestown Foundation, December18,2019.https://jamestown.org/program/russian-pmcs-in-the-syrian-civil-war-from-slavonic-corps-to-wagner-group-and-beyond/.

130 Michael Kofman and Mathew Rojansky, 'What Kind of Victory for Russian in Syria?', *Military Review*, January 2018. https://www.armyupress.army.mil/Journals/Military-Review/Online-Exclusive/2018-OLE/Russia-in-Syria/.

131 Mattathias Schwartz, 'Hillary Clinton Acknowledges Saudi Terror Financing in Hacked Email, Hinting at Tougher Approach', *The Intercept*, October 16, 2016. https://theintercept.com/2016/10/12/hillary-clinton-acknowledges-saudi-terror-financing-in-hacked-email-hinting-at-tougher-approach/.

132 Natasha Bertrand, 'State Department Officials are "Baffled" by John Kerry's Latest Comments that have "Muddied the Waters" in Syria', *Business Insider*, July 12, 2016. https://www.businessinsider.com/john-kerry-jaysh-al-islam-ahrar-al-sham-syria-2016-7.

133 'Isis "Losing Control" of Palmyra as Syrian Troops Backed by Russian Air Strikes Approach Ancient City', *Independent*, March 26, 2016.

134 Laila Bassam et al., 'Battle of Aleppo Ends after Years of Bloodshed with Rebel Withdrawal', Reuters, December 13, 2016. https://www.reuters.com/article/idUSKBN1420H5/.

135 Neil MacFarquhar and David Sanger, 'Russia Sends Bombers to Syria Using Base in Iran', *The New York Times*, August 16, 2016. https://www.nytimes.com/2016/08/17/world/middleeast/russiairan-base-syria.html.

136 'Reactions to Russia's Use of Nojeh Base', *Donya-e Eqtesad*, August 18, 2016. https://www.donya-e-eqtesad.com/fa/tiny/news-1065040.

137 'Russia, Iran, Turkey set up Syria De-escalation Zones for at Least Six Months: Memorandum', Reuters, May 2017. https://www.reuters.com/article/idUSKBN1820Co/.

138 'Iran Fires Missile at ISIL Positions in Eastern Syria', Al Jazeera, June 19, 2017. https://www.Al Jazeera.com/news/2017/6/19/iran-fires-missiles-at-isil-positions-in-eastern-syria; see also https://www.haaretz.com/middle-east-news/2017-06-21/ty-article/irans-missile-attack-on-syria-failed-5-missed-3-landed-in-iraq/0000017f-ebaa-dof7-a9ff-efefac810000.

139 See 'Report: Israel Treating al-Qaida Fighters Wounded in Syria Civil War', *Jerusalem Post*, 13 March, 2015. https://www.jpost.com/Middle-East/Report-Israel-treating-al-Qaida-fighters-wounded-in-Syria-civil-war-393862. Iranian sources refer to this article as 'proof' that the US and Israel supported terrorists in Syria.

140 Qasem Soleimani's letter to Ayatollah Khamenei and Khamenei's response, November 11, 2017. Khamenei.ir. https://farsi.khamenei.ir/message-content?id=38249.

141 'Syrian Army and Allies Capture Last Major ISIS-held Town in Syria – Reports', RT, November 8, 2017. https://www.rt.com/news/409274-syrian-army-capture-last-isis-town/.

142 Personal interview with Ambassador Robert Ford, October 2, 2022.

143 Mark Landler, Helene Cooper, and Eric Schmitt, 'Trump to Withdraw U.S. Forces from Syria, Declaring "We Have Won Against ISIS"', *The New York Times*, December 19, 2018.

144 Joel Gehrke, 'Rex Tillerson: "Crucial" to Maintain US Military Presence in Syria', *Washington Examiner*, January 17, 2017. https://www.washingtonexaminer.com/news/292974/rex-tillerson-crucial-to-maintain-us-military-presence-in-syria/.

145 'Top Trump Adviser: US, Israel, Russia All Want Iran Out of Syria', *The Times of Israel*, August 19, 2018. https://www.timesofisrael.com/top-trump-adviser-us-israel-russia-all-want-iran-out-of-syria/.

146 Eran Etzion, 'The Day after Soleimani: Israel Contemplates "Success Leveraging"', Middle East Institute, January 27, 2020.

147 Shimon Shapira, 'Iran Launches "Hizbullah Syria", to Open a New Front Against Israel on the Golan Heights', *Jerusalem Center for Public Affairs*, Vol. 14, No. 16, June 2, 2014. https://jcpa.org/article/iran-hizbullah-syria-front/.

148 Ibid.

149 As quoted in Grajewski, 'The Evolution of Russian and Iranian Cooperation in Syria'.

150 Mostafa Islami, 'Why Did Israel Attack Syria?', Khabarneqar Defa-ye Moghaddas, April 10, 2018. https://defapress.ir/286101.

151 'Names of the Martyrs of the Airport Attack', *Tahavolat-e Jahan-e Islam*, April 10, 2018. https://iswnews.com/10038/.

152 Ibid.

153 'Exclusive Talk with Mohammad Ali Sobhani' [former director general of the Middle East department of the Ministry of Foreign Affairs], Jamaran News, January 29, 2024. https://www.jamaran.news/fa/tiny/news-1621557.

154 Judah Gross, 'IDF Reveals "Operation Chess": Its Effort to Keep Iranian Reprisals in Check', *The Times of Israel*, May 11, 2018. https://www.timesofisrael.com/idf-reveals-operation-chess-its-effort-to-thwart-iranian-reprisals-from-syria/.

155 Oula A. Alrifai, 'In the Service of Ideology: Iran's Religious and Socioeconomic Activities in Syria', Washington Institute for Near East Studies, Policy Notes 100, March 14, 2021. https://www.washingtoninstitute.org/policy-analysis/service-ideology-irans-religious-and-socioeconomic-activities-syria.

156 Fulton, et al., 'Iranian Strategy in Syria', p. 10.

157 Shimon Shapira, 'Iran Plans to Take Over Syria', *Jerusalem Center for Public Affairs*, Vol. 13, No. 10, May 5, 2013. https://jcpa.org/article/

irans-plans-to-take-over-syria/. Years later, he wrote about the Iranian conquest of Syria: Jacques Neriah and Shimon Shapira, 'The Iranian Conquest of Syria', *Jerusalem Center for Public Affairs*, No. 626, August 14, 2019. https://jcpa.org/article/the-iranian-conquest-of-syria/.

158 David Lesch, 'Iran Is Taking Over Syria: Can Anyone Stop It?' *The New York Times*, August 29, 2017. https://www.nytimes.com/2017/08/29/opinion/iran-syria.html.

159 United Nations Human Rights, June 28, 2022. https://www.ohchr.org/en/press-releases/2022/06/un-human-rights-office-estimates-more-306000-civilians-were-killed-over-10.

160 Alfoneh and Eisenstadt, 'Iranian Casualties in Syria and the Strategic Logic of Intervention'.

161 David Adesnik, 'Iran Spends $16 Billion Annually to Support Terrorists and Rogue Regimes', Foundation for Defense of Democracies, January 10, 2018.https://www.fdd.org/analysis/2018/01/10/iran-spends-16-billion-annually-to-support-terrorists-and-rogue-regimes/

162 'Falahatpisheh's Unambiguous Words: We Gave 30 Billion Dollars to Syria, We Have to Get it Back', *Hamshahrionline*, May 20, 2020. hamshahrionline.ir/x6nXY.

163 Michael Jansen, 'Iranian Support of Assad Regime in Syria Amounts to Billions', *The Irish Times*, January 11, 2015. https://www.irishtimes.com/news/world/middle-east/iranian-support-of-assad-regime-in-syria-amounts-to-billions-1.2246378.

164 Hamidreza Azizi and Leonid Issaev, 'Russian and Iranian Economic Interests in Syria (Pre-2012 and Intra-war Period), Geneva Center for Security Policy, February 2019. https://dam.gcsp.ch/files/2y1onlGNuebJ3zh4kU5wS7N66uuFm35TYDmJjO9jyzKVQYbDoO7vybkfq.

165 'The Minister of Tourism of Syria Emphasized the Expansion of Relations with Iran', IRNA, December 2, 2010. www.irna.ir/news/6136628/.

166 'Rahim Safavi: Iran's Expenses in the Syrian War Should be Returned', *Euronews*, February 17, 2018. https://per.euronews.com/2018/02/17/rahim-safavi-iran-to-return-its-costs-in-syrian-civil-war.

167 US Department of State, Caesar Syria Civilian Protection Act, June 17, 2020. https://2017-2021.state.gov/caesar-syria-civilian-protection-act/index.html.

168 Sinan Hatahet, *Russia and Iran: Economic Influence in Syria*. Research Paper. Chatham House, March 2019. https://www.chathamhouse.org/sites/default/files/publications/research/2019-03-08RussiaAndIranEconomicInfluenceInSyria.pdf?fbclid=IwAR2VzV4QdFeVBknWM7OODmMH1B8kt7u_foxgdYzceEyNoqtTZ5izYxnDMEI.

169 'Majles Deputy: Putin and Assad Will Betray Us', BBC Persian, June 27, 2018. https://www.bbc.com/persian/iran-44630393.

170 'Iran to Play Leading Role in Syria Refinery Project', *Financial Tribune*, September 26, 2017.https://financialtribune.com/articles/energy/73170/iran-to-play-leading-role-in-syria-refinery-project.

171 Azizi and Issaev, 'Russian and Iranian Economic Interests in Syria', pp. 4–5.

172 'Negotiations between Tehran and Damascus to Build Housing in Syria', IRNA, August 25, 2020. www.irna.ir/news/83921546/.

7 Iran and the Yemen Policy: Operating in the Grey Zone

1 'US Maximum Pressure Has Turned into *"Maximum Deceit"'*, *Tehran Times*, September 15, 2019.

2 Taylor Hanna, David K. Bohl, and Jonathan D. Moyer, *Assessing the Impact of War in Yemen*. United Nations Development Programme, 2021, p. 12. https://www.undp.org/sites/g/files/zskgke326/files/2022-09/Impact%20of%20War%20Report%203%20-%20QR_o.pdf.

3 C.E. Bosworth, 'Abna', *Encyclopedia Iranica*, https://iranicaonline.org/articles/abna-term.

4 Stephen W. Day, *Regionalism and Rebellion in Yemen: A Troubled National Union*. Cambridge University Press, 2012, p. 31.

5 'Zaydi Shiites; The Most Political Sect of Shiism: Ideological Foundations', Conversation with Dr Qasem Zaeri, Mehr News, July 4, 2015. mehrnews.com/xwf7v. Zaeri posits that the main distinction between Twelvers and Zaydis lies in the latter's rejection of *taqiyyah*, which permits concealing one's beliefs under the threat of death or injury.

6 For the history of modern Yemen see Paul Dresch, *A History of Modern Yemen*. Cambridge University Press, 2000.

7 Details of this Western-led alliance against the republicans are chronicled in Asher Orkaby, *Beyond the Arab Cold War: The International History of the Yemen Civil War, 1962--68*. Oxford University Press, 2017, p. 18.

8 Letter from the Shah of Iran to President Johnson, January 7, 1964. https://history.state.gov/historicaldocuments/frus1964-68v22/d2.

9 Bruce Riedel, 'John F. Kennedy's Yemen Crisis', Brookings, December 13, 2021. https://www.brookings.edu/essay/john-f-kennedys-yemen-crisis/.

10 Central Intelligence Agency, Directorate of Intelligence, 'The Shah of Iran and His Policies in the Aftermath of the Arab-Israeli War', August 18, 1967, p.3. https://www.cia.gov/readingroom/docs/CIA-RDP79T00826A002400140001-4.pdf.

11 Mohammad Jafar Chamankar, 'The Commission of Militarism of Pahlavi II and its Effect on Iranian Foreign Policies' (in Persian), *Historical Investigations* (University of Esfahan), Vol. 2, No. 4, January 2011. https://jhr.ui.ac.ir/article_16530.html.

12 Orkaby, *Beyond the Arab Cold War.*

13 Ibid., pp. 112–33

14 Sadif Esmailpour, 'The Impact of Iran's Islamic Revolution Discourse on Yemen's Houthi Movement', Part 3, Taghrib News, January 24, 2018. https://www.taghribnews.com/fa/article/306426/. Parts 3 and 4 of Esmailpour's four-part article are particularly useful.

15 The group was formerly known as the Popular Front for the Liberation of the Occupied Arabian Gulf. See Fred Halliday, *Arabia without Sultans.* Saqi Books, 2001.

16 Central Intelligence Agency, 'Staff Note, Middle East Africa South Asia', June 26, 1975. https://www.cia.gov/readingroom/docs/CIA-RDP79T00865A001200270002-9.pdf.

17 Central Intelligence Agency, 'The President's Daily Brief', March 12, 1976. https://www.cia.gov/readingroom/document/0006007695.

18 Ali Reza Zaker Esfahani, 'Iran and the Players in Dhofar', Political Studies and Research Institute, no date. http://pahlaviha.pchi.ir/show.php?page=contents&id=1669#.

19 Central Intelligence Agency, April 5, 1977. https://www.cia.gov/reading-room/docs/CIA-RDP81B00401R002500160002-9.pdf.

20 Mohsen Showqi, 'Damavand Operation', *Hamshahrionline*, November 17, 2020. https://newspaper.hamshahrionline.ir/id/115960/.

21 Mohammad Jafar Chamankhar, 'Opposition of the Anti-Shah Groups and Organizations against the War in Dhofar', Institute for Iranian Contemporary Historical Studies, Tehran, no date. http://www.iichs.ir/Modules/Content/Other/Print.aspx?id=164. Mohsen Showqi, 'Damavand Operation', *Hamshahrionline*, November 17, 2020. https://newspaper.hamshahrionline.ir/id/115960/.

22 'Yemen', in *Iran's Networks of Influence in the Middle East, Strategic Dossier*, International Institute for Strategic Studies (IISS), 2019, pp. 159–61. https://www.iiss.org/publications/strategic-dossiers/iran-dossier. This is an excellent source of information and analysis on the evolution of Iran-Houthi relations.

23 Daryoush Jalali, one of the Iranian pilots who was released during the Shah's rule, was later executed by the Islamic Republic for involvement in the Nouzeh coup. See also Mostafa Showqi, 'Damavand Operation', *Hamshahrionline*, November 17, 2020. https://newspaper.hamshahrionline.ir/id/115960/.

24 'Documents of Non-Iraqi Prisoners in the Imposed War', Rasekhoon, October 3, 2020. https://rasekhoon.net/faq/show/1544022.

25 Sadif Esmailpour, 'The Impact of Iran's Islamic Revolution Discourse on Yemen's Houthi Movement', Part 3, Taghrib News, January 24, 2018. https://www.taghribnews.com/fa/article/306426/.

26 Central Intelligence Agency, Directorate of Intelligence, 'Near East and South Asia Review: Supplement', August 15, 1986. https://www.cia.gov/readingroom/document/cia-rdp05s02029r000300820004-0.

27 Ibid.

28 Ibid.

29 Maysaa S. Al-Deen, 'Yemen's War-torn Rivalry for Religious Education', Carnegie Endowment for International Peace, June 7, 2021. https://carnegieendowment.org/2021/06/07/yemen-s-war-torn-rivalries-for-religious-education-pub-84651.

30 On the impact of tribal politics on Yemen and on the Houthis movement, see two excellent sources: Stephen Day, 'Understanding the Regional Divisions of Yemen', in Stephen Day, *Regionalism and Rebellion Yemen: A Troubled National Union*. Cambridge University Press, 2012, pp. 22–52; Marieke Brandt, 'Sufyān's "Hybrid" War: Tribal Politics during the Hūthī Conflict', *Journal of Arabian Studies*, Vol. 3, No. 1, 2013, pp. 120–38.

31 The impact of the Islamic Revolution on the Houthi movement has been thoroughly studied in Iran. See Mohsen Nasr Esphahani, 'The Effect of the Discourse of the Islamic Revolution on the Identity of Yemeni Shiites with an Emphasis on the Houthi Movement', *Scientific Journal of the Study of Islamic Awakening*, Vol. 11, No. 1, April 21, 2022, pp. 55–75. https://www.iabaj.ir/article_149604.html; Jallil Dara and Mahmood Babaei, 'Rereading Yemen's Ansarullah Movement in the Context of Iran's Islamic Republic', *Islamic Revolution Research*, Vol. 4, No. 4, January 2016, pp. 129–50. http://www.roir.ir/article_62877.html.

32 'Ansarallah Movement from Its Inception Until Now: Hossein al-Houthi's Trip to Iran', Holy Defense News, March 13, 2015. https://dnws.ir/000BEd.

33 Ibid.

34 Saddif Esmailpour, 'The Impact of Iran's Islamic Revolution's Discourse on the Yemen's Houthi Movement', Part 3, Taghrib News, January 21, 2018. https://www.taghribnews.com/fa/article/306426. See also Part 4, https://www.taghribnews.com/fa/article/306481/.

35 Mahjoob Zwieri, 'Iran and Political Dynamism in the Arab World: The Case of Yemen', *Digest of Middle East Studies*, Vol. 25, No. 1, pp. 4–18.

36 Zahra Soliemanipour, 'History of Iran–Yemen Relations (in Particular towards Houthis): Yemen's Place in Iran's Foreign Policy', OurPresident.ir. https://tinyurl.com/364xcmcw.

37 Saddif Esmailpour, 'The Impact of Iran's Islamic Revolution Discourse on Yemen's Houthi Movement', Part 3, Taghrib News, January 21, 2018 and Part 4, January 24, 2018. https://www.taghribnews.com/fa/article/306426/.

38 'President Ali Abdullah Saleh's Meeting with the Leader of the Revolution', Khamneini.ir, April 18, 2000. https://farsi.khamenei.ir/news-content?id= 11503.

39 Iran's President Khatami Visits Yemen: No Noticeable Excitement', Confidential Telegraph, May 28, 2003. https://wikileaks.org/plusd/ cables/03SANAA1190_a.html.

40 Holy Defense News, March 13, 2015. Also see Victoria Clark, *Yemen: Dancing on the Heads of Snakes*. Yale University Press, 2010, p. 249.

41 'Hizballah and the Houthis: Different Goals and Ideology', November 18, 2009. https://wikileaks.org/plusd/cables/09SANAA2079_a.html.

42 Jeremy M. Sharp, 'Yemen: Civil War and Regional Intervention', Congressional Research Service (CRS) Report, R43960, Washington, DC, September 17, 2019, p. 2.

43 'Saudi Cleric Muhammad Al-Arifi Vilifies Shiites, Calling Iraqi Ayatollah Sistani "an Infidel"', MEMRI, December 11, 2009. https://www.memri.org/ tv/saudi-cleric-muhammad-al-arifi-vilifies-shiites-calling-iraqi- ayatollah-sistani-infidel.

44 'Written Message of the President of Yemen to the Supreme Leader', Khamenei.ir, March 7, 2007. https://farsi.khamenei.ir/news-content?id=244

45 Iran, too, began a propaganda campaign against the Yemeni government and its support for what it called Wahhabisation. 'The Slaughter of Yemen's Shias (Houthis) at the Hands of the Wahabis', Tabnak, June 8, 2008. https:// www.tabnak.ir/000370.

46 'Iranian–Yemeni Relations Strained by Sa'ada War', December 13, 2009. https://wikileaks.org/plusd/cables/09SANAA2205_a.html.

47 Ibid.

48 'Yemen Accuses Iran of Backing Shiite Rebels', May 24, 2007, https://wikile- aks.org/gifiles/docs/33/330861_-os-yemen-iran-yemen-accuses-iran-of- backing-shiite-rebels-.html.

49 'Al-Houthi Rebellion: No End in Sight', July 14, 2008. https://wikileaks.org/ plusd/cables/08SANAA1165_a.html.

50 'Iran in Yemen: Tehran's Shadow Looms Large, but Footprint is Small', September 12, 2009. https://wikileaks.org/plusd/cables/09SANAA1662_a.html.

51 'Saudi Strikes in Yemen: An Invitation to Iran', November 16, 2009. Cleared by Ambassador Stephen Seche. https://wikileaks.org/plusd/cables/09SANA A2070_a.html.

52 Ibid.

53 'Growing Saudi Alarm over Threats from Yemen', October 21, 2009. https://wikileaks.org/plusd/cables/09RIYADH1396_a.html.

54 'Saudi Interior Ministry Offers Assessment of Yemen's Security', February 7, 2010. By Ambassador James B. Smith. https://wikileaks.org/plusd/cables/10RIYADH160_a.html.

55 'Saudi Military Operations against the Houthis Continue', December 7, 2009. https://wikileaks.org/plusd/cables/09RIYADH1593_a.html.

56 'Hizballah and the Houthis: Different Goals and Ideology', November 18, 2009. https://wikileaks.org/plusd/cables/09SANAA2079_a.html.

57 'Who Are the Houthis, Part Two: How Are They Fighting?', December 9, 2009, from Stephen Seche. https://wikileaks.org/plusd/cables/09SANAA2186_a.html. Until 2009 the US had no clear understanding of Houthis' relationship with Iran.

58 'Iran in Yemen: Tehran's Shadow Looms Large, but Footprint is Small', September 12, 2009. https://wikileaks.org/plusd/cables/09SANAA1662_a.html.

59 '(US) Secretary Clinton's January 22, 2010 Conversation with Yemeni Foreign Minister Abu Bakr Al-Qirbi', January 30, 2010. https://wikileaks.org/plusd/cables/10STATE9668_a.html.

60 'Iranian–Yemeni Relations Strained by Sa'ada War', December 13, 2009. https://wikileaks.org/plusd/cables/09SANAA2205_a.html.

61 Conversation with an Iranian professor teaching in Tehran who has requested anonymity. Tampa, December 8, 2016.

62 In addition to the sources cited in this chapter, I have benefited from the analysis of the following articles. Dina Esfandiary and Ariane Tabatabai, 'Yemen: An Opportunity for Iran–Saudi Dialogue?', *Washington Quarterly*, Vol. 39, No. 2, July 25, 2016, pp. 155–74; Thomas Juneau, 'How War in Yemen Transformed the Iran–Houthi Partnership', *Studies in Conflict and Terrorism*, July 30, 2021. https://t.co/hnsl5TIvf4; Thomas Juneau, 'Iran's Policy toward the Houthis in Yemen: A Limited Return on a Modest Investment', *International Affairs*, Vol. 92, No. 3, 2016, pp. 647–63; Alex Vatanka, 'Iran's Yemen Play: What Tehran Wants – and What it Doesn't', *Foreign Affairs*, 4 March 2015. http://www.foreignaffairs.com/articles/Iran/2015-03-04/irans-yemen-play; Andrew Terrill, 'Iranian Involvement in Yemen', *Orbis*, Vol. 58, No. 3, Summer 2014, pp. 429–40; and Seyyed Ali Nejat, 'Iran's Foreign Policy and the New Developments in the Middle East' (in Persian), *Journal of Politics*, Vol. 1, No. 4, Winter 2015.

63 GCC Initiative 23/11/2011. https://www.peaceagreements.org/view/1401/.

64 'Saudi Interior Ministry Offers Assessment of Yemen's Security', February 7, 2010. https://wikileaks.org/plusd/cables/10RIYADH160_a.html.

65 Maged al-Madhaji. 'How Yemen's Post-2011 Transitional Phase Ended in War', Sana'a Center for Strategic Studies, May 19, 2016. https://sanaacenter.org/publications/main-publications/39.

66 'Growing Saudi Alarm over Threats from Yemen', October 21, 2009. https://wikileaks.org/plusd/cables/09RIYADH1396_a.html.

67 Maged al-Madhaji, 'How Yemen's Post-2011 Transitional Phase Ended in War'. Sana'a Center for Strategic Studies, May 19, 2016. https://sanaacenter.org/publications/main-publications/39.

68 Resolution 2201, February 15, 2215. https://www.un.org/press/en/2015/sc11781.doc.htm#:~:text=Through%20the%20unanimous%20adoption%20of,they%20refrain%20from%20further%20unilateral.

69 Final report of the Panel of Experts on Yemen established pursuant to Security Council Resolution 2140, 2014, January 22, 2016, p. 11. https://reliefweb.int/sites/reliefweb.int/files/resources/N1600299.pdf.

70 'The Results of the 2-week Visit of the Houthi Government Delegation to Tehran: Iran is Building a Power Plant in Yemen', *Asr-e Iran*, March 14, 2015. asriran.com/001cm4.

71 Final report of the Panel of Experts on Yemen established pursuant to Security Council Resolution 2140, 2014, January 22, 2016, p. 15. https://reliefweb.int/sites/reliefweb.int/files/resources/N1500825.pdf.

72 'Yemen's President and Houthis Reach Agreement', Al Jazeera, January 22, 2015. https://www.Al Jazeera.com/news/2015/1/22/yemens-president-and-houthis-reach-agreement.

73 United Nations Security Council, 'Letter dated 27 January 2017 from the Panel of Experts on Yemen addressed to the President of the Security Council', January 31, 2017, p. 2. http://www.securitycouncilreport.org/atf/cf/%7B65BFCF9B-6D27-4E9C-8CD3-CF6E4FF96FF9%7D/s_2017_81.pdf.

74 'It is Not Forbidden to Have Relations with Iran', *Donya-e Eqtesad*, May 10, 2017. https://tinyurl.com/4aeaxmua; 'Iran Has No Presence in Yemen', *Donya-e Eqtesad*, November 28, 2017. https://donya-e-eqtesad.com/fa/tiny/news-3320540.

75 Khamenei.ir, July 18, 2015. https://farsi.khamenei.ir/speech-content?id=43276.

76 Ben Hubbard, 'Dialogue with Iran is Impossible, Saudi Arabia's Defense Minister Says', *The New York Times*, May 2, 2017. https://www.nytimes.com/2017/05/02/world/middleeast/saudi-arabia-iran-defense-minister.html.

77 Peter Salisbury, 'Yemen and the Saudi–Iranian "Cold War"', Research paper. London: Chatham House, Royal Institute of International Affairs, February 2015.

78 Ben Hubbard, (May 2, 2017).

79 Thomas Friedman, 'Saudi Arabia's Arab Spring', November 23, 2017. Interview with Mohammad bin Salman. https://www.nytimes.com/2017/11/23/opinion/saudi-prince-mbs-arab-spring.html.

80 Andrew Terrill, 'The Saudi–Iran Rivalry and the Future of the Middle East', Strategic Studies Institute, December 2011.

81 Robin Wright, 'Saudi Arabia's Game of Thrones', *The New Yorker*, June 22, 2017.   https://www.newyorker.com/news/news-desk/saudi-arabias-game-of-thrones.

82 'Letter dated 25 January 2019 from the Panel of Experts on Yemen addressed to the President of the Security Council', January 25, 2019, p. 3. https://www.securitycouncilreport.org/atf/cf/%7B65BFCF9B-6D27-4E9C-8CD3-CF6E4FF96FF9%7D/s_2019_83.pdf.

83 Letter dated 25 January 2022 from the Panel of Experts on Yemen addressed to the President of the Security Council, January 26, 2021, p. 39.

84 Ibid., p. 252.

85 Khamenei.ir. https://farsi.khamenei.ir/speech-content?id=43276 1394/04/20.

86 'Zarif's Letter to UN Secretary-General over Yemen Crisis', *ILNA*, November 11, 2017. https://www.ilna.news/Section-politics-3/561509-zarif-letter-to-un-secretary-general-over-yemen-crisis.

87 UN Resolution 2216, April 14, 2015. https://documents-dds-ny.un.org/doc/UNDOC/GEN/N15/103/72/PDF/N1510372.pdf?OpenElement.

88 Letter dated 27 January 2020 from the Panel of Experts on Yemen addressed to the President of the Security Council, April 28, 2020, p. 8.

89 Letter dated 22 January 2016 from the Panel of Experts on Yemen established pursuant to Security Council resolution 2140 (2014) addressed to the President of the Security Council, January 26, 2016, p. 3.

90 Letter dated 25 January 2019 from the Panel of Experts on Yemen addressed to the President of the Security Council, p. 3. https://documents-dds-ny.un.org/doc/UNDOC/GEN/N19/006/48/PDF/N1900648.pdf?OpenElement.

91 Letter dated 27 January 2017 from the Panel of Experts on Yemen addressed to the President of the Security Council, January 31, 2017, p. 27.

92 Yara Bayoumy and Mohammed Ghobari, 'Iranian Support Seen Crucial for Yemen's Houthis', Reuters, December 15, 2014. https://www.reuters.com/article/idUSKBN0JT17A/.

93 Letter dated 20 February 2015 from the Panel of Experts on Yemen established pursuant to Security Council resolution 2140 (2014) addressed to the President of the Security Council, February 20, 2015.

94 Matthew Levitt, 'Hezbollah's Pivot toward the Gulf', *CTC Sentinel*, Vol. 9, No. 8, August 2016. https://ctc.usma.edu/hezbollahs-pivot-toward-the-gulf/.

95 The comment was made by Mohammad Ali Jafari, IRGC Commander. Parisa Hafezi and John Irish, 'Iran Willing to Push for Ceasefire in Yemen Talks with European Powers', Reuters, May 29, 2018. https://www.reuters.com/article/us-iran-europe-yemen/iran-willing-to-push-for-ceasefire-in-yemen-talks-with-european-powers-idUSKCN1IU1FO.

96 Letter dated 26 January 2018 from the Panel of Experts on Yemen mandated by Security Council resolution 2342 (2017) addressed to the President of the Security Council, January 26, 2018, p. 30.

97 Letter dated 27 January 2017 from the Panel of Experts on Yemen addressed to the President of the Security Council, January 31, 2017. p. 26. https://www.securitycouncilreport.org/atf/cf/%7B65BFCF9B-6D27-4E9C-8CD3-CF6E4FF96FF9%7D/s_2017_81.pdf.

98 Iran's Letter to the President of the Security Council, September 29, 2016. https://documents-dds-ny.un.org/doc/UNDOC/GEN/N16/302/50/PDF/N1630250.pdf?OpenElement.

99 David D. Kirkpatrick, 'Saudi Arabia Charges Iran with "Act of War", Raising Threat of Military Clash', The New York Times, November 6, 2017. https://www.nytimes.com/2017/11/06/world/middleeast/yemen-saudi-iran-missile.html.

100 Letter dated 26 January 2018 from the Panel of Experts on Yemen mandated by Security Council resolution 2342 (2017) addressed to the President of the Security Council, January 26, 2018, p. 3. and David D. Kirkpatrick, 'Saudi Arabia Charges Iran with "Act of War", Raising Threat of Military Clash', The New York Times, November 6, 2017. https://www.nytimes.com/2017/11/06/world/middleeast/yemen-saudi-iran-missile.html.

101 Ben Hubbard and Nick Cumming-Bruce, 'Rebels in Yemen Fire Second Ballistic Missile at Saudi Capital', The New York Times, December 19, 2017. https://www.nytimes.com/2017/12/19/world/middleeast/yemen-rebels-missile-riyadh.html.

102 Ibid.

103 Jean-Loup C. Samaan, 'Missiles, Drones, and the Houthis in Yemen', Parameters, Carlisle Barracks, Vol. 50, Issue 1, Spring 2020, p. 56.

104 Azin Sahabi 'Where is the Source of Yemen's Ansarallah Missile Power?', IRNA, December 30, 1403. https://www.irna.ir/news/84617474/.

105 UN Report, 2018, p. 152.

106 Khamenei.ir, January 30, 2018. https://farsi.khamenei.ir/speech-content?id=43276 1396/11/10.

107 For a good discussion of Iran's role in training the Houthis in irregular warfare, see Seth Jones, Jared Thompson, Danielle Ngo et al., 'The Iranian and Houthi War against Saudi Arabia', Center for Strategic and

International Studies, December 2021. https://www.csis.org/analysis/iranian-and-houthi-war-against-saudi-arabia.

108 'Iran's Response to Ali Abdullah Saleh's Secret Contact with Iran', Shia News, June 19, 2016. https://www.shia-news.com/fa/news/130949.

109 'Saudi's Main Agent is Killed', *Kayhan*, December 4, 2017. https://kayhan.ir/fa/news/120275/.

110 'Saudi's Allegation Against Iran Following the Killing of Ali Abdullah Saleh', Alef, December 5, 2017. https://www.alef.ir/news/3960914018.html.

111 Ben Hubbard, Palko Karasz and Stanley Reed, 'Two Major Saudi Oil Installations Hit by Drone Strike, and US Blames Iran', *The New York Times*, September 14, 2019. https://www.nytimes.com/2019/09/14/world/middleeast/saudi-arabia-refineries-drone-attack.html.

112 Uzi Rubin, 'Saudi Arabia's Black September', Jerusalem Institute for Strategy and Security, October 15, 2019. https://jiss.org.il/en/rubin-saudi-arabias-black-september/.

113 'Saudi Arabia Oil Attacks: UN "Unable to Confirm Iranian Involvement"', BBC, December 11, 2019. https://www.bbc.com/news/world-middle-east-50742224.

114 'Missiles Used to Attack Saudi Arabia of "Iranian Origin": UN', Al Jazeera, June12,2020.https://www.aljazeera.com/news/2020/6/12/missiles-used-to-attack-saudi-arabia-of-iranian-origin-un.

115 Ben Hubbard, et al. (November 25, 2019).

116 Reuters Staff, 'Special Report: "Time to Take Out Our Swords" – Inside Iran's Plot to Attack Saudi Arabia', November 25, 2019. https://www.reuters.com/article/us-saudi-aramco-attacks-iran-exclusive-idUSKBN1YN299/.

117 'Iran Supplied Houthis with Weapons Technology, Says Senior IRGC Official', *The National*, April 23, 2021. https://www.thenationalnews.com/mena/iran-supplied-yemen-with-weapons-technology-says-senior-irgc-official-1.1209431.

118 'Houthis' Reaction to Qasemi's Comments about Iran's Presence in Yemen', *DW*, April 24, 2021. https://tinyurl.com/377fdx6c.

119 Letter dated 22 January 2021 from the Panel of Experts on Yemen addressed to the President of the Security Council, January 25, 2021, p. 12.

120 Ibid.

121 Resolution 2624 (2022) Adopted by the Security Council at its 8981st meeting, February 28, 2022. https://www.securitycouncilreport.org/atf/cf/%7B65BFCF9B-6D27-4E9C-8CD3-CF6E4FF96FF9%7D/S_RES_2624.pdf.

122 'Houthis Have Fired 430 Missiles, 851 Drones at Saudi Arabia Since 2015 – Saudi-led Coalition', Reuters, December 26, 2021. https://www.reuters.

com/world/middle-east/houthis-have-fired-430-missiles-851-drones-saudi-arabia-since-2015-saudi-led-2021-12-26/.

123 Letter dated 26 January 2018 from the Panel of Experts on Yemen mandated by Security Council Resolution 2342 (2017) addressed to the President of the Security Council, p. 2. https://reliefweb.int/sites/reliefweb.int/files/resources/N1800513.pdf.

124 Jeffrey S. Bachman, 'A "Synchronised Attack" on Life: The Saudi-led Coalition's "Hidden and Holistic" Genocide in Yemen and the Shared Responsibility of the US and UK', *Third World Quarterly*, Vol. 40, Issue 2, January 2019, pp. 298–316. https://www.tandfonline.com/doi/full/10.1080/01436597.2018.1539910?scroll=top&needAccess=true.

125 Tom Stevenson, 'Saudi's Coalition in Yemen: Militias and Mercenaries Backed by Western Firepower', *Middle East Eye*, March 28, 2019. https://www.middleeasteye.net/fr/news/hundreds-columbian-mercenaries-fight-saudi-led-coalition-yemen-964433925; Aram Roston, 'A Middle East Monarchy Hired American Ex-Soldiers to Kill Its Political Enemies: This Could Be the Future of War', *BuzzFeed News*, October 16, 2018. https://www.buzzfeednews.com/article/aramroston/mercenaries-assassination-us-yemen-uae-spear-golan-dahlan.

126 For an excellent and short analysis of the US policy towards Yemen, see Bruce Riedel, *America and the Yemens: A Complex and Tragic Encounter*, Brookings Institution Press, 2023.

127 Robert Malley and Stephen Pompa, 'Accomplice to Carnage: How America Enables War in Yemen', *Foreign Affairs*, March/April 2021. https://www.foreignaffairs.com/articles/united-states/2021-02-09/how-america-enables-war-yemen. This is a thoughtful piece about how the US became entangled in the civil war.

128 Edward Wong, 'U.S. Fails to Assess Civilian Deaths in Yemen War, Internal Report Says', *The New York Times*, June 7, 2022 https://www.nytimes.com/2022/06/07/us/politics/saudi-yemen-war-us-weapons.html.

129 Letter dated 22 January 2021 from the Panel of Experts on Yemen addressed to the President of the Security Council, January 25, 2021, p. 2.

130 See Michael W. Hanna and Peter Salisbury, 'The Shattering of Yemen: Why Ending the War Is More Difficult Than Ever', *Foreign Affairs*, April 19, 2021. https://www.foreignaffairs.com/united-states/shattering-yemen.

131 Letter dated 27 January 2020 from the Panel of Experts on Yemen addressed to the President of the Security Council, January 27, 2020, p. 17.

132 'Truce Test: The Huthis and Yemen's War of Narrative', *Crisis Group*, April 29, 2022. https://www.crisisgroup.org/middle-east-north-africa/gulf-and-arabian-peninsula/yemen/233-truce-test-huthis-and-yemens-war-narratives.

133 'Statements in the Meeting with Officials of the System', Khamenei.ir, April 12, 2022. https://farsi.khamenei.ir/speech-content?id=50037.

134 Jess Diez, 'Yemen's Government Calls for Support against Houthis', Middle East Council, November 29, 2022. https://mepc.org/commentaries/yemens-government-calls-support-against-houthis/.

135 'US Navy Seizes Massive Shipment of Ammo, Explosive Material in Gulf of Oman', *Task & Purpose*, December 3, 2022, https://taskandpurpose.com/news/us-navy-ammo-explosive-material-gulf-of-oman/.

136 Jonathan Landay and Doina Chiacu. 'Iran Still Smuggling Weapons, Narcotics to Yemen, U.S. Envoy Says', Reuters, May 11, 2023. https://www.reuters.com/world/middle-east/iran-continues-smuggle-weapons-narcotics-yemen-us-envoy-2023-05-11/.

137 Bruce Riedel, 'In Yemen, Iran Outsmarts Saudi Arabia Again', Brookings, December 6, 2017. https://www.brookings.edu/articles/in-yemen-iran-outsmarts-saudi-arabia-again/.

138 Ari Heistein and Elisha Stoin, 'Out of Sight, Out of Mind? Understanding the Houthis Threat to Israel', Institute for National Security Studies, April 27, 2021. https://www.inss.org.il/publication/the-houthi-threat-to-israel/. They wrote that: 'Despite their rhetoric, the Houthis do not appear to have taken a decision to strike Israel, and they might never decide to do so.'

139 Letter dated 25 January 2022 from the Panel of Experts on Yemen addressed to the President of the Security Council. https://www.security-councilreport.org/atf/cf/%7B65BFCF9B-6D27-4E9C-8CD3-CF6E4FF96FF9%7D/S_2022_50.pdf.

140 Kristin Smith Diwan, Hussein Ibish, Peter Salisbury, Stephen A. Seche, Omar H. Rahman, and Karen E. Young, 'The Geoeconomics of Reconstruction in Yemen', Arab Gulf States Institute in Washington, 2018. https://agsiw.org/wp-content/uploads/2018/11/Yemen_UAESF_ONLINE.pdf.

8 Iran's Evolving Relations with Hamas and the Palestine Islamic Jihad

1 Ehud Barak, 'Israel Must Decide Where It's Going – and Who Should Lead It There', *Foreign Affairs*, March 1, 2024. https://www.foreignaffairs.com/israel/israel-must-decide-where-its-going-ehud-barak.

2 All the statistics are by Julia Frankel, 'Half a Year into the War in Gaza, Here's a Look at the Conflict by the Numbers', Associated Press, April 6, 2024. https://apnews.com/article/israel-hamas-gaza-war-statistics-95a6407fac94e9d589be234708cd5005.

3 'The Islamic Republic's Support for Palestine is Compatible with the Constitution', *Hamshahrionline*, December 3, 2023. https://tinyurl.com/25a5h8nn.

4 For Gaza's historical importance, see Jean-Pierre Filiu, 'Why Gaza Matters: Since Antiquity, the Territory Has Shaped the Quest for Power in the Middle East', *Foreign Affairs*, January 1, 2024. https://www.foreignaffairs.com/middle-east/why-gaza-matters?utm_medium=social.

5 Neil MacGregor, '2600 Years of History in One Object', February 29, 2012. https://www.ted.com/talks/neil_macgregor_2600_years_of_history_in_one_object?subtitle=en. The transcript of this interesting lecture is included.

6 For the Islamic Republic's short version of Pahlavi Iran's relationship with Israel see, Hossein Molavi, 'Markaz-e Asnad-e Enqelab Islami' [The History of the Evolution of Pahlavi's Relations with the Zionist Regime], Tehran, February 9, 2016. https://tinyurl.com/y99afzkj.

7 William Shawcross, *The Shah's Last Ride: The Fate of an Ally*. Simon & Schuster, 1988, pp. 80–81. Shawcross provides no source for this claim but writes of having seen the collaborating document.

8 For an Iranian perspective, see Ali Fallahnezhad, *Monasebat-e Iran va Esra'il dar Dore-ye Pahlavi-e Dovvom* [Iran's Relations with Israel During the Second Pahlavi Period]. Tehran, 1982.

9 Directorate of Intelligence, 'Israel and Iran: The Ties that Bind', October 7, 1985. https://www.cia.gov/readingroom/docs/CIA-RDP85T01058R000506980002-7.pdf.

10 Avi Shlaim, *The Iron Wall*. W.W. Norton, 2011, p. 195, as quoted in Dalia Dassa Kaye, Ali Reza Nader and Parisa Roshan, *Israel and Iran: A Dangerous Rivalry*. Rand, 2011, p. 10.

11 Gholam Afkhami, *The Life and Times of the Shah*. University of California Press, 2009, p. 384.

12 Central Intelligence Bulletin, *Daily Brief*, January 3, 1960. https://www.cia.gov/readingroom/docs/CIA-RDP79T00975A004900010001-6.pdf.

13 Central Intelligence Bulletin, *Daily Brief*, July 25, 1960. https://www.cia.gov/readingroom/docs/CENTRAL%20INTELLIGENCE%20BULL%5B15799045%5D.pdf.

14 Hamid Enayat, *Modern Islamic Political Thought*. University of Texas Press, 1982, p. 50.

15 David Menashri, 'Israeli Relations with Iran: The Pahlavi Period', *Encyclopedia Iranica*. https://www.iranicaonline.org/articles/Israel-i-relations-with-iran#pt1.

16 Directorate of Intelligence, 'Intelligence Memorandum: The Shah of Iran and His Policies in the Aftermath of the Arab–Israeli War', August 18,

1967. https://www.cia.gov/readingroom/docs/CIA-RDP79T00826
A002400140001-4.pdf.

17 Central Intelligence Agency, 'Assessments of the Middle East Situation',
June 9, 1967. https://www.cia.gov/readingroom/docs/CIA-RDP79T00975
A004900010001-6.pdf.

18 Directorate of Intelligence, 'Israel and Iran: The Ties that Bind', October 7,
1985. https://www.cia.gov/readingroom/docs/CIA-RDP85T01058
R000506980002-7.pdf.

19 Abdolreza Hooshang Mahdavi, *Iranian Foreign Policy under the Pahlavis* (in
Persian). Alborz, 1998, p. 284.

20 Directorate of Intelligence, 'Israel and Iran: The Ties that Bind', October 7,
1985. https://www.cia.gov/readingroom/docs/CIA-RDP85T01058R
000506980002-7.pdf.

21 David Green, 'Friends to Foes: How Iran and Israel Turned into Archenemies',
Haaretz, May 8, 2018. https://www.haaretz.com/middle-east-news/
iran/2018-05-08/ty-article-magazine/how-israel-and-iran-went-from-allies-
to-enemies/0000017f-f633-d887-a7ff-fef71e7f0000.

22 See Sohrab Sobhani, *The Pragmatic Entente: Israeli–Iranian Relations, 1948–
1988*. Praeger, 1989.

23 Central Intelligence Agency, Directorate of Intelligence, 'Iran's Mediatory
Role in Middle East', May 19, 1975. CIA-RDP85T00353R00010070008-0.

24 Ibid.

25 Security Council Report. https://www.securitycouncilreport.org/un-docu-
ments/document/ip-a-res-3379.php.

26 See Mike Wallace's interview with the Shah of Iran, *60 Minutes*, CBS. For the
transcript of the controversial interview, see: 'The Shah on Israel, Corruption,
Torture', *The New York Times*, October 22, 1976. https://www.nytimes.
com/1976/10/22/archives/the-shah-on-israel-corruption-torture-and.
html.

27 The bilateral relations were so friendly that Jason Brodsky believes they should
be used as a model for the Abraham Accords. Jason Brodsky, 'Israel's Ties with
Pre-revolutionary Iran Provided a Roadmap for the Abraham Accords',
Middle East Institute, June 7, 2023. https://www.mei.edu/publications/
israels-ties-pre-revolutionary-iran-provided-road-map-abraham-accords.

28 Masoud Kuhestani 'Iran–Israel Relations during Dr Mosaddegh's Rule',
Faslname-ye Tarikh-e Rawabet-e Khareji No. 15, 1882, pp. 105–60. https://
ensani.ir/file/download/article/20101119144054-193.pdf.

29 See, for example, 'Why Did the Mosaddegh Cabinet Revoke Israel's
Recognition?', Center for Studies of Modern History, May 9, 2017. https://
iichs.ir/vdca.onyk49nme5k14.html.

30 Central Intelligence Agency, National Foreign Assessment Center, November 20, 1978. https://www.cia.gov/readingroom/docs/CIA-RDP80 T00634A000500010002-9.pdf.

31 Ruhollah Khomeini, *Islam and Revolution: Writings and Declarations of Imam Khomeini*, translated and annotated by Hamid Algar. Mizan Press, 1981, p. 50.

32 This book, authored by Akram Zuaiter, a former Jordan ambassador, was first published in 1964; *The Fate of Palestine or the Dark Record of Colonialism*, trans. by Ali Akbar Hashemi Rafsanjani was published in Qom in 1985.

33 Ali Fallahnezhad, p. 150.

34 Imam Khomeini portal. April 15, 1967. Author's translation. It was written in Najaf, Iraq. http://www.imam-khomeini.ir/fa/n22199.

35 https://farsi.rouhollah.ir/library/sahifeh-imam-khomeini/vol/2/page/199.

36 For a good discussion of the ideas of Al-e Ahmad, Shariati and others about Israel, see Seyyed Ali Alavi, *Iran and Palestine: Past, Present, Future*. Routledge, 2011. A shorter version of this insightful source on Iran's relations with Hamas and the PIJ, which I have used in this chapter, is available in his 'Iran's Relations with Palestine: Past, Present, Future', Arab Center for Research and Policy Studies, June 11, 2021. See also Jalal Al-e Ahmad, *Safar be Israeel* [Journey to Israel]. Nika, 2023.

37 'For the First Time, the Letter by the Iranian Intellectuals Is Released', Tarikhe Irani, October 29, 2023. The letter is from SAVAK's file. http://tarikhirani.ir/fa/news/8899.

38 'Ayatollah Khomeini's Letter to Yasar Arafat from Najaf, Iraq', Imam Khomeini portal, September 19, 1978. http://www.imam-khomeini.ir/fa/c207_41758/. According to the CIA, Khomeini 'repeatedly accused the Israelis of providing troops to protect the Shah's regime during the fall and winter of 1978'. Central Intelligence Agency, Intelligence Assessment, 'New Directions in Iranian Foreign Policy', March 1979. https://www.cia.gov/readingroom/docs/CIA-RDP81B00401R000500100036-0.pdf.

39 Farnoosh Ram, 'Israeli Government Files', Radio Farda, March 2, 2023. https://www.radiofarda.com/a/israeli-documents-about-pahlavi-rule-in-iran/32282876.html.

40 Latife Reda, 'Origins of the Islamic Republic's Strategic Approaches to Power and Regional Politics: The Palestinian–Israeli Conflict in Khomeini's Discourse', *Middle East Critique*, Vol. 25, No. 2, 2016, p. 182.

41 For a good discussion of the ideological and strategic reasons for the Islamic Republic's commitment to the Palestinian cause, see Amal Saad-Ghorayeb, 'An Examination of the Ideological, Political and Strategic Causes of Iran's Commitment to the Palestinian Cause', Conflicts Forum, Beirut, Lebanon,

July 2011. https://www.conflictsforum.org/wp-content/uploads/2012/03/Monograph-IranCommitmentPalestine.pdf.

42 Abbas Milani, *The Shah*. Palgrave Macmillan, 2011, pp. 326–8. Milani writes that he had personally seen the copy of the cheque and the letters exchanged between Arafat and the Shah. These documents were given to him by Ambassador Ardeshir Zahedi, Iran's former foreign minister.

43 Imam Khomeini portal. http://www.imam-khomeini.ir/fa/n25380. Author's translation.

44 Central Intelligence Agency, Intelligence Assessment, 'New Directions in Iranian Foreign Policy', March 1979. https://www.cia.gov/readingroom/docs/CIA-RDP81B00401R000500100036-0.pdf.

45 Trita Parsi, *Treacherous Alliance*, p. 84. This is an excellent source on the Iran–Israel relationship. See also Trita Parsi, 'Israel–Iranian Relations Assessed: Strategic Competition from the Power Cycle Perspective', *Iranian Studies*, Vol. 38, No. 2, 2005, pp. 247–69.

46 *Sahife-ye Nour: The Collection of Imam Khomeini's Guidance*, Vol. 8. Vezarat-e Ershad Islami, 1361/ 1983, p. 229.

47 Central Intelligence Agency, 'Palestinian Presence in Iran', August 1, 1980. https://www.cia.gov/readingroom/docs/CIA-RDP85T00287R0001 01850001-8.pdf.

48 Central Intelligence Agency, 'Secret Spoke, NONFORN/NONCONTRACT/ORCON', November 21, 1979. https://www.cia.gov/readingroom/docs/CIA-RDP81B00401R000500130031-2.pdf.

49 Central Intelligence Agency, 'Iran: New Arab Alignments', December 12, 1980. https://www.cia.gov/readingroom/docs/CIA-RDP81B00401 R000500110004-4.pdf.

50 'Revisiting Ayatollah Khamenei's Historic Warning to Arafat', Khabaronline, February 2, 2020. khabaronline.ir/xftFf.

51 Hossein Bastani, 'The Undisclosed Aspects of the Iranian Government's File on Ahmad Motevaselian', BBC Persian, July 7, 2020. https://www.bbc.com/persian/iran-features-53320271.

52 Trita Parsi, *Treacherous Alliance*, pp. 110–35.

53 See Farhad Rezaei and Ronen Cohen, 'Iran's Nuclear Program and the Israeli–Iranian Rivalry in the Post Revolutionary Era', *British Journal of Middle Eastern Studies*, Vol. 41, No. 4, p. 446. For why Ayatollah Khomeini allegedly agreed to buy weapons from Israel, see Mansour Farhang, 'The Iran–Israel Connection', *Arab Studies Quarterly*, Winter 1989, Vol. 11, No. 1, pp. 85–98.

54 Trita Parsi, *Treacherous Alliance*, pp. 110–35.

55 David Menashri, 'Iran, Israel and the Middle East Conflict', *Israel Affairs*, Vol. 12, Issue 2, 2006, pp. 107–22. Menashri argued that Iran had adopted

a pragmatic approach in its foreign policy, except in its dealings with Israel.

56 For details, see Trita Parsi, 'Israel–Iranian Relations Assessed', p. 249.

57 Razani and Cohen, p. 448, as quoted in Scott Peterson, 'Imminent Iran Nuclear Threat?', *Christian Science Monitor*, November 8, 2011.

58 For the importance of deterrence in Iran–Israel relations, see Nora Maher, 'Balancing Deterrence: Iran–Israel Relations in Turbulent Middle East', *Review of Economics and Political Science*, Vol. 8, No. 3, 2003, pp. 226–45.

59 Nader Entessar, 'Israel and Iran's National Security', *Journal of South Asian and Middle Eastern Studies*, Vol. 27, No. 4, Summer 2004.

60 Masoud Nedafat, 'The Tale of a Compromise', Khamenei.ir, September 17, 2014. https://farsi.khamenei.ir/others-report?id=27576.

61 Ibid.

62 W.A. Rivera, 'The Strategic Culture of Resistance', *Journal of Advanced Military Studies Strategic Culture*, 2022, pp. 49–68. https://www.usmcu.edu/Portals/218/JAMS_SpecialIssueStrategicCultureofResistance.pdf. Rivera is one of a few experts who have recognised the importance of the narrative of resistance in Palestinian and Iranian narratives.

63 Doron Itzchakov, 'Ayatollah Khomeini's Approach to the Palestinian–Israeli Conflict and its Longstanding Ramifications', *Israel Affairs*. The original date is not given.

64 For an Iranian perspective on the Islamic Republic's relationship with Hamas and PIJ, see Ebrahim Abassi and Zeynab Tabrizi, 'Review of Iran's Relationship with the Hamas Movement and Islamic Jihad After the Islamic Awakening', *Journal of Political and International Relations*, Vol. 6, No. 20, 2016, pp. 32–70, and Hossein Masoud Nia and Saeed Ghorbani Tazekandi, 'The Impact of the Islamic Republic on the Formation of the Islamic Jihad in Palestine', *Political Science Quarterly*, Azad University (Karaj Branch), Vol. 12, No. 37, pp. 97–119. Both articles, written in Persian, have useful background information on the PIJ that I have used in this chapter.

65 On the history and evolution of the PIJ, see Erik Skare, *A History of Palestinian Islamic Jihad: Faith, Awareness, and Revolution in the Middle East*. Cambridge University Press, 2021; and Meir Hatnia, *Islam and Salvation in Palestine: The Islamic Jihad Movement*. Syracuse University Press, 2001.

66 For an Israeli perspective, see Yossi Mansharof, 'The Relationship Between Iran and Palestinian Islamic Jihad', Jerusalem Institute for Strategy and Security, February 17, 2020.

67 'Martyr Shaqaqi's Struggle Epitomized the Islamic Revolution', *IRNA*, October 26, 2021. https://irna.ir/xjGqjJ.

68 See Fazel Sharou. 'The Practical Impact of Imam Khomeini's Thoughts and Revolution' (in Persian), Khomeini portal, February 10, 2018. http://www.imam-khomeini.ir/fa/n127377/; and Anwar Abuteh, 'The Impact of Imam Khomeini and the Islamic Revolution on the Thoughts and Actions of the Palestine Islamic Jihad' (in Persian), Khomeini portal, 2000, pp. 126–47. http://www.imam-khomeini.ir/fa/c78_127228/.

69 'What was Imam Khomeini's Ruling to Fathi Shaqaqi about How to Fight Israel?', Tasnim, May 19, 2018. https://tn.ai/1729266.

70 Robert Fisk, 'The Doctor Who Finds Death a Laughing Matter', *Independent*, January 30, 1995. Fisk does not reveal the source for his claim of Iran's financial support to the PIJ. https://www.independent.co.uk/news/world/the-doctor-who-finds-death-a-laughing-matter-1570442.html.

71 'Martyr Fathi al-Shaqaqi's Speech at the Commemoration Ceremony of Imam Khomeini's Death', Political Studies and Research Institute, June 10, 1989. https://psri.ir/?id=dos6mcta.

72 'Fathi Shaqaqi: Don't Kill Him in Damascus', *Al Jazeera*, January 17, 2018. https://www.Al Jazeera.com/program/al-jazeera-world/2018/1/17/fathi-shaqaqi-dont-kill-him-in-damascus/.

73 'Issuing the Announcement of the Office of the Supreme Leader to Commemorate the efforts of the Martyr Dr Fathi al Shaqaqi', Khamenei portal, October 31, 1995. https://www.leader.ir/fa/content/1198/.

74 Ynetnews, December 7, 2022. https://www.ynetnews.com/articles/0,7340, L-3484933,00.html.

75 Lee Gancman, 'Iran-backed Jihadi Group Claims it's Operating in West Bank, Jerusalem', January 14, 2016. https://www.timesofisrael.com/iran-backed-jihadi-group-claims-expansion-to-west-bank-jerusalem/.

76 For a brief history of Iran's relationship with Hamas, see Mathew Levitt, 'The Hamas–Iran Relationship', *Jerusalem Strategic Tribune*, November 2023. For a Palestinian perspective on Hamas, see Tareq Baconi, *Hamas Contained: A History of Palestinian Resistance*. Stanford University Press, 2022.

77 Paul Brykczynski, 'Radical Islam and the Nation: The Relationship between Religion and Nationalism in the Political Thought of Hassan al-Banna and Sayyid Qutb', *History of Intellectual Cultures*, Vol. 5, No. 1, 2005. https://journalhosting.ucalgary.ca/index.php/hic/article/view/68891.

78 *Sharh-e Esm: The Biography of Ayatollah Seyyed Ali Khamenei*, with Hedayat Behboodi. Tehran, 2013, pp. 277–88.

79 'Charter of the Islamic Resistance Movement (Hamas) of Palestine, translated by Muhammad al-Maqdisi', *Journal of Palestine Studies*, Vol. 22, No. 4, Summer, 1993, p. 122. https://www.palestine-studies.org/sites/default/files/attachments/jps-articles/2538093.pdf.

80 'Meeting with Yasin', Khamenei portal, May 2, 1998. https://www.leader.ir/fa/content/1613.

81 For a balanced analysis of the Islamisation of Palestinian politics and the beginning of the Hamas–Tehran relationship, see Meir Litvak, 'The Islamization of the Palestinian–Israeli Conflict: The Case of Hamas', *Middle Eastern Studies*, Vol. 14, No. 1, January 1998, pp. 148–63.

82 For a useful overview of Iran's relations with Hamas, see 'Iran and the Palestinians in Gaza', *The Iran Primer*, November 2, 2023. https://iranprimer. usip.org/blog/2023/nov/02/iran-and-palestinians-gaza.

83 CIA, *The World Factbook*. https://www.cia.gov/the-world-factbook/coun-tries/gaza-strip/.

84 James Bennet, 'Seized Arms Would Have Vastly Extended Arafat Arsenal', *The New York Times*, January 12, 2002. https://www.nytimes.com/2002/01/ 12/world/seized-arms-would-have-vastly-extended-arafat-arsenal.html.

85 Douglas Frantz and James Risen, 'A Nation Challenged', *The New York Times*, March 24, 2002. https://www.nytimes.com/2002/03/24/world/ nation-challenged-terrorism-secret-iran-arafat-connection-seen-fueling-mideast.html.

86 Jonathan D. Halevi, 'The Hamas Regime in the Gaza Strip: An Iranian Satellite that Threatens Regional Stability', in *Iran's Race for regional Supremacy: Strategic Implications for the Middle East*, Jerusalem Center for Public Affairs, 2008, pp. 74–81, and Jonathan Schanzer, 'Hamas as Tehran's Agent', *Middle East Quarterly*, Vol. 29, No. 3, Summer 2022. https://www. meforum.org/63270/hamas-as-tehran-agent.

87 On Hamas's independence from Tehran, see Ahmed Madani and Mohammad Muttaqien, 'The Relationship between the Islamic Republic of Iran and the Palestinian Hamas Movement and its Impact on the Palestinian Issue', *People: International Journal of Social Sciences*, Vol. 4, No. 2, pp. 56–66.

88 'Hamas Political Leaders Leave Syria for Egypt and Qatar', BBC, February 28, 2012. https://www.bbc.com/news/world-middle-east-17192278.

89 William Both, 'Iran's Post-sanctions Windfall May Not Benefit Hamas', *Washington Post*, August 31, 2011. https://www.washingtonpost.com/ world/will-irans-post-sanctions-windfall-benefit-hamas-maybe-not/2015/ 08/30/08d0c62c-481e-11e5-9f53-d1e3ddfd0cda_story.html.

90 'Haniyeh Trip Tehran Highlights Hamas Rift', *The Jerusalem Post*, February 12,2012.https://www.jpost.com/middle-east/haniyeh-trip-tehran-highlights-hamas-rift#google_vignette.

91 'The Secret about Iran's Support for Hamas during the Syrian Sedition', *Farsnews*, August 21, 2022. http://fna.ir/1q0aye.

92 *The Jerusalem Post*, (February 12, 2012).

93 'Khaled Mashal's Conversation with Al Jazeera', Mehr News, August 13, 2022. https://www.mehrnews.com/news/5561847.

94 'Restoration of Hamas's Relationship with Hamas and Iran', Tasnim, October 19, 2022. https://www.tasnimnews.com/fa/news/1401/07/27/2790795.

95 For details, see 'Repairing Hamas–Syria Relations: Step by Step from Tehran to Damascus', Tasnim, October 19, 2022. https://tn.ai/2790795.

96 For an Israeli perspective on why Hamas sought to repair its relations with Iran, see Michael Segall, 'Iran and Hamas Reconnect', Jerusalem Center for Public Affairs, September 25, 2017.

97 'Yahya Al-Sinwar; Get to Know the Mysterious Man of Hamas whom Israel Fears Dead and Alive', Jamaran News, October 12, 2023. https://www.jamaran.news/fa/tiny/news-1610826.

98 'Today, Iran is Our Biggest Supporter', ISNA, August 29, 2017. https://www.isna.ir/news/96060703879/.

99 'Hamas Leader in Gaza: Ties with Iran Now "Fantastic"; We're Preparing Battle for Palestine', The Times of Israel, August 28, 2017. https://www.timesofisrael.com/hamas-leader-in-gaza-ties-with-iran-now-fantastic-were-preparing-battle-for-palestine/.

100 'Restoration of Hamas's Relationship with Hamas and Iran', Tasnim, October 19, 2022. https://tn.ai/2790795.

101 'Hamas's New Steps to Improve Relations with Iran and Syria', Tabnak, July 20, 2022. https://www.tabnak.ir/fa/news/912808/.

102 'Video: Ismail Haniyeh Thanks Iran, Seyar-e Al Quds Thanks Iran' (in Persian), Tahavolat-e Jahan-e Islam, May 21, 2021. https://iswnews.com/46992/.

103 'The Details of the Conversation of the "Seyyed of Resistance" [Nasrallah] with Al-Mayadeen Network', IRIB News Agency, December 28, 2020. https://www.iribnews.ir/ooCS5a.

104 Nathan Sales, 'Tehran's International Targets: Assessing Iranian Terror Sponsorship', Washington Institute for Near East Policy, November 13, 2018. https://www.washingtoninstitute.org/policy-analysis/tehrans-international-targets-assessing-iranian-terror-sponsorship.

105 'Senior Hamas Official's Narrative about Meeting Commander Soleimani', Jamaran News, December 28, 2020. https://www.jamaran.news/fa/tiny/news-1489026.

106 Claire Parker and Adam Taylor, 'What Weapons do Palestinian Militants in the Gaza Strip Have and How Powerful Are They?', Washington Post, May 13, 2021. https://www.washingtonpost.com/world/2021/05/13/faq-hamas-missiles/.

107 Ibid.

108 Charlie Szrom, 'Iran–Hamas Relationship in 2008', Critical Threats, American Enterprise Institute, February 18, 2009. https://www.critical-threats.org/analysis/iran-hamas-relationship-in-2008.

109 The Palestinian Information Center (PIC), 'Martryed Zavari and Companion Built Thirty Drones Before the Furqan War (2009 Israel–Hamas war)', April 30, 2017. https://farsi.palinfo.com/news/2017/4/30/.

110 'Speech to the People of Qom', Khamanei.ir, January 8, 2020. https://farsi.khamenei.ir/speech-content?id=44628.

111 'The Meaningful Words of Commander Soleimani in a Meeting with the Delegation of the Hamas Movement in Tehran', Khabaronline, March 17, 2016. khabaronline.ir/x6rFc.

112 Ibid.

113 Ibid.

114 'Qasem Soleimani Placed No Preconditions', Mashregh News, April 2022. mshrgh.ir/813417.

115 'Jimmy Carter: Give Hamas a Chance', *CNN*, February 2, 2006. https://edition.cnn.com/2006/WORLD/meast/02/01/carter.hamas/.

116 Mark Mazzetti and Ronen Bergman, 'Buying Quiet: Inside the Israeli Plan that Propped Up Hamas', *The New York Times*, December 10, 2023. https://www.nytimes.com/2023/12/10/world/middleeast/israel-qatar-money-prop-up-hamas.html.

117 Aluf Benn, 'Israel's Self-destruction: Netanyahu, the Palestinians, and the Price of Neglect', *Foreign Affairs*, March–April 2024. https://www.foreignaffairs.com/israel/israels-netanyahu-self-destruction.

118 Ibid.

119 Ibid.

120 Ehud Barak, *Foreign Affairs*, (March 1, 2024).

121 Mark Mazzetti and Ronen Bergman, 'Buying Quiet: Inside the Israeli Plan that Propped Up Hamas', *The New York Times*, December 10, 2023. https://www.nytimes.com/2023/12/10/world/middleeast/israel-qatar-money-prop-up-hamas.html.

122 The more assistance Iran provided Hamas, the more intense the Iran–Israel shadow war became. See Jonathan Spyer, 'Israel's Secret War Against Iran is Widening', *Foreign Policy*, September 7, 2018. https://foreignpolicy.com/2018/09/07/israels-secret-war-against-iran-is-widening/.

123 Report of the United Nations Fact-finding Mission on the Gaza Conflict, 2009. https://documents-dds-ny.un.org/doc/UNDOC/GEN/G09/158/66/PDF/G0915866.pdf?OpenElement, p.20.

124 Alavi, *Iran and Palestine: Past, Present, Future.*

125 *Doulat*, February 1, 2009. https://dolat.ir/detail/174825.

126 'How Commander Soleimani Armed the Palestinians in the 22-day War: The Role of Haj Qasem in Designing Tunnels and Missile Factories', Tasnim, January 18, 2021. https://tn.ai/2435105.

127 Embassy of the Islamic Republic of Iran, Stockholm, January 3, 2021. https://stockholm.mfa.ir/portal/newsview/622978.

128 'Zarghami's Narrative of Missile Making Training in Gaza', Tabnak, November 22, 2023. The site provides the video of Zarghami's statements. https://www.tabnak.ir/0053mQ.

129 'What was the Role of Sardar Soleimani in Arming the Gaza Strip? From the Idea of Digging a Tunnel to a Missile Factory', Tasnim, October 10, 2023. https://tn.ai/2969283.

130 Ibid.

131 'The Role of Commander Soleimani in Building Tunnels in Gaza', *Hamshahrionline*, November 15, 2023. hamshahrionline.ir/x8Snp.

132 Ibid.

133 'Report of the Independent Commission of Inquiry Established Pursuant to Human Rights Council Resolution S-21/1', September 25, 2019. https://www.un.org/unispal/document/auto-insert-185919/.

134 Ibid.

135 Ruth Eglash, 'Israel Says it Stopped Iranian Arms Shipment Destined for Gaza Strip', *Washington Post*, March 5, 2014. https://www.washingtonpost.com/world/middle_east/israel-says-it-stopped-iranian-arms-shipment-destined-for-gaza-strip/2014/03/05/0614bd20-a46f-11e3-8466-d34c45176ob9_story.html.

136 'Iran, Hezbollah Coordinated Gaza Fighting in Joint War Room – Report', *The Times of Israel*, May 29, 2021. https://www.timesofisrael.com/iran-hamas-and-hezbollah-coordinated-gaza-fighting-in-joint-war-room-report/.

137 Office for the Protection and Propagation of Ayatollah Khamenei's Works, Tehran, October 22, 2023. https://farsi.khamenei.ir/others-dialog?id=54112.

138 For the comments made by various Iranian officials about the Hamas attack on Israel in October 2023, see 'Israel–Hamas War: Iran's Role and Comments', *The Iran Primer*, October 28, 2024, https://iranprimer.usip.org/blog/2023/oct/10/israel-hamas-war-iran-comments.

139 Biden's remarks after October 7. https://www.whitehouse.gov/briefing-room/speeches-remarks/2023/10/18/remarks-by-president-biden-on-the-october-7th-terrorist-attacks-and-the-resilience-of-the-state-of-israel-and-its-people-tel-aviv-israel/.

140 Summer Said, et al., 'Iran Helped Plot Attack on Israel Over Several Weeks', *Wall Street Journal*, October 8, 2023. https://www.wsj.com/world/middle-east/iran-israel-hamas-strike-planning-bbe07b25?mod=article.

141 US Department of State, 'Secretary Antony J. Blinken with David Muir of World News Tonight', October 12, 2023. https://www.state.gov/secretary-antony-j-blinken-with-david-muir-of-world-news-tonight/.

142 Benjamin Weinthal, 'Iran's Arch-terrorist was Architect of Hamas Massacre of 1,300 People: Report', *Fox News*, October 15, 2023. https://www.foxnews.com/world/irans-arch-terrorist-architect-hamas-massacre-1300-people-report.

143 *The Times of Israel*, October 28, 2023. https://www.timesofisrael.com/live-blog_entry/netanyahu-cant-say-for-certain-if-iran-was-involved-in-planning-october-7-attacks/.

144 Dan De Luce and Lis Cavazuti, 'Gaza is Plagued by Poverty, but Hamas Has no Shortage of Cash. Where Does it Come From?', *NBC News*, October 25, 2023. https://www.nbcnews.com/news/world/gaza-plagued-poverty-hamas-no-shortage-cash-come-rcna121099.

145 Jo Becker and Justin Scheck, 'Israel Found the Hamas Money Machine Years Ago. Nobody Turned it Off', *The New York Times*, December 16, 2023. https://www.nytimes.com/2023/12/16/world/europe/israel-hamas-money-finance-turkey-intelligence-attacks.html.

146 Mark Mazetti and Ronen Bergman, *The New York Times*, (December 10, 2023).

147 On the October attack and how it reshaped the Middle East landscape, see Maria Fantappie and Vali Nasr, 'The War That Remade the Middle East: How Washington Can Stabilize a Transformed Region', *Foreign Affairs*, November 20, 2023. https://www.foreignaffairs.com/middle-east/war-remade-middle-east-fantappie-nasr. On how Tehran views the crisis, see Sina Toosi, 'How Iran Really Sees the Israel–Hamas War', *Foreign Policy*, November 2, 2023. https://foreignpolicy.com/2023/11/02/how-iran-really-sees-the-israel-hamas-war/, and Devorah Margolin and Mathew Levitt, 'The Road to October 7: Hamas' Long Game, Clarified', *CTC Sentinel* (Combating Terrorism Center, West Point), Vol. 10, Issue 11, October/November 2023, https://ctc.westpoint.edu/the-road-to-october-7-hamas-long-game-clarified/.

148 'Iran: Oct. 7 Attack was Revenge for Killing of Soleimani in 2020; Hamas: No it Wasn't', *The Times of Israel*, December 25, 2023. https://www.timesofisrael.com/irans-guard-corps-hamas-oct-7-attack-was-revenge-for-killing-of-soleimani-in-2020/.

149 'What Was the Connection Between Hamas's Operation Against Israel and Commander Soleimani?', Fararu, November 8, 2023. https://fararu.com/fa/print/681060.

150 Samia Nakhool and Laila Bassam, 'Who is Mohammad Deif, the HAMAS Commander Behind the Attack on Israel', Reuters, October 11, 2023. https://www.reuters.com/world/middle-east/how-secretive-hamas-commander-masterminded-attack-israel-2023-10-10/.

151 'What Did Commander Soleimani Say about the Brain Behind Hamas's Attack?', *Etemad Online*, October 18, 2023. https://www.etemadonline.

com/tiny/news-636571. The letter is in Arabic. See *Raja News*, October 7, 2023. http://rajanews.com/node/371841.

152   Mohammad Ayatollahi Tabaar, 'Why Iran is Gambling on Hamas: Tehran's Strategy to Weaken Israel and Divide the Region', *Foreign Affairs*, November 1, 2023. https://www.foreignaffairs.com/middle-east/why-iran-gambling-hamas; Hamidreza Azizi, 'How Iran and Its Allies Hope to Save Hamas', *War on the Rocks*, November 16, 2023.

153   On the role of the Axis of Resistance during the Gaza crisis, see Narges Bajoghli and Vali Nasr, 'How the War in Gaza Revived the Axis of Resistance: Iran and Its Allies Are Fighting with Missiles and Memes', *Foreign Affairs*, January 17, 2024. https://www.foreignaffairs.com/united-states/how-war-gaza-revived-axis-resistance.

154   '"Overshadow Gaza Crimes": World Reacts to US Attacks on Iraq and Syria', *Al-Jazeera*, February 3, 2024. https://www.Al Jazeera.com/news/2024/2/3/overshadow-gaza-crimes-world-reacts-to-us-attacks-on-iraq-and-syria.

155   Farnaz Fassihi and Eric Schmitt, 'Iran and U.S. Held Secret Talks on Proxy Attacks and Cease-fire', *The New York Times*, March 15, 2024. https://www.nytimes.com/2024/03/15/world/middleeast/iran-us-secret-talks.html.

156   Emanuel Fabian, 'Iran Vows Revenge after Senior IRGC Officer Slain in Alleged Israeli Strike in Syria', *The Times of Israel*, December 25, 2023. https://www.timesofisrael.com/senior-iran-revolutionary-guards-officer-slain-in-alleged-israeli-strike-on-damascus/.

157   'Details of Seyyed Razi Mousavi's Martyrdom', Mehr News, December 25, 2023. mehrnews.com/x33P9w.

158   Herb Keinon, 'Israel's Killing of Zahedi: Taking the Fight to the Iranian Head of the Octopus – Analysis', *The Jerusalem Post*, April 3, 20024. https://www.jpost.com/opinion/article-794998.

159   Farnaz Fassihi, 'What We Know about the Iranian Commanders Killed by Israel in Syria', *The New York Times*, April 2, 2024. https://www.nytimes.com/2024/04/02/world/middleeast/iran-commanders-syria-strike-israel.html.

160   'Iran Attacks Israel with Over 300 Drones, Missiles: What You Need to Know', *Al Jazeera*, April 15, 2024. https://www.Al Jazeera.com/news/2024/4/14/iran-attacks-israel-with-over-300-drones-missiles-what-you-need-to-know.

161   Zachary Kellenborn, 'Swarm Talk: Understanding Drone Typology', Modern War Institute of West Point, October 12, 2021. https://mwi.west-point.edu/swarm-talk-understanding-drone-typology/.

162   'General Salami: The Va'deh-e Sadeq is an Outstanding Illustration of Our New Dealing with the Zionist Regime', *Al Jazeera*, April 15, 2024. Tom Spender, 'What Was in Wave of Iranian attacks and How Were They

Thwarted?' BBC, April 15, 2024. https://www.bbc.com/news/world-middle-east-68811273.

163 *Khabar-e Rooz*, April 14, 2024. https://tinyurl.com/3mpj33du.

164 Tom Spender, 'What Was in Wave of Iranian Attacks and How Were They Thwarted?', BBC News, April 15, 2024. https://www.bbc.com/news/world-middle-east-68811273.

165 'The Leader of the Revolution's Appreciation for the Performance of the Armed Forces in Recent Events', Tasnim, April 21, 2024. https://tn.ai/3072466.

166 Sean Seddon and Daniele Palumbo, 'What We Know about Israel's Missile Attack on Iran', BBC News, April 19, 2024. https://www.bbc.com/news/world-middle-east-68853402.

167 Yonah J. Bob, 'Israeli Drone Attack on Iranian Weapons Factory Was Phenomenal Success – Sources', *The Jerusalem Post*, January 29, 2023. https://www.jpost.com/middle-east/iran-news/article-729959.

168 'The Meaningful Words of Commander Soleimani in a Meeting with the Delegation of the Hamas Movement in Tehran', *Khabaronline*, March 17, 2016. khabaronline.ir/x6rFc.

169 'Exclusive Talk with Mohammad Ali Sobhani [former Director General of the Middle East of the Ministry of Foreign Affairs]', Jamaran News, January 29, 2024. https://www.jamaran.news/fa/tiny/news-1621557.

Conclusion: Iranian Regional Policies at a Perilous Crossroads

1 The ranking does not consider the possession of nuclear weapons or a country's ability to utilise proxy groups to advance its agenda, which is a critical aspect of Iran's power projection. Sinead Baker and Thibault Spirlet, 'The World's Most Powerful Militaries in 2023, Ranked', December 18, 2023. https://www.businessinsider.com/ranked-world-most-powerful-militaries-2023-firepower-us-china-russia-2023-5#17-iran-9.

2 Benoit Faucon, 'Iran's Rise as Global Arms Supplier Vexes U.S. and Its Allies', *Wall Street Journal*, February 16, 2024. https://www.wsj.com/world/irans-rise-as-global-arms-supplier-vexes-u-s-and-its-allies-6f205083.

3 William Burns, 'Spycraft and Statecraft', *Foreign Affairs*, March/April 2024. He writes: 'the key to Israeli – and the region's security – is dealing with Iran'.

4 Central Intelligence Agency, 'Briefing Papers for Visit of General Nematollah Nasiri', April 28, 1975, https://www.cia.gov/readingroom/docs/CIA-RDP85T00353R000100270011-5.pdf.

5 Colin Gray, *Irregular Enemies and the Essence of Strategy: Can the American Way of War Adapt?* US Army War College Press, March 2006, p. 39.

6 Colin Gray, *Irregular Enemies and the Essence of Strategy: Can the American Way of War Adapt?* US Army War College Press, March 2006.

7 David Singer et al., 'US and Iran Battle through Proxies, Warily Avoiding Each Other', *The New York Times*, January 14, 2024. https://www.nytimes.com/2024/01/14/world/middleeast/us-iran-mideast-war.html.

8 Scott Peterson, 'How Iran, the Mideast's New Superpower, is Expanding its Footprint Across the Region – and What it Means', *Christian Science Monitor*, December 17, 207.

9 See Scott Harr, 'Trans-rational: Iran's Transitional Strategy for Dominance and Why it Cannot Survive Great Power Competition', *Military Review*, March–April 2020, pp. 77–84, and Ofira Selikar, 'Iran's Geopolitics and Revolutionary Export: The Promises and Limits of the Proxy Empire', *Orbis* (Foreign Policy Research Institute), Winter 2021, pp. 152–71.

10 See: https://oec.world/en/profile/bilateral-country/irn/partner/irq.

11 See: https://oec.world/en/profile/bilateral-country/irn/partner/syr; https://oec.world/en/profile/bilateral-country/irn/partner/lbn; https://oec.world/en/profile/bilateral-country/yem/partner/irn.

12 The estimates for Iran's military expenditures are provided in the chapters on Iraq, Lebanon, Syria, Yemen, and Gaza.

13 In 2021, Iran's total defence budget was approximately 2.3 per cent of its GDP, compared to 11.1 per cent in 1978, the last year of the Shah's rule. https://www.macrotrends.net/global-metrics/countries/IRN/iran/military-spending-defense-budget.

14 Arash Azizi, 'What if Iran Already Has the Bomb?', *The Atlantic*, May 26, 2024. https://www.theatlantic.com/international/archive/2024/05/iran-nuclear-program-threat/678514/.

15 See the excellent work by Narges Bajoghli, Vali Nasr, and Djavad Salehi-Isfahani. *How Sanctions Work: Iran and the Impact of Economic Warfare.* Stanford University Press, 2024.

16 World Bank. https://data.worldbank.org/indicator/NY.GDP.PCAP.CD?locations=IR.

17 Ali Vaez, 'The Long Twilight of the Islamic Republic: Iran's Transformational Season of Protest', *Foreign Affairs*, February 2, 2023. https://www.foreignaffairs.com/iran/long-twilight-islamic-republic.

Index

al-Abadi, Dr Haider 86–7, 88, 97–8
Abbas, Mahmoud 223, 228
Abbasid Caliphate 8–9, 162
Abdalhadi, Ahmad 230–1
Abdelsalam, Mohammad 199
Abraham Accords (2020) 248, 328 n. 27
Abu Kamal 166–7
Abu Nidal Organization 112
Abu Omar 149
Achaemenid empire 8, 42, 103, 203, 293 n. 6
al-Adeeb, Ali 87
Afghanistan 31, 35, 38, 72, 73–4, 90, 159–60, 171, 214
Al-e Ahmad, Jalal 209
Ahmadinejad, Mahmoud 38, 151, 214
Airborne Warning and Control System, US 58
Alawi, Ayad 77, 87
Alawites 146, 156
Aleppo 162, 164–5
Algiers Accords (1975/81) 27, 44–6, 47, 70–1, 140, 207
Alimi, Rashad al 199
Amal (Hope) militia 107, 108–9, 111–12, 115–16, 121–2, 124, 127, 132, 145

Ames, Robert 118
Amini, Mahsa 252
Amiri, Hadi al 87, 91
Anglo-Russian Convention (1907) 9
Ansar-e Islam 77
Ansarallah, *see* Houthis
anti-Americanism 7–71
anti-Shah militant Islamists 108–10
Arab League 150
Arab Spring 145–50, 154, 184, 185–6, 192, 222–3
Arabian Peninsula 3, 42, 175, 176–7
Arafat, Yasser 209, 210–15, 217, 220, 221, 330 n. 42
Araqchi, Abbas 161
Argov, Shlomo 112
al-Arifi, Mohammad 182
Armacost, Michael 62
Armitage, Richard 103
Arvand Rood (Shatt al-Arab) 44, 45, 48, 51, 61, 69
Asa'ib Ahl al-Haq 93, 159
al-Askari Shrine, Samarra 83
Aslah party 199
Assad, Bashar 138–9, 145–6, 150–3, 154–7, 164–5

agrees to prisoner swap 308 n. 69
concessions to Russia 172
fall of 163
Hamas and 222, 225
Kadhimi and 98
Khamenei and 146–50, 158–9, 171
opposition to 34, 160–2
Quds Force and 244
retains power 170
Saudi Arabia and 190
Syrian army and 154
US and 247
withdraws troops from Lebanon 127
al-Assad, Col Riad 151, 153
Assad, Hafez 37, 59, 114, 115, 121, 139–42,
 144, 145, 217
Assad, Rifaat 113, 141
Assadi, Mohammad Jafar 162
Assembly of Experts for Leadership 37,
 123
Astana peace process (2017) 165
Austria 50
Avaei, Seyyed Ahmad 141
Avicenna 8
Awda, Abd al Aziz 216
Axis of Resistance 5, 33, 92, 136, 154, 200,
 225, 234–5, 238, 241, 244–5
Ayn al-Assad airbase 96
Azerbaijan 12, 248
Azhari, Gen Gholamreza 21

Ba'ath party 49, 76, 139
Bab al-Mandab Strait 175, 198, 201, 245
Badr al-Din al-Houthi 180
Badr Brigade, see Badr Organisation
Badr, Mohammad al 175–6
Badr Organisation 53, 86, 90, 91, 180
Baghdad 42, 46–7, 96
Baghdad International Airport 1, 96, 98
Baghdad Pact (1955) 45
al-Baghdadi, Abu Bakr 88–9, 162
Bahrain 32, 147, 185, 248
Bakhtiyar, Shapour 24, 49
Bakhtiyar, Gen Teymur 45, 106, 293 n. 18
al-Bakr, Ahmed Hassan 49
Balfour Declaration (1917) 204
Ban Ki-Moon 151, 160, 161
Bani Sadr, Abol Hassan 52
al-Banna, Hassan 216
Barak, Ehud 112–13, 126, 202, 229
Barzani, Masoud 92–4

Barzani, Mustafa 46, 47, 207, 276 n. 27
Baseej organisation 51–2
Baskerville, Howard 12
Basra 54–5, 63, 86–7
Bazargan, Mehdi 25–6, 29, 34, 108, 109
Beckwith, Col Charles 27
Begin, Menachem 58
Beheshti, Mohammad 110
Beirut barracks bombings (1983) 118–19
Beirut car bombing (2013) 156
Beirut port blast (2020) 135
Beit Lid massacre (1995) 218
Ben Ali, Zine El Abidine 147
Ben-Gurion, David 205
Berri, Nabih 116, 122, 132
Biden, Joe 198, 232, 233
black markets 59, 184, 191
Blair, Tony 100
'Bloody November' (2019) 252
Bolton, John 168
Bonyadi, Behrooz 172
Bostan-e Iran (Iran's Garden) 103
Bouazizi, Mohammad 147
Bremmer, Paul 76
Britain 12–13
 Balfour Declaration 204
 establish Iraq 10, 43, 72
 Iran and 14
 Persian Gulf withdrawal 18
 revolutionary wars 50
 Saudi Arabia and 198
 support for Iraq 42, 43, 44
 support for Israel 236
 withdrawal from Persian Gulf 45
 Yemen and 175, 176, 190
British Empire 10–11, 12
Brodsky, Jason 328 n. 27
Brown, Gen George S. 19
Brzezinski, Zbigniew 26
Buckley, William 59
Buenos Aires 125
Burns, William 241
Bush, George H.W. 70
Bush, George W. 34, 39, 74, 76, 85, 100,
 221

Caesar Syria Civilian Protection Act (2019)
 172
Camp Ashraf, Diyala 84
Camp David Accords (1978) 210
Carter Doctrine (1980) 31

Carter, Jimmy 2, 20, 26–7, 31, 58, 228
ceasefires 66, 197–200, 283 n. 115
Chalabi, Ahmad 77
Chamoun, Camille 105
Chamran, Mustafa 109, 111, 140
Chechnya 163
chemical weapons 54–5, 57, 61, 64–5, 67,
 156–7
China 34, 172, 177, 249
Christians 104, 106, 117, 146
Churchill, Winston 10, 13, 275 n. 7
CIA 45–50, 61–2, 120–1
 on Amal 111
 Ames murder 118
 Buckley held captive 59
 on Hamas 221
 on Iraq 51
 Israel and 207
 on Mohammad Reza 176
 North Yemen 179
 operations 152
 Reagan and 120
 reports 19, 21, 206, 211, 241
Clapper, James 157
Clinton, Bill 37
Clinton, Hillary 164, 184
Coalition Provisional Authority 76
Cold War 7, 13, 15, 25, 60, 163, 213
Conoco 37, 168
Constantinople Protocol (1913) 44
constitution, Iranian (1979) 27, 30, 31
Cooper, Scott 110
Council of the Islamic Revolution 28
Crocker, Ryan 86, 244
cross-border raid (2006) 102
Curzon, Lord George 10
Cyrus the Great 203–4

Dabbagh, Nezam Omar 93
Daesh, see ISIS
Daoud, Qassim 289 n. 71
D'Arcy, William Knox 10
al Dawa party 49, 52–3, 80
de Mistura, Staffan 171
deep state 28–30, 37, 38, 39, 111, 148
Dehghan, Hossein 116, 298 n. 77
Deif, Mohammed 224, 234
Deir ez-Zor 166, 168
demonstrations 20, 135, 147, 151, 252
deterrence mechanism 238–9
Dhofar 19, 177–8, 242

Directorate of Intelligence 122
Documents from the U.S. Espionage Den 27
Dodge, David 115
Dome air defence system 231
drones, US 95–6, 98
Duelfer, Charles 79

economic growth 19
Egypt:
 1952 coup 104–5
 Arab Spring 222
 Iran and 107, 109
 Israel and 213, 228
 Mubarak 147
 Muslim Brotherhood 222, 224
 Saudi Arabia and 197
 Six-Day War 41, 206
 Suez Canal 13
 Syria and 139, 142
 uprising 185
 Yemen and 176
Eisenhower, Gen Dwight 13, 105
embargoes 27, 34, 49, 56, 58, 68, 206
Erbil 86, 92, 93, 96

factional rivalry, and regional policies
 35–40
Fadlallah, Mohammad Hossein 120
Faisal I 43, 275 n. 7
Faisal II 44
Al-Fajr VIII operation (1986) 61
Falahatpisheh, Heshmatollah 165, 171
Fallujah 88, 91
famine 9–10
Fatemiyoun group 159–60
fatwas 43, 90–2
Faw Peninsula 61–4
First World War 9, 42, 175
Fisk Robert 217
Foley, James 89
Ford, Robert 157, 167
Foreign Military Sales (FMS) 18
foreign policy 28–30, 36–8, 250–3, 270
 n. 22
foundations, aid 115, 191
France:
 Bani Sadr and 52
 Lebanon and 104, 117, 126, 134
 NATO member 57
 Nusayrids and 146
 revolutionary wars 31, 50

supplies weapons to Iraq 55
support for Israel 236
Frangieh, Suleiman 107
Free Syrian Army (FSA) 153
French Revolution (1789–99) 50

Gaddafi, Hannibal 110
Gaddafi, Muammar 108, 110, 147, 163
Gaza Strip 202–3, 215–17
  financial aid from Qatar 233
  Hamas in 223, 224, 225–32, 233–4
  Iran and 31, 214, 246
  Israel in 241, 247
  militants in 149, 215, 222, 243
  Muslim Brotherhood 219
  PA in 213
  population 221
  Soleimani and 90
GDP (gross domestic product) 135, 252,
  340 n. 13
Gemayel, Amine 117
Geneva conferences (2012/14) 150–1,
  160–1
Genghis Khan 8
geostrategic rivalry (with US/Israel)
  116–17, 166–7
Germany 11
Ghaani, Gen Ismail 97
Ghalioun, Burhan 148, 149
Ghouta chemical attack (2013) 156–7
Golan Heights 140, 169
Goldberg, Jeffrey 126
Goldsmith, Leon 146
Gray, Colin 243
Green Movement (2009) 38–9, 152, 227,
  251
Grey Zone 173–201
Grunberg, Hans 199
Gulf Cooperation Council (GCC) Initiative
  186–7, 188
Gulf War, First (1990–1) 37, 69–71, 213,
  243
Gulf War, Second (2003–11) 75–87,
  99–100
Guterres, António 196

Hadi, Abd Rabbuh Mansur 186–7, 188–9,
  191, 197, 199
Hadidchi-Dabbagh, Marziyeh 141
Haiat, Lior 233
Haifa 130

Hajizadeh, Amir Ali 96
Hakim, Mohammad Baqer 74
Halabja 64
Haley, Nikki R. 194
Halutz, Gen Dan 102, 129
Hamad, Ghazi 223
Hamadani, Gen Hossein 138, 153–5
Hamas 33, 128, 149, 202–48, 335 n. 122
Hamas-led attack (7 October 2023) 202,
  229, 232–5
Hamdan, Osama 230
Hammadi, Sa'dun 48
Hanit, INS (2006 attack) 130
Haniyeh, Ismail 223, 224, 225, 228
Harakat al-Mahrumin 107
Hariri, Rafic 126–7
Hashd al-Sha'bi 90, 93, 94, 98, 99
Hashemi, Mehdi 61
Hazam, Colonel 87
Heidari, Reza 191
Hersh, Seymour 130
Hezbollah:
  Gaza War 230
  Houthis and 193
  Iran's key strategic asset 102–37, 149,
    155, 190, 243, 247
  IRGC and 156
  Khomeini and 111–13
  leaders 75
  in Lebanon 32, 36, 52, 101, 243, 244
  low-intensity warfare against Israel 168
  PIJ and 217
  post Hamas-led attack 234, 235
  Rafsanjani and 59–60
  Saudi Arabia and 194
  Soleimani and 231
  Syria and 145
  Yemen and 187
Hezbollah–Israel War (2006) 126–32
Higgins, Lt. Col William 122
Hijab, Riyad 170
Hill, Chris 79–80, 82
Hodeidah 181, 188
Hormuz, Strait of 55, 62, 95, 201, 245
Hosseini, Kochek 115
House Joint Resolution 216 62
al-Houthi, Abdul Malik 181
al-Houthi, Hossein Badr al-Din 179–81
Houthis 37, 173–4, 178–201, 219, 235, 243,
  247, 326 n. 138
Hoveyda, Amir Abbas 104, 209

Hulagu Khan 9
human rights violations 3, 19–20, 79, 198, 201
Huntington, Samuel 3
Hussein, Saddam:
  al Dawa and 52–3
  Algiers Accords and 47
  ambitions 67
  Barzani and 46
  CIA report on war aid 284 n. 129
  human rights abuses 79
  invades Kuwait 69–71
  Iran and 41, 244, 274 n. 1
  Khalid and 278 n. 53
  Khomeini and 54
  MEK and 83–4
  miscalculating Iran invasion 48–51
  Mohammad Reza Shah and 277 n. 39
  overthrowing 74, 75
  pariah 73
  Pollack on 278 n. 55
  Rumsfeld visits 57
  Saleh and 188
  Sana'a and 179
  Shia crackdown 81
  Soviet Union and 46, 50
  statue toppled 72
  Syria and 143

Ibn Taymiyya 146
Imam Khomeini Relief Committee 115
Imperial Armed Forces 49, 50, 68, 76
India 9, 19, 35
Indian Ocean 19, 201
insecurity, fear of 34–5, 146
inter-Shia War 86–7
intifada (uprising) 77, 213, 217, 219, 234
Iran Air Flight 655 incident (1988) 65
'Iran–Contra' affair (1985–7) 59–60
Iran hostage crisis (1980) 50, 51, 56, 58
Iran–Iraq War (1980–88) 31–2, 41–71, 111–13, 211–12
  cost of 247
  covert network 33, 75
  neutrality during 218
  Syria during 143–4
  weapons 245
  Yemen during 179
Iran Study Group 85–6
Iranian coup d'état (1953) 11–15

Iraq:
  attacks by 235
  'axis of evil' with Iran and North Korea 74
  Barzani and 207
  established 10, 43, 72
  fatwas 90–2
  foreign debts 69
  Governing Council 77
  insurgency and state formation in 76–7, 79
  Iran and 17, 19, 214, 243, 244
  Iran–Iraq War 31–2, 33, 35, 36, 41–71
  Iran's exports to 100, 246
  Iran's strategic goals/threat perception 73–6
  Iran's success/failure in 99–101
  Israel and 213
  Kurds and 242
  miscalculating Iran invasion 48–51
  'no peace, no war' state with Iran 69
  ongoing civil war 39
  Palestinian militants and 208
  pre-revolutionary Iran's uneasy relations with 42–4
  US and 145, 247
  US invasion of (2003) 38, 72, 75, 214, 243
  Yemen and 177
Iraq War veterans, US 100
Iraqi insurgency (2003–11) 75–87, 99–100
Iraqi military coup (1958) 44–5
Iraqi National Congress 80
Iraqi National Intelligence Services 77
ISIS (Islamic State of Iraq and Syria) 87–95, 149–50, 161–2
  defeat 98
  members 155, 163
  threat posed by 164–5, 166–8, 244
  weakened 170, 249
Islamic Revolution (1979) 14, 23, 29, 31–2, 243
Islamic Revolutionary Guard Corps (IRGC) 1–2, 32–3, 52–4, 192–3
  Aerospace Force 96
  American embassy in Tehran 23
  building 29, 77, 243
  comes of age 66–9
  commanders 38, 141–2, 153, 154, 196, 235, 237, 298 n. 77

goes to Syria and Lebanon 113–16, 144
Hamas and 232–3
Hezbollah and 32, 156
in Iraq 91–2
ISIS and 166
Israeli air strike against 169
al-Mahdi visited by 97
PLO and 211
protest deaths 38
Rafsanjani and 37
secrecy 30
Sinwar and 224
speedboat fleet 63
trains al Dawa party 52
Yemen and 187
Islamic Supreme Council of Iraq (ISCI) 80
Islamisation of Palestinian politics 212–21
Ismail I 103
Israel 107–8
    anti-Israel discourse in the clerical
        establishment 207–9
    Gaza and 233
    geostrategic rivalry with 116–17, 166–9
    Hamas and 202–48, 225, 226
    Hamas-led attack (7 October 2023) 202,
        229, 232–5
    Hezbollah–Israel War 126–32
    Hezbollah operations against 102–3, 115
    invades Lebanon 112–13
    in Iraqi Kurdistan 94
    Iraqi Kurds and 46
    IRGC and 144
    Lebanese prisoners 59
    Lebanon and 110, 114, 117, 119
    nuclear arms 35
    possibility of regional war 235–8
    Six-Day War 41
    strategies against Iran 248
    Syria and 148, 152, 168–9
    undermining 111
    wars with Hamas 229–30
Israel Defense Forces (IDF) 102, 131, 133,
    218, 227–8
Izz al-Din Qassam Brigades 202, 219, 221,
    223, 224–5, 227, 234
Qassam Brigades 223, 227, 234

al-Jaafari, Ibrahim 80–1
Jabal Amil 104
Jadid, Salah 139
Jafari, Gen Mohammad Ali 153, 323 n. 95

Jalali, Daryoush 317 n. 23
Jamal, Shuja 160
Jannati, Ahmad 123
Jannati, Ali 141
Jaysh al-Islam 164
Jaysh al-Mahdi (Mahdi Army) 78, 86, 87
Jews 58, 146, 203–4, 207, 217
Jihad 89, 118, 149, 150, 155, 159, 202–53,
    234
Johnson, David 119, 131
Johnson, Lyndon 45, 176
Joint Comprehensive Plan of Action
    (JPCOA) 39, 95
Jordan 41, 152, 176, 213, 235, 236
June Uprising (1963) 16

Kadhimi, Mustafa al 97–9
Karami, Omar 127
Karbala 97
Karine A ship 74
Karroubi, Mehdi 38
Karzai, Hamid 74
Kashani, Abolghasem 208
Kata'ib Hezbollah 90, 91, 93, 96, 159
Kennedy, John F. 15, 88
Kerry, John 158, 164
Khaddam, Abdul Halim 140, 143
Khalid, King 278 n. 53
Al Khalifa dynasty 147
Khamenei, Ali 29–30, 211–12, 214–15
    on 2019 demonstrations 135
    Assad and 138, 158
    assassination of Shaqaqi 218
    authorised collaboration with the US 73
    becomes Supreme Leader 37
    Berri and 132
    on chemical weapons 158
    demonstrations against 252
    depictions of 103
    foreign policy 241
    Gaza War 230
    on Hadi 188
    Hamadani and 154
    Hamas and 203, 219–21, 232
    Haniyeh visits 223, 224, 225
    Hezbollah and 121–3, 127–8, 136
    Iran's rise 243–4
    ISIS and 89
    Israel and 214
    issue of succession 251
    Lebanon and 123–6

al-Maliki and 78–9, 85, 88
meets al-Sudani 99
post Hamas-led attack 236, 237
power and deterrence 32, 35
Rafsanjani and 39
regional policies 39
on Sadat 215
Sadr visits 99
Saleh and 181, 182, 195
Salman on 190
Saudi Arabia and 191, 199
Sharif Imami on 270 n. 22
on Soleimani 226
Soleimani and 1–2, 96, 130–1, 167
supports Assad 146–50
Supreme Defence Council 54
threat to enemies 166
UN and 195
US sanctions 95
Kharazi, Kamal 248
Khark Island 55
Khashoggi, Jamal 198
Khatami, Mohammad 37–8, 39, 73, 181
Khaz'al bin al-Ka'bi 44
Khoeiniha, Mohammad Mousavi 26
Khomeini, Ruhollah Mousavi:
    accepts ceasefire 66, 283 n. 115
    anti-Israel politics 208–9
    and anti-Shah Islamists 140–1
    Arafat and 209
    armed neighbourhood committees 154–5
    arrest and exile 16
    becomes Supreme Leader 25
    death 36
    deep state and 28–30
    depictions of 103
    fear of insecurity 34–5
    fights for democratic rights 20
    foreign policy 241
    H. Assad and 140, 142
    on Hezbollah 122
    Hussein and 49
    Imperial Armed Forces and 76–7
    on Iraq 55
    IRGC and 114
    Jews and 58
    on Lebanon 118
    MEK and 83
    national stage debut 15–17
    pan-Shiism and Hezbollah 111–13,
        135–6

PLO and 210–12
    political alliance with Syria 139–40, 142–3
    power and deterrence 32
    presiding over revolution 21–2
    radical foreign policy and 36
    Saddam 'US proxy' 56
    Sadr and 110
    Shaqaqi and 216, 217, 218
    and Shia organisations 112–13
    shrine attacked 94, 166
    takes war into Iraqi territory 53–4
    Tehran Hostage Crisis 24–5, 26, 27
    trust of IRGC 68
    US weapons 58–60
    war initiatives 51–2
    writes to clerics in Iran 20
    Yemen and 180
    Kashf al-Asrar 15
Khomeini, Ahmad 26
Khorramshahr 51, 53, 113
Khouri, Rami 136
Khuzestan 43–4, 45, 105, 139, 149, 278 n. 55
Khwarizmi 8
Kirkuk 94, 96
Kissinger, Henry 3
Kober, Avi 131
Kosari, Mohammad 234
Kuperwasser, Yossi 229
Kurdish Regional Government (KRG)
        92–4, 98, 248
Kurdistan 12, 47, 64, 154
Kurdistan Democratic Party 46
Kurds, Iraqi 46–8, 64–5, 73, 92–4, 99, 148,
        242
Kurds, Syrian 148, 165, 168, 170, 247
Kuwait 32, 35, 55, 62–3, 69–71, 145
Kuwait embassy bombings (1983) 53

Laingen, Bruce 28
Landis, Joshua 167
Larijani, Ali 183
Latakia 152, 156, 163–4, 172
League of Nations 43
Lebanese National Movement 117
Lebanon:
    and anti-Shah Islamists 140–1
    Bakhtiyar and 293 n. 18
    Buckley held captive in 59
    Hezbollah established in 32, 36, 52, 91,
        101
    intelligence service 120

Iran and 31, 37, 214
Iran's power play in 102–37
militias and Shia activists 68
Multinational Force in 297 n. 67
Palestinian militants and 208
pan-Arabism in 18
Soleimani and 90
Syria withdraws troops 145
TWA Flight 847 hijack 59
US and 247
War of Liberation 123
Leffler, Melvyn 34
Leftists guerillas 24
Lesch, David 170
Levant, the 3, 42, 52, 103, 104, 116, 143,
    150, 151, 163, 169, 226, 227
Levitt, Mathew 137
Liberation Movement of Iran 25, 108, 109
Libya 147, 185
Lubrani, Uri 47, 108, 209

McFarlane, Robert 58–60
Machiavelli, Niccolò 4
McKenzie, Gen Kenneth F. 2, 96
Mclean, Neil 176
Madrid Conference (1991) 145, 218
al-Mahdi, Adel Abdul 95, 97, 98
Mahdi Army, see Jaysh al-Mahdi
al Majid, Ali Hassan 65
Majles 16, 37, 38, 44, 52, 166, 230
Majnoon Islands 54
al-Maliki, Nouri 78–9, 81–2, 84–8, 90
Malta 218
Mansur, Hassan Ali 16, 17
Maraghei, Mohammad Sa'ed 204–5
Maronites 104, 106, 115, 134, 299 n. 93
martyrdom 33, 96, 119, 123, 137, 181, 230,
    234
Mashal, Khaled 223, 224, 227
Masjedi, Iraj 91
Mattis, Gen Jim 153, 168
May 17 Agreement (1983) 117
Mediterranean Sea 148, 152
Menashri, David 206
Mesbahi, Mohiaddin 33
Mesopotamia 42
Milani, Abbas 330 n. 42
Mill, John Stuart 6
Millspaugh, Arthur 12
Moghaddam, Hassan Tehrani 144
Mohammad Reza Shah 12–13, 17–22,
    205–10, 250–1

air force legacy 51
Algiers Accords 44–6, 47, 48
Arafat and 330 n. 42
Bakhtiyar and 293 n. 18
cancer treatment in US 26
Egypt and 105
exile and death 21
faces criticism for purchase of US
    weapons 19
foreign and security decisions 30
foreign policy 30, 241–2
Hussein and 277 n. 39
Iraqi Kurds and 46–8
Lebanese civil war 107–8
Lebanon and 104
Maraghei and 205
meets Carter 2
on Nasser 105
oil exports 250
overthrown 47
Sadr meets 107
and Shia empowerment 103–5
Syria and 139–40
and the two Yemens 174–8
uneasy alliance with Israel 203–7
US and 7
Mohandes (Jamal Jaffar Mohammad
    Abumahdi) 90–1
Mohtashamipour, Ali Akbar 112
Mojahedin-e Khalq (MEK) 66, 83, 84, 144
Montazeri, Hossein-Ali 61
Montazeri, Mohammad 112
Morsi, Mohammad 222–3, 224
Mosaddegh, Mohammad 13–14, 208
Mossad 46–8, 205, 207, 218
Mosul 88, 89, 91, 162, 166
Motevaselian, Ahmad 113, 115, 296 n. 58
Mottaki, Manuchehr 184
Mousavi, Mir Hossein 29, 38
Mousavi, Gen Razi 235
Mousavi, Seyyed Abbas 112, 123, 125
Mubarak, Hosni 147, 222
Mughniyeh, Imad 102, 128, 231
Muslim Brotherhood 113–14, 148, 149,
    216, 219–20, 222, 224
Muslim militias 117
Mutawakkilite Kingdom 175

Nader Shah 9, 177
Naguib, Mohammad 104
Najaf 16, 79, 97
Najaf Hawza 42–3, 106

al-Nakhaleh, Ziyad 231
Nasrallah, Hassan:
  cautions Americans 75
  Dehghan and 116
  false rumours about 130
  Khamenei and 123, 132
  Khomeini and 112
  Lebanon and 125
  'secret war room' 102
  Soleimani and 128–9, 154, 225
  on Syria 149
Nasser, Gamal Abdel 18, 44, 104–5, 107,
  109, 139, 176, 205–6, 220
National Intelligence Council 118
national interest, Iran's 248–50
National Security Decision Directive
  (NSDD 139) 56
NATO 39, 57, 147, 241
Netanyahu, Benjamin 228–9, 232, 233
Nixon, Richard 14, 18, 47, 177
Nojeh air base, Hamadan 165
Nojeh coup plot (1980) 49
Non-Aggression Treaty (1962) 17
Non-Aligned Movement 25, 211
North Africa 164
North Korea 74
North, Lt Col Oliver 60
North Yemen, see Yemen
Northern Alliance 73–4
Norton, Richard 137
nuclear power 34, 35, 39, 169, 339 n. 1
Nusayr al Bakri al Numayri, Muhammad
  Ibn 146
Nusayrids 146
al-Nusra Front 155, 156, 157, 161, 165

Obama, Barack 87, 88, 148, 157–8, 167,
  197–8
oil industry 15, 18, 67
  exports 54, 250
  facilities 10, 13–14, 166, 168, 173,
    195–7
  'tankers' war' 55–6, 61, 62–3, 206
Olmert, Ehud 129, 132–3
Oman 19, 32, 35, 177–8, 197
Organization of Petroleum Exporting
  Countries (OPEC) 18, 250
Oslo Accords (1993/5) 213, 214, 215, 218,
  221, 228
Ottoman empire 9, 42, 44, 104, 175, 275
  n. 7
Oveissi, Gen Gholam Ali 50

Pahlavi dynasty 10, 44, 141
Pakistan 19, 35, 171, 197, 250
Palestine 117, 145, 149, 202–53
Palestine Liberation Organization (PLO)
  203, 209–13, 216, 221, 223–4, 228
  Lebanon and 107, 112, 116, 133
Palestinian Authority (PA) 74, 213, 221,
  223, 228
Palestinian Islamic Jihad (PIJ) 33, 203,
  214–19, 221, 222, 227, 228–31, 245,
  247
Palestinians, Lebanese 107, 110, 114, 121–2
Palmyra 162, 164
pan-Arabism 17, 18, 44, 104–5, 105, 107,
  206, 242
pan-Islamic principles 36, 111
pan-Shia principles 36, 111–13, 136
Parthian empire 8, 42
Pashaei, Mujtaba 46, 105–6
peacekeepers, UN 109
Pejman, Isa 47
Peres, Shimon 213
Persian empire 42, 44, 174, 203–4
Persian Gulf 3, 9, 17–19, 31–2, 35, 37,
  42–3, 45, 46, 50, 145, 172
  'tankers' war' 55–6, 61, 62–3
Peshmerga, Kurdish (militias) 47, 93, 94
Phalange 117
Pollack, Kenneth 278 n. 55
Pompeo, Mike 39, 96, 173, 195
Popular Committees 155, 187
Popular Front for the Liberation of Oman
  177
Popular Mobilisation Units (PMU) 90–2,
  96, 98
  see also Hashd al-Sha'bi
Power, Samantha 165
Provisional Revolutionary Government 25,
  109, 111
Prussia 50
Putin, Vladimir 162–3, 164

Qaboos bin Said 177
Qadar, Gen Mansur 106, 108, 205
al-Qaeda 73, 77, 82–3, 88, 89, 155, 182,
  188
Qajar dynasty 9, 10, 44, 104
Qaradawi, Yusuf al 149
Qasem, Brig Abdul al-Karim 44, 196
Qasr-e Shirin, Treaty of (1639) 42
Qassam Brigades, see Izz al-Din al-Qassam
  Brigades

Qatar 32, 35, 152–3
  financial aid to proxies 161, 164, 233
  Hamas and 149, 222, 223, 228
Qavam, Ahmad 12
al-Qirbi, Abu Bakr 184
Qom 106, 179, 208
Quds Force 74, 97, 127, 128, 227, 235, 244
al Qusayr 156, 157
Qutb, Sayyid Ibrahim Husayn 220

Rabin, Yitzhak 213
Rafiqdoust, Mohsen 143–4
Rafsanjani, Ali Akbar Hashemi 37–9, 54,
  59–60, 65, 66, 70–1, 121, 158–9
Rafsanjani, Hashemi 208
Raisi, Ebrahim 99, 203
Rapid Deployment Force, 31
Raqqa 155, 162, 166
Razoux, Pierre 60, 278 n. 53
Reagan, Ronald 27, 56, 57, 58–60, 61,
  63–4, 118, 120
Red Army 12
Red Sea 74, 183, 200, 234
regional network, building a 51–3
regional policies 240–53
  factional rivalry and 35–40
  national interest and 248–50
  revolutionary 23–40
Revolutionary Courts 29
revolutionary wars (1792–1802) 50
Reza Shah 10–12, 15–16, 30, 43–4, 48
Rezaei, Mohsen 54, 62, 64, 67
Rice, Condoleezza 131
Riedel, Bruce 50
rise, Iran's 242–8
  sustainability/effective deterrence 245–8
Riyadh Agreement (2019) 199
Rouhani, Hassan 39, 64, 225
al-Rubai, Mowaffak 81
Rumsfeld, Donald 57
Russia 9–10, 31, 34, 160–6, 168–9
  cannot be trusted 60
  investment opportunities 172
  Iran and 13
  Iran's 'pivot' towards 13, 34, 249
  -made weaponry 59, 143, 230
  menace of communism 43
  Obama and 157
  PLO and 221
  presence in Syria 170
  revolutions 31

Sadat, Anwar 48, 107, 110, 215
Sadr, Imam Musa 103, 105–10, 135, 140,
  141, 146
al-Sadr, Mohammad Baqer 49
Sadr, Muqtada 78–80, 86–7, 98–9
Sadr Special Groups 78–9
Safavi, Gen Rahim 141–2, 171
Safavid empire 9, 42, 103–4, 149
Salami, Gen Hossein 96, 196, 237
Saleh, Ali Abdullah 147, 178–83, 185, 186,
  188, 195
Salem, Hisham 219
Sales, Nathan 225
al-Sallal, Abdullah 175
Salman, Mohammad bin 99, 150, 189, 190,
  194, 197, 198
Samuel B. Roberts, USS 63
Sana'a 174, 175, 179, 183, 184, 186–8, 191,
  192
Sanjabi, Karim 209
Saraya al-Quds Brigades 216–17
Sassanid empire 8, 42, 103, 174
Saudi Arabia 152–3, 160–1, 189–90, 200–1
  Arab Spring 147
  B. Assad and 145, 190
  Britain and 198
  CIA and 120, 298 n. 77
  credibility 89
  Egypt and 197
  financial and logistic support to ISIL
    161, 164
  GCC and 32
  Hamas and 223
  Hezbollah and 194
  Iraq and 50, 69
  ISIS and 166
  Israel and 248
  Khamenei and 191, 199
  Lebanon and 123–4, 134
  oil facilities hit 173, 195
  Sadr visits 99
  Soleimani and 150
  'tankers' war' 55
  Twin Pillars policy 18
  US bases in 35
  Western arms 192
  Yemen and 176, 177, 181–8, 193–9, 219
  Zaydis in 175
SAVAK–CIA–Mossad axis 46–8
SAVAK (secret police) 105–6, 109–10
  Bakhtiyar and 293 n. 18

Carter and 20
creation 15, 205
Iraqi Kurds and 46–8
Khamenei and 220
Motevaselian and 296 n. 58
Rafsanjani and 208
Sazeman-e Makhsous-e Ettehad va Amal
    (Special Group for Unity and Action)
    109
Seche, Stephen 182
Second World War 11, 68
sectarian civil war, Iran and the 81–4
Al Shabab al-Moumeneen 180
Shabak 229
Shahlai, Abdulreza 265 n. 1
al-Shahwani, Gen Mohammad
    Abdullah 77
Shallah, Ramadan Abdullah 218, 230
Shamkhani, Adm Ali 89
Shapira, Brig Gen Shimon 170, 298 n. 77
Shaqaqi, Fathi 216–18, 227
al-Shaqfa, Mohammad Riad 148
Shariati, Ali 209
Sharif Imami, Jafar 270 n. 22
Sharif, Ramazan 233–4
Shatt al-Arab Treaty (1937) 44, 45–6
Sheikholeslam, Hossein 119, 123
Shekarchi, Brig Gen Abolfazl 196
Shia Afghans 159–60
Shia clerics 14, 17, 33, 208
Shia Internationalism 155–6
Shia organisations 49, 52, 75–6, 112
Shiism 50, 68, 103–4, 108, 109, 110, 135–6,
    149, 219
Shirazi, Gen Ali Sayyad 114, 115
Shirazi, Hassan Mahdi 146
Shirazi, Mohammad-Taqi 43
Shultz, George 117
Sick, Gary 58
Simon, William 19
Sinai II Agreements (1975) 206
Sinwar, Yahya 202, 224–5, 232
el-Sisi, Gen Abdel Fattah 224
Sistani, Ali 79, 88, 90, 91, 167, 182
Six-Day War (1967) 41, 206
Slim, Randa 125, 156
Sobhani, Mohammad Ali 169
Soleimani, Gen Qasem 1–2, 126–31
    arming of Hamas and PIJ 225–32
    Assad and 152, 170
    assassination of 96, 97–8, 245

Barzani and 92–3
Daoud on 289 n. 71
Deif and 234
Gaza War 230–1
Hamadani and 138
Hezbollah and 156
Irani people and 150
Iran's rise 243–4
ISIS and 88–9, 90–1, 167
Khamenei and 39
Khatami and 38
al-Maliki and 78–9
Mughniyeh escorts 102
on Palestine 238–9
Peshmerga and 94
precedence for military over diplomacy
    148
rise of 214
Russian–Iranian tactical alliance 162
Sadr visits 99
statue of 103
Syrian armed forces 153–4
Yemen and 185
Somalia 176
South Yemen, see Yemen
Southern Transitional Council 198–9
Sovereignty:
    Arvand Rood 44, 45, 46, 48, 51
    Iran's 8–15, 24, 77, 214, 236, 248–9
    Lebanon's 117, 119, 124
    Syria's 167
    Yemen's 187, 199
Soviet Union
    disintegration of 37, 163, 213
    Hussein and 46, 50
    influence 12, 45, 47, 48, 57, 59
    invasion of Afghanistan 35, 50
    Iran and 214
    Non-Aggression Treaty 17
    threat posed by 15, 16, 57, 242
    Yemen and 176, 177
    see also Russia
Sri Lanka 19
Stark, USS 63
Status of Forces Agreement (SOFA) 16, 17,
    84–5
Strategic Framework Agreement (SFA)
    84–5
strategic goals:
    power and deterrence 30–5
    student protests 14, 38

al-Sudani, Mohammad Shia 99
Suez Canal 13, 105, 200, 201
Sunni organisations 33, 164, 203, 215, 245
Supreme Council of Islamic Revolution in
    Iraq (SCIRI) 53, 74, 80
Supreme Defence Council 51, 54
Supreme Islamic Shia Council 106
Supreme National Security Council 29–30,
    89, 148
Syria:
    Assad agrees to prisoner swap 308 n. 69
    attacks by 235
    closure of Iraq's oil pipelines 55
    Egypt and 105, 139, 142
    Hamas and 222–3, 232
    Hezbollah and 126–7
    hybrid warfare 153–5
    internally displaced citizens 155
    Iran and 214
    Iran's alliance with 33, 36, 52, 134,
        138–72, 243
    Iran's strategic partnership with 31, 145
    IRGC in 32, 113–16
    Lebanon and 107, 117, 124
    ongoing civil war 34, 39, 146–53, 155,
        170–1, 223, 244, 247
    Palestinian militants and 208
    Reagan and 57
    sale of weapons to Iran 143–4
    Six-Day War 41
    Soleimani and 90
    'sponsoring terrorism' 118
    withdraws troops from Lebanon 145
Syrian Democratic Forces (SDF) 161, 167
Syrian Free Army 151
Syrian National Council 148

Tabaar, Mohammad Ayatollahi 270 n. 12
tabun (nerve agent) 54–5
Ta'eb, Mehdi 149
Taif Agreement (1989) 124, 299 n. 93
Talabani, Jalal 81, 93
Taliban government 73–4
Tartus 140, 163
Tehran Hostage Crisis (1979–81) 23–8, 111
Thalweg Doctrine 44, 48
Tikrit 91
Tillerson, Rex 95, 168
TOW missiles 60
Truman, Harry S. 12, 13

Trump, Donald 167–8, 251–2
    Israeli US embassy 227
    JPCOA nuclear deal 34, 39, 95
    sanctions set by 172
    Saudi Arabia and 190, 198
    on Soleimani 1
    threat towards Iran 2
Tudeh party 14, 27, 45
al-Tufayli, Subhi 115, 122–3
Tunisia 147, 185, 226
Turkey 35, 94, 152, 161, 165, 204
TWA Flight 847 hijack (1985) 59–60,
    120–1
Twelver Shiism 174, 180, 183
Twin Pillars policy 18
Tyre headquarters bombings (1982–3) 117
Tzur, Brig Gen Guy 103

Ukraine International Airlines Flight
    disaster (2020) 2
Umar ibn Khattab, Caliph 8
UN Security Council 75
    Resolutions 55, 126, 132, 157, 163, 192,
        195, 204, 207
United Arab Emirates (UAE) 32, 35, 145,
    152, 198–9, 248
United Arab Republic 105
United Iraqi Alliance 80
United Nations General Assembly 32
United Nations Interim Force in Lebanon
    (UNIFIL) 122
United Nations (UN):
    envoys to Syria 171
    Gaza and 233
    Panel of Experts 191, 192–3, 194, 196,
        199
    reports 173, 231–2
    sanctions 73
    Syrian crisis 150
    Zarif and 191–2
US embassy attack, Baghdad (2019) 96
US embassy, Tehran 2, 7
US–Iraq strategic agreements 84–6
US Mission 7, 98

Vahidi, Brig Gen Ahmad 134
Velayat-e Faqih 27, 52
Velayati, Ali Akbar 182
Vietnam War 18
Vincennes, USS 65

Wahhabism 89, 179, 180
Walt, Stephen 33, 142
Weir, Rev Benjamin 60
West Bank 213, 217, 228
Winograd Committee 133
Woman, Life, Freedom movement 252
Woodward, Bob 120
Wright, Robin 49

Yassin, Ahmed 219, 220, 227
Yazdi, Ebrahim 24, 109
Yemen 244–5
    Hamas and 223
    Iran and the civil war in 190–2
    Iran operating in the Grey Zone 31,
        173–201
    modern history 175–8
    North Yemen 18, 173, 175–9, 242
    ongoing civil war 39, 173–201, 242
    Saleh and 147
    South Yemen 175, 177–8, 187, 199
    support for 247
Yom Kippur War (1973) 140, 206

Zahar, Mahmood 225
Zahedi, Ardeshir 104, 108, 140–1, 277
    n. 33, 330 n. 42
Zahedi, Gen Mohammad Reza 235, 236
al Zaidi, Muntadhar 85
Zarghami, Ezzatollah 230
Zarif, Mohammad Javad 162–3
    on Afghans 160
    IRGC and 30, 96
    on ISIS 89
    on Pompeo 173
    on Saudi Arabia 194
    Soleimani on 227
    on Syria 148
    UN and 191–2
al-Zarqawi, Abu Musab 82–3
al-Zawari, Mohammad 226
Zaydi Shias 174–5, 175, 179, 181
Zeynab, Hazrat 141
Zeynabiyoun group 159–60
Zionism 167, 204, 207–8, 212, 215, 226,
    232, 237
Zu'ayyin, Yusuf 139

About the Author

Mohsen M. Milani completed his high school, undergraduate, and graduate education in California, earning his PhD from the University of Southern California. He is currently a professor of comparative politics at the University of South Florida. He has served as a fellow at Harvard, Oxford, and the Foscari University in Venice, Italy. Widely published and a dynamic public speaker, his advice has been sought by government and non-government entities. He is frequently interviewed by international media.